James Morton was for twenty-five years a solicitor primarily involved in defence work. He is now one of the UK's leading crime experts. He is the author of *Gangland*, *Gangland Volume 2*, *Gangland International*, *Bent Coppers*, *Supergrasses and Informers*, *A Calendar of Killing*, *Sex, Crimes and Misdemeanours* and *East End Gangland*. James Morton has also co-written *Mad Frank* and its sequel, *Mad Frank and Friends*, the memories of the celebrated villain Frankie Fraser.

GANGLAND TODAY

James Morton

timewarner
paperbacks

A *Time Warner* Paperback

First published in Great Britain in 2002 by Time Warner Books
This edition published by Time Warner Paperbacks in 2003

A CIP catalogue record for this book
is available from the British Library.

ISBN 0 7515 3162 6

Typeset by Palimpsest Book Production Limited
Polmont, Stirlingshire
Printed and bound in Great Britain by
Clays Ltd, St Ives plc

Time Warner Books UK
Brettenham House
Lancaster Place
London WC2E 7EN

www.TimeWarnerBooks.co.uk

For Dock Bateson with love and, once more, with unquantifiable thanks

Contents

Introduction

In the first year of the new century, what may turn out to be one of the last of the great traditional robberies – to rank with the Great Train Robbery, the Boston and London Brinks-Mat snatches, the Nice Bank Robbery and the Victorian Sporting Club heist in Melbourne – went belly-up. Many would have thought that with the increase in security techniques this sort of caper had become extinct; but the aim was to steal, in broad daylight, a collection of De Beers diamonds including the Millennium Star on show at the ill-fated Millennium Dome in Greenwich.

At about 9.30 a.m. on 7 November 2000, when there were fewer than 100 visitors at the Dome, a team of masked robbers used a JCB to break through gates in the perimeter fence. Once inside, armed with sledgehammers and a nail-gun which was said to be capable of penetrating one-inch-thick solid steel, they made for the Money Zone where the Star and other jewels including the 27-carat Heart of Eternity lived. In a manoeuvre reminiscent of the great days of Billy Tobin, they then used the excavator to break the shutters, at the same time releasing smoke bombs.[1] To use a term of the trade it was a ready-eye, and the police swooped. The diamonds had been replaced the night before with copies. It was speculated that either there was a ready buyer or that the gems would be broken up and sold in the Middle East. Had the raid succeeded, the value of the stolen diamonds, said Martin Heslop QC prosecuting, would have been 'a conservative £2,000 million'. According to Heslop, Robert Adams, Raymond Betson, Aldo Ciarrocchi and William Cockram had manned the digger while Kevin Meredith was the pilot of a speedboat waiting at the nearby Queen Elizabeth pier to take them and the diamonds across the river. Wayne Taylor was alleged to have been involved in the planning of the job along with Terry Millman, another member of the team, who had died while on remand.

Millman had bought a boat in the name of 'Mr Diamond' from a marina shop in Whitstable, keeping the receipt in his spectacles case. All identification marks had been removed from the boat and it had been moored at a pier close to the Dome. Millman had also bought the nail-gun for cash in Southwark, paying £762.

On the day, initially things went well. The robbers crashed into the Dome with their JCB digger driven by Raymond Betson, wearing body armour and carrying a stink-bomb and ammonia to squirt at anyone who tried to intervene. The team set off smoke grenades as they entered the vault.

---

[1] In the 1970s Billy Tobin led a highly successful team of armed robbers who on the occasion when they were captured in November 1980 were using a mobile crane to rob a security van of £1 million. They were the victims of a police informant. Tobin received 16 years.

According to the prosecution, William Cockram fired the nail-gun into the glass cabinet and Robert Adams followed up with a sledgehammer. And then, to use a term of art, it all came on top. One of the bottles of ammonia burst and the men were having breathing difficulties. Worse, there were no fewer than 40 firearms officers inside the Dome and another 80 outside. 'It was 12 inches from pay day. It would have been a good Christmas,' Robert Adams is alleged to have said to an officer.

When the trial began Robert Adams, Raymond Betson, Aldo Ciarrocchi and William Cockram all pleaded guilty to conspiracy to steal but not conspiracy to rob. Kevin Meredith and Wayne Taylor pleaded not guilty to either conspiracy. On 10 December 2001 Judge Michael Coombe ruled that Wayne Taylor had no case to answer on the charges of conspiracy to rob and steal and he was discharged. Outside the court he said he had been telling the police he had nothing to do with the robbery for the last year, and now he was considering suing 'for all I can'.

During the prosecution case, allegations were made that security at the Dome was lax and a police officer had offered inside help, something he denied. These allegations were never substantiated, and were merely part of the defence strategy. Now, when Cockram gave evidence, the picture became a little clearer. The job, he said, had been planned by a man named Tony who was built like the footballer turned actor, Vinnie Jones. Tony, he claimed, had been involved with security at the Dome and, together with the police officer, was offering inside help.

On the day of the raid Tony had been driving in a van

in convoy behind the JCB, but suddenly veered off towards Greenwich. The plan was for them all to rendezvous behind the Mayflower public house in Rotherhithe, where they would exchange the diamonds for cash. The team had arranged to wear body armour because, said Cockram:

> Criminals shoot – somebody was shot for a mobile phone the other day – you cannot trust people. We were double-crossed but in a different way.[2]

His part in the raid had, indeed, been to shoot the nail-gun to break the glass and for this he was to be paid £100,000.

> From hitting the gates of the Dome in the JCB to getting to the other side of the Thames in the boat would have been five minutes maximum. The police would not have got there in time.

When first approached he had gone with his daughter and grandson in September 2000 to reconnoitre. He had thought the raid was pie in the sky, but then been amazed at how little security there was. The raid had been deliberately timed so that there would be few (if any) tourists about.

Even in the last decade, the face of organised crime has

---

[2] The mobile telephone was a reference to a young girl shot in the head in the East End the previous week after she had handed over her mobile telephone to an armed robber. She had suffered a fractured skull but she survived. In January 2002, a Home Office report showed that the previous year 710,000 mobile telephones, each worth between £10 and £60 to the thieves, were stolen – almost double the previous year's total. Some 500,000 were taken from children aged between 11 and 15. It was suggested that black youth gangs preying on white youths accounted for most of the crime. Apparently it was thought to be 'out of order' to steal from girls.

been changing dramatically both in Britain and abroad. Drug dealing is still the market leader, but there has been a substantial shift towards people-smuggling, regarded as safer and more lucrative and which leads back to other old-fashioned crimes such as extortion and enforced prostitution. Also it has brought what is called cybercrime with, increasingly, identity theft.

New organisations have sprung up to replace what twenty years ago was the monopoly of the old-time working-class gangster. There are new but very organised, capable and ruthless kids on the block. For example, a decade ago there was little Turkish crime in Britain; now they have cornered much of the heroin market. Five years ago there was no Albanian crime in this country; now they are recognised as being more powerful than the Russian *mafiya*, who are thought not to have made quite the impression originally expected of them.

In October 1999 *The Times* published a list of what it called the 'dirtiest dozen on the planet'; major criminals, some of whom might also be masquerading as politicians. They all deserve a preliminary mention, but most are dealt with later in more detail. One immediate exception is Charles Taylor, simply because he falls into that ravine between patriotism on the one hand and expediency and organised crime on the other. To dispose of him straight away, Taylor, an American–Liberian, took an economics degree before becoming a director in the military government in Liberia in 1980. Unfortunately there was some difficulty over the whereabouts of nearly $1 million and he fled to the US where he was imprisoned. He broke out using a hacksaw and, like so many professional criminals before him including the great *soi-disant* Count Victor Lustig, with the help of bed-sheets. He then disappeared for five years. By now it was politics, and the United States suggested he had been cuddling up to Libya. His invasion of Liberia in 1989, when he seized the diamond, gold and timber regions in the north of the country, led to a seven-year civil war in which 150,000 were killed. He then became the country's 'elected' President.

Another on the list who sadly fails to qualify is Arkan (Zelko Raznatovic), the Serbian patriot who began his days as a contract assassin and later became a bank robber and gunrunner before being indicted as a war criminal. He was assassinated in January 2000 in a Belgrade hotel, along with his trusted friend Manda Mandik.

General Khun Sa's early career was documented in *Gangland International* but this freedom fighter, who at one time controlled 60 per cent of the world's heroin and is thought to have a private army of some 25,000, is now nearly 90. While he has 'surrendered' to the Burmese military junta, he enjoys his old age in his lakeside mountain home.

As for the remainder on *The Times'* list – the Unabomber, Theodore Kaczynski, excepted – they all feature in one way or another. Strictly in alphabetical order they are Tommy Adams, of the North London family, now released from his eight-year sentence; Henry Loazia Ceballos, 'The Scorpion', of the Cali cartel; the Budapest-based Semion Mogilevich, 'The Red Don'; Bernardo Provenzano, 'The Tractor', on the run in Sicily for 35 years and sentenced to 100 years in his absence; the Rodriguez brothers of the Cali cartel; Charles Sobhraj, almost a one-man Indian crime wave, now living in France; and the current Indian Bandit King, Veerappan, as well as the head of the largest of the yakuza operations. They and the many others in this book are testimony to the belief that, for a large chunk of the time, crime does indeed pay.

As with other books on organised crime, the problem of just what constitutes a gang arises. Over the years criminologists have destroyed forests in trying to set out comprehensive definitions, but some help arose in the decision of the First Circuit in the case of Samuel Patrick who was a member of the notorious Boston Intervale Posse youth gang.[3] The gang's prime source of income in the first half of the 1990s was selling crack. The question was whether, for the purpose of a conviction under RICO, Intervale was an 'enterprise'. Patrick was named by his co-accused, Jason Arthur – who, of course, may well have been seeking to lessen his own involvement – as 'chief' and 'top dog'. It was Patrick who decided who could sell drugs, where and which rivals were to be eliminated. He was the No. 1 dealer in the pyramid, selling on to Arthur who in turn sold it to the ranks. Intervale had colours and signs, something of a hierarchy and held brain-storming (if that is the right word) sessions to work out how to deal with rivals and the police. Patrick's argument was that Intervale was simply a loose connection of young drug entrepreneurs and there was nothing organised about it. The First Circuit was having none of it and ruled that 'enterprise' meant an ongoing formal or informal organisation of associates who function as a continuing unit for a common purpose, which is probably as good

[3] *US v Patrick*, 991387.

a definition as any for an organised crime gang. No doubt Patrick and Arthur, whose attempt at distancing himself did him no good, will appeal the decision. Each received life.

Here, in Britain, the National Criminal Intelligence Service (NCIS) defined the criteria for an organised crime group as being at least three in number, with prolonged or indefinite criminal activity, motivated by profit or power and with serious criminal offences being committed. Given that definition, NCIS believed there were no fewer than 930 organised crime groups active in the United Kingdom. In 2000, 56 per cent of the groups were thought to be involved in drug trafficking.

With apologies to NCIS, gangs do not have to be long-running affairs. They can be an *ad hoc* arrangement as when, on 13 December 2000, a group of prisoners led by George Rivas escaped from the maximum-security Connally Unit in Kenedy, south of San Antonio, in a prison pick-up truck along with sixteen stolen weapons. Known as the Rivas Gang after their leader, they were a motley and thoroughly dangerous collection of murderers and rapists. They had overpowered staff when they returned from the maintenance room and, dressed in their uniforms, over a 2½-hour period obtained access to the prison tower where they stole the guns. No check had been made to establish their identities at any time. They left behind a note: 'You haven't heard the last of us.'

Two days later two of the gang robbed a Radio Shack in Houston, some 200 miles away, taking walkie-talkies and police radio scanners with them. Then on Christmas Eve there was a mass raid on a sports shop near Dallas. This time the haul was $75,000, along with another 25 weapons and ammunition. The toll included a police officer, Aubrey Hawkins, shot 11 times, six in the head, and also run over. Now it was almost certain that if recaptured and convicted they would receive the death penalty. As usual, sightings came in across the state – in pool halls, fast-food outlets and public libraries from New York City to Mississippi. The general opinion, however, was that the men were heading for Mexico. General opinion was wrong.

Four of the men, now known as 'The Malevolent Seven' after the heroes of John Sturges's film, were caught in Woodland Park some 50 miles south of Denver after the manager of the Coachlight trailer park told the police that they had been staying there since the beginning of the year. He had seen them on the television programme *America's Most Wanted*. Three, including Rivas, were arrested when they drove to a nearby petrol station, and a fourth when he left the mobile home. By now the trailer had been surrounded by police and a fifth man, rapist Larry Harper, shot himself during negotiations for his surrender. The police had tried to persuade him to talk to his father.

The remaining two men, Patrick Murphy and Donald Newbury, came out of the Holiday Inn in Colorado Springs on 24 January after a night of negotiating. As part of the terms of their surrender they were each given five minutes on a CNN affiliate where they took the opportunity to complain about the Texan judicial and penal system.

Rivas, as leader, had managed to maintain discipline and kept the gang together, but this probably led to their recapture. Despite the fact that they played religious music and socialised with the other trailer dwellers, a group of seven men together was bound to stand out. Although keen to say they had tried to keep violence to the minimum, there were no regrets expressed over the death of the officer. Had the men split up in the remote mountains, probably they would have attracted little notice. At least they had outrun the prison service's 'rule of three' – that all escapees were recaptured within three days and three miles of the prison.[4]

When I wrote *Gangland* in 1991 I received a number of calls and letters suggesting there was a serious omission. 'You know who the biggest gang is?' I was asked by one caller. 'The coppers,' I was told without waiting for a reply. So now I have included an account of some of the more interesting examples of police misconduct throughout the world over recent years, linking their behaviour to organised crime in one form or another.

Once again I have tried to concentrate on crime for outright profit but, as always, dividing lines are not totally clear and, as I have said before, today's terrorists are tomorrow's freedom fighters and next month's oldest allies. It is impossible not to link the former Taliban regime in Afghanistan and Osama Bin Laden's Al-Qaeda, along with the growing of poppies there to provide opium, with organised crime. Afghanistan is the source of 90 per cent of the

[4] For accounts of the escape, man-hunt and recapture see for example the *Guardian*, 12 January; *New York Times*, 23 January 2001. Theirs was not the first mass prison escape from Death Row. On 31 May 1894, prisoners who became known as 'The Mecklenburgh Six' escaped from the correctional facility of that name near Boydton, Va. Two were captured within 19 hours and the last was recaptured 19 days later. They had not killed anyone during their relatively brief period of freedom. See Joe Jackson and William Burke jnr, *Dead Run*.

heroin imported illegally into Britain, and shortly after the 11 September outrage it was believed that the Taliban had a stockpile of some 3,000 tons of opium which would condense into 300 tons of raw heroin with a street value in London of £20 billion.

In 2000 the Taliban had bowed to international pressure and banned the planting of poppy seeds, although it was thought that in the event of an attack on the country the ban would be lifted. Now, after the war, US officials believed that the real aim of the Taliban was to establish a firmer grip on the market. The reduction in production from 3,656 tons to 74 tons in 2001 had driven up the prices, but the stock-pile ensured there was sufficient to avoid a shortage. After a 'fire sale' at the start of the war, things stabilised once again. In addition to the search for Bin Laden there was also a search for the opium stockpiles, but there are conflicting reports as to the current state of the market.[5]

It was also thought that Bin Laden had seen the sale of drugs not only as a source of revenue but as a way of under-mining Western society. If so, he was doing reasonably well. There are an estimated 295,000 heroin users in Britain, with an annual value of £2,313 million of the drug sold.[6]

Given the profit rule, organisations such as Abu Sayyaf, a kidnapping gang in the Philippines which is said to be campaigning for a Muslim state in the south, may not qualify either, though its activities are certainly worth noting in passing. In 2000 this gang took 24 hostages at a Malaysian

---

[5] *Financial Times*, 10 January 2002.
[6] *Drug Misuse Declared in 2000: Results from the British Crime Survey.*

resort and extorted millions in ransom. Other exploits which may be attributed to it include the hijacking of a ferry on 24 May 2001. Two days before that two staff members of the Pearl Farm Resort were killed when they fought off a number of gunmen carrying assault rifles and, on 27 May 2001, 20 people including three Americans were kidnapped at the £150-a-night Dos Palmas Island Resort at Honda Bay in Palawan province nearly 400 miles south-west of Manila. Guests and staff were rounded up as they ate breakfast. The gang fled in a speed-boat which was thought to have been heading for the rebel stronghold on islands in the Sulawesi Sea.

Then there is the vexed question of when the IRA and the various satellite paramilitary organisations cross the profit line. The third raid in less than 30 years on the ill-fated art collection at Russborough House in County Wicklow begun by Sir Alfred Beit, nephew of the German co-founder (with Cecil Rhodes) of the diamond company De Beers, is another example of the difficulty in separating crime pure if not simple from political crime. On 26 April 1974 the gallery was raided by the British heiress, Dr Rose Dugdale, when 19 paintings were stolen. On this occasion the raid was linked with the transfer of the Price sisters from British prisons and efforts to obtain the release of Dugdale's husband Eddie Gallagher who had been sentenced for the kidnapping of Dr Tiede Herrema. In 1986 Martin Cahill, 'The General', later executed by the IRA, led a very successful raid, while a raid on 26 June 2001 netted, for the third time, Gainsborough's portrait of Madame Pacelli. Now it was thought that the theft might have been part of a Provisional IRA effort to raise cash to launch a new terror campaign following the then effective collapse of the Good Friday agreement. However, it may have been for less altruistic reasons.[7]

According to some reports many members of the IRA may be described as urban gangsters, taxing drug dealers and taking reprisals if they default in payment of their protection money.[8] There have been other reports that the organisation has been promised money by FARC in return for training its members in urban guerrilla warfare. In September three Irishmen, including Niall Connelly – accredited by the Cuban government with being Sinn Fein's representative in Havana – were arrested in Colombia with false passports. Despite the fact that over the years the IRA has aided, abetted and foiled the major Dublin gangsters of the period, they themselves cannot really qualify for inclusion. Elsewhere the National Liberation Movement for Kosova (LKCK) is believed to have obtained funding from drug trafficking. I have also avoided any close inspection of neo-Nazi and other Fascist groups such as the Oregon-based *Holle Katzen* (Hell Cats), thought to be responsible for a series of hate crimes and the attempted bombing of a bridge in Junction City.

When I wrote *Gangland International* it was still relatively easy to compartmentalise gangs, certainly during the first eighty years of the last century. There were clearly defined territories. Gangs maintained control of cities, of suburbs, even only of streets, but they rarely encroached on another's

---

[7] Part of the ill-fated Beit collection came and went again in September 2002. First Rubens' *Head of a Man* was found after long police negotiations and then off went five more pictures from the collection, including two more Rubens. This time the thieves escaped with them in a four-wheel drive vehicle across a field.
[8] Andrew Alderson, Jeremy McDermott and Ted Oliver, 'Gangsters, not freedom fighters', in the *Sunday Telegraph*, 19 August 2001.

city. Members may have transferred to other organisations but, by and large, it was all fairly parochial. As a rule they played by themselves. Now things have changed out of all recognition. The ease of transport has something to do with it but the growth of drug trafficking has been a very different matter. To make mega-money nowadays it is not sufficient to have a small street operation. National and international links must be forged, first to buy, then to distribute and finally to launder. Now, to chart the activities of any halfway self-respecting organisation, it is necessary to look at their relationship with gangs in other countries. At home one example is the links between Ireland and Holland.

Another good example comes from a drugs raid in Canada which shows how things swirl around. In May 2001 the RCMP revealed details *of Operation Chevalin*. The unravelling of a hashish smuggling ring began on 21 October 2000 when a couple were stopped at the Rock Island border crossing from Vermont. Customs officials believed they looked nervous and gave evasive answers to routine questions. When they were searched, $136,832 was found taped to their bodies and hidden in clothes and luggage.

The drugs themselves had begun their journey in Pakistan and been sent to India, from where they went to Europe, South America and Jamaica. The police allege that the Canadian brokers were Ernest Pitt and his wife, Suzan Renaud, from Lennoxville, near Montreal. The drugs entered the country probably at Dorval or Pearson airports in containers – in one case 836 kg of liquid hashish were found in boxes of spices for jerk beef. The police claim the suppliers were Indian nationals from India and Portugal.

Pitt was alleged to have sold the drugs to three rings in Montreal, including one headed by the missing Louis 'Melou' Roy of the elite Hell's Angels chapter, the Nomads. The proceeds were then sent to Indians in Toronto and Mississauga and the money converted into American dollars before being transferred to Pakistan, India and the United Arab Emirates. Pitt was arrested in France; Roy had been missing for nearly a year.[9]

As a result it is not possible to compartmentalise gangs completely, and there will consequently be some overlapping. For example, Israeli gangs can no longer be considered in isolation from Europe and America or the Russian *mafiya*. I have nevertheless maintained more or less the same structure as in *Gangland International*, looking at the various countries and cities. However, I have included a final section which considers trends in organised crime – those which have faded away, those which have lasted centuries and others which are relatively new.

To avoid undue repetition in the chapters and also to help readers who have never encountered the labyrinthine comings and goings, particularly in New York, I am setting out a very brief history of the so-called Five Families there. It is probably convenient if I also summarise the history of the London gangs from the 1920s when the Italian Mob, the Sabinis from Saffron Hill, Clerkenwell, were the most powerful of organisations which also included the long-running Irish gang from the docks, the Watney Street Mob, and their Jewish rivals from Aldgate.

In the 1920s the White family from King's Cross were

[9] See *Globe and Mail*, 17 May 2001.

local supporters of Darby Sabini; but eventually, when Sabini was unable to control the disparate Jewish and other elements in his organisation, a split of territory was agreed and the Whites took over the King's Cross district which adjoins Clerkenwell. In the Second World War many of the Sabini family and their supporters were interned and their control, which had extended into the West End, disappeared. The Whites were never strong and in 1947 an alliance between Jack Spot, the Jewish gangster from the East End, and Billy Hill, from Holborn, drove them out of London. Spot and Hill maintained a benign reign until a quarrel in 1954 led to a series of assaults and prosecutions. Spot was defeated and Hill more or less retired. Now the Kray Twins took over the East End and whole chunks of London nightlife. South of the river, Charles and Eddie Richardson controlled things, but they went to prison in 1966 to be followed three years later by the Krays. For years London was without any effective old-fashioned blue-collar family in control, but then the Arif brothers – originally from Cyprus, who had married into South London families – took over that area. By the 1990s the top firm in London was accepted to be the one run by the shadowy Adams family from North London. The Krays had never established themselves as anything much more than a local enterprise and, although Charlie Richardson had mining interests in Namibia, it was the Adams family which really took London crime to international levels.

As for New York's Five Families, the euphemistic and sanitising name for the gangs of organised criminals who controlled the city, they were (in alphabetical order) the

Bonanno, the Colombo, the Gambino, the Genovese and the Lucchese. During the years since the wars of the 1930s they would form and split alliances, interfere with each other's affairs and wage war internally and on each other. Almost at the end of the century, nevertheless they remained identifiable entities.

In the 1990s the line-up was more or less as follows: John Gotti jnr – in the absence of his imprisoned father – and Peter Gotti were said to be running the Gambino Family, regarded as the strongest, of which Nicholas Corozzo was thought to be acting street boss. Vincente 'The Chin' Gigante, boss of the Genovese, had lost a long battle to stay out of prison and finally surrendered in 1996. The ranks of the Lucchese Family had been seriously depleted; with Vittorio Amuso in federal prison and likely to remain there, it was now thought to be run by a triumvirate headed by pigeon-fancier Steven Crea. The Family, believed now to have under a hundred members, had lost a considerable amount of its interests in the garment industry to the Gambinos. The Colombos were hardly any stronger, with both former leaders serving life imprisonment, and day-to-day control alleged to be in the hands of Joe 'T' Tomasello. The Family had been ravaged over the previous three years, with more than 100 members arrested or convicted. They had also lost one of their prime sources of income, the skimming of gasoline taxes, which in recent years had been shared with the New York Russian *mafiya*. The Bonannos were similarly weakened, with one-time boss Joseph Massina now out on parole and forbidden to associate with known criminals. This was now thought to be the weakest of the once glorious

Five Families.[10] They may all seem to have been irrevocably weakened, but there were plenty of members still seeking to lead.

I have also tried to avoid undue repetition over other organisations, simply explaining the previous history of some of the gangs and players in what I hope are manageable footnotes. In a number of cases defendants will have been acquitted or convicted and sentenced between completion and the publication of this book. Some may also have had their convictions overturned or lost their appeals. I will endeavour to follow their progress in any subsequent editions. As always I am happy to consider applications from supporters of those whom they think merit inclusion over some of the present incumbents.

My thanks, as always, are due to many people, some of whom have asked not to be named. I am as grateful to them as I am to Al Alschuler, Tish Armstrong, Michel Auger, Michael and Pamela Bailey, Frankie Bateson, Jeremy Beadle, J. P. Bean, Susan Bell, Joe Beltrami, Barbara Boote, Keith Bottomley, Paul Brown, Duncan Campbell, Joanne Coen, Stan Cohen, the late Clive Coleman, Nicholas Cowdery QC, Nils Christie, John Clitheroe, Dave Critchley, Jeanne Damirgian, Don DeKieffer, James Dubro, Walter Easey, Clifford and Marie Elmer of Clifford Elmer Books, Roger Foligot, Frank Fraser, Jim Freeman, Rita Fry, Cornelia Fuchs, Adrian Garrett, Jonathan Goodman, Stefania Grant, Wilf Gregg, Richard

---

[10] Joseph Bonanno, the founding father of the Bonanno Family, died on 11 May 2002 in Arizona at the age of 97. For a run-down on the history of the Five Families from the wars of the 1930s, see James Morton, *Gangland International*, Chapter 8.

Harvey, Frances Hegarty, Brian Hilliard, Susan Jarvis of the University of Nevada, Linda Jourgensen, John Kay, Thomas Kilpatrick of the Chicago Crime Commission, Anne Kmieck of the Cleveland Police Historical Museum, Stephen Komie, Edward Kovacic, Albert Krieger, James LaRossa, Loretta Lay, Francine Levitov, Barbara Levy, Susannah Lobez, Jean Maund, Cal McCrystal, Susan McNeary, Peter McSweeney, Christopher Murphy, Neil Murray, C. B. Niland, Clive Norris, John O'Hair, Judge John O'Meally, William Pizzi, Maurice Punch, John Rigbey, William F. Roehmer III, Laura Rosenberg, Bruce Reynolds, Gerald Shargel, Linda Silverman, Joe Swickard, Edda Tasiemka, Jane Thompson, Tony Thompson, Richard Whittington-Egan, Paul Williams, Linda Wright and Caroll Yap.

I would also like to thank police and law officers past and present of a number of jurisdictions and the staff at libraries around the world, particularly the New York, Chicago and Detroit Public Libraries and the Newspaper Library at Colindale, many of whom went out of their way to find me material and, even more importantly, to show me how the viewing machines worked. Obviously, without all of them this book would have been even more imperfect. Such errors as appear are mine alone.

Again, this book could not possibly even have been started without the promise of unfailing and tireless help and support from Dock Bateson. It was a promise she more than fulfilled.

GREAT BRITAIN

1

The Krays and their Aftermath

At the beginning of the millennium the old guard – the Krays, Freddie Foreman, Charlie Richardson, Frank Fraser and others from the 1960s – had, in one way or another, more or less retired from active duty. Ronnie Kray was dead and, reunited with his brain which had originally been kept for study, buried in the family grave in Chingford. While in Broadmoor he had suffered a heart attack. Reggie and his elder brother Charlie were in prison. Reggie had been unable to obtain parole from his life sentence back in 1969 for the killing of Jack 'The Hat' McVitie. Charlie had been released in the 1970s but now he was back inside.

Shortly after Ronnie Kray's funeral, Charlie had run into serious trouble. He was by now 69 and his son, Gary, who had emotional problems throughout his life, had just died of cancer at the age of 44.[1] Charlie, released in 1975 from his 10-year sentence for assisting in the disposal of the body of Jack McVitie, from then on had wheeled and dealt, variously selling cutlery at the Ideal Home Exhibition and managing a pop group. He had also acted as consultant on the film *The Krays*, something which caused trouble in the Kray family who did not think he had obtained the best deal for any of them. Now he was charged with conspiracy to sell cocaine worth £39 million to under-cover police officers. It was a charge greeted with ridicule amongst the Underworld, who regarded Kray as a pathetic old man trading off the names of his younger brothers for hand-outs for old times' sake. It was said he had been unable to pay for Gary's funeral, the money for this coming from Reggie.

The police version was that here was a man still deeply involved in the Underworld, and who had been investigated on at least three occasions. There were unproven allegations linking him to amphetamines, counterfeit videos and fake coins. He had neither a bank account nor a credit card; he never claimed benefits. This, said the police, showed that he was still an operator with whom to be reckoned.

Kray cannot have been totally broke because he had offices down the Commercial Road and, unless he was doing it as a favour, Ronnie O'Sullivan snr, father of the world-class snooker champion, was said to have serviced Charlie Kray's car. O'Sullivan himself was jailed for life in September 1992 for the killing of Bruce Bryan in a night-club brawl in Stocks Nightclub, Chelsea, in October 1991. Bryan had been with Angela Mills,

---

[1] John Pearson in his *The Cult of Violence* suggests the cause of death was from AIDS.

the one-time girlfriend of Charlie Kray. According to the prosecution evidence, Edward O'Brien and O'Sullivan were making racist taunts and singing football songs. A fight broke out and O'Sullivan allegedly produced a hunting knife with which he stabbed Bryan who had hit him with a champagne bottle. O'Sullivan was then alleged to have kicked Bryan in the head as he was on the ground. Although O'Sullivan claimed mistaken identity he was convicted, and also received 16 years for affray.

The police in the Kray drugs case were recruited from provincial forces and at Charlie Kray's 70th birthday party he had been introduced by an unknowing Patsy Manning to 'Jack', an undercover officer posing as a businessman dealing in drugs. This, say his supporters, was his first mistake. Many saw Kray as being out of touch with the real harsh world. Frank Fraser, who gave evidence on Kray's behalf, points out:

> There was no problem in saying, 'This is Tom, this is Dick and this is Harry' and having a chat, but once Charlie'd started talking serious what he should have said is, 'What's your surname?' 'Can't tell you.' 'Who do you know?' Any bona fide villain would ask. It shows you what an idiot Charlie was. And if you're dealing in anything serious like a robbery or anything then, if the man can't put up names of people he's worked with or won't tell you his name, you know the score and it's, 'On your bike, get back to your local police station.' You are brought up automatically to ask questions and protect yourself. It's instilled in you from the time you're ten years old. Charlie simply didn't have a clue about life. That's how simple he was.[2]

[2] Frank Fraser, *Mad Frank and Friends*, p. 229.

In subsequent taped conversations Kray offered to supply 5 kg of 92 per cent pure cocaine every fortnight for up to two years. If the deal had gone ahead he and his associates would have grossed £8 million. His defence was that he was stringing the potential purchasers along in the hope of conning money from them. He told the court:

> All my life I have advised people never to be involved in drugs. I swear on my son's grave I have never handled drugs in my life. Juries have got it wrong for me before and this jury has got it wrong.

Judge Carroll was not convinced and, sentencing him to 12 years imprisonment on 23 June 1997, he commented:

> There was never a real question of entrapment by those officers but, when caught, you cried foul. I am pleased to say this jury saw through that hollow cry.

Robert Field received 9 years and Robert Gould 5 for their respective parts in the affair. For a time it was thought that Charlie Kray might have his conviction quashed or at least have his sentence cut but, on 12 February 1999, his appeals against both conviction and sentence were rejected. He had been given leave to appeal the previous November. Now the court said that it was 'unpersuaded that the judge was wrong in attributing to Kray a central role in this affair'. He could seek his release on licence once he had served half his sentence, said Lord Justice Ian Kennedy. When it came to it these apparently encouraging words never actually assisted Charlie Kray.

Nipper Read, the nemesis of the family, saw him through less than rose-coloured spectacles:

> He had always been considered as the mildest of the three brothers and I know he was devoted to his son Gary who had serious emotional problems and who died just before the smuggling plot. But, in fact, he didn't need to use violence. The mere use of his name coupled with his brothers' reputation was sufficient to enforce his demands. After his release from serving his sentence for the disposal of the body of Jack McVitie, he lived well and always managed to maintain an expensive lifestyle.[3]

Efforts had been made to persuade Reggie Kray to give evidence on his brother's behalf, but he declined. There was soon better news for the brothers, however. On 14 July 1997 a well-educated and successful businesswoman, 37-year-old Roberta Jones, joined the list of women who have married long-serving prisoners when she became Reggie Kray's second wife in a ceremony at Maidstone prison. The occasion was celebrated by a laser-show on the prison walls. Two years on from the marriage the campaign to have Reggie released had again gathered momentum, but had shown no signs of moving the Home Secretary. Kray was still held as a Category C prisoner and it was generally thought that Category D status and a move to an open prison would be a prerequisite before any release on licence.

Then in the summer of 2000 Charlie Kray was taken seriously ill with heart trouble, and he was moved to the Isle of

---

[3] Conversation with the author, May 2000.

Wight so that he could be visited by his brother. He died in Parkhurst on April 2000 and was given a funeral which, if anything, was larger than the one for Ronnie Kray. A poem said to be by Reggie Kray was read:

> Do not stand at my grave and cry
> I am not there. I did not die.
> I am a thousand winds that blow.
> I am diamond glints on snow.[4]

At the graveside Frankie Fraser called for three cheers for Reggie and the crowd responded enthusiastically. Kray was allowed to see the graves of other members of his family before, with mounting cries of 'Take the cuffs off' echoing around the cemetery, he climbed back into the car and was driven away.

In early 2001 Charlie Kray was linked by the police to the murder of businessman Donald Urquhart who had been shot in Marylebone High Street on 2 January 1993. The hitman, Graeme West, received life imprisonment but the contractor had never been charged. Now, when two men were arrested in London and released after questioning, the police said that Kray might have been an adviser after the murder. At one time it was thought that Urquhart was killed over an international gun-running and drug-smuggling operation, but it is much more likely to have been over a business deal which had soured. After his death, a will was found

---

[4] Far from being by Reggie Kray, the poem is believed to have been written many years ago by an unknown author. In 1991 a copy was found in the possessions of a soldier killed in Ulster. In the first and second lines Kray substituted the words 'cry' and 'die' for 'weep' and 'sleep'.

which left his property to his lawyer and business associate Jonathan Levene, himself the son of a prominent barrister. Levene then went to Switzerland.

It has also been suggested that Kray arranged the contract in 1977 when Barbara Gaul, the estranged wife of Maltese property developer John Gaul, was shot outside a public house in Patcham, near Brighton.[5]

Reggie Kray did not survive his elder brother long. By the summer of 2000 he was suffering from prostate cancer. Sent from prison to a hospital, with only a matter of days to live he was released on licence. He remained in hospital in Norwich, unable even to walk by the river and certainly unable to return to the East End.

In an interview for which the BBC was reputed to have paid £280,000, the dying Kray admitted there had been one more murder. This was almost certainly that of Mad Teddy Smith – writer and homosexual friend of the brothers, particularly Ronnie – who had been acquitted with them of demanding money with menaces in their take-over of the Hideaway Club. The probability was that Teddy Smith had been killed, following a dispute with Ronnie Kray, over a boy in Steeple Bay, Kent.[6]

When Reggie Kray died on 1 October 2000 his funeral

---

[5] For an account of the killing of Barbara Gaul and the career of John Gaul see James Morton, *Gangland*, pp. 254–6. For an account of the killing of Donald Urquhart see James Morton, *A Calendar of Killing*, p. 2.

[6] As with many people who disappeared there have been probable and improbable sightings. Frank Fraser writes that Smith went to Australia; he had the story from a newspaper vendor in Chancery Lane who sheltered Smith after he had fallen out with the Krays. See F. Fraser, *Mad Frank's Diary*. There were a number of other 'disappeareds', one of whom – Jack Frost, who had been Ronnie Kray's driver and was long thought to have been killed – turned up alive and well on a television programme in January 2002.

was much more muted than that of his siblings. Instead of an expected crowd of over 10,000 a considerably lower but still respectable estimated 3,000 turned up. Instead of pallbearers from the past, these now included Tony Mortimer, a former East 17 singer, and Bradley Allardyce, a former armed robber whom Reggie had met in prison.

Nor was there a full complement of other former villains. Fraser was there along with the Great Train Robber Bruce Reynolds and the then media celebrity Dave Courtney, who had been acquitted in the Charlie Kray drug trial and who in 2001 would also be acquitted of conspiracy to plant drugs on a woman involved in a custody battle with her former husband. Absentees included Barbara Windsor, Charlie Kray's one-time girlfriend, who nevertheless sent roses, and Freddie Foreman who had been sentenced to 10 years' imprisonment for helping to clear up after the death of McVitie.

Kray's wife Roberta had wanted a smaller funeral, not an old-time gangster parade, but Foreman's absence was attributable in part to the bad taste left in a number of elderly mouths after he appeared on television to say that he had in fact killed another acknowledged Kray victim, the 'Mad Axeman' Frank Mitchell, on their behalf. This was something of which he and the Twins had been acquitted in their second trial. In the interview he said:

Ronnie and Reggie was ill and looking it. Rings under their eyes and worried sick. Mitchell was talking about going round to their house and saying he was going to hold them responsible if he got arrested. He said he would not go in quietly. He would take six or seven coppers

with him. He said he was not prepared to spend the rest
of his life in prison.

According to Foreman, the Krays had had a meeting at Harry
Hopwood's flat to which Albert Donaghue was called.
Donaghue was not a party to what went on, nor was
Hopwood. Both were excluded from the actual discussion,
but afterwards Charlie Kray approached Donaghue and said
it had been decided to take Mitchell down to Kent to spend
Christmas with Ronnie. 'We need you to get him out of the
flat and away from the girl because Ronnie don't like women
tramping over his house.'

The Krays were getting seriously worried as they were
looking at a period of imprisonment for helping in the escape
and harbouring Mitchell. Foreman also clearly established
the Krays' complete involvement, saying, 'They called me in
as I was the more professional.' As for the actual slaying he
had this to offer:

Alfie Gerard was with me. He was a good man to have
with you to get it done as quick as possible. It was all
over in seconds. If you're sitting on a cold winter's night
in the back of a van waiting to commit the horrible crime
it's not very nice. It's not something you get pleasure out
of doing. It's got to be done properly and mercifully and
as quickly as possible. As soon as it was over and done
with the better. I know that sounds very clinical and cold-
blooded. I was Frank Mitchell's final executioner.[7]

[7] *The Krays: Unfinished Business* (Part One) transmitted 13 January 2000; *The
Krays: Inside the Firm* (Part Two) transmitted 17 January 2000. Alf Gerard died
in Brighton in 1981.

Was the confession true? It matched, in almost all respects, the evidence given by Albert Donaghue at the trial. Nipper Read certainly believed it was:

> I think Freddie Foreman was very, very convincing about throwing the bodies into the shipping lanes off Newhaven. He and some friends had run a watch smuggling business between Belgium, France and this country and they used to combine one bit of business with another. He did it rather better than the people who tied up Jack Buggy and threw him overboard. They did that much too close to shore and he surfaced.[8]

The police took the matter seriously and arrested Foreman who had already given a substantially similar account in his book *Respect*. In the end it was announced that no charges would be preferred.

In the spring of 2001 Foreman successfully underwent by-pass surgery and was then signed up, along with Tony Lambrianou and Dave Courtney, to promote Thomas Pink's range of 170 shirts aimed at a core clientele of 30–40-year-old professionals.[9]

In the November it was announced that Reggie Kray had left an estate worth £210,000. Eighty per cent was to go to his widow Roberta. The remainder was to be divided between burglar Paul Henry, who had once shared a cell with Kray

---

[8] For an account of the death of Jack Buggy and the investigation into his killing see L. Read and J. Morton, *Nipper: The Man Who Nicked The Krays*.

[9] One hundred and seventy denotes the number of threads in the Italian fabric from which the shirts are made. *Wall Street Journal Europe*, 5 September 2001.

and who described their relationship as that of 'father and son', and Bradley Allardyce and his wife Donna. Allardyce, who had served a 12-year sentence for armed robbery, had been Kray's best man when he married Roberta. All three were warned that they would forfeit their share of the estate if they published his letters or contacted the media to sell their stories without the permission of his trustees.[10]

[10] For an account of Allardyce's relationship with Kray see John Pearson, *The Cult of Violence*.

2

Gone to Graveyards

As for other old-timers, many have also died. The roll-call of men from the Great Train Robbery now includes Charlie Wilson (shot in Spain), Buster Edwards (suicide), Roy James (heart attack), Brian Field (car accident) and William Boal (cancer). Ronnie Biggs, who had escaped from Wandsworth prison and ended up in Brazil, successfully avoiding kidnapping and attempts to extradite him, had a stroke in 2000 and almost lost the power of speech. In May 2001, in a deal with the *Sun* and no doubt hankering after the benefits of the National Health Service, Biggs was flown back to England where he was promptly remanded to Belmarsh prison. He did not remain there long, for within a matter of weeks he suffered another stroke. He was taken to a hospital where he was chained to a warder, presumably in case some of his geriatric old friends decided to stage a daring raid, pop him in a wheelchair and take him down in the nearest lift which was working. Either that or someone was making a political statement. He was eventually unchained and went back to Belmarsh where he was reported to be in very poor health. Since then he has been in and out of hospital, but the Home Secretary has announced that however poor his health may be it is not sufficiently poor for his release on humanitarian grounds.[1]

Meanwhile speculation continued, 40 years after the event, as to who was also on the robbery but had not been caught, and also who actually ended up with the money. It is almost certain that three others involved were never arrested, and a good deal of fun has been had trying to name them without running into libel difficulties. Journalist Peta Fordham, wife of barrister Wilfrid who appeared for a number of the defendants in the case, had an interesting unpublished story about one possible person:

> As many people know, more men than were arrested were involved in the Great Mail Train Robbery. One of these was 'Michael'. The son of a banker father, he was half English and had been to an English public school. He had got into crime partly for 'kicks' and partly because he was a social misfit.

[1] One way of avoiding extradition from Brazil, as Biggs discovered all those years ago, is to be the parent of a child born in the country. Gloria Trevi, once known as the Madonna of Mexico and now wanted in that country on charges that she sexually abused groupies touring with her band, was discovered to be five months pregnant after being in segregation in prison for two years. It is thought she managed this seemingly magical feat by the use of a gynaecological syringe filled with semen belonging either to her manager Sergio Andrade, who is also facing extradition, or a Brazilian drug smuggler. The Justice Minister Jose Gregori said under the circumstances Ms Trevi would not be allowed to benefit from the provisions.

After the GMTR he went down to the Côte d'Azur (he was then rich) where he picked up with an old pal from the RAF, a French crook nicknamed 'Mesclun' and, together with Mesclun's young nephew, came back to England to do a rather odd safe-deposit robbery. This was fixed from France and the inference is that wanted papers were there since the thieves were allowed to keep the valuables (or at least most of them). In the course of this they killed a man. He was another of the GMTR gang and had tried to get in on the act: he may have been up to blackmail. They got away with the lot.

Michael then got himself on to one of the biggest jewellery raids of recent years. But there he left a finger-print. Which did not matter at the time, as Scotland Yard had no record of him. It did subsequently.

There followed a period of boredom and then a message came through from his French contacts (who I assume are not very high-grade Mafia, themselves often hired to do jobs) to open a safe in one of the embassies in London. This was done; but there was a dispute when one of the gang, who spoke Polish, realised that it was a list of some 2,000 names that their hirers were after – a bit much even for Michael – and in the row Mesclun got killed and Michael shot someone.

He then realised what he had done but thought he could bluff his way out. However, at this point he received a call from the Special Branch of Scotland Yard. They had identified the fingerprint with one on the gun he had dropped. He was given the chance of leading the Yard to his employers, if and when they contacted him. But the condition was that he should leave the country perma-nently. Or risk long imprisonment. (The Yard, Special Branch, no doubt wanted to keep everything discreet but they had to square the ordinary Branch.)

Michael just couldn't play straight. He got his next orders to go to Athens, and await instructions. The order came through. He was to take a certain plane. He had actually checked in when a contact arrived, told him plans were altered and ordered him to return to Rome. He protested that his luggage was already on board. He was informed that this was all arranged: someone else would be travelling on his ticket and his luggage would be forwarded to him in France. His master's orders were law.

So he obeyed. As he got out of the plane at Rome, he saw the headlines. It was the doomed Comet that he had been ordered to leave and he had been the cat's paw for the appalling disaster. He realised that his masters had known of his treachery all the time: this was their pay-off, to use him in such a way that he could never face the world again. His name was among the dead: he had no passport and no legal existence: he could not return to England, he could not bring the murderers to justice: there was nothing more left to him. He hired a car and went up into the hills behind Coursegoules, where they had had their headquarters. There was no one there. He drove to a lonely part and blew his brains out/or went over a precipice – I am not sure which.

It all sounds like the first draft of a treatment for a film but she continues:

My last contact with him was after the jewel-raid. The rest I have had to piece together from other informants. There is a lot of girl-stuff and various family disownings and so forth. I think disclosure of his villainies, at that time, might have caused some sort of political or financial scandal.

Many of the surviving old-time villains, the most prolific of whom is Frank Fraser with five books, also started literary careers. Fraser was followed by his former victim, Eric Mason, whom he chopped with an axe before leaving him wrapped in a blanket outside the London Hospital, with two books. Bruce Reynolds has republished his *Autobiography of a Thief* and Dave Courtney (in between his acquittals at the Central Criminal and other courts) has written three volumes.

Others in print include Biggs, with part of a novel to his credit, and Barbara Windsor's former husband, Ronnie Knight, alleged to have been behind the Security Express Robbery and to have organised the killing of Tony Zomparelli in the Golden Goose pinball arcade in Old Compton Street in revenge for the death of his own brother David. His revised edition of *Black Knight* now accepted that he had contracted Nicky Gerard, son of the legendary (but himself long-deceased) Alf, to undertake the execution.

Another face from the 1960s surfaced albeit briefly and foolishly in London. In August 1966 Harry Roberts, along with John Duddy and Jack Witney, killed three policemen – DC David Wombwell, Sergeant Christopher Head and PC Geoffrey Fox – in Shepherd's Bush when they were being subjected to some routine questioning. Duddy and Witney were soon caught but Roberts, who had learned survival techniques while in the Army, led the police a dance for three months before he was found in Epping Forest, that home-from-home for missing (but mainly dead) people. Roberts was fortunate not to have been tried for murder earlier when a man he had badly beaten died after the statutory period of one year and a day, so automatically reducing matters to manslaughter at worst. For the Shepherd's Bush killing he was sentenced to life imprisonment with a recommendation that he serve at least 30 years. It was unlikely, said the judge, that any Home Secretary would consider his release. But, despite Roberts trying to escape over twenty times, Jack Straw approved his release on licence in April 2000. By this time Duddy had died in prison and Witney, already released, had been killed in 1999 in never fully explained circumstances in Bristol.

As part of his pre-release training Roberts was sent to an open prison near Sudbury, Derbyshire, and allowed out on day-release to work at an animal sanctuary. He was now 65. After a little while he failed to appear at the sanctuary and was later spotted by an off-duty police officer in London with what were euphemistically described as 'some very unsavoury people'. It transpired that he had also been taking driving lessons. On 3 October Roberts was transferred to Lincoln and a full-scale inquiry into his behaviour was launched. It is unlikely that the present or any Home Secretary in the foreseeable future will show Roberts the compassion awarded by Mr Straw.[2]

Over the Easter Bank Holiday 1983, a team led by John Knight carried out what came to be called the Great Bank Note Raid: £7 million was removed from the Security Express headquarters in Curtain Road, Shoreditch, East London, when six masked bandits burst in at about 10.30 a.m. One

---

[2] In recent years Sudbury open prison has rather suffered from the behaviour of inmates out on day-release. In 1999 kidnapper and rapist Clive Barwell was convicted of serious assaults, and in July 2001 Mark Leicester admitted the murder of Margaret Thomson. Both had been on day-release at the time the crimes were committed.

guard had petrol poured over him and was threatened that, if he did not give them the combination for the safe, he would become a human torch.

As with the Great Train Robbery, it was a job which had been on offer for some years and had taken a considerable time in the planning. The Security Express building, known as Fort Knox, was thought to be a virtually impregnable fortress. The underwriters put up the then staggering sum of £500,000 as a reward, but it was police work which paid off. One of the men involved had been under observation for some time and when he was being questioned about another major robbery he told the police he had stored Security Express money at his home. This led to the arrest of an Allen Opiola who was later given three years and three months with a recommendation he serve this in police custody. He became a principal witness against the Knight family.

Ronnie Knight was not charged at the time, but on 10 June 1985 John and James Knight (Ronnie's brothers) and Billy Hickson were three of five men jailed over the robbery. John Knight received 22 years and James 8 years for handling stolen monies; Hickson received 6 years.

With his new wife, Ronnie Knight went to live in Spain, one of the so-called Famous Five unwilling to return to England. It was reduced to four with the conviction of Frederick Foreman who in 1990 received a 9-year sentence for handling part of the Security Express monies.

On 2 May 1994 Knight, in some disgrace on the Costa because his high profile was bringing no favours to anyone, eventually returned to England courtesy of the *Sun* newspaper which, it was said, had paid his family up to £185,000 for the story. He was charged with robbery and dishonest handling. For months gossip circulated in the Underworld that Knight was going to tell all in return for a deal, and what a story that might have been. In the end, however, he remained staunch and received 5 years for dishonestly handling part of the proceeds.

Then on 6 July 2000 Knight, now living with a relatively new girlfriend in Barnet, rather fell from grace. At Hendon Magistrates' Court, he was convicted of shoplifting items worth some £40 including a packet of salmon, a tube of hand cream and some goods from the delicatessen counter at the Waitrose store in Brent Cross. He was fined £200 and costs.

The remaining three of those suspected of taking part in the Security Express robbery who are still in Spain include Ronald Everett, also once a close friend of the Twins. His companions on the Costa are John James Mason, who was acquitted of conspiracy in the £8 million robbery of the Bank of America in 1976, and Clifford Saxe, one-time landlord of the Fox in Kingsland Road, Hackney, where the robbery is said to have been planned.[3]

In January 2001 Saxe, now aged 74 and said to have failing

---

[3] By the 1990s Spain was no longer as safe a home for the ex-pat criminal. The Spanish police were co-operating in extradition proceedings and there was a new and more violent element from the Northeast and Glasgow sunning themselves. On 24 April 1990 Charles Wilson, convicted of the 1963 Great Train Robbery, was shot at his villa outside Marbella. His death was linked to that of Roy Adkins who was shot in the American Hotel, Amsterdam, on 28 November that year. Adkins had been selling stolen emeralds on behalf of Colombians. One of Wilson's killers, Danny Roff, had previously been jailed in Spain over forged currency. In turn he was killed in Bromley, Kent, on 24 March 1997.

Meanwhile things were looking brighter for the former mayor of Marbella, Jesus Gil y Gil, currently facing fraud and money-laundering charges. A number of important original documents lodged at court disappeared in August 2001. An inside job, alleged the prosecution.

eyesight and a heart condition, was arrested in a flat in Fuengirola. He was said to have fallen foul of the Costa del Sol's new zero tolerance organised by police chief Florentina Villabona. Mason was said to have gone to Panama and Everett was in prison in Madrid awaiting extradition. Saxe had told a local journalist 'I am too old to run. They know where I am. So they can come and get me when they want.' Saxe died in early 2002 before the extradition process could be completed.

Two months later Jack Straw, then the Home Secretary, signed an extradition agreement which might lead to suspect fugitives being brought back to England within weeks rather than months or years.

It was thought that there were up to 36 suspected criminals who might be extradited. One of them was Mickey Greene, named from time to time – and when Kenneth Noye was not holding down that position – as being the most wanted man in, or rather out of, Britain. Greene has been on the run for some 20 years, suspected of a variety of drugs and money-laundering offences.

Greene began his career as a bank robber in the late 1960s with the notorious supergrass Bertie Smalls and the Wembley Mob. He served 9 out of 18 years for the Ilford bank robbery and after his release was one of the first to realise how much money could be made buying Krugerrands without VAT, smelting the gold and reselling with VAT added. He moved between Morocco and France where, in his absence in 1987, a Paris court sentenced him to 17 years. Gold bullion and cocaine along with a stolen Rolls-Royce had been found, but not Greene, at his flat.

He was next found by the FBI in Beverly Hills in 1990,

where he had rented the flat of an unsuspecting Rod Stewart. While being taken to Paris to serve his sentence, he took advantage of the stopover at Shannon to leave the plane and disappear into the Irish countryside. Next he bought a house for £250,000 in Kilcock, County Kildare, but he left after suggestions that he might be kidnapped by the IRA and held to ransom. He had come to general notice when he knocked down a pedestrian, a local taxi-driver, Joe White, and his details were given in court. It was believed that he had buried a good deal of his money in Spain and a surveillance operation was set up on his friend John Traynor, at one time suspected of being involved in the murder of the Irish journalist, Veronica Guerin. It was then thought that Greene would be extradited to England to face drug charges, but the Spanish authorities declined to grant a warrant. His next stop perhaps should have been France, but at the end of 2001 he was reported to be safe in Northern Cyprus.

Rather less safe was Greene's former friend, the Greek Cypriot Michael Michael, said to be in 'enormous danger', to which many a criminal would add 'and rightly so'. Giving a new dimension to the word 'bubble' he had just been revealed as Britain's and possibly the world's biggest super-grass, dwarfing the exploits of Bertie Smalls and Maurice O'Mahoney and possibly rivalling those of Sammy Gravano.

His evidence resulted in the conviction of 34 men and women who were jailed for a total of over 170 years, and as a result of his co-operation 26 drug organisations were said to have been smashed. Now in December 2001 Michael was sentenced to 6 years before being lost, possibly abroad, in a witness protection programme which might cost up to £2 million. His sentence followed his plea of guilty to smuggling £132 million of cannabis and cocaine into Britain. By his co-operation he had saved himself 18 years on the tariff, but in return he was said to have a £4 million contract on his head.

For some years there had been talk in the Underworld of the biggest of the biggest supergrasses and, as is usually the case, it proved to be correct. Michael had been arrested in April 1998, which made him eligible for release in April of 2002 even if he did not obtain parole. Born Constantine Michael, the son of a Birmingham shoemaker, in 1957, he first studied fashion at Southgate Technical College and then bookkeeping, although he never qualified.

His criminal career had begun in 1989 with a mortgage fraud and in return for a reduced sentence he agreed to become a registered police informant. It was then that he met his current partner, Lynn, who had a substantial knowledge of the vice trade, and together they set up a chain of saunas in and around North London which, at their peak, were said to be netting £500,000 a year.

According to Michael, he met the celebrated Greene through Lynn whose son had been at the same school as Greene's. Underworld sources tend to discount this, believing he must have had a lower-level entry into the trade. Says one East End face:

> To start off with Mickey would be like having your first drink by going into a pub and ordering a bottle of Dom

Perignon as a starting point. He'd have to have met someone lower down as his starting point; someone who knew the Adamses or the Reillys. I know these people. Mickey's a very suspicious person. He's not a fool. He didn't get his money talking to people like Michael. That said, they get very big in the drug trade very quickly because of the money. A lot of information had been given to people about him even before he was nicked.[4]

Whoever is correct, Michael maintained he was sucked into Greene's empire and things were made easier for him because his handler, DC Paul Carpenter, had been giving him information to pass on in return for £10,000. Michael claimed that Carpenter urged him to move from cannabis to the highly lucrative cocaine trade, but Carpenter has denied this and has been cleared of corruption.

Nevertheless Nicholas Loraine-Smith, for the prosecution at Michael's trial, told the Woolwich Crown Court:

Michael Michael would provide him [Carpenter] with information some of which led to arrests. In turn Paul Carpenter provided him with information which was of great use to the enterprise and some of which was sold on to other criminals. Michael Michael obtained from Paul Carpenter some customs information about Michael Greene which he passed on to him. Paul Carpenter was

[4] Conversation with author, 20 December 2001. Certainly drug dealers may progress swiftly up the ladder. A 2001 Home Office report showed that in a matter of six weeks an individual could progress from club dealing to become a middleman making £10,000 through his own network. At this stage he would be selling between 1,000 and 3,000 Ecstasy tablets a week, a pound of amphetamine, a few ounces of cocaine and some cannabis. *The Times*, 31 January 2001.

paid large sums of money, up to £10,000 per week according to Michael, and was provided with a wealth of information, some of which he'd put into the police system.

Judge Michael Carroll accepted this:

> I have no doubt whatsoever that for the purpose of this sentence you received assistance and encouragement from a corrupt person to carry out and carry on the plan. I am satisfied, however, there were mutual benefits for both of you over that arrangement.

In the four years from 1994 Michael's network brought 19,000 kg of cannabis and 110 kg of cocaine into the country. One of the methods of importing was to use trucks belonging to Marks & Spencer. Another was to use a tourist coach fitted with hidden compartments. As the tourists came to London to sightsee, they had no idea they were almost literally sitting on their weight in drugs. He sold drugs on credit, and cash was sent back to his suppliers less a 2 per cent commission. Money was laundered through a back-room money exchange near Marble Arch.

It was the Customs and Excise which proved to be Michael's downfall. He fell into a surveillance operation in April 1998 and members of his team were caught unloading 16 kg of cocaine and 2,900 kg of cannabis on an industrial site in Hatfield. From there it was a short step to his home in Radlett where, holding a .9mm pistol which he then tried to hide in a wardrobe, he was surrounded by Customs officers. Inside his home, apart from the pistol, was a money-counting machine, £800,000 in cash and, best of all, detailed records of his dealing. Now he began to talk, and about 250 hours of tapes were used.

Apart from his colleague, Mark Hooper, who arranged for the drugs to be distributed and who received 21 years after Michael gave evidence against him, he implicated his 62-year-old mother Maria, who was never charged, and his brother Xanthos, who turned Queen's Evidence and received 4½ years for carrying in the region of £80 million across the Channel. He went on to name Lynn, who also became a grass and received a two-year suspended sentence; Janice Marlborough, who helped run the brothels and handled cash, who became a supergrass and received four years; his lover Sue Richards who did not and received 12 months; and the former Page Three girl Tracey Kirby who drew three years. She had been one of the laundresses taking packets of £200,000 to Europe. Apparently she used some of her wages for beauty treatments.

Most importantly, however, it was the Underworld figures about whom Michael talked, including Kenneth Noye and Greene. Greene he named as being behind the killings of Solly Nahome, alleged to be the financial brain for the Adams family, and their strong-arm man Gilbert Wynter. He claimed that two men, one Stephen McGoldrick, a friend of 'Mad' Frank Fraser, were Spanish-based suppliers and men of utmost violence. McGoldrick was held in custody for four months before the charges against him were dismissed. Richard Hannigan was not so fortunate; he was facing charges of importing 13,000 kg of cannabis when he killed himself in prison. Michael also named a solicitor's managing clerk, suggesting he had laundered money; the man was charged, but the allegation was dropped in September 2001.

There was even a flashback to the celebrated Guinness trial of 1990 when Ernest Saunders, Gerald Ronson, Anthony Parnes and Sir Jack Lyons were convicted over an alleged share fraud support scheme in a takeover battle for Distillers. In a video-link shown in the Court of Appeal in December 2001, Michael claimed he had been approached by a man who told him that he was a relative of a member of the jury and was open to bribery. Michael said he was the middleman in what would have been a £1 million attempt, but he told the court he had never spoken to Michael.[5]

Michael's downfall as a witness came about because of his meticulous business records. Asked to explain certain initials, he tried to provide a cover for a relation and claimed they referred to a second person. Exposed as a liar, his reliability as a witness was at an end.

When it came to it, in January 2003 Michael was ordered to repay nearly £70,000. His wife Lynn was made the subject of a nominal 1p confiscation order. Michael was released from his sentence a year earlier and is reported to be living abroad.

Overall there has not been a high mortality rate amongst British supergrasses; at least not a published one. However, grasses such as Darren Nicholls (now known as Bloggs 19), who gave evidence in a triple killing in Essex, and Michael Michael,

[5] Tony Thompson, 'Downfall of the Supergrass who thought he was untouchable' in the *Observer*, 23 December 2001.

do not always simply get discredited.[6] They may end up dead; very often through their own fault. James Lawson, or rather Peter McNeil to give him his correct name, was one of these.

On 10 February 1998 McNeil, whose informing activities had been of nearly the highest quality, was shot. He had been a key informant in the 1985 trial at the Old Bailey involving a member of the Detroit Mafia. Arrested in Colombia in 1985 for his part in a £20 million cocaine deal, McNeil had rolled over, naming David Medin from Detroit who was arrested as he went to Grays, Essex, loaded with 36 kg of the drug. He too became an informant and in 1988 John O'Boye, another American, was sentenced to 18 years. Two other men received 10 apiece and McNeil became James Lawson.

At about 8 p.m. he opened the door of his rented detached four-bedroomed house and was shot. He died 90 minutes later on the operating table at the North Hampshire Hospital in Basingstoke. McNeil had not been hiding his light under a bushel. Over the years he had made a number of enemies from his dealings in expensive cars and drugs, and had also been supplying doormen for clubs in the Midlands. A compulsive womaniser, he had attracted displeasure from the husbands and boyfriends of a number of women. Perhaps worst of all, he had been unable to keep his mouth shut; he was forever boasting of his role as an informant and of the amount of cash he carried with him.

---

[6] Tony Thompson, *Bloggs 19*. In the Protected Witness Units designed to take prisoners who are giving evidence for or assistance to the police in cases of serious crime, all inmates are known to staff as Bloggs, followed by a number. Their true names and reasons for being in the PWU are, in theory, known only to senior management.

It was, said the prosecution, a domestic affair. McNeil had been involved not only with Lynn, the girlfriend of car dealer James Clelland, but also another former girlfriend. In December 1998 Clelland arrived at McNeil's house making threats, for which he was remanded in custody. The prosecution's case was that while on remand Clelland passed details of McNeil to two brothers and asked them to sort matters out. There were, of course, many others with a grudge against McNeil, and Clelland was acquitted after a three-week trial. Given the nature of McNeil, his death may not have had anything to do with being a supergrass, and Bloggs 19 and Michael Michael may breathe again.

On the plus side for the oldies, Eddie Richardson, who had been jailed for 25 years in a £30 million cocaine and cannabis plot, was released in September 2001; he was then 64. As for his elder brother, Charlie, there was talk of making a film setting the record straight, and Richardson had agreed to co-operate in the film in the event of its being made. A company called Midas Films had been set up in July 2000 to attract £5 million but the stock, requiring a minimum investment of £2,000 per investor, was under-subscribed and the offer was continually repeated.[7]

Some old-time villains, however, had very definitely not retired voluntarily. One was the 57-year-old Tommy Hole, a top-class villain of the 1960s and 1970s, who found to his cost that even though there may no longer be the seriously active old-fashioned East End gangs and families of 30 years

---

[7] *Guardian*, 3 November 2001.

ago, it can still be a dangerous place even to visit. On 5 December 1999 he and Joey 'The Crow' Evans, two years younger, along with a third man who survived and made himself scarce, were shot dead at the Beckton Arms, Beckton, while they were watching television on the pub's giant screen. The balaclava-wearing killers waited until 3.20 p.m. when the pub was emptying and six shots were fired at point-blank range, killing 'The Crow' first and then Hole as he tried to flee.[8]

At around 5.10 p.m. on 19 April 2001 there was an echo of the celebrated Tibbs case of the early 1970s when Lennie Naylor, whose father Stanley had received 12 years for his part in the affair, was gunned down outside his home in Istead Rise, Kent, which was fast becoming commuter-land for London's upper-echelon criminals. Naylor jnr, who described himself as a businessman, had been arrested in June 1996 for attempted murder, but the charge was dropped when the victim of a machete attack in the East End refused to co-operate with the police. Lennie Naylor then served a 7-year sentence for drug dealing. Now he was shot four times as he stepped out of his white Rover in his own driveway. Naylor was well known, and disliked, for his habit of failing to pay for services and goods offered to him.

[8] For the ramifications of these killings which may have stemmed back 20 years, see James Morton, *East End Gangland*.

3

Friends and Enemies

The Brindles and the Dalys

Another feud which rumbled on over the years was that
between the Brindle family of David, George, Patrick and
Tony, who contrary to many reports are not closely related
to 'Mad' Frank Fraser, and the Dalys formerly of South
London. It appears to have begun in August 1990 when
two associates of the Brindles threatened John Daly in the
Queen Elizabeth public house in Walworth. Ahmet
Abdullah, 'Turkish Abbi', then lured a friend of the Brindles,
Stephen Dalligan, into a club basement and shot him.
Dalligan survived. Ahmet Abdullah was then shot in March
1991 in a William Hill betting shop in Bagshot Street,
Walworth. A drug dealer, he was closely related to the very

powerful Arif family who were known enemies of the Brindles.

It seems that Abbi knew he was in difficulties because he was pleading with his attackers not to kill him. He grabbed one of the other men in the shop as a temporary shield and managed to get outside before being shot again. Two of the Brindle brothers, Tony and Patrick, were charged with his murder. Witnesses were allowed to give evidence from behind screens, and only had to give numbers not their names. Some never made it to court. One witness killed himself. Part of the prosecution's case was that Abbi had made something by way of a dying declaration to the effect that the Brindles had killed him.

Tony Brindle said he never knew Abbi from Adam and at the time the man was killed he'd been playing cards and drinking in the Bell in East Street, Walworth. Patrick Brindle did not give evidence, and they were acquitted in May 1992.

Things did not end there, however. A third brother, David, was killed while drinking in the Bell one evening in August 1991, and the man who was simply standing next to him was shot as well. No one was arrested for that shooting, but it was thought to be connected to a beating given to Peter Daly by the old Richardson gang member Jimmy Moody, when he ventured into the Queen Elizabeth. It was suggested that the gunman was Moody and that his was a pre-emptive strike. Moody had escaped from Brixton and later would himself be shot in East London.

In early 1995 the fourth Brindle brother, George, survived being shot from a passing van. Then later that year, in the September, Tony was ambushed and shot outside his home in

Christopher Close, Rotherhithe. The prosecution alleged that this was a hit set up by George Mitchell, a drug dealer in Dublin known as 'The Penguin', on behalf of Peter Daly who had been financing him. The gunman was Dubliner Michael Boyle who was arrested by the police on the spot. The police had been waiting for some time to foil the attempt on Brindle's life.

Boyle had had a long, if ultimately unsuccessful, criminal career.[1] Born into a respectable family in 1946, his father was a sergeant in the Irish army and his mother a legal secretary. He had been well educated and had played both hurling and football for County Wicklow. He worked initially as a builder's labourer, but then began to mix with the local thieves and was soon out burgling. In February 1969 he picked up 22 months for an assortment of burglaries and thefts, followed by another six months in March and again in May. By the October he had graduated, if not with honours: he received 4 years after holding a widow at gunpoint in her Shankhill home. After his release it was back to serious crime. Witnesses were intimidated; his enemies had their homes fired on; banks were robbed.

He absconded from the Central Criminal Courts in Dublin during his trial for robbery in April 1975, when he was allowed to go to the lavatory where he collected a pistol left for him in the cistern. He was caught two months later at Punchestown races, and in 1976 he was jailed for 10 years. Released in 1982, he then took up the increasingly popular sport of kidnapping and in early 1983 was alleged

---

[1] For an account of the career of Michael Boyle and his association with George Mitchell, 'The Penguin', see Paul Williams' excellent *Gangland*.

to have been responsible for six of them, none of which were reported to the police. The ransoms paid were significant but not impossible to raise, and these included £25,000 paid by a businessman for the return of his wife. This time, however, once the woman had been released the man called the Gardai. The kidnapping had been a fairly amateur affair because Boyle – who had nearly run out of petrol on his way to collect the ransom – put in £10 of petrol, leaving £20 at the forecourt. Though not a difficult matter for the Gardai to identify Boyle, it was far more difficult proving he had committed the kidnapping, particularly since a barrister gave him an alibi. He was released without charge.

Boyle's downfall came about when he kidnapped the son of a solicitor from Enniskerry on 9 August 1983. Around 10 o'clock in the evening, the 14-year-old boy was feeding the dogs when Boyle appeared and, holding a gun to his head, ordered him back inside. When the boy's parents arrived it was the solicitor who was kidnapped, taken to a forest near Kilpedder, County Wicklow, and taped to a tree. A ransom was paid and he was released but Boyle, who had been under surveillance, was arrested on 16 August. He showed the Gardai where the kidnap money was hidden and, charged with false imprisonment, incredibly was released on bail. He was remanded until 21 October, on the morning of which he kidnapped Alma Manina at gunpoint, telling her husband Robert that if he wished to see her alive he would have to pay £60,000. After a call to say two men were acting suspiciously at Stylebawn, Boyle was arrested. Alma Manina was released unharmed. Boyle, convinced he would receive a life sentence, asked the police to shoot him. But he had been overly pessimistic and was sentenced to only 12 years.

He was out and about again in the early 1990s, when he was leading a protection racket against wealthy landlords and businessmen. On 4 July 1993 the library of the Earl of Meath was gutted by fire and shortly afterwards the Earl received a demand to ensure such a thing did not happen again. Over the next two years Boyle was thought to have been a moving figure behind another sixteen armed robberies and kidnappings. He was finally arrested on 22 February 1994 after the hijacking of a lorry-load of vodka shortly before Christmas. The Director of Public Prosecutions ultimately decided that there was not enough evidence to go to court, but Boyle had made an independent decision: he would talk to the police. Now he was given the cover name of Pius O'Callaghan.

What the Gardai had in mind was the arrest of Peter Daly's friend George Mitchell, 'The Penguin', whom they considered even more trouble than Boyle. Amongst other things, Boyle told the police about the possibility of a hit on Tony Brindle – contracted, he said, by Mitchell. He was advised to have nothing to do with it. Nevertheless, during the summer of 1995 he was making his way between Dublin and London.

Boyle decided to have his shot, so to speak, on 20 September 1995. At 7.30 a.m. he took up a position in a stolen van outside Brindle's home and waited. At 10.42 Brindle came out and walked to his parked car. The police had thought Boyle would come out of his van and that was when they planned to arrest him, but he did no such thing and, firing from inside, he hit Brindle in the elbow, chest and both thighs. It was only when Brindle turned and tried to reach the safety of his house that Boyle leaped from the van and in turn was shot by police marksmen who hit him five times, also in the elbow and chest.

At his trial in January 1997 Boyle claimed that he had been 'allowed' to shoot Brindle and that the police knew everything. He had certainly not intended to kill the man, merely kneecap him. The blame lay with 'The Penguin' who, he claimed, had threatened to kill Boyle's girlfriend's young daughter if he did not carry out the contract. The story did not wholly appeal to the jury. Boyle received three life sentences for attempted murder and a co-defendant, David Roads, who had been keeping the guns for him, was sentenced to 10 years' imprisonment.

In April 2001 David Roads was killed in an alleyway off Cowper Road in Kingston. He was in Latchmere House near Richmond finishing off his sentence, working on day release. The supposition was that he had been followed on his way back as he tried to get there before the 10 o'clock curfew. He was shot twice in the head. In breach of prison regulations he had a car, which was parked a little way from the prison, and a mobile telephone on which he had called his son at 9.51 p.m.

Six months later in the October, Tony Brindle's action against the Metropolitan Police – claiming that they owed a duty of care and had failed to tell him his life was in danger – was heard in the High Court. He had been granted legal aid to commence it. After the attack he had spent a fortnight in hospital. Now he suffered severe shock, distress and had palpitations, insomnia, and both the inability to concentrate and difficulty in breathing. He had, it was claimed, been a labourer earning £200 a week but now was unable to work.

Friends and Enemies, Old and New

Some from a generation younger, but keeping up the traditions of their elders, were retired on a temporary but long-term basis. On 22 May 2000, Charlie Tozer, then aged 47, and Francis Pope, two years older, from the Camden Town Mob, both of whom had convictions going back to the 1960s, were jailed for 30 years apiece. After a series of abortive trials, they had been convicted of attempting to rob a security guard, Stephen Sturgeon, at a Safeways store in Bow in August 1997 and causing him grievous bodily harm. In his evidence Sturgeon told the court that he had been punched so hard that his helmet was knocked off. He had then been dragged from the store to the security van. One of the men had grinned and said, 'Shoot him anyway.' He had been shot through the hand and the bullet had gone into his thigh. The pair were also convicted of robbing the Nationwide Building Society in Kentish Town the following month.

Just as old-time bandits in America dreamed of retirement to Mexico, Tozer and Pope wanted to retire to Spain. In the meantime they had celebrated their robberies singing 'Pennies from Heaven' at parties in London hotels. Paraphrasing the time-honoured words of Mr Justice Melford Stevenson when he sentenced the Krays, Judge Peter Beaumont told them,

'The time has come for the public to have a long rest from your activities.'

The senior family of the post-Kray generation also had its troubles again when, on 20 May 1999, Bekir Arif, known as 'The Duke', received 23 years for his part in a conspiracy to supply 1,000 kg of heroin said to be worth £12.5 million. He joined his brothers, Dennis who was serving 22 years and Mehmet 4 less following an armed robbery in 1991. The Arifs had come from Northern Cyprus and, settling in South East London, quickly bonded with the other local families. By the 1980s they were thought to be the single most powerful family, with control over pubs and clubs and interests in property.

On 27 November 1990 Dennis and Mehmet Arif had ambushed a Securicor van parked on a garage forecourt in Reigate, Surrey, and in turn been ambushed by the police. The van was due to deliver £¾ million to various branches of Barclays Bank and the woman guard and a colleague had stopped to buy drinks from a café. Mehmet Arif and his brother-in-law Anthony Downer had thrown down their guns; but when old-timer robber Kenny Baker shot at the police they returned fire, killing him. Mehmet Arif pleaded guilty. Dennis Arif ran the difficult defence of duress, saying that Baker had threatened to shoot him if he did not repay some £60,000 of gambling debts. To establish this he effectively had to show that he or his family had been in an immediate life-threatening situation with no opportunity to report the matter to the police. He was unsuccessful. It did not help that he and Baker had been at an Arif wedding reception held at the Savoy earlier in the year which had also been attended by the cream of South London families – the Frasers, Colemans, Whites, Hiscocks and Adamses. He was convicted at a re-trial after the first jury disagreed, one woman juror saying later that she had feared for her life in the event of a conviction.

Previously, Bekir Arif had been convicted back in May 1977 when his brother Osar Arif was acquitted of the murder of a security guard, David Cross; £103,000 had been stolen from a security van on the A2. Bekir received 5 years for disposing of guns found in the Surrey Docks.

Now at his 1999 trial he told the jury that over the years he had been nothing more than a Del-Boy businessman – a reference to the loveable rogue in the television comedy series of working-class vagabondage *Only Fools and Horses* – running a second-hand car business, with no knowledge of any drugs deal. The police and the trial judge thought differently. They had recorded hundreds of hours of surveillance tapes of the operation, including conversations between Arif and a supplier. 'Your role was plainly that of a principal and your conduct was as cynical and dishonest as has been your defence. In my view there is no mitigation,' said Judge Geoffrey Grigson. The 62-year-old Joey Hartfield and Leslie Lucas each received 13 years' imprisonment and driver Patrick Molloy four.

There was also a reminder of the late 1970s great drug-smuggling murder case, the Mr Asia trial, when on 28 July 1999 Charles Russell waved to the court after he and three others were sentenced at the Old Bailey. In 1979 it was Russell who supplied the .38 revolver which was used to shoot New Zealander Martin Johnstone – known as Mr Asia, because of his drug connections there – before he was dumped in a Lancashire quarry. Johnstone's hands had been cut off and his face disfigured to avoid identification. Unfortunately for his killers, they omitted to remove a medallion Johnstone wore around his neck. Russell pleaded guilty to murder and received life imprisonment along with a concurrent sentence of 11 years.[2]

After his release he imported some 50 kg of cocaine from Peru via a bogus wood-shipping firm; it was hidden in parquet flooring and shipped to Estonia via Rotterdam, Hamburg and Felixstowe. The intention was that the consignment should be unloaded in Rotterdam on to a smaller boat, but in March 1997 it was unloaded in Felixstowe where Customs officers found the drugs in the container. Twenty-five wooden planks had been cut in half, hollowed out and glued back together with plastic tubing containing cocaine. The cocaine was then switched for rock salt and sent on its way where it was seized in the Baltic.

Russell's new trial was fraught. In the first, held at Southwark Crown Court, the jury disagreed after 16 days; at the first re-trial at the Old Bailey, it was alleged that one of the defendants had deliberately disclosed a co-accused's bad character, so undermining his defence. The third trial ended after six days of jury deliberations. The total cost of the trials was in the region of £4.5 million. Russell received 22 years and two of his co-accused – Miguel Wong, a Peruvian

[2] Prosecuting counsel in the case, Michael Maguire, died in December 2001. When, after one of the defendants had complained about the cold conditions at Lancaster Castle where the trial was being held, he was asked his opinion, he replied, 'None of the defendants are as cold as Mr Johnstone.'

businessman, and James Bierne, originally from Ireland – were sentenced to 18 years each. A fourth man who was not named received 20 years.

In March 2001 it was announced by the government that a new crime agency was to be set up by 2003 to investigate suspected criminals and confiscate their assets including houses, cars and cash. In newspaper reports Bekir Arif was listed in the top half-dozen of the country's wealthiest criminals. In his case one of his assets would have been his box at the Arsenal Football Club – altogether more modest in proportion than that of his brother, Dogan, who once owned Fisher Athletic, a non-league football club.

Brinks-Mat Revisited

Over the years there have been echoes of the London Brinks-Mat bullion robbery, following which Kenneth Noye was acquitted of killing a police officer. On 26 November 1983 at 6.40 a.m., the then biggest of the biggest of robberies took place when £26 million in gold was lifted from the Brinks-Mat warehouse on the Heathrow trading estate. Its ramifications would still be running in the twenty-first century. The guards were threatened – one with castration, others had petrol poured over them, another was coshed for not producing keys sufficiently speedily. The gang drove off with 6,400 bars of gold waiting to be sent to the Middle and Far East. It was clearly an inside job and it was really only a matter of days before the police latched on to the last guard to arrive that morning – Tony Black – who missed the robbery because he was ten minutes late for work. Black confessed. His sister was living with Brian Robinson, another of the number of villains known over the years as 'The Colonel'.[3] Black also identified two more of the team, Tony White and Michael McAvoy.

In December 1984 Robinson and McAvoy received 25 years each. White was acquitted. Later there was said to be £50,000 on offer to free McAvoy and Robinson; but, if the rumour was true, it came to nothing. Black, who had given evidence for the Crown, was handed a 6-year sentence.

For McAvoy there was still the problem of how to protect his interests. A very large amount of property was missing and in the way of things this could attract a great many high quality predators. It was essential that he have people on the outside whom he could trust to help him. Two such individuals were Brian Perry, who ran a minicab agency, and John 'Little Legs' Lloyd who now lived with Jeannie Savage, the former wife of the celebrated Mickey Ishmael. In turn they recruited Kenneth Noye who soon came under police surveillance with, at one time, John Fordham – dressed in a balaclava helmet and combat fatigues – placed in the grounds of Noye's house. The officer was stabbed to death, but Noye

---

[3] Robinson was one of a number of criminals known as 'The Colonel' of whom there may be several around at any one time. He had been on the Williams & Glyn's robbery in 1978 and had benefited through the mistakes of the No. 5 Regional Crime Squad. The most famous example is Ronnie Kray and another is George Copley. It was Copley who was instrumental in sabotaging the efforts of the Squad when in June 1981 he and Frankie Fraser jnr were on trial at Oxford on charges of robbery. Three months previously a Sergeant Pook visited him in Reading jail and was secretly taped by Copley in a conversation in which Pook confirmed an offer that if Copley was to admit his part in the Williams & Glyn's robbery and also give evidence of corruption against certain London detectives, he would receive only a 5-year sentence. The tape was produced at the trial and the case was stopped. It was 'hopelessly compromised', said Stephen Wooler for the Director of Public Prosecutions.

was acquitted, having told the court he had been in fear of this masked man in his grounds. However, he received the maximum of 14 years after being convicted of handling some of the bullion.

Then, at about 11.15 p.m. on 19 May 1996, Noye was alleged to have been involved in a road-rage killing. Stephen Cameron was stabbed to death in a road-rage incident at the Swanley interchange while his fiancée, a girl completely unconnected to crime, watched helplessly. Noye promptly disappeared. Later it was suggested in the Underworld that, while the meeting was itself accidental, Cameron did in fact know Noye.

The L-registration Land Rover Discovery involved in the incident was registered to an Anthony Francis of Bexley, South London, and Anthony Francis was a name Noye had been known to use. Immediately an 'all persons' bulletin went out on him and, like Lord Lucan, he was spotted across the Continent, in Portugal, the Canaries, Spain of course, Moscow, and by the end of the year he was reported to be safe from extradition in Northern Cyprus. This was probably just as well for him because his name cropped up at the Southwark Crown Court where it was alleged he was a principal in a plan – along with his old friend John Lloyd – to break the bank card scheme in Great Britain. Lloyd received 5 years after pleading guilty.

The prosecution alleged that Lloyd and Noye had established a worldwide network of criminals in order to set up a card fraud on a global scale. It was claimed that the profits would have been in the nature of hundreds of millions of pounds. Their undoing came about when they tried to recruit a computer expert, Martin Grant, who had previously been sentenced to 16 years for trying to burn his wife and child to death. While he was being rehabilitated he was persuaded by a Paul Kidd to take a job at a garage, and there pressure was put on him. He contacted a prison chaplain and former policeman John Bourne. Kidd also received 5 years in the scam. It was said that there was a £100,000 contract on the life of Grant.

Meanwhile, Noye's name was being linked to a number of other deaths over the years. It was not suggested that he had either killed them or instigated their deaths, rather that they had crossed his path. The first was Barbara Harold, who received fatal injuries in a parcel-bomb attack. A friend of Noye's had quarrelled with her and her husband over a tax bill after buying their Spanish villa. The second was Alan 'Taffy' Holmes, a former member of the Serious Crime Squad who had worked on Noye's case in the aftermath of the Brinks-Mat robbery. He shot himself in the garden of his Croydon home after apparently being questioned by the Scotland Yard Complaints Division. The third was garage owner Nick Whiting, who had been kidnapped and then killed in Essex, and the fourth another former Scotland Yard officer, Sydney Wink, who had renumbered guns used in the Brinks-Mat robbery. He too committed suicide. The fifth was builder Keith Hedley who was suspected of, but never charged with, laundering the Brinks money. He was shot dead on his yacht in Corfu harbour on 26 September 1996 as he chased away gunmen.

All kinds of ideas were put forward as to where Noye might be, and indeed in early 1997 it was suggested that the

Underworld had considered him far too dangerous to be allowed to survive and so, like many of his predecessors, he had been taken out in a damage limitation exercise.[4] However, Noye's arrest in Cadiz in September 1998 showed that this was far from the case. He was duly retrieved from Spain and appeared at the Old Bailey where it was suggested that he would not get a fair trial because of the notoriety he had acquired both through the Fordham case and after his disappearance. That argument was quickly rejected and much of the case against him for killing Stephen Cameron came from a seemingly independent eye-witness, Alan Decabral, who was driving his Rolls-Royce at Swanley at the time. He told the jury that he saw a look on Noye's face after the stabbing which seemed to him as though Noye was saying, 'That sorted him out. You have got yours, mate.' All very compelling stuff. Noye was duly convicted and received life imprisonment.

Alan Decabral turned out to be another who died after crossing Noye's path. Although there is no suggestion whatsoever that Noye had anything to do with his death, Decabral did not long survive the trial and it very quickly became clear that he was by no means all he had seemed to be.

On 6 October 2000 he was shot twice in the back of the head as he sat in his black Peugeot 205 at lunchtime outside a Halfords store in the Warre Retail Park, Ashford, Kent. He had been waiting for his son, who found him slumped in the front passenger seat. A witness said that Decabral had been calling out, 'Please don't shoot me.' He had apparently been receiving death threats.

[4] *Evening Standard*, 9 January 1997.

Now it emerged that Decabral was not just a businessman who traded in vintage cars and motorbikes. He also traded in drugs, and was a long-standing associate of the Hell's Angels. Drugs and up to 60 guns had been found by police in three separate raids on his home during the previous 18 months, and he had also been involved in smuggling drink and tobacco. His £350,000 home was unmortgaged and, when raided in the months before his death, he was found to have £100,000 in cash in the house. He had been banned from one of his local pubs.

It might have been thought that the discrediting, albeit posthumously, of Decabral – who was the only witness to have suggested vengeance by Noye – would have helped in the appeal. Now Anne-Marie Decabral came forward to say that her former husband was not only a drug dealer but also a liar. The Court of Appeal would have nothing of it. Decabral was only a piece in the jigsaw, and there were 17 other witnesses. Even if Decabral's evidence was disregarded, 'the only proper conclusion one can come to is that the jury would come to exactly the same verdict', said the Lord Chief Justice.

As for the Brinks-Mat gold, a great portion of which was still missing, in February 2001 the police started a search of a timber merchant's premises in Hastings. However, nothing connected to the robbery was found.

Another name from the Brinks-Mat case turned up at the Old Bailey in 2000. After the robbery the prosecution had got nowhere with their case against John Palmer, known as Goldfinger, when it was alleged that he had smelted down some of the missing gold. Since then he had surfaced in the newspapers from time to time, particularly when he was shown on a television documentary offering to clean up cash for Khun Sa, the drug warlord from the Golden Triangle.[5]

Now he was charged with fraud in excess of £30 million. The prosecution claimed that many of his victims were time-share owners who had been led to believe that the apartments which they already owned could be readily sold at up to 600 per cent profit if they bought a new one at one of Palmer's resorts. Inducements to go to see the new apartments included scratch cards for the punters to play – and as for the cards themselves they could not lose. Once they had fallen for the sales pitches – which could last all day – the prospective purchasers were often taken to the bank to get the necessary cash or persuaded to hand over all their small change. The promised sales of their apartments, for which they paid a registration fee of up to £90 per flat, never materialised and Eurorentals, another of Palmer's companies which also cleared £400,000 in registration fees, failed to rent out any properties on the owners' behalf. Those who had taken out mortgages with Palmer's finance company, Caldon, lost their payments and deposit if they failed to maintain their repayments, which ran at 80 per cent interest.

Palmer defended himself and, in a long and bitter battle, he clashed repeatedly with the retired officer Commander Roy Ramm who claimed Palmer was a super-criminal. Palmer maintained he was simply a misunderstood businessman who was suffering from the backlash following the Brinks-Mat robbery, accepting that he was no angel but still maintaining he was no gangster.

[5] See *Sunday Express*, 8 September 1996.

On 18 May 2001 Palmer was convicted and five days later was sentenced to 8 years' imprisonment. It was claimed that he had swindled some 17,000 tourists, from pensioners to barristers, out of an estimated £30 million. Half of the alleged victims were said to be British. On 10 April 2002 Palmer's preliminary appeal that his conviction should be quashed on the technical ground that the indictment had not been properly signed was rejected by the Court of Appeal. Meanwhile, pending other appeals he was ordered to pay a record £35.5 million under compensation and confiscation orders. At the end of July 2002 the Court of Appeal quashed the confiscation order, ruling that the law on confiscation had been breached.

Throughout the trial, during which the jury retired for 21 days, Palmer wore body armour against (so it was said) potential reprisals from members of the Brinks-Mat robbery team. On one occasion Palmer's right-hand man, Brendan Hannon, a former Catholic priest and later used-car salesman, was alleged to have fled from Tenerife after death threats and a fire-bomb attack on his villa. In September 2000 Hannon had received four years and four months after he admitted conspiring with Palmer. Then, in a separate trial, five directors of Palmer's companies received sentences of up to 18 months. Palmer's long-term girlfriend was also convicted and received a suspended sentence, but the jury disagreed in relation to Palmer's nephew, Andrew, and he was discharged.[6]

Palmer was born in Birmingham in the late 1940s, one

---

[6] See numerous newspaper reports including *Independent*, 19 May 2001, and *Daily Mail*, 19 May 2001.

of seven children, and when he left school at the age of 14 he was only just able to read and write. He began work selling paraffin door-to-door and then progressed through scrap-metal and second-hand cars into gold. With only a single conviction for handling a stolen car in 1973, he was a partner with a coin dealer in Mayfair specialising in Krugerrands.

In 1980 he received a suspended sentence after warehouses containing furniture had been burned down, but it was following the Brinks-Mat robbery that the police raided his home in Bath and came away with some of the stolen gold which had been smelted in his back garden. By then he was in Tenerife. He was expelled in 1986 and, after being refused entry into Brazil, returned to England where he was subsequently acquitted of dishonestly handling the bullion. He received another suspended sentence over a mortgage fraud and then, after paying some £360,000 in a settlement with the insurance company's loss adjusters over the gold, he returned in triumph to his timeshare business in Tenerife.

In 1994 Palmer was under investigation by the television journalist Roger Cook and allegedly told an American private investigator, posing as a drug baron's middleman, that he could launder £75 million and sell guns if the man would supply foreign hitmen for use in Britain. Recorded on video, Palmer also allegedly told him that he had a warehouse containing £750,000 worth of medical supplies following an insurance fraud. At one time Palmer had ranked 51st in the *Sunday Times*' list of the richest men in Britain, but then slumped to a still very respectable 105th in April 2001.

But where had Noye been all the time he was on the run,

and how had he got there in the first place? The answer to the second half of the question was that he had been helped by his old friend John Palmer. Immediately after the 1996 incident at Swanley, Noye had made a flurry of calls on his mobile telephone and one of these had been to Palmer. Noye then made his way to his friend's estate in the West Country and from there, on 20 May, he was helicoptered to a golf course Palmer owned in Normandy. From there they went together to Paris and one of Palmer's employees flew them to Madrid. It was off to Tenerife and then the trail petered out. What had Noye been doing while he was abroad? His biographer, the crime writer Wensley Clarkson, suggests that Noye flew in and out of Britain and that, living on the Costa de la Luz on the Atlantic coast of Spain, he set up a drug-running scheme with a Gibraltarian dealer.[7]

It was after Palmer's imprisonment that more stories of the timeshare business in the Canaries began to emerge. There were allegations that his timeshare empire had been run by fear, and that women working for rival timeshare touts had been hung by their heels over balconies. It was not the first time that time-shares on the islands had been looked at askance. There had been troubles in the 1980s, some of which may have contributed to the death of the Newcastle hardman Viv Graham, whose demise may also have been connected to the death of his arch-rival, Andy Winder, who died in Tenerife in 1993.

The 34-year-old Winder had been in charge of the touts for a major timeshare company in Los Cristianos, Tenerife. Having taken over touting in Lanzarote and Gran Canaria,

---

[7] Wensley Clarkson, *Killer on the Road*.

he now wanted control of South Tenerife, an area which had been the fiefdom of another hardman said to have bitten off a rival's nose before leaving for Portugal.[8]

One version of that story tells of a savage bare-knuckle fight between Graham and Winder after which Graham, who had needed substantial surgery, placed a £10,000 contract on the body-builder. Winder is said to have taken out a bizarre form of insurance or at least revenge in the form of a £30,000 contract on Graham to be executed only after his own death, which came in late September 1993.

There had also been a fight involving four other 'very large men' at a timeshare in Tenerife. It appears that Winder had tried to stab a man from Teesside, and when others intervened he stabbed them as well. A shot was fired and Winder fell dead.

Now the police were investigating the 1999 death of Julie Woodward, a property dealer from Nottingham who was found dead from head injuries in her home in the Los Cristianos development. In February 2001 her sister wrote to the *Tenerife Times* appealing for help in solving the murder. Another killing was the shooting of a timeshare security guard at the Playa de las Americas. One of the bad beatings was suffered by a man, who lost the sight of an eye following an attack in a public house lavatory, also in the Playa de las Americas. He claimed that a Doncaster hitman, Michael Standing, had been sent to kill him. The next day Standing

---

[8] Along with the Costa del Crime, Portugal has long been a haunt of English gangsters. According to a report in the *Guardian*, a group arrived in the late 1980s and 'until recently' were taking £1,000 a week off the managers of Vale Vavio on the promise of not breaking the legs of their timeshare salesmen. Nick Davies, 'Who killed Rachel?' in *Guardian Weekend*, 14 August 1993.

was found hanging by his shirt in a courthouse cell near the airport; he was said to have died from asphyxia.[9]

Yet another name from Brinks-Mat came and went when Brian Perry, who had been entrusted with placing McAvoy's money and for his pains was sentenced to 9 years for dishonestly handling part of the proceeds, was shot in Bermondsey on 16 November 2001. Now Perry was 63 years old and was running the Blue Car minicab firm in Creedon House. Over the years he had been suspected of not having accounted for money deposited with him for safe-keeping on behalf of one of the robbers. At his 1992 trial he received a letter saying that if he believed he was safe because of the long sentences handed out he was signing his own death warrant. But while in prison he is thought to have convinced people that he had not misappropriated the money entrusted to him. On his release he built up his cab firm and made a series of intelligent property investments. But, as was said in the killing of another man not connected with the Brinks-Mat case, 'Everyone in the manor knew it was on top except him.'

Perry was killed by a masked gunman as he stepped from his car, the keys still in his hand. 'He had really upset some serious people,' says one London face. It was thought that a number of other people might well be concerned about their reaching pensionable age. One suggestion as to the identity of the killer was that he was the nephew of a member of a well-known and much feared team of London hitmen from the 1960s.

[9] *Sunday Telegraph*, 27 May 2001.

Brian Wright, known as Uncle or the Milkman because he always delivered, was not at the Central Criminal Court to see his nephew Brian Wright jnr and other members of his worldwide drug-smuggling gang sentenced in June 2002. He had avoided arrest back in February 1999 and fled to Northern Cyprus. The gang was said to have imported £300 million worth of cocaine. The hunt for Wright and his team began in September 1996 when bad weather caused a converted trawler *Sea Mist* to change course and shelter at Cork. Customs found drugs valued at around £80 million on board. Drugs were being picked up from the sea in the Caribbean and brought to Britain after being transferred to boats that had been hired for day trips. Wright had considerable interests in racing and was the intimate of top-class jockeys whom he used to gain information on the running of horses. The drug money was partly laundered through gambling on fixed races. In all, nine people were convicted in Britain. According to the autobiography of former top National Hunt jockey Graham Bradley:

> When there is a breath of scandal within racing there is only one name that comes up. Just as the Krays were meant to be behind every protection racket that operated in London during the Sixties, his name is the first into the frame whenever there is a hint of corruption.[10]

In all, 15 people were sentenced in English, Irish and American courts. Brian Wright jnr received 16 years, whilst

[10] Graham Bradley, *The Wayward Lad*; *The Times*, 15 June 2002; *Guardian*, 15 June 2002.

Ian Kiernan went down for 20 years and Paul Rogers, who crewed the smuggling yachts, received a year less. As for Brian Wright, he fled Northern Cyprus shortly before he would have become the first British person to be deported. He left behind his BMW in a supermarket car park and is thought to have made his way to the Middle East. Although there is no suggestion that Bradley knew of Wright's operation, for his part in supplying information he was warned off for eight years by the Jockey Club. A decision which he has appealed against.

4

The Police

In a curious way, police corruption so far as perjury and falsifying evidence are concerned can only flourish with the tacit help of lawyers and the judiciary. It is their role in this aspect of the judicial process to support the police and iron out problems with their evidence. Corruption was rife in England in the 1950s and 1960s and has still not been completely eradicated.

The name of Kenneth Noye, which has run through the courts like a thread over the last two decades, again appeared – this time in his absence – in the trial of DC John Donald who pleaded guilty at the Old Bailey on 29 February and four months later was sentenced to a total of 11 years. Donald had agreed to take £11,000 from Kevin Cressey for passing on information relating to a surveillance operation on Noye, as well as taking a further down payment of £18,000 for removing surveillance logs on Cressey. The case also involved one of the sons of the notorious 'Mad' Frank Fraser and stretched back to 1992.

In September that year, during a long-running observation, Cressey was seen taking a box and laundry bag from the boot of Fraser's car. Both of them were arrested and 55 kg of cannabis were found. Cressey was also found to have a deposit box containing £8,000. Fraser was given bail and when the case against him and Cressey was dismissed at the magistrates' court he went to Spain. The reason for the dismissal was that the surveillance logs were withheld because of their sensitivity. Meanwhile Cressey had taken the prudent step of working as a registered police informant, and Donald and another officer were designated to be his handlers.

The dismissal of a case in a magistrates' court is not always the final decision, and six months later the Crown Prosecution Service had put its act together and made some decisions. The previously withheld log would be disclosed, and Cressey was to be recharged. Unsurprisingly he was not pleased. He met with Donald and told him that another criminal had put up £500 for information about the surveillance. He also took the precaution of arranging for the BBC's *Panorama* team to film and tape his meetings with Donald, something they did for the next six months. There was something of a flurry of excitement when it was announced that the programme was to be shown, and Donald was arrested the following day when he went to Croydon Police Station.

His was not an unusual story, and one which again pointed to the unwillingness of other officers to see ill or even anything suspicious in the actions of a colleague.

On 4 February 2000 another in a long line of dishonest police officers went to prison. Detective Constable Neil Putnam received 3 years 11 months at the Old Bailey after pleading guilty to 16 counts of drug possession and acts tending or intended to pervert the course of justice. His was perhaps a sad story and, in the end, he fared rather better than his co-defendant Evelyn Fleckney, thought to be Britain's first female drugs baron, who went to prison for 4½ years.

In fact, as it all came out, Evelyn Fleckney was a drug dealer who at one time had an affair with one of Putnam's colleagues and liked to be known as the Chairman of the Board. She recycled drugs seized in police raids, selling on quantities of cannabis, heroin and cocaine and sharing the profits, alleged the prosecution, with a number of other officers. She was also a long-time police informer and in 1990 an officer named Robert Clark had become her handler at the South East Regional Crime Squad (SERCS) based in Dulwich. She later had an affair with him, twice becoming pregnant. Fairly soon Clark was giving drugs to Fleckney, and in 1991 after Putnam joined the SERCS she tipped off Clark that a light aeroplane was going to drop a quantity of cannabis near Fletching, Sussex. Clark seized several blocks and later gave Putnam £300. This was the first time he had accepted corrupt money and he did it, the court was told, because he wanted to be accepted. Later he was given £2,000 after a raid on a public golf club and the seizure of more drugs. In 1995 Putnam was given a further £500 after a cocaine raid on the car park of a public house.

Then in 1998 Fleckney was sent to prison for 15 years

for drug dealing. Working from her nondescript house in Tunbridge Wells, she would take her young son to school before returning to her business of distributing cocaine, cannabis and Ecstasy imported via Portugal throughout south-east England. It was said she had ruled her empire with a rod of iron: 'Go and find another bird that can get what I get. I could have a million pills if I wanted,' she is reputed to have declared.

Three weeks later she decided to tell all, or most of it. Putnam also decided to co-operate in a police inquiry after becoming a born-again Christian, and both were set fair to become supergrasses. This, said the judge, knocked two-thirds off their sentences. In the case of Evelyn Fleckney, her sentence was made concurrent with the 15 years.[1]

As a general rule police officers stoutly deny any miscon-duct when questioned in criminal trials, but an exception was DC Colin Goring who admitted during a murder trial at the Old Bailey in the same month that Fleckney and Putnam were sentenced that he had been a cannabis user for ten years and had later become addicted to cocaine. Samson Teshome was accused of the murder of Adiane Teane, a single mother and Ethiopian refugee, at her flat in Dalston in November 1998. His defence was that he had been set up for the murder by a ruthless North London drugs gang. Stephen Kamlish, for the defence, suggested that the detective had been shielding the real killers because they were supplying him with cocaine – something Colin Goring denied.

[1] *The Times*, 3 March 1998; *Evening Standard*, 4 February 2000; *Guardian*, 5 February 2000.

Goring told the judge that he had become involved with a woman in East London (whom he refused to name) after being sent to investigate a burglary at her home. She had, he said, needed a counsellor. They had sex and she began to supply him with cannabis. Later her son supplied him with cocaine. It was only in November 1999, when he found he was overdrawn by £7,000, that he decided to give up the drug and had not touched it since.[2]

Shortly after Fleckney and Putnam saw the light, they were followed into court in April by an ex-Flying Squad officer who had also volunteered to give evidence against his former colleagues. DC Terence McGuiness received 9 years after admitting crimes which included burglary, perverting the course of justice, theft, and conspiracy to supply cannabis.

Like so many officers before him, he had put together a 'first aid kit' including a balaclava and an imitation gun to be planted on suspects. He had been caught in 1997 in a sting with another officer, Kevin Garner, involving £200,000 of cannabis, when CIB officers planted 80 bars of cannabis inside a bathroom cabinet in a flat in East London and McGuiness and Garner were filmed taking it. Garner also began helping the anti-corruption unit CIB3.

McGuiness had been working on his own account since at least 1992, when he took £500 from a senior officer who had been drying out money dumped in woods after a security van robbery. It was freewheeling all the way after that. The same year he went to Brighton, where he was given £50 from £1,500 unrecovered from the robbers. He was learning

[2] *The Times*, 22 February 2000.

quickly. Asked to guard £300,000 recovered after a lorry theft, he took 30 bags containing £3,000 for himself.[3]

The McGuiness–Garner case had repercussions when in July 2000 Michael Brown, Anthony Taylor and Kevin Martin – who had been convicted of robbing a jeweller's shop in Edmonton and received 10 years apiece – were freed by the Court of Appeal. In the raid, in which the men had constantly denied taking part, £6,000 was stolen after the jeweller had been immobilised with a stun-gun. Garner was the officer who said he had found the stun-gun in a search of Kevin Martin's flat which took place nine months after the robbery. McGuiness was also there during the search. The men's first appeal had been dismissed in June 1996. Now the Appeal Court judges said that it was surprising that such an incriminating object would be found 'so ill concealed after a surprise raid'. Nor were the judges by any means happy about the 'surprising' way in which a fingerprint had been matched several months after the robbery.

The rest of the officers in the Evelyn Fleckney case were finally dealt with in August 2000. By this time her lover Robert Clark had received 12 years and his partner Detective Sergeant Drury one less. During their affair Clark and Fleckney had appeared together at police functions, and the court was told that a number of officers knew who Fleckney was but turned a blind eye. Once, when she was arrested on a drink-drive charge, Clark had ordered an inspector to release her. Three other officers received sentences of up to 42 months each.

[3] *The Times*, 7 April 2000.

In June 2002 a Home Office report suggested that the fight against crime was being hindered by a new breed of corrupt police officers. It was thought that corruption was on a more individual basis rather than the endemic corruption of some squads in the 1960s and 1970s. Officers with a known weakness, such as a marriage breakdown or a penchant for drink or drugs, or those having financial problems, are targeted. 'Individual compromise' was the key phrase.[4]

At least some secrets of Scotland Yard were divulged during the trial of the private investigator Jonathan Rees, who owned a firm called Law and Commercial, jeweller Simon James and the often-acquitted-gangster-turned-media-personality Dave Courtney. On the other hand, perhaps they were not. The allegation against the three was that they had conspired along with the former Detective Constable Austin Warnes to plant 15 wraps of cocaine in James's wife Kim's Fiat Punto in the hope, first, that she would be jailed and second, that as a result she would lose custody of their two-year-old son.

Part of the story, alleged the prosecution, was that Dave Courtney was a registered police informant – something which, if it were true, would have ruined his status in the Underworld. He had made nine court appearances in the last 15 years and had been acquitted on every occasion. Warnes, who pleaded guilty, was alleged to have told his superiors that he had received information from his registered informant Courtney. Not right, said Courtney. He had been

4 Police Corruption in England and Wales: An Assessment of Current Evidence.

involved in a 100 per cent corrupt relationship with Warnes over a 15-year period which involved recruiting fake inform- ants, obtaining information from the police computer and wrecking the case for the prosecution. Warnes received 4 years and Rees and Simon James 6 apiece. Courtney recorded his tenth successive acquittal. Afterwards he denied he had ever been an informer and said, 'I have always had faith in the British justice system.'[5]

The name Jonathan Rees might have struck a chord in the minds of crime spotters. It was his partner Daniel Morgan who had been killed in the car park of the Golden Lion pub in Sydenham. He had been axed to death.

[5] *Observer*, 17 December 2000.

5

Kidnapping and Prostitution

Kidnappers

By 2000 kidnapping had become one of the crimes of choice, regarded as much less dangerous (for the kidnapper, that is) than an armed robbery. As for the victim, on statistics available it would seem that some 7 per cent of victims were released without payment and a further 3 per cent escaped. Of those who had no insurance against kidnapping some 10 per cent were killed, a figure which was reduced to 1 per cent if insurance was in place. In the years 1991–8 Colombia – where, just as Britain has had a drugs tsar, there is a kidnapping tsar – led the list of most dangerous countries with a staggering 4,040 kidnappings, followed by Mexico (656) and

Brazil (523). In fifteenth place, Turkey boasted a modest 28. Other countries regarded as highly dangerous for businessmen included Algeria, India, the former Soviet Union, the Philippines, Nigeria and a clutch of other South American countries. The victim of a kidnapping in Mexico could expect the situation to be nasty and brutish but relatively short. In Colombia there would be protracted negotiations, and there has been a high likelihood of a fatal outcome in Chechnya.

Short of rescue with the victim still in possession of all his faculties, payment of between 10 and 20 per cent of the original demand could be considered satisfactory. The lowest payment was thought to be £500 and the highest a reputed $64 million. Worldwide, ransom money paid was estimated to be around £235 million.

In Britain, kidnappings by triads of illegal immigrants and holding them against further payments from their relatives in China were one example of the sport. In 1996 a chef was kidnapped at Hendon tube station and held for twelve days before being released by the Organised Crime Group. During his captivity he had been given a cup of boiled rice every two days and made to crawl on the floor and bark like a dog while his captors kicked him. He was a great deal more fortunate than John O'Grady who was kidnapped in 1988 by Dessie O'Hare, the so-called 'Border Fox', who received 40 years imprisonment. Not only had he kidnapped the Irish dentist but he had also cut off his fingers. O'Hare said he had been acting from political motives.

The kidnapping of members of rival gangs has become increasingly common, with argument over payments for drugs as one of the causes. In 1997 a man was kidnapped outside Hounslow tube station. Called down to London to discuss the non-payment of a £40,000 debt, he had been put in a van and then attacked with a stun-gun. During his time as a hostage he was moved to various addresses in the Hounslow area and given shots from an adapted vacuum cleaner. When found by the police, he had suffered extensive burns, cuts and a broken nose. Five men and a woman were arrested. The man may have escaped relatively lightly because the next year brothers Wayne and Shane Scotland received sentences of life imprisonment after they had kidnapped and shot a 19-year-old disc jockey in Edmonton, North London, over a drugs dispute.

There was also a trend towards kidnapping a person not for money but as a hostage to persuade his colleagues to co-operate in some scheme or other, as when in April 2000 a man was held in Wembley after associates of his had become involved in an insurance fraud.

In September 2000 the 21-year-old Merion Martin told Middlesex Guildhall Crown Court how he had been kidnapped, driven to an open spot and shown a shallow grave. In the dock were Jason Germain, Christopher Whitcomb and Eugene Vatsallo who, said Martin, had held him for 18 hours. The problem had arisen, he said, over a deal for dodgy laptop computers. The three men provided him with the money, but when he went to buy the machines he was robbed of his rucksack full of cash. According to the prosecution Germain and Martin then met with Vatsallo, a night-club owner, and went to Cardiff to collect Whitcomb. After being shown the grave Martin was told, he said, that he would be set alight. Once the fire was out, he would be cut into pieces and buried in concrete. He persuaded them to allow him to ring up his father, who alerted the police. The trio were followed to an hotel in Kent where the police used stun-guns in the arrest. The defence claimed that the whole thing had been planned by Martin and Vatsallo was acquitted. The other men received three years each, with the judge commenting that he was sure the whole story had not emerged.

In December 1999, 19 men and women received a total of 200 years after they had seized five people from flats in Plumstead and Billericay and held them in Acton for eight days. The kidnappers had been acting in concert with Snakeshead gangs from Fujian province in China.

In September 2000 the police raided Spinnaker House in Byng Street on the Isle of Dogs and released seven women and two men who had been abducted and held in a two-bedroomed maisonette there. Another man who managed to escape had raised the alarm. The police said that there were a number of Chinese gangs operating in London who specialised in kidnapping illegal immigrants whom they had previously brought into the country and then demanding yet more money from their families in China.[1]

Late May 2002 saw an outbreak of violence in the Chinese community. A well-known restaurant in Bayswater had its windows smashed, and in another a cache of machetes, hand-guns and a machine-pistol were found. There was a major fight in Newport Place in the heart of Chinatown. One man was taken to hospital with injuries caused by a meat cleaver.

---

[1] *Daily Telegraph*, 8 September 2000.

The police thought the trouble was brought about by the Snakeheads – notorious people smugglers – trying to muscle in on the action, rather than by traditional triad interests.

In 2000 there was a worldwide reported total of kidnappings of rather over 1,700, while in the United Kingdom the kidnap business grew 500 per cent that year. In January 2001 the Metropolitan Police investigated 11 cases. Courses at a cost of £15,000 a head were held to teach potential victims the best way to survive, while specially trained bodyguards were available at £1,200 a day depending on the area and length of time required.

In August 2001 four members of a Russian *mafiya* kidnap gang were sentenced to a total of 37 years after twice kidnapping Semeon Agadjanov from his home in Kent. The first time the Moscow businessman had handed over £375,000 and promised a further £1 million. When this did not materialise he was kidnapped a second time, burned with cigarettes, chained to a lavatory and kicked in the face. This time he was freed by Scotland Yard's Kidnap and Specialist Investigation Squad. Perhaps the most curious and alarming feature of the case was that the four men were described by their lawyers as 'businessmen' and as having no previous convictions.

Prostitutes

In September 2000 one of the more unlikely controllers of prostitution was ordered to hand over more than £2 million which she had earned from three London saunas – the Aqua Sauna, the Lanacombe Sauna and the Ishka Bath – in which women smuggled from Thailand and Eastern Europe worked. The 64-year-old Josephine Daly, who appeared in court at Inner London Sessions in a wheelchair, pleaded guilty to controlling prostitutes between 1996 and 1997. As she was wheeled past a bank of flowers and plants from well-wishers including customers – 'Keep smiling, the end is near' and 'I hope this small token of flowers shows that some of us support you' – she said that she had only pleaded guilty to save her daughter, Emilia Tawaih, who had been charged with her but against whom the prosecution offered no evidence.

> The police surveillance showed that around 1,500 men were going each week into the saunas. Undercover officers paid a £10 entrance fee. They were then invited to choose a woman and a variety of sexual experiences was offered. In the time-honoured words of newspaper reporters, at that moment they made their excuses and left. The prostitutes, who lived in a 60-room hostel also owned by Daly, were allowed to keep any money they earned. The sauna receptionists took her the door money to her home in Crouch End. The police, in whose magazines Daly advertised, regarded her as being in the top flight of London's whoremongers. It was later suggested that a well-known East London family was trying to arrange a take-over of her saunas one of which was licensed to provide 'special treatment'.[2]

Curiously, a woman of the same name but who was no relation – Mary Daly, 'Madame Stiletto' – had died the same year

[2] *Evening Standard*, 2 August 2000.

Josephine Daly appeared in court. Mary Daly was regarded as *the* biggest of London's whoremongers.

> People often said that Mary Daly reminded them of Madge, the downtrodden little shrew who sometimes sits at the feet of the comedian Dame Edna Everage, quivering nervously, serving no great purpose other than to be the butt of the Dame's cruellest barbs. Mary Daly was small and old and thin, she wore carpet slippers and baggy cardigans, and she liked to sit with her ankles crossed and her elbows gathered in her lap. The smoke from her Silk Cut would drift slowly across her cheek, adding yet another layer to the yellow-brown streak which its predecessors had already painted over the years across the loose grey fringe of her hair.[3]

In fact, 'downtrodden' was by no means a word to apply to her. She grew up in Islington between the wars, and for a short time had had a relationship with Jimmy Essex, a former London face who holds the doubtful distinction of being one of the relatively few people to be charged with murder on two separate occasions and to be acquitted on both.[4]

Given the increasing freedom in sexual relations in the second half of the twentieth century, it might have been expected that, in Britain at least, prostitution would effectively have been wiped out. This is far from the case. One of the more curious aspects of prostitution, which is linked inexorably to people-smuggling, emerged at the beginning

---

[3] Nick Davies, *Dark Heart*, p. 250.
[4] In fact he was convicted of manslaughter. For various episodes in Essex's life see Frank Fraser, *Mad Frank*, *Mad Frank's Friends* and *Mad Frank's Diary*.

of 2001 with the news that in the two previous years about 50 West African and Chinese girls, some as young as 12, had been kidnapped or persuaded to leave a refuge in Sussex where they were sheltering.

Having arrived in England, the girls had been released into the care of 'relatives' or 'sponsors' whose documentation was later found to be false. They had arrived under the impression that they would be working as domestics; the reality was that in many cases they would be working in brothels, very likely in and around Turin.

One thought was that they feared threats of voodoo revenge if they did not go with their sponsors. Some of the girls said that before leaving Africa they had had part of their head hair as well as their pubic hair cut off. They had also been required to give up their underpants and parings from their nails. These samples would then be used as a form of control over them.[5]

[5] *Daily Telegraph*, 9 March 2001.

6

The A Team

Meanwhile the North London teams seem mostly to have been keeping their heads out of the range of police fire if not each other's. Allegedly the most powerful is the tightly knit Adams family, known as the A Team, said to comprise a number of brothers and cousins, and to have built up a multi-million-pound empire based on gun and drug running involving shipments from Eastern Europe and Israel to Britain and Ireland. Terry, Patrick and Tommy Adams were amongst the eleven children of Florence and George Adams and, so it was said, they gained their expertise at the feet of the old Italian families in Clerkenwell.

The first the outside world heard of them was almost in passing when in 1985 Tommy Adams was acquitted of handling some of the proceeds from the celebrated Brinks-Mat robbery. In 1993 another brother Patrick, known as Patsy, was acquitted of involvement in the importation of 3.5 tons of cannabis estimated to be worth £25 million. His co-defendant received 11 years. He was also acquitted of another offence involving drugs, claiming that a gun and a full set of body armour belonged to his wife.

The *cognoscenti* had known of them for years, however, and wondered why the police had taken no steps to crush the team in its infancy. Now the Adamses were beginning to acquire the reputation of being untouchable. The Kray Twins had acquired that kind of reputation before their arrest at the end of the 1960s when it was said that if a complaint was made against them, by the time the complainant walked out of the police station they would know. Perhaps the police did have a grander plan. In October 1996 it was reported that, following the unwelcome attentions of MI5 under orders to liquidate the Adams empire, the family was selling up – six night-clubs including two in Chelsea and The Angel were said to have been sold, and they had disposed of interests in pubs and restaurants. In early 1997 it was rumoured that the senior members of the family had moved to Spain.

In 1988 one supposed member of the A Team, Wayne Hurran, had been convicted of murder and armed robbery after shooting a boy in the street. In the mid-1990s a story circulated that for his own safety he had been kept in various segregation units throughout the country, but was now about to be released and had turned informer against the family. If this was ever true, he seems to have changed his mind.[1]

He came into the limelight again in August 1995 when

---

[1] John Gibb, 'The Gang Stars' in *Evening Standard*, 3 January 1997.

he told the *Daily Mirror* that he had shot two men dead and ordered the killing of a third while in prison. He was, he said, wiping the slate clean before he came out of jail.[2]

The first of Hurran's victims to be killed was Gary Hutchings, whom he shot in Islington in 1986 over a domestic matter. The second was in August the same year when he killed Frank Moody, the doorman of the Willows public house in Bermondsey. This was for an alleged slight to his cousin whom Moody had punched, knocking her teeth out. The third was the one he organised from prison. This time the victim was David Foley, a minicab boss, and again it was a domestic dispute. Foley was killed outside the Northumberland Arms in King's Cross in July 1994. Hurran also admitted to some 65 more robberies committed, he said, in London and on the South Coast. He was never prosecuted.

The Adamses, rightly or not, were considered by members of the Underworld as a group to be feared. One noted thief, asked if he would say anything about them off the record, said he wanted to say, on the record, that he had nothing to say.

Another had said earlier:

They are today's equivalent of the Krays and the Richardsons. Say a man owes you £15,000 for a legit piece of business, then he goes to the Xs and says he doesn't want to pay. They say they'll get you off his back for £5,000 and they do. I'm not frightened but I'm not going up against them. Why don't the police do something about

---

[2] *Daily Mirror*, 21 August 1995.

them? I don't know. There's three of them on bail at the moment. One for a big drugs thing and the others for possessing shooters. Maybe the police have a grander plan. I don't know.[3]

Some have not been happy with their style in allegedly using black criminals to do the dirty work. Others, however, speak well of their generosity:

When I had just come out I was introduced to Tommy and he simply said, 'I've heard about you' and pulled out all the money he had on him and told me if I needed more I was to see him. When I counted it out it came to £300.[4]

When, in 1991, Frank Fraser was shot outside Turnmills night-club in Camden Town it was suggested – something which he denied – that this was over an unhappy, unsuccessful drug involvement with the family. He said it was undercover police. The family did not deign to make any comment. Freddie Foreman was also stated to have been at the sharp end of the Adams family's attention. It was suggested, but later found to be false, that his son had been attacked by Adams men in Spain. Foreman received messages of support and loyalty from the London and Essex Underworld including, it was said, the Rileys and the Arifs, and a meeting was arranged at a club in the Finchley Road where an accommodation was reached.

[3] James Morton, *Gangland*, p. 324.
[4] Conversation with author, May 1999.

It was shortly after the Fraser shooting that John McVicar, the former East End hardman turned sociologist and writer for *Punch*, was again told of the folly of writing stories about the family. Apparently he had previously been visited in 1987, and this time the messenger shrugged and warned him, 'John, it saddens me to say it, and I hope it won't go further, but if I were you I'd purchase some insurance, get in some target practice and be very, very careful of big trail bikes in your immediate vicinity.'

Over the years reports began to surface of a struggle between the Adams family and that of the Rileys, brothers based in the Kentish Town area. There had been a major skirmish in January 1990 when there was a shooting in Huntingdon Street near The Angel, Islington. The whole matter was thought to have been finally resolved in March 1996, it was said substantially in favour of the Adamses, following a gun-battle in Finsbury Square in the City.[5]

Perhaps on the principle of giving dogs bad names, over the last 15 years a number of incidents have been laid at the Adams family's door without any evidence to support them. These have included blame for the death of Terry Gooderham, found shot in his black Mercedes together with his girlfriend Maxine Arnold in Epping Forest on 22 December 1989. Gooderham had been a stocktaker for a number of clubs, and amongst the suggestions on offer was the disappearance of £150,000 said euphemistically to have been 're-directed'.

Some laid the actual killing at the feet of the by-now-deceased Jimmy Moody, a former associate of the Richardsons,

[5] John Gibb, *Evening Standard*, 3 January 1997.

who was himself shot dead on 1 June 1993.[6] But there again
it was argued it might just as easily have been undertaken
by an Adams associate, Gilbert Wynter.

It has also been alleged but never proved that the family
were involved in the murder of Claude Moseley, the former
junior British high-jump champion who was stabbed to death
with a Samurai sword, more or less slicing him in half, over
a drugs deal in 1994. Whoever was responsible, it was
thought that Moseley had been lax in his accounting methods.
A 22-year-old received three months for contempt when he
refused to testify against Gilbert Wynter. This man, who was
serving a 5-year sentence for armed robbery, had originally
made a statement claiming he witnessed the murder which
took place in his house while he was on the run from prison.
The case against Wynter was dropped. Said Judge Coombe:

> It is terrible that a man who can commit this kind of
> crime can get away with it because another man refuses
> to do his duty and give evidence. If a murderer gets away
> with it they are likely to kill again until men have the
> courage to give evidence.[7]

But there again, some will argue that the judge did not have
to live and work in the area.

Gilbert Wynter also freelanced, running the lucrative
doorman trade. He walked with a limp after being hit by a
police car in 1992. His former girlfriend, Dee, said he spoke

[6] For an account of Jimmy Moody's life and death see Cal McCrystal, 'The Hit
at the Royal Hotel', in *Independent on Sunday*, 8 August 1993. For a more personal
account see Frank Fraser, *Mad Frank*.
[7] 17 February 1995.

a lot about God but – backing things each way – also used African oils to keep him from harm. His mother was said to be some sort of Obeah princess. Both he and Solly Nahome (see below) were thought to have been double-crossing the family.[8]

In September 1998, Sean 'Tommy' Adams was reported to have left the dock laughing after being jailed for 7½ years for his part in an £8 million drug-smuggling operation. An additional £1 million confiscation order was not thought to present any great problem because the family was reputed to have assets of £50 million. As it was, the police could find no single bank account held by him. One suggestion for his conviction was that he had been freelancing and, with no family help forthcoming, this was a lesson not to act without the family's authority. A meeting was said to have taken place in Belmarsh prison, where he was on remand, when the facts of life were explained to him in words of one syllable. Two of his old schoolfriends, Michael Papamichael and Edward Wilkinson, received 6 and 9 years respectively. [9]

Now the newspapers turned on the Adamses. 'Britain's Biggest Crime Family' said John Twomey in the *Daily Express*. There were suggestions that the family had originated the 'two-on-a-bike' hit in which the pillion passenger shoots the victim. At best they can only have imported it to England, because it has been a trademark of South American killing for decades.

---

[8] John McVicar in *Punch*, 31 July 1999.
[9] See Jo-Ann Goodwin, 'The Curse of the Untouchables' in *Daily Mail*, 19 August 2000; Dean Nelson, 'Adams Family Values' in *Gear*, September 2000.

Clearly, however, the family was having difficulties at the time. Gilbert Wynter simply disappeared in the March and almost immediately after the imprisonment of Tommy Adams, Solly Nahome – a Hatton garden diamond buyer said to be the family's money adviser – was shot dead outside his Finchley home by a black gunman. It was thought that Nahome and Wynter had been playing dangerous games on more than one side of a fence. The story in the Underworld was that Wynter was strangled but his body, if indeed he is dead, has never been recovered.

Immediately there were suggestions that a gang war would follow and that Patrick Adams had been seen at Heathrow amid speculation that he had returned from Spain to exercise some control over matters. Certainly in the weeks that followed no gang war broke out. Instead the family became involved in the financing of a very smart and fashionable night-club in the East End.

In 1999 one of their close friends, Christopher McCormack, was acquitted of causing grievous bodily harm to the financier David McKenzie. It was alleged at the Old Bailey that McKenzie had borrowed money from Terry Adams, said to be the family's chief executive, and was summoned to a house in Finchley, North London. Describing Terry Adams, McKenzie said:

> Everyone stood up when he walked in. He looked like a star . . . a cross between Liberace and Peter Stringfellow. He was immaculately dressed in a long black coat and white frilly shirt. He was completely in command.

McKenzie claimed that an attack later took place at the home of John Potter, Terry Adams' brother-in-law, in Islington. It was accepted that there had been an attack in which McKenzie's ribs were broken and he suffered knife wounds to his face. His nose and left ear were left flapping; tendons in his wrist were cut. The jury, who deliberated for a day, accepted John Potter's version of the incident that the attack had been carried out by a complete stranger. Allegations that McKenzie's blood was on Christopher McCormack's jacket were explained by the fact that he had broken up a fight between the financier and another man at an earlier meeting, and that was when it became stained.

But reports of the family's permanent exile proved premature when in 1999 the Crown Prosecution Service found to its horror that Mark Herbert, son of a retired Scotland Yard detective, had sold them a list of 33 informers.

The prosecution at the Old Bailey claimed that while Herbert had been moonlighting as a bouncer in a South-West London night-club to supplement his £14,000 a year CPS salary, he had been passing information. This included tip-offs about 12 forthcoming arrests, including that of an alleged enforcer for the family. But when that man was arrested there was no sign of evidence at his home and he was acquitted. Herbert had also passed over details of two brothers from South London who were said to be in dispute with the family and to have contracts worth £250,000 on their heads.

In 1998 Herbert was a junior clerk working on a team investigating the brothers. He told the jury that he had passed on the information because he was fearful for his life and that of his fiancée. In fact he had received £1,000 for the information which he had accessed from computers. He was sentenced to 6 years' imprisonment. His co-accused, Kevin Sumer, who was alleged to be the conduit, was acquitted. He told the court that he had simply been humouring Herbert when agreeing to show the lists to the Adams family; as far as he was concerned, the lists were bound for the police. The prosecution had alleged that a bag passed to his friend Billy Isaacs contained the lists. In fact, said Sumer, the bag contained wedding photographs. He had no idea that Isaacs knew the Adams family. It was thought that Herbert would be kept in some form of segregation in prison both to protect him and also to prevent him from passing on more information which he might have memorised.

In September 2000 the *News of the World* survey of Britain's wealthy criminals listed Tommy Adams as the second wealthiest behind Curtis Warren.[10] Despite efforts to keep out of the public eye the family continued to make the news, however. In November 2001 the remains of Scott Bradfield were discovered in two suitcases found behind a conference centre in Torremolinos. An attempt had been made to burn them, but on 26 October the remains were found when the fire brigade was called to the site. Bradfield's arms and legs were stuffed into a pink Samsonite case, with his head and

---

[10] *News of the World*, 17 September 2000. If the story is accurate, Warren's wealth or at least earnings were probably matched, if not overtaken, by those of Andrew Billimore, a former guide at Ely Cathedral who, when he received 20 years at Norwich Crown Court in September 2000, was thought to have grossed £640 million. This was the figure calculated by detectives after a remand prisoner said that Billimore had told him he was bringing in cocaine from the Netherlands at £20,000 a kilo and Colombia at £4,000 less. *Independent*, 19 September 2000.

torso in another. It appeared that he had been badly beaten before being killed.

Bradfield, a friend of the family, disappeared after the shooting of James Gaspa at his home in Islington on 8 May 2000. He had been seen with Gaspa the day before the murder, but disappeared almost immediately after. Bradfield was thought to have been working as a barman in the Marbella area and the British police were about to request his extradition.[11] Now there was speculation as to whether he had been killed to prevent him talking if he was returned to Britain. Another theory was that he had been dealing in drugs in Spain and his death was a warning to competitors.

Whichever is the case, Bradfield's death added to the list of British criminals dating back to the 1970s – such as the robber-turned-informer John Moriarty, and Charlie Mitchell who defected from the Krays – who have died on the south coast of Spain.[12]

In May 2002 Tommy Adams was released from his sentence after his wife paid £1 million, reportedly in two instalments of cash, in settlement of a court order.[13]

---

[11] *The Times*, 3 December 2001; *Independent*, 4 December 2001.
[12] John Moriarty, a bank robber of the 1960s, was a known supergrass. Mitchell, who had worked with the Krays and been arrested with them, crossed over during the committal proceedings at Bow Street. He was also a noted greyhound and horse doper.
[13] *Sunday Times*, 5 May 2002.

7

Turks and Yardies

The Turkish Mafia in London

In June 2001 Scotland Yard announced that fatal shootings in London were running at five a month for the year to date. Non-fatal shootings in April and May had totalled 46, and the number of fatal shootings had risen to 13. It was thought that over 20 contracts had been taken out on gangland rivals, with professional gunmen charging a relatively modest £20,000 a hit. Five of the recent killings were believed to have been linked to Yardie crack-cocaine wars and others to the London Turkish mafia.

On Bank Holiday Sunday in May 2001 Hasan Mamali and Sama Mustafa were shot and killed in Balmes Road, Hoxton, having gone there with two other men in a white BMW.

Mamali was shot in the back of the head; when Mustafa tried to run away, he was shot in the back, chest and head, and probably shot twice more as he lay on the ground.

It was thought that they might have tried to rip off someone in the heroin trade and had paid the price. They had certainly fallen foul of powerful Turkish mafia figures. The belief is that there are three or four established main Turkish mafia crime families in London with links to Turkish organised crime and quasi-terrorist organisations such as the Grey Wolves. People, as well as drugs, are smuggled, and the main run for the latter is from Afghanistan through Turkey into the Low Countries.

The first Turkish mafia killing in London is thought to have been that of 33-year-old Memet Kaygisiz, shot dead on 17 March 1994 while playing backgammon at a Turkish club in Islington. He probably entered the drug trade by financing a stake through people-smuggling, a trade which had been growing since the early 1990s. Kaygisiz had been bringing them in through Dover in a cramped truck with instructions to say, if they were found, that they wished to claim asylum. The fee was what now seems to be a modest £3,500. Before his death he had also been an associate of Farok Koroglu, convicted in 1995 of importing £7 million worth of heroin into Britain.

The next year there was the death of a Turkish Cypriot found shot in a car park only a matter of hours after his arrival in the country. This was followed by the killing of Hassan Bilgi, found shot in a field in Kent; the post-mortem showed that prior to his death he had been tied up. There were also reports of a number of disappearances in Turkey and Northern Cyprus by dealers returning from London.

Then in 1996 came the death of Mustafa Zarif. He had fallen foul of one of the Turkish gangs and been dragged from his car at gunpoint, said the prosecution, by Arkin Izzigil and Tan Onbassi. He was pushed to the ground and garrotted; his grave had already been dug for him. At their trial at the Central Criminal Court the men denied the murder, suggesting that it had been carried out by another man who had now fled to Northern Cyprus which has no extradition treaty with Britain.

From such little acorns do big oak trees grow. The Turkish control of an estimated 80 per cent of the heroin market began in a small way with what the National Criminal Intelligence Service described as 'a corner-shop operation'.[1] At the beginning 5 kg was a large amount for them, but in a short period of time the gangs were in a position to import very substantial quantities and to have devised a marketing plan in which free samples were handed out in inner cities. By the late 1990s substantial amounts of Turkish imported heroin were being seized – 230 kg from a warehouse in Barking, another 250 kg in a North London warehouse traced after a surveillance operation, and a further 200 kg by chance. From time to time senior players were caught and prosecuted. They were thought to have taken over control from Pakistani and Indian traffickers in the previous decade.

In 1996 David Nevzat Telliagaoglu from Sussex received 25 years for masterminding a smuggling operation. Having

---

[1] Quoted in David Connett and Michard Gillard, 'Turkish gangs seize control of Britain's heroin trade' in *Observer*, 27 July 1997.

come to England on the back of serving 5 years of a 9-year sentence in Germany, again for drug smuggling, he then tried to arrange the supply of Turkish heroin to the United States in return for the supply of Colombian cocaine to Britain. When this was not successful he arranged the smuggling of 90 kg of heroin worth an estimated £10 million at street level from Holland. It had been concealed under the floor of a horsebox.

That year, on 2 August, Muslum Simsek received 30 years at Southwark Crown Court and Aki Aksu, from Bounds Green, 20 years, after their convictions for using a pensioners' tour bus to ship 50 kg consignments of heroin into London.

The Turkish control of the heroin market in London has resulted in at least 20 deaths in the last four years. One of the more recent was that of Oguzhan Ozdemir, from Enfield, shot dead in July 2001. Most have been members of Turkish Cypriot gangs who battled each other, but there have been signs that they are now banding together and/or forming alliances to repel Albanian and Pakistani interests. At the end of the month three members of the African Crew were jailed for their part in a gang war which was thought to have accounted for five deaths. The Crew had bought from Turkish dealers and then sided with them in a war with a West Indian gang from Lambeth which was seen to be encroaching on their operations. There were also signs of a rapid expansion in the heroin market, bringing with it rising purity and falling prices. By the summer of 2001 the street price of a kilo of heroin was down to around £13,000, a fall of £2,000 from the beginning of the year.

Now there were reckoned to be about 900 gangs engaged

in drug trafficking, immigration fraud and money laundering, with estimates of turnover ranging from £8 billion to a staggering £50 billion. The estimated consumption of heroin by British addicts was 30 tons, while only two tons were seized annually. British consumption of cocaine is estimated at between 25 and 40 tons, with the bulk coming from Colombia via Spain.

There are continuing signs of the inroads Turkish gangs are making into the heroin trade in North London. In July 2002 two gangs of gunmen fought a pitched battle outside Wood Green police station in which 20 shots were fired. In the following five months there were over 300 arrests in and around the main thoroughfare, Green Lanes, whilst in November another Green Lanes battle which began in the Dostlar Social Club left one dead and four seriously injured. In January 2003 over 500 police took part in *Operation Narita*, swooping on members of a Turkish family alleged to be involved in the importation of Afghan heroin. Part of the trouble was thought to stem from the imprisonment of Huseyin Baybasin, the so-called 'Heroin Emperor', jailed for 20 years in Holland in 2001, and a battle for control of his vacated territory. It has been estimated that over half of all Turkish and Kurdish shopkeepers in London have been obliged to pay protection money of up to £10,000 a year.[2]

The new kids in the game were reported to be Asian crime gangs fighting for a share of the trade. It was estimated that South Asian gangs now accounted for some 20 per cent of the trafficking of heroin across Europe and into Britain. In

[2] See Tony Thompson, 'Heroin "Emperor" brings terror to UK streets' in *Observer*, 17 November 2002.

England, Bradford, with its major links to Pakistan and Afghanistan, has become a centre of the Asian heroin trade.[3]

Yardies, Crews and Posses

On the street, no one really talks about Yardies any more. That's not what they call themselves. It's all crews and posses. Deputy Assistant Commissioner Mike Fuller.[4]

It is probably not unfair to say that Scotland Yard never really came to terms with how to deal with the Yardies in the 1980s and has never quite made up the lost ground ever since. The last decade has been littered with bodies left by Yardies or their like, some of whom have actually been brought to England to help clear up drug and gang problems. Instead they have slipped the leash and gone off on sprees of their own at considerable cost to the community.

The Yardies in Britain can be traced back to about 1980, and their arrival followed their involvement with the political struggles in Jamaica over the years since that island's independence in 1962. There in the 1970s the various political leaders, just as in New York 90 years previously, had used street gangs to garner power.

In the Jamaican election campaign of 1980 when they supported Michael Manley's People's National Party, Yardies were blamed for up to 500 murders. When that regime was toppled by the more moderate Labour Party they fled first to New York and Miami and then further afield, including

[3] Keith Dovkants, 'The New Godfathers' in *Evening Standard*, 26 July 2002.
[4] Quoted in the *Observer*, 26 August 2001.

England. Suggestions as to the meaning of their name are diffuse. The yard can mean home in general, a patch of territory or manor, Jamaica more specifically and a dock area in Kingston quite specifically.[5]

Back at the end of the 1980s, membership of the senior ranks in London was confined to between 30 and 40 men from Jamaica who were said to rule their members with iron discipline. They were then reported as having established a base in Railton Road, the scene of the Brixton riots in 1981, running protection in the shebeens, and also prostitution, illegal gambling and drugs. Two years later they were reported as having moved the scene of their operations to the All Saints Road area of Notting Hill.

Twenty years on, the situation had deteriorated to the extent that the Metropolitan Police *Operation Trident*, which targets 'black-on-black' crime, was investigating contract killings carried out for as little as £200. In Lambeth there were over 400 gun-related incidents in a year, and these were just the cases which came to the notice of the police. By the end of August 2001 there had been 25 gun deaths. One problem with Jamaican gunmen coming and going seemingly at will was the loophole in Britain's none too strict immigration rules. Visitors from Jamaica needed only to apply to the British High Commission there for an entry clearance certificate. Sheer weight of numbers at airports made a filtering process almost impossible. With stricter controls on entry into the United States, the United Kingdom had become the country of choice for anyone wanted in Kingston.

[5] In American prison slang it can also mean the exercise area.

Back in Kingston in areas such as Tivoli Gardens, Rema and Hannah Town, the drugs gangs had long outgrown their political masters and operated freely, with regular shootings between gangs such as the Lock City Crew, the Fatherless Crew, and Nah Live Fi' Nutton Crew racking up 700 murders by the middle of September 2001. Just as the 1920s gangsters such as Dutch Schultz and Al Capone curried favour with the general public by hosting community parties and making highly publicised charitable donations, so have the Kingston Dons. Parents are given money for textbooks and school uniforms and the children from the ghettos are said to be the best dressed in the city.

Again, just as streets in New York and London have over the years belonged to gangs, where to be caught crossing the demarcation line has meant a severe beating at best, the same applies between Tivoli and Rema territory. 'I would come out in a box,' says one Tivoli youth worker.

Now more Jamaican influence is alleged to be spreading to London, where part of Brixton is known as Little Tivoli and parts of Harlesden are said to have been informally renamed after areas loyal to the People's National Party.

One of the more recent and notorious of escapees is Hopeton Eric Brown, known variously as Sandokan, Angel, Anthony Briscoe and Devon Foster. In March 2001 he was thought to be back in Britain after killing two people in Jamaica. He had not been used as an inside man. Instead, rather unfortunately, he had been released from prison by mistake.

In 1995 he and the remainder of his gang shot dead a drug dealer in St Paul, Minnesota, and also shot his girlfriend twice in the head; she survived. The gang was indicted for murder and attempted murder in 1999, and in June 2000 Brown was in Britain where he was arrested after being heard boasting about his part in drug trafficking in general and the shooting in particular. He was expected to be extradited but unfortunately, because of an administrative error, he was released from prison two days before he was due to be collected by the American authorities.

Six months later in January 2001 he was in Jamaica, where he shot a man dead for leaning on his car and allegedly killed a second man who was hit by a stray bullet. Within the month he was seen in London again. He was placed on the FBI 'Ten Most Wanted Fugitives' list in March 2001, by which time he had run up seven aliases and three street names.

Although there are still a number of Jamaican gunmen working in the Yardie milieu, it is now considered that the majority of hitmen amongst the so-called Yardies are British-born black criminals.

What has alarmed the police and public is the indiscriminate way in which the gunmen operate. In July 2000 a gunman opened fire outside Chicago's, a night-club in Peckham, hitting nine people. The club was in a district known by locals as the Front Line because of the 24-hour drug dealings which took place. From 1997, 18 black people were murdered in Brent, 21 in Hackney and Haringey and a further 29 in Lewisham and Lambeth. At least 23 of the 1999 murders were thought to be the work of Yardies.

In 2001 up to April there had been ten 'black-on-black' murders compared with 16 in all of 2000, mostly resulting from wars in the £1 billion a year crack-cocaine trade. In London, by the middle of September there had been 25 gun murders and 37 shootings.

In April 2001 Wayne Henry and Corey Wright, both from North London, were ambushed as they left Chimes night-club – formerly the Krays' Regency Club in Stoke Newington – in a blue BMW convertible. They were shot, as was the driver who, dying, lost control of the car and ploughed into three women pedestrians before hitting a bus.[6]

The Yardies appeared to have ratched things up a notch when at the end of June 2001 the bodies of Ray Anthony Samuels and Godfrey Owen Scott, who shared an address in Regents Close, Stoke Newington, were found within 24 hours of each other. Scott was the more fortunate; he was merely shot in Hainault Road, Leytonstone, on Friday 29 June. Samuels, whose body was found in Epping Forest a day later, was thought to have been tortured, skinned and had his tongue cut out, a symbol (it was said) that he had fallen foul of major players.[7] Scotland Yard was then in a race to find what were described as two 'dead men walking': two Jamaicans known only as Bubba and Lapper, friends of Samuels and Scott. The police did not know if the men had fled or were already dead.

Another escalation in Yardie violence came about when on 9 July a man who worked in a branch of Domino's Pizza was shot during a raid when £2,000 was stolen. The robbers,

---

[6] Justin Davenport, 'Who pulls the trigger in London's gun war' in *Evening Standard*, 13 June 2001.
[7] *Evening Standard*, 9 July 2001.

all armed, demanded money when the shop managers at the branch in Egerton Street, Stamford Hill, returned to their cars with the night's takings. The money was handed over but the victim was then shot in the stomach.

Then in the early autumn of 2001, amidst arguments over the admission of asylum seekers generally, came the news that one alleged Yardie was seeking asylum from his police-protected hospital bed to which he had been confined since June, having been shot in the mouth and neck while in Brixton. He had entered Britain legally but had overstayed his visa before the incident in which he lost the use of his arms and legs. He was being guarded 24 hours a day by a five-man firearms squad at a monthly cost said to be around £100,000.[8]

'The bravest woman in Britain', said Judge Martin Stephens of 22-year-old Sophie Lewis, who was shot four times in the head and upper body in an attempt to prevent her giving evidence against her former boyfriend, Rickey Sweeney of the London version of the Lock City Crew. The 20-year-old Sweeney from Colindale had spoken to her of his killing a rival, Dean Roberts, in a tit-for-tat shooting in 1999. When he learned that she would be giving evidence, Sweeney ordered her execution. In March 2001 he was convicted of killing Roberts and jailed for life. From his cell he had ordered Trevor Hamilton and Shimei Yungsam to kill her, and on 18 January 2002 they both received 18 years for attempted murder. An attempt on Ms Lewis' life had also been made

[8] *Sunday Telegraph*, 9 September 2001.

when she was shot while on holiday in Jamaica. The judge's comments came at a time when the police claimed that thousands of people were avoiding conviction because of the fears of victims and witnesses who were being intimidated.

Although the big profits are in cocaine smuggling into Britain, there is still a regular trade in marijuana. At the beginning of September Justin Davenport of the *Evening Standard* watched as a series of English women were sentenced in Jamaica for efforts to export the drug. A single mother from Birmingham, with two children and pregnant with a third, received a fine of £4,000 and 18 months' imprisonment for attempting to smuggle 23 lbs of cannabis designed to look like breadfruit and oranges. If the fine was paid she would serve only four months. She said she had been given the packages by friends after visiting her ill grandfather and had not checked them. A woman from Brixton had cannabis disguised as cheese; her story and sentence were the same. Another from Enfield appears not to have been displeased with her 6 months hard labour after being found with 63 lbs of the drug. Over sixty women out of a total of about 110 British people were currently serving sentences in Kingston. In the spring of 2000 the overall figure had been a bare 15.

As a rule the couriers of hard drugs, of whom there can be a number on any plane – at one time, 11 appeared to be the record from one British Airways flight – travel business class. The profits may be reduced but the chance of detection is seen as less.

Apart from those who secrete the drugs in the vagina or anus – a risky business since death is highly likely if the condom in which they are contained bursts – there are some who have used rum bottles, soap, an artificial leg and somewhat bizarrely, since the woman claimed ignorance, in the wig she was wearing.

By the autumn of 2001 a kilo of cocaine brought to the Caribbean by plane and dropped to await collection by high-speed boats known as 'go-fasts' would fetch £125,000 in Britain, with a wholesale price of £25,000. In America the street value was nearer $30,000. Apart from the flight and possibly a holiday, the courier would receive £1,000 for a successful run. It is not unknown for a courier to be deliberately exposed to Customs officers so as to enable others on the flight to pass unnoticed.

Now, not only were traditional blue-collar criminals using the Thames but so were the Yardies. In November 2001 Lee Woolcock and Matthew Woodcraft, both from Essex, were convicted at the Old Bailey, following a swoop by marine officers. The operation was said to have been part of a multi-million-pound international drug-smuggling syndicate involving Yardie gangs from Jamaica.

Cannabis had been fixed to the underside of the ship MC *Pigi* as it lay at anchor in Kingston Harbour, Jamaica. Woolcock and Woodcraft were arrested at night in February 2001 as they were recovering the cannabis from a container vessel which had docked near Silvertown, East London. They were seized literally when their heads popped out of the water as they surfaced after diving under the ship.

This was one of the successes of *Operation Trident*, launched in 1998 following the Stephen Lawrence inquiry. Originally designed as an intelligence-gathering operation with the increasing number of 'black-on-black' gun crimes, in 2000 it expanded to an operational command unit. Because of the differing police methods of classifying gun crime, it is not possible to say accurately how many gun-related offences there are annually throughout the country and, of course, by no means all of them are black related.[9] They do, however, make up a significant proportion. It is thought that there may be as many as 300,000 weapons in circulation, and the Metropolitan Police collected some 700 weapons in the 18 months to August 2001.

Another success for *Operation Trident* came at the end of 2001 when in December a good percentage of passengers on a flight from Kingston to London were arrested on landing. No fewer than 23 people were held on suspicion of importing drugs. One woman was said to have swallowed 94 thumb-sized packages of cocaine with a street value of around £70,000.[10]

At the beginning of 2002 there were calls for the visa laws to be changed in an attempt to stop the huge amount of smuggling by Jamaican groups. There were suggestions that 30 kg of a drug might be smuggled in on each flight. Certainly,

---

[9] The Stephen Lawrence Inquiry, chaired by Sir William Macpherson, followed the outcry over the killing of a teenager at a South London bus stop by white youths in 1993. A number of boys were arrested and charged but, for a variety of reasons, the case against them collapsed. There were allegations of negligence and bad faith against some of the officers involved in the investigation and an inquiry was held. The report condemned what it described as institutional racism in the Metropolitan Police. Crimes may be recorded as gun-related by some forces even though no gun is used. This can occur where, for example, the attacker holds a piece of wood to the victim's head and tells him it is a gun. One recorded instance involved a banana wrapped in a handkerchief. It does not make it any the less frightening for the victim however.

[10] *Evening Standard*, 5 December 2001.

cocaine seizures were up; in December 2001 600 kg were found at Liverpool docks. Out of 4,023 people convicted of drug smuggling or awaiting trial, 795 were women, and of these 311 were Jamaican nationals.[11]

A former face, who had served a sentence for murder and who later became a successful author, explains why there is so much violence in the drug industry:

The reason for the increase in violence is that the drugs industry is run on credit. I don't mean on street level but the wholesale level. Nobody pays cash for crack, cocaine or heroin. Everything is given out on credit, on bail as they say. Now, if somebody decides not to pay you can't go to law so you've got to find a way of compelling them to pay you. That's where the violence comes in.

If people think they can run off with your products or the service you provide and not pay you they will do so. So, many firms have to have somebody on them who is willing to be violent or even go so far as to kill someone.

The danger is if you want to talk and the other side wants to go to war straightaway you are the one that gets shot. So especially nowadays especially in certain areas it's shoot first, talk afterwards.

Virtually anyone can set up as a firm. £40,000 will buy you an incredible amount of power. You are an incredible someone and they'll come and fight behind your flag.

There is no boss of bosses in England. In London some firms are perceived to be stronger than others. In the final analysis there are a lot of dangerous little firms about.

---

[11] *Daily Mail*, 4 January 2F002. See also Sissy Gascoigne, 'Confessions of a naïve drug smuggler' in the *Independent*, 7 January 2002, who tells just how easy it is to get caught up in an alarming situation.

Dave Courtney believes that in Brixton in the summer of 2001 there were 20 crack houses being run by five firms, and that they robbed each other:

> If you wasn't a drug dealer, you was a drug robber. Drugs has bred a different class of robber. The average cracksman[12] has to find £500 a day to feed his habit. He has to go out and rob.

At the end of 2002 and the beginning of 2003 it became clear just how little impact the gun controls – imposed after the Dunblane shooting of schoolchildren by a deranged man[13] – had made, particularly on black organised crime. In a temporary amnesty 23,000 firearms were handed in. It had little lasting effect and between 1996 and 2001 gun crime rose by 26 per cent. In 2002 there were something in the region of 9,000 known firearm offences. There are about 25 gun-related offences daily. The number of illegally owned guns in the country is impossible to estimate but suggestions range from a quarter of a million to 10 million. There is also the problem of weapons such as the Brocock ME .38 Magnum air pistol, costing around £120, which for £70 can be converted to fire bullets.

---

[12] In the sense of crack user rather than the old-fashioned safebreaker. The quotations are from the television programme *Gangsters*, Channel 5, 31 July and 7 August 2001.
[13] In March 1996 Thomas Hamilton shot dead 16 children and their teacher at a primary school in Dunblane, Scotland. Following a symbolic crusade, handguns over .22 in calibre were banned and then, under the new Labour government, all remaining handguns were also banned.

At the beginning of 2003 Eli Hall, wanted for questioning over the shooting of two police officers, holed up for 11 days with a hostage for much of that time in Marvin Street, Hackney before he shot himself. During the siege the police allowed food to be sent in and subsequently arrested a man for allegedly trying to smuggle drugs to Hall in a Kentucky Fried Chicken package. His brother Dean Hall, who is serving eight years for drugs and firearms offences, was alleged to be part of the 10-strong Africa Crew.

Lottery money is not always well spent. Members of the Underground G Crew had used a charity, set up to help deprived young children, to provide a base for themselves in North London. The gang's base was at Staples Corner, with storerooms near the Welsh Harp reservoir from where guns, masks, post office and traffic wardens' uniforms, axes and surveillance equipment were retrieved by the police. The co-leaders of the gang, Orson de Silva and his uncle Emmanuel de Silva, received 24 and 23 years respectively after being convicted of raids on security vans and a post office. Antonio Bryan received 26 years; he had also been involved in a second gang which targeted clients of hotels such as the Ritz. The clients were seen leaving the hotels, were then followed and might be watched for up to 18 months before their homes were invaded. In one raid one of the team used his teeth to pull off a diamond ring from the finger of a victim.

Strictly speaking not Yardies, but nevertheless very tiresome people, at the end of 2002 the Muswell Hill Mob, a group of black teenagers who specialised in armed car-jackings in North London, were jailed. Part of their undoing was to pose in Capone-like suits with fake weapons for their communal photograph, *à la* The Wild Bunch. The photograph was taken at a studio in the Trocadero complex in Piccadilly where they took the opportunity to decamp with two of the photographer's Colt six-shooter props. They left behind a baseball cap and, of course, the negatives. Daniel Willoughby, Robert George and Anthony Cunningham received 11 years and Colin Palmer 9½ years.

One of the crimes which created a temporary stir at the beginning of 2003 was the shooting of four young women at a New Year's Eve party outside the Uniseven Studios hairdressing salon on Churchill Row in the Aston district of Birmingham. Two of them, the 18-year-old Charlene Ellis and Latisha Shakespear, a year younger, were killed in the attack. They were thought to be innocent bystanders in part of the long-running war between the Johnson Crew, named after a café, and the Burger Bar Boys from a fast-food outfit in the Lozelles area of the city. The two gangs have maintained a 10-year feud with Birchfield Road – the front line. In 1997 a number of members of the Johnson Crew were convicted of the murder of disc jockey Jason Wharton in Handsworth, and of armed robbery, but far from dismantling the gang the convictions have given it some added kudos and membership is said to be around the 200 mark, with the Burger Bar Boys totalling about half that number. More recent incidents have included the 2001 killing of Corey Wayne Allen, a member of the Johnson Crew, shot with his own gun outside a local club. A man was charged but acquitted after the prosecution witnesses retracted their statements. Then in April 2002 Ashi Walker, a Burger Bar Boy, was gunned down in a hail of 30 bullets in a drive-by shooting in the Edgbaston district of the city. In December 2002 another Burger Bar Boy, Yohanne Martin, was killed in his Mercedes in West Bromwich. Two years earlier he had been acquitted of murder but had served a four-year sentence for illegal possession of a gun. His killer escaped in a BMW.

By the time of the burial of Charlene Ellis the Burger Bar Boys had claimed responsibility for the murders, saying they were in revenge for Martin's death. And if the police ever manage to eliminate the Johnson-Burgers there are plenty of other gangs in the city, including the Champagne Crew, the Badder Boys and the Rally Close Crew, all from the Edgbaston area.

There were also signs that cities without any great tradition of major crime were being targeted by London, Manchester – where 13 young men have been killed in gang warfare since 1999 – and Birmingham gangs. Just after 7 p.m. on New Year's Day 2003, Lester Divers, a night-club promoter and regarded as one of the players in Sheffield's burgeoning drug trade, was shot at the wheel of his Lexus, parked outside his home in Freedom Road.

The Yardies have apparently infiltrated markets such as Bedford and university towns. In July 2002 Rupert Foster was jailed for six years for supplying crack in Cambridge. His conviction came two days before a raid on a council flat that was being used as a crack house in the city. The standard method of infiltration in Cambridge is no different from that in Sheffield. Single mothers with a known crack habit are targeted. As they fall more and more into debt with their dealer their homes are taken over for use as crack houses. The increase in the use of crack has brought with it an increase in shoplifting and burglary to provide money for drugs. In May 2002 Andrew Clay, said to have been responsible for a fifth of all burglaries in Cambridge and supporting a £300-a-day habit, was jailed for 4½ years. In six months he had committed more than 230 crimes in and around the city.

Even worse, it was reported that the girlfriends of two suspected Yardie gangsters had been given jobs as police civilian workers. One was said to have been present at a briefing of an undercover operation targeting her boyfriend.[14] Worst of all, a Yardie who had boasted of killing seven women in Jamaica was used by Scotland Yard as an informer. Delroy Denton had come to Britain using his brother's passport. In 1993 he was arrested in Brixton for possessing a knife and drugs. Rather than be deported he turned undercover informer, but things quickly went bad. In December 1994 he was charged with raping a 15-year-old schoolgirl but the charges were dropped. Then in April 1995 he raped and killed Marcia Lawes, stabbing her 19 times. In October 2002 her family was given permission by the Court of Appeal to sue the police and the Home Office over her death.

[14] *Evening Standard*, 10 October 2002.

8

The North and North West

If London has had its fair share of shootings in recent years, so has Leeds. In the spring of 2000 there were seven incidents in a month, climaxing on 14 April with the death of 33-year-old Frank Birley in Sugar Well Road. Birley, also known as Frank Gatt, had recently been released after serving a 14-year sentence for armed robbery in Blackpool in which a 78-year-old woman and her 53-year-old daughter were taken hostage during a siege.

This time he was accidentally shot while he was out on what was described as a punishment raid. His fellow punisher slipped and the gun went off as he fell, hitting Birley and a young man. There were suggestions that a contract had been taken out on Birley by men who had moved into his empire in his enforced absence. Birley was, it was thought, trying to re-establish himself. There were the usual floral tributes placed against the wall where he fell including one which, perhaps over-egging the pudding, described him as King of New York.

Others who were shot in the weeks before Birley included a bouncer who was wounded in the legs outside the Chained Bull public house in Moortown on 11 March. This was followed five days later by the death of car dealer Craig Mirfield, shot through the windscreen of his car in Oakwood Lane, Gipton. The next day 29-year-old Clifton 'Junior' Bryan survived a shooting in Chapeltown Road. Despite two pistol bullets in his stomach and a back peppered with shotgun blast he managed to get himself to hospital. He had survived another attack when, seven years earlier, he was ambushed and shot outside the St James's University Hospital in the east of the city. On 12 April a man was shot when he answered his door-bell in Hares Road. He too survived, as did another man shot in Old Colton the same day. Three days after Birley's death, the body of a 36-year-old man was found in the backyard of the Leeds Rifleman public house, also in the east of Leeds.

It was alleged that Bryan's earlier shooting in December 1993 had come about because of previous unacceptable behaviour in the drug-dealing community in the Chapeltown area. He and a Robert Samuels had, it was alleged, kidnapped a teenager, Mark Smith, and then blackmailed his associates into paying £2,900 as a deposit against his release. The reason for his kidnapping was that he had assaulted a woman friend of theirs, Michelle Midgeley. A further £700 was due to be paid over and now Bryan and Samuels went to a Chapeltown bank to meet Smith. There was, however, no Smith but instead a car which followed them and, when they stopped, said the prosecution, '. . . pulled alongside and someone fired off a double-barrelled shotgun'. Samuels was badly injured and Bryan thought he was dead. He drove him to the hospital where, when they reached the Chancellor's Wing, the gunmen opened fire again.

In fact Clifton 'Junior' Bryan did not last long after the March attack. At around 5.50 a.m. on 15 May his body was found with that of another man laid out in a P-registration Rover in the Harehills area. It was thought they had been killed the night before.

There was something of a lull in proceedings before one man died and five were injured in a gun battle outside the Hayfield Club. It was two miles away from the Wilson's Arms in Seacroft where, on 22 July 2001, children playing games during a pub disco were ordered to lie on the floor by a masked gunman who shot and killed the former Sheffield, Castleford and Wakefield rugby league player, David Nelson. Known to be a heavy gambler, Nelson had also been shot and slightly wounded outside the pub on the previous Thursday, but had not reported the incident to the police. This time, however, the gunman shot Nelson in the head and, when Joseph Montgomery tried to intervene by throwing a beer glass at the assailant, he was shot and killed as well.

Nor was Manchester to be left behind. During the 1980s when the Gooch–Pepperhill turf wars were being fought, the city had become known as Gunchester. Now following a period of relative quiet it seemed as though the Gooch and the New Gooch were re-establishing themselves.

The current outbreak stems back to July 1999 when Martin Bennett, previously convicted for drug trafficking, was shot dead outside his home in Moss Side. His death was followed three days later by that of Dorrie McKie, shot when five men on mountain bikes ambushed the car in Hulme in which he and a friend were sitting. The friend survived. Anthony Cook, described as an up-and-coming gangster, lasted only a week longer when he was shot dead after a high-speed car chase. In January 2000 businessman Roger Ormsby was found shot dead as he sat in the driver's seat of his BMW in a Moss Side alleyway.

Two of the seven shot dead since the summer of 1999, Gabriel Egharevba and Simon Brown, were not regarded as being gang members. On 14 January, the 17-year-old Egharevba was shot in a motorcycle killing. He had been in Longsight, on his mountain bike, on his way to his mother's. Simon Brown was ambushed at the end of a Christmas party as he left the Old Library Centre in Cheetham. In April 2001 the police rounded up 15 men, three of whom were questioned about a series of gangland killings, but another innocent bystander was shot the following month. This time pensioner Alice Carroll survived being shot in the back after being caught in the cross-fire between two groups of youths on mountain bikes as they fought, again in the Longsight area of the city.

Overall, Manchester continued to live up to its nicknames Gunchester and Gangchester. In June 2001 five members of the Gooch Close gang were jailed for over 43 years for firearms offences. A second trial followed in January 2002 and this time Thomas Wesley Pitt, the leader of the Pitt Bull Crew, received life imprisonment after he was convicted of one gang murder, three attempted murders and various drugs and firearms offences. In June 2002 four members of the Pitt Bull Crew received life imprisonment for the murder in March

2001 of a Levenshulme taxi driver. Two of them were also convicted of attempted murder, kidnapping and wounding. Another man received 15 years for kidnapping, wounding and a firearms offence.

The Gooch Gang started life around 1988 and took its name from Gooch Close where a number of members lived. It has around 65 members all under 25 years of age, a very small percentage of which are girls. The Dodington Gang, which is half that in strength and emerged in the same year, is 100 per cent male. It also has an exclusively under-25-year-old membership, as does the Longsight Crew with around the same membership tally as the Gooch Gang. Again it is 100 per cent male, although it came to prominence in the middle 1990s. The Pitt Bull Crew is the smallest of all, but has a significant minority female membership. It is the newest of the gangs, coming to notice in 1999, and has only about 25 members. Females are not front-line players, but are used in the traditional supporting role of minding houses and carrying weapons for the male members. Roughly a quarter of the Pitt Bull Crew are white, whereas the Dodington Gang is exclusively Afro-Caribbean. Gang members are becoming younger, with 13- and 14-year-olds being shot and wounded as they chase the £600 a day to be made from dealing the Cris life, a reference to the sought-after Cristal champagne. As one boy said, 'Why did I want to work for £4, £5 an hour?'[1]

---

[1] Jane Drinkwater, 'I had to leave or I'd be dead' in the *Guardian*, 10 September 2002; Ian Burrell, 'Bystanders caught in cross-fire' in the *Independent*, 19 October 2002.

There were also fears that Liverpool might be on the verge of another war similar to the one following the murder of David Ungi in 1995. The current spate of killings appears to have resulted from loss of face and perceived disrespect rather than the more usual fight for control of the night-club doors and therefore the city's drug trade. Now, in May 2001, Stephen Lawler died after being shot following a party in Netherley. A corporal in the King's Regiment, Peter Clarke, was arrested and while he was awaiting trial his brother Ian was killed in the September – hit by up to seven shots as he sat in his car at traffic lights in the Tuebrook area. On 12 October Stephen Lawler's brother, Tony, out shopping with his elderly mother in the Netherley district, was chased over waste ground and killed. Four men had jumped out of a blue Ford Transit van at about 6.30 p.m. as he parked his car. The van was later found, burned out, in Woolton Park. Eleven-year-old Darren Carley, who had just left a chip shop, was hit by a stray bullet and underwent a seven-hour operation to pin bones at the top of his leg.

In a curious way it was the Ungi war which had led to the fall of another Liverpudlian, Curtis 'Cocky' Warren. Born in the city in 1963, he had worked his way up through the criminal ranks first as a thief and then a mugger. He also produced a slight variation on the traditional rolling of prostitutes' clients. The girls were threatened with violence to ensure their co-operation, one being told her throat would be cut if she did not co-operate with him. In March 1982 Warren, together with his friend Johnny Phillips, appeared at Liverpool Crown Court after one girl and her client had been attacked but had managed to drive to a police station.

Phillips received 3 years and Warren 2. Their youth, said the judge, had saved them from longer sentences.

After prison Warren turned to armed robbery, and in the spring of 1983 he took part in a raid on a Liverpool post office. Pamela Walsh, a housewife, saw what was happening and bravely, if foolishly, decided to have a go and attacked one of the robbers. She received a fractured skull for her trouble when the man lashed at her with the stock of his shotgun, but made a full recovery and later was awarded the Provincial Police Gold Medal Award.[2] Warren was awarded 5 years.

He was out and about in the mid-1980s using – along with his friends, Johnny Phillips, Mark 'Sonny Boy' Osu and Paul Uchegbu – the International Café in Granby Street as an unofficial headquarters, but international was a word which would epitomise Warren's career. In April 1988 he received a surprisingly lenient 30 days at Chur Cantonal Court in Switzerland after a shopkeeper in the town had been knocked to the ground when her till was rifled and £1,300 stolen.

By now he was also a small-time drug dealer; not yet in the league of the Liverpool greats such as Tommy Comerford and the Showers brothers, but working his way up nevertheless.

In the autumn of 1988 Uchegbu took up ram raiding and, along with Osu, the following spring received a total of 14 years. They had been working with Delroy Showers, who

---

[2] Her injuries did not deter Mrs Walsh. A year later she chased and helped to detain a suspected burglar.

was sentenced to 5 years for receiving stolen property.

By now the senior Liverpool criminals, a generation or half a generation older than Warren, had realised the benefits of Amsterdam and he followed the likes of Stan Carnall trading in a city where any drug could be obtained on very favourable terms. When Carnall was arrested and sentenced Warren's name and voice cropped up repeatedly in transcripts of telephone conversations, but he was never linked to the man he called the 'Big Fella'.

Even Warren's biographers are not clear how he made the transition from a relatively small dealer into the big time, but his name cropped up again in 1991 in *Operation Bruise* involving an informer, Graham Titley, though again he was not arrested. Warren also became involved with the Ghanaian Joseph Kassar, who wanted to move lead in the form of ingots from Venezuela, and met Brian Charrington who over the years would wreak havoc with the English criminal justice system. Charrington, then in his mid-thirties and described as oozing charm, raced offshore powerboats and owned a flying school, two private planes, a yacht and a variety of high-profile cars. In fact the ingots were used merely as a cover for drugs; inside each lump was a steel box containing cocaine. The prosecution would allege that Warren had supervised the South American end of the drug loading. One consignment of the drugs ended in a warehouse in Stoke. Customs officers had drilled into lead ingots and they believed Charrington was the organiser of the shipment. On 29 March 1992 they arrested both Kassar and Warren.

On 26 June 1992 Customs officers were waiting as Charrington landed in his private aircraft at Teesside airport.

At his home was £2 million in cash contaminated with traces of almost all major drugs. There were also details of a £4.5 million payment to a salesman known to be working with a Colombian cartel.

Charrington had been fancied as a major player since 1989. One of his runs had involved smuggling cannabis in beer crates with the aid of innocent day-trippers to France. Drugs to the value of £500,000 were confiscated. In 1990 a Danish skipper, convicted of trying to export £5 million of drugs from Denmark, named Charrington as being implicated in the scheme. There was also a tale that he had been smuggling cocaine into Britain by using corrupt airport baggage handlers to remove the bags containing the drug from the conveyor and so thwart any investigation.

It appears that members of the drug wing of the No. 2 (North East) Regional Crime Squad had been working with Customs to prepare a case against him. Unfortunately, it seems not to have been mentioned that quite apart from being Target One, Charrington was also the *Numero Uno* police informant. The moment he was arrested the police went to his rescue, and if need be they would give evidence in his defence.

The Customs officers in the Charrington case complained that, far from producing major drug-related arrests, he had only implicated small-time if professional criminals. Gilbert Gray QC, the barrister for Charrington, asked for and was granted a meeting with Sir Nicholas Lyell, the Attorney General. Five weeks later, on 28 January 1993, all charges against Charrington were withdrawn by the Crown Prosecution Service. He and ten others had been due to be committed for trial to the Crown Court. In their turn the police complained that the bust of Charrington pre-empted a major strike against a Colombian cartel.

The trial, whose ten defendants included Warren and Joseph Kassar, was scheduled for Manchester Crown Court. However, after the escape from Strangeways of a major drug dealer and later a Warren helpmate, Stanley Mee, it was transferred to Newcastle. It was a fiasco, principally because Charrington was not around to give evidence and was believed to be in Hong Kong. The trial began in April 1993 and at the end of the prosecution case a submission that Warren had no case to answer was upheld. In January 1994 the only person to be convicted for his part in the whole affair was Joseph Kassar, described by the trial judge, Mr Justice May, as 'not one of the principal organisers, but very much a middleman'. He received 24 years. According to the *Observer*, one of the police officers involved in thwarting the Customs inquiry left the force in January 1993 and in the September drove to Spain with his wife, a serving police constable, in an £87,000 BMW registered to Charrington.[3]

---

[3] In fact this is not uncommon practice. For example, in January 1989 Detective Superintendent Martin Lundy was allowed to give evidence *in camera* on behalf of his protégé, supergrass Roy Garner, and towards the end of 1994 a major furore broke out when it was discovered that Commander John Allinson, former head of operations at Scotland Yard, had privately intervened at the trial of a man linked to a contract killing. During the search for the killer of Donald Urquhart, shot in 1992 in a professional hit, a suspect's home in Sussex was raided and detectives found a huge cache of arms and ammunition. Allinson gave evidence in the judge's private room, saying that the man had helped to solve a major robbery 10 years previously. This was a move which pleased neither London nor Sussex detectives. In the end the weapons were confiscated and the man fined. As for Charrington, in November 1976 it was reported that he was suing the Chief Constable of Cleveland, claiming £1 million in reward money.

It was after *Operation Singer* that Warren assumed the role of drug supremo of Liverpool. It was then that *Operation Crayfish* was established with the aim of toppling another major Liverpool dealer but, in November 1993, Warren was recognised at Burtonwood Service Station near Warrington where a Turkish lorry driver, Hidayet Sucu, was under observation. Sucu was later arrested at Scratchwood Service Station on the M1 where, after his lorry was dismantled, it was found he was carrying 180 kg of very high-quality heroin. He later received 16 years' imprisonment. But Warren had been unfortunate. It might be that his presence at Scratchwood was wholly incidental, but it was enough to put him close to the centre of *Operation Crayfish*.

He was also unfortunate that, in 1995, a black-versus-white gang war broke out in Liverpool with the participants lined up from the Granby area against those principally from the Dingle area of Liverpool 8. It did not directly involve him but it involved his close friend Johnny Phillips and attracted a great deal of unwanted police attention. By all accounts there were a number of separate incidents which caused the trouble, the first of these being the shooting of bouncers at the State club on the evening of Christmas Day 1994 by Darren Delahunty. He and another man had been ejected earlier in the evening and Delahunty returned with a pistol, firing at the bouncers seven times. He was later sentenced to 15 years for the attack. The police responded with *Operation Aladdin*, investigating drug dealing, arson, kidnapping and protection by the so-called door security agencies. Seventeen people were arrested.

A longer-standing problem also occurred with the shooting

of a black bouncer and his employer. The bouncer had knocked out the member of a prominent white family and revenge had been promised. It was, as the Italians say, a dish best eaten cold because it was a year later when the bouncer and his employer were shot at as they got out of a parked car. The employer suspected the white family was behind the trouble and went to Manchester to obtain weapons. It was into this mess that, partly through pride and partly because of a genuine desire to resolve matters, Phillips stepped. He tried to mediate and failed.

In February 1995 Colin Fitzgibbon was shot in the back as he walked through the Kensington area of Liverpool. His attackers were suspected of being members of what the police called the Black Caucus, and three men were arrested including 'Sonny Boy' Osu. The charges were dropped over a year later.

Then came the take-over by Johnny Phillips of Cheers, a wine bar which belied its name on Aigburth Road in what had once been the Conservative club. White regulars, including relations of Fitzgibbon, were declared *persona non grata*. One of the men was second-hand car dealer and former amateur boxer, David Ungi, whose mother Vera had been a Fitzgibbon before her marriage.[4] The matter was to be resolved in the time-honoured method of a one-on-one, no weapons used, straightener. Traditionally the winner and loser would shake hands after the event and things would

---

[4] His father, a Maltese, had died in an accident many years earlier. For a full account of the war see Tony Barnes et al., *Cocky*; David James Smith, 'The Mersey Killers' in *Sunday Times*, 14 July 1996. Smith subscribes to the knuckleduster story, saying that Phillips' seconds protested but were warned off.

return to normal. Rather in the manner of agreements for old-time prize fights, a place had to be settled; Phillips suggested a spot near the Toxteth Sports Centre, but this was too far out of Ungi territory and too near a black-controlled one. He countered with the car park of the Golden Gloves gymnasium, where the fight took place on 20 March 1995.

The handshake did not happen in this instance, however. Ungi knocked down Phillips, who refused to accept his defeat, claiming Ungi had worn skin gloves concealing a knuckleduster.

The next day Ungi was shot at outside his home. He survived that attack but not the next when on 1 May, at around 5.30 p.m., he slowed at a junction in Toxteth and found his Volkswagen Passat blocked by a Golf. Words were exchanged and Ungi was shot. He was found to be dead on arrival at the Royal Liverpool University Hospital. His brother Ronnie appealed for witnesses. That night Cheers was wrecked. The next day it was torched and two days after that shots were fired at six houses in Halewood, a neighbouring suburb. Phillips went to the police station, provided an alibi and flew to Jamaica.

During that month the number of shootings rose. Ricardo Rowe, questioned over the Ungi killing and released without charge, was shot in the hand in Vic's gymnasium on 9 May. Within a week three more people were shot.[5]

Colin Ungi was found in body armour carrying a Tokarev pistol. He had, he said, been going to buy a cake. He and

---

[5] For a full account of the feud and the police response see Tony Barnes et al., *Cocky*, Chapter 10.

his brother Brian would be charged with the attempted murder of Rowe. That evening there was rioting in Toxteth. A year later no evidence was offered on the charge of attempted murder but Brian Ungi, who had a previous conviction for manslaughter, received a year for possessing a pistol. Johnny Phillips, returning from the Caribbean, was charged with the attempted murder of David Ungi in the first shooting. Meanwhile the shootings continued throughout areas of the city. On 21 March 1996 Phillips was shot in the thigh as he returned his daughter to his wife's home in Toxteth. He survived.

Edward Shaw received 5 years after being found in a car with two sub-machine guns. It was alleged he had said he was being forced by the Ungis to mind them, but he denied this, saying the police had suggested the name to him. In the middle of June, Stephen Anderson was shot and killed in Moses Street; this was the fourteenth recorded shooting since Ungi's death. The police then took the step of naming two men they wished to interview in connection with Ungi's death; neither of them had been much in evidence in the district since the killing and both were thought to be in Jamaica. It did not stop someone shooting at one man's home soon after his name was circulated. Warren was questioned, both over the disappearance of the pair and the original shooting, but was released. In September Phillips was arrested and charged with causing damage to police vehicles and assaulting officers. The next month he was acquitted of the charge of attempted murder.

At the inquest on David Ungi on 23 October 1996, a verdict of unlawful killing was returned. When the coroner,

Roy Barter, asked the investigating officer whether it was true that handguns could be hired by the day, DCI Alan Buckley replied, 'That is what our intelligence suggests.'

All this unwelcome police interest in the activities of the city had been too much for Warren and he disappeared from the scene, re-surfacing in early 1996 at 'Bakara', 53 Hoofstradt, Sassenheim, a town halfway between Amsterdam and The Hague. It was from here that his downfall was plotted by *Operation Crayfish* with the help of the Dutch police. They had established wire-taps on Warren – legal under Dutch law, provided the tapped person is notified after six months – as he went about his way setting up connections with Colombian and Turkish gangs, becoming one of the half-dozen men in Europe who had established such a position. In the autumn of 1996, while a huge consignment of cocaine from Colombia was being finalised by Stephen Mee, the Dutch and English police combined in a series of raids in Holland and the North West. At 5 a.m. on 24 October Curtis was arrested at his home. In raids in the Netherlands and England 1,500 kg of cannabis resin, 60 kg of heroin, 50 kg of Ecstasy and, along with a number of weapons, £370,000 in guilders were seized. In addition a further 400 kg of cocaine were found in a container during the numerous raids.

Warren, Mee and their lawyers bitterly fought the evidence obtained by the wire-taps, but on 19 June Mee received 7 years and Warren 12. Other minor players were sentenced to a year upwards.

Warren's time in Nieuw Vosseveld prison has not been without incident. On 15 September 1999 he was attacked by a Turkish criminal serving a sentence for murder. The

Turk was taken to hospital where he died of a brain haemorrhage. To compound his problems, an application was made in Holland to strip Warren of assets totalling around £20 million.

Some other old faces were also back in the dock. In 1972 the major Liverpool criminal, John Haase, had received 7 years for post office robberies following evidence given by a Northern supergrass, Roy Grantham. In 1980 he was acquitted of attempted murder when a rival, Tony Murray, failed to attend court after being shot in the leg with a pump-action shotgun. In 1982 Haase went down for 14 years for armed robbery. It was back inside again in 1993 and it was then that he became a police informant. He and his co-defendant and nephew, Paul Bennett, were arrested in 1993 and charged over smuggling £15 million of heroin from Turkey to Liverpool. By the time in 1995 when Haase was sentenced to 18 years for drug offences, he was regarded as being of such value to the police that a year later the then Home Secretary, Michael Howard, authorised his and his nephew's release. He had enabled the police to retrieve in excess of 150 illegal firearms including Kalashnikov and Armalite rifles, Thompson and Uzi sub-machine guns and Bren guns as well as large quantities of drugs.

That was the end of Haase's standing in the criminal community; before then he had been much admired. Shortly after his release he telephoned the London villain Frank Fraser to ask him to come to his wedding. Fraser's then girl-friend, Marilyn Wisbey, a daughter of Thomas Wisbey from the Great Train Robbery, had already sung at the wedding of Haase's daughter.

I said, 'No, on your bike.' He said, 'You calling me a grass?' and I said, 'Yes, I am.' It broke my heart because I liked him so much. 'I'm not having nothing to do with you.'[6]

In 1999 when Haase was running a security company as a front for supplying guns to criminals and money laundering, he was arrested after one of his workmen had planted a listening device on the firm's premises. Haase was heard arranging for an employee, Heath Grimes, to deliver an Uzi, a Smith & Wesson and 200 rounds of ammunition to Walter Kirkwood. In February 2001 Haase received a total of 13 years. Grimes and Kirkwood were sentenced to 4 and 3 years respectively.

The same month saw at least the temporary end of the career of Merseyside company owner 38-year-old Edward Gray of Honeys Green Lane, West Derby, Liverpool, known as 'The Bear' and, with a fortune reputed to be in the region of £20 million, one of Britain's richest criminals. Understandably he was less than pleased when he was convicted at the city's Crown Court and sentenced to 24 years' imprisonment for supplying £2.5 million of heroin and Ecstasy. 'I hope you die of AIDS,' he told the jury. Gray had been the subject of a 14-month surveillance by the National Crime Squad who recruited a profoundly deaf person to read his lips as he gave the orders for a deal.

In August 1999 John Prendergast, riding an old police BMW motorcycle, was being escorted by Gray's car towards

[6] Frank Fraser, *Mad Frank and Friends*, p. 218. The same book also has more details on Roy Grantham's prison life.

the M62 on his way to collect half a kilo of heroin. They saw a police car and swerved on to the M62. A chase followed and Prendergast was found in possession of the heroin. Gray and another defendant, Simon Smart, were stopped at Coquelles on the French side of the Channel Tunnel the next day. Smart received 7 years and his stepfather, Paul Russell, 14. On 11 April 2001 at Liverpool Crown Court, Gray was ordered to repay £417,343, part of his accumulated proceeds of crime.

Gray, who ran a small taxi firm and who, throughout his trial, maintained his innocence, was said to have owned a red Ferrari Spyder, an Alfa Romeo, a BMW convertible, a Lexus and a customised Toyota Landcruiser. Apart from his home in Honeys Green Lane which had an indoor pool, he had properties in three other streets in the area. In a report by the National Crime Squad on the investigations into Gray and another Liverpool gangster named Mark Lilley, the Director General William Hughes commented: 'During the year we also successfully disrupted or dismantled 253 criminal organisations of which 206 were drug-related.'

The disruption of Lilley's organisation may have been successful, but the actual detention proved less so. A 6 ft, 20-stone man from Earlestown, St Helens, described as 'the worst type of drug dealer', Lilley had been trapped by listening devices in his home. During his trial, while on bail for drug and gun offences, he absconded and received 25 years in his absence.

An interesting case occurred when a kidnapping, which seems to have arisen from the settling of scores, took place

on Merseyside in November 1998. It is also an example of
the application of the 20 per cent of demand rule, which is
often sufficient to obtain the release of the victim in kidnapping cases.

In the previous October Charles Seiga, a former Liverpool
restaurant owner, had been acquitted of the killing of 36-
year-old George Bromley, described as a security consultant,
who had been involved in running teams of doormen at
Liverpool clubs. As he sat eating a meal at Seiga's home, a
gunman entered through the patio doors and shot him. It
was suggested that Seiga had set up the killing.

On 20 November 1998 Seiga left his home in the West
Derby area of the city about 9 a.m. to buy a morning newspaper and was kidnapped by armed men. Over the next 30
hours he made a series of increasingly frantic calls to his
brother Joe, saying he was being held and that a ransom of
£100,000 was being demanded. It was believed that the
kidnappers would accept drugs as payment instead of cash.
First, £10,000 in cash was raised by relatives and handed to
a man in a street near Wavertree police station. Seiga then
telephoned his brother to say that the kidnappers regarded
this as only a down payment. A further £7,000 was handed
over. Eventually, after having had scalding water poured on
him and suffering cuts and bruises to his face and wrist where
he had been tied, he was released. Two men were later
arrested in the Wavertree district and a handgun and sawn-
off shotgun were found. The Merseyside police were keen to
play down any suggestion that there might be a connection
between the kidnapping and drugs. 'On Merseyside, drugs
are more myth than reality,' said Assistant Chief Constable

Mike Baxter, pointing out that in the previous two years incidents involving firearms had fallen by half. Not everyone was convinced about the myth and reality.[7]

In fact it transpired that the kidnapping had been a fairly amateurish affair, if nonetheless frightening for Seiga. While he was on remand awaiting trial over the murder of Bromley he had met Alan Lea in prison. Lea decided that the Seiga family had money and when Seiga went to a meeting with him he was kidnapped. Lea and Brian Airey appeared in the Liverpool Crown Court in June 1999.

The National Crime Squad has identified two tiers of criminal – the 'core nominal' and the 'current nominal'. The former is described as a major criminal of international, national or regional significance believed to be involved in the commission of crime at the highest level. The current nominal, although regarded as a serious criminal, has yet to reach the upper echelons of crime. The NCS estimates that there are around 300 core nominals in England and Wales, with the highest number concentrated in Greater London followed by Liverpool. There were reports that the five richest Mr Bigs in Britain had assets totalling over £204 million. It was all so very different from the view in 1994–5 that there was no single indigenous Mr Big, let alone five.[8]

And, on the subject of absconding criminals, two of Britain's most wanted men had been on the run for some length of time. Many thought that the old-fashioned bank robbery was – except for petty criminals and drug addicts –

[7] *Guardian*, 23 November 1998.
[8] Home Affairs Committee, *Organised Crime*, p. xvi, H.M.S.O..

a thing of the past, but in recent years Michael Lydon and Richard Dalton (son of the well-known boxing promoter Mike Dalton) have proved them wrong. Both were found guilty in their absence of breaking into banks overnight, waiting for the staff to arrive and then crashing through the ceiling. They were thought to have netted at least £300,000 from raids in Lincolnshire, Nottinghamshire and all over Yorkshire.

Charged with robbery and now with a number of convictions behind them, they were given bail and skipped in the last days of their trial at Hull. In August 2001, in their absence they were sentenced to 18 and 15 years respectively. A third man, Patrick Middlebrook, who did not abscond, received 15 years. Almost immediately a series of raids on banks and post offices in South Yorkshire in which the same technique was used took place. The police thought that now perhaps there was more than one gang involved.

Lydon and Dalton, both from Grimsby, were linked to an armed robber who committed suicide in his cell in Doncaster prison in October 2000. Kevin Garvin, who was accused of blackmail and kidnap, hanged himself. The family of a supermarket manager in Lincoln had been kidnapped by robbers who demanded £326,000 as a ransom.[9]

The new boys started young – none much younger than the 14-year-old boy known as the Kinder Surprise Kid who ran an embryonic drugs empire in Rhyl, the town in which James Hanratty, the A6 murderer, once claimed an alibi. At the beginning of August 2001 this boy from Liverpool began

[9] *The Star*, 23 August 2001.

a two-year sentence for supplying heroin and crack-cocaine in the town. Hiding the drugs in Kinder Surprise eggs, he would take orders on a mobile telephone and be chauffeured to the meetings, often near the Asda superstore in Kinmel Bay just out of the town, and often minded by two body-guards. He was happy with the store's long opening hours and his customers could telephone from 11 until late. When arrested by the police, he claimed that he had been kidnapped and forced to sell drugs after going on holiday with a man who had lived near the family home in Liverpool. He main-tained that he had been thrown through a plate-glass window, slashed with a knife and hit by a car. However, the pros-ecution took the view that he was the master of his own destiny. He had not attended school for over a year and, apparently, had not been much missed. Finally, he had been trapped by an undercover operation when he offered detec-tives bags of heroin and cocaine.[10]

---

[10] *Guardian*, 4 August 2001. Two days later, in another example of early begin-ners, a 17-year-old from Islington became the first person charged in Britain with possession of the Chinese-made AR-15 rifle capable of firing between 700 and 950 rounds a minute. In the car in which he was travelling there was also a sawn-off shotgun and 100 armour-piercing, titanium core 'full metal jacket' bullets. *Evening Standard*, 6 August 2001.

9

Scotland

Nor have things been anything approaching stable in Glasgow, where a variety of interests have converged since the bad beating of Billy Thompson in August 2000. Observers of Thompson said that the heroin addict could 'talk the talk but never walk the walk'. He was stabbed twice in the head and three times in the body and then suffered a kicking and stamping as he left a shop 200 yards from his home at Provanmill. Within the week Robert Morrison was charged with attempted murder.

Billy Thompson's legendary father, Arthur, was the King of Glasgow crime until his death. Arthur, once a high-quality safebreaker, survived both the attentions of the rival Welsh family and a charge of murder. In 1966 a bomb had exploded in his MG and his mother-in-law was killed. In reprisal he drove his car at the van of Patrick Welsh and James Goldie, whom he suspected of the killing, forcing it off the road and into a lamp-post and killing both of them.

Billy's brother Fat Boy, Arthur Thompson jnr, had been killed in 1985. Rather against his father's wishes he had established himself as a major drug dealer, operating his Barlanark Boys from Blackpool until he was jailed for 11 years.

He was killed outside the family home, known as The Ponderosa, in 1991 when he was out on home leave. For a time the Barlanark Boys had paid him his wages while he was in prison but, as is often the case, others involved took a less altruistic view. On the morning of Fat Boy's funeral, Bobby Glover's and Joe 'Bananas' Hanlon's bodies were found in a car on the route of the cortège. Each had been shot in the head. At first it was suggested that Arthur Thompson snr had arranged the contract, but the prevailing view is that it was done as a present for him by a local bar owner, but without his knowledge. Thompson, on the eve of his son's funeral, was invited to view their bodies. He is said to have remarked on later occasions, 'I was given it. But it didn't suit me.'

Arthur Thompson snr died following a heart attack in 1993, and from that time what remained of his empire – and with it the effective control of the Glasgow Underworld – was up for grabs.

One heir was Paul Ferris – acquitted, after a long and bitter court case, of the murders of Hanlon and Glover. However, in July 1998 he received a 10-year sentence at the Old Bailey after he was convicted of being involved – along with Londoner, John Ackerman, who turned informer – in the supply of arms and explosives. Initially Ferris said he thought the box he had been carrying contained counterfeit money and false passports, but he then wrote to the *Daily Record* saying that he considered he had been caught fair and square. His position was not helped by the fact that he had been regarded as a police informer himself, something he bitterly denied:

> This sham that I am a police informer, tout and grass is information being given out without any validity as I have never, ever, grassed anyone and there is not ONE person who is either in prison or out that can say I put them in jail.[1]

This had not stopped an earlier contract, reputedly worth £100,000, being placed on Ferris by a major drug dealer serving a sentence who blamed Ferris for his predicament. The contract came to nothing after the *Daily Record* gave the name of the proposed gunman. A second contract put on Ferris after he had failed to pay for certain drugs was subsequently called off after an accommodation had been reached.

Ferris had been brought up in the best of criminal traditions. His father served a sentence for armed robbery and later for tax evasion; in 1977 his brother was convicted at Northampton of the murder of Alan Thompson.[2] Ferris, who at one time worked for Arthur Thompson – who, he maintained, had also been a police informer – had fallen foul of

---

[1] *Daily Record*, 29 July 1998.
[2] In 1993 Billy Ferris escaped from a prison escort after being given time out of Perth prison to see his ill father. He was recaptured in Blackpool two months later and had two years added to his sentence. See *Daily Record*, 24 July 1988.

the Welsh family at an early age. He claimed that some of the brothers had bullied him badly at school and that later he had slashed John Welsh, cutting him from ear to ear, as a reprisal for earlier times.

Ferris also claimed that he and another Glasgow hardman, Tam Bagan, left Thompson's organisation because they had been shown a lack of respect. Bagan, who had served a sentence for the shooting of two brothers at Easterhouse and had received 12 years for armed robbery in 1995, had worked for Thompson after the shooting. Now he maintained that he had been set up over that robbery and that, with a new Mr Big running Glasgow, he and the police were in each other's pockets. He also asserted that ambitious young policemen were trapped by Mr Big who would arrange for a small-time criminal to be arrested as 'a body'. From then on the officer, knowing that it had in effect been a false arrest, would be in Mr Big's pocket.

His allegations against seven Strathclyde police officers, unconnected with the later Rae trial, provoked a long-running inquiry during which Bagan was seen up to 50 times by senior policemen and at the end of which the officers were exonerated.[3]

The previous year another top Glasgow man came under observation after a bus containing members of a youth football team had been stopped on the M74 near Hamilton and was found to contain 89 kg of cannabis worth in the region of £260,000. It was suggested that the team had been cynically used to divert suspicion. Thomas McGraw,

---

[3] See e.g. *Scotland on Sunday*, 21 April 1996.

known as 'The Licensee', was acquitted after the jury returned a non-proven verdict on charges that he had bank-rolled the smuggling ring bringing cannabis into Scotland from Spain.

McGraw, who at the time had no visible means of support, lived in a £300,000 home which had security systems worth £10,000. He had also financed a public house in Donegal as well as the Caravel in Barlanark. His brother-in-law, John Healy, who had been found at Heathrow airport with £150,000 which was confiscated, received 10 years. McGraw left the court in Edinburgh in a car and was thought to be heading for Tenerife where he was said to be purchasing a share in a development complex. It was said a contract had been taken out on him by those less than happy with the story that he also had been a police informer for many years. He had been handled by at least two detectives for some time but then, said 'an insider':

> . . . as time went on McGraw spoke to just about every-body. He was marking a lot of cards and police were able to make arrests because of him.[4]

An informer could be expected to make 10 per cent of money or property recovered.

McGraw's earlier career had been as the owner of Fifti Ices which, appropriately enough, owned more than 50 vehicles leased out to vendors of ice-creams who sold them mainly on Glasgow estates. It was during the so-called Ice Cream

---

[4] *Daily Record*, 14 July 1998.

Wars, described as a free market economy gone wild, that a Second World War grenade was thrown into his Barlanark public house. The culmination of the wars was said to have been an arson attack on a tenement flat in Glasgow in which six people died. Thomas Campbell and Joseph Steele were convicted in 1984 and throughout their sentences protested their innocence. They were convicted largely on the evidence of a Billy Love who later claimed that he had lied. At one time in 1996 the pair were released on bail after the Scottish Secretary referred the case to the Criminal Court of Appeal, but on 10 February 1998 the Law Lords said there was no reasonable explanation as to why Love had changed his mind. Now, in the middle of December 2001, the men were back in court yet again after the Scottish Criminal Cases Review Commission once more referred their cases to the Court of Appeal. Again they were released on bail. It was thought that the new evidence would include an allegation that once Love had agreed to give evidence, charges of armed robbery against him were dropped.

During his trial for drug smuggling, McGraw's counsel Donald Finlay QC had suggested that much of his original money came from the time when he was running the ice-cream vans – one of which his wife, Margaret, had driven.[5]

His lack of involvement in crime was something McGraw was keen to establish, pointing out that while he might not have paid his tax immediately, his income derived not from drugs but from an empire of 600 taxi-cabs, Mac's Cabs, which

---

[5] For an account of the Ice Cream Wars see Douglas Skelton and Lisa Brownlie, *Frightener*; James Morton, *Gangland 2*.

had originally operated from a site next to the Caravel. In February 2000 he was reported to be selling his business to another company.

Others suggested that McGraw might be in fear of his life and that he had hired two Bosnian Serb ex-soldiers as his bodyguards before selling up and going to live in the Canary Islands. If he did go, in April 2001 he was back at his home in the east end of Glasgow with no minders and, according to reporter Ron McKenna:

> Gone are the dark-rimmed spectacles and grey suit that gave him a bookish, almost weedy look. He is tanned, wearing jeans and a T-shirt which shows off the tattoos all the way up his arm and his full head of wild grey hair is no longer combed smooth. It gives him, I notice, a younger and alarmingly vigorous appearance.[6]

However, not everyone was enchanted to see him back and there were reports that in July 2001 shots were fired at his home.

Another who had left for the sun was businessman Pat Sweeney who had the misfortune to become involved with the girlfriend of Ian McDonald, known as Blink because it was said he would kill you in the blink of an eye. While McDonald was serving a 16-year sentence for a bank raid in Torquay in which a shotgun was fired, Sheila McGourlay began a relationship with Sweeney, something of which McDonald understandably did not approve. McDonald was

---

[6] Ron McKenna, 'Killer Instinct' in *The Scotsman*, 11 April 2001.

released from Shotts prison in November, driven away in a white limousine. In February 2001, Sweeney said that he was in fear of his life, and he had only escaped an attack when cars blocked his drive by driving his Jeep at them to clear a path. He had not returned home.[7]

Shortly after McGraw's trial came the death of Manny O'Donnell, found shot in a lovers' lane with his body wrapped in a tarpaulin. He had made a number of enemies and one of his problems seems to have been over a club in Dublin which he owned in partnership. It was said he had tried to take out a £50,000 contract against his former partner. After O'Donnell's death the man was reported to have said that it was regrettable in the sense that he had not been there to see it.

O'Donnell's lawyer Jack Quar was found hanging from the banisters in his office some days before the discovery of O'Donnell's body. The verdict was that he had committed suicide, but there were suggestions in the Underworld that he had been murdered after O'Donnell gave him £100,000 from £250,000 he had stolen from a drug baron. Certainly Quar had had financial difficulties, he had sold a substantial house, and at the time of his death was living in a £40,000 ground-floor former council flat.

In March 2001 Robert Morrison and Christopher Irvine were acquitted of the attempted murder of Billy Thompson but convicted of assault. The attack seems to have followed a request by Thompson for £3. Both men had kicked and stamped on Thompson whose skull was smashed. Unable to

[7] *Daily Record*, 10 February 2001.

give evidence at the trial, he was in a unit for the long-term brain damaged.[8]

Allegedly keeping things going for Paul Ferris was the jailed drugs baron, Martin Hamilton. He had been jailed for life in 2000 after being found guilty in the High Court in Inverness following a long-running fight for control of the Glasgow and Edinburgh drugs markets. According to the prosecution, rivals were set on fire, stabbed and scalded with boiling water. The trial had been moved from Edinburgh where Hamilton had connections.[9]

Then, in March 2001, Hamilton's former running mate, Joe Hart, a man with convictions for violence and dishonesty, was attacked as he left the Telford Arms in Drylaw. Two carloads of men, one from Glasgow and the other from Edinburgh, were said to have been involved in the assault. One of them carried a machete and Hart was struck several times. He discharged himself the next day and declined to speak with the police about his possible assailants. A police insider was quoted as saying:

There was not much sleep lost when we heard that Joe had been done in. He's had it coming for a long time.

---

[8] Morrison was sentenced to 8 years' imprisonment and Irvine received 5. A neurosurgeon said that Thompson's skull was like a shattered and smashed eggshell. At the time of the trial he could only respond to the simplest commands. *Daily Record*, 30 March 2001.
[9] The links between various strata of crime showed up when the body of 34-year-old Jeremy Earls was found on 8 August 2001 in his first-floor flat in Lincoln. He had shot himself. Earls was in fact Andrew Walker, a career criminal with links to members of the upper echelons of organised crime such as Paul Ferris, whom he had visited in Frankland prison in July. In 1994 Earls and an associate, Gary Skinner, were arrested at Seething airfield near Bungay, Suffolk. They had flown from Holland and 19 kg of drugs and 5,000 Ecstasy tablets were found. Earls was acquitted but Skinner received an 8-year sentence.

> The hunt for the attackers is not our top priority. Joe
> wasn't keen to talk about what happened – he seemed
> more interested in a revenge attack.[10]

One suggested explanation for the attack was that it had been
ordered by a man serving a life sentence. He had supplied drugs
to Hart who, once the man was sent down, declined to pay.

Echoes from the Ice Cream Wars rumbled on. John Linton,
a campaigner for the release of Campbell and Steele, was
found shot dead behind the Roadhouse public house in
Easterhouse in April 1996. He had long been convinced that
they were the fall guys for someone else's crime and, as part
of his campaign, in 1994 he had broken into the House of
Commons and hidden protest leaflets in various offices. No
one was ever charged with his murder, but suspicions fell
on another man involved in the Ice Cream Wars.

Then, at about 3 a.m. on 28 December 1998, Glasgow
hardman George Edgar was shot in Crownpoint Road,
Bridgetown, after leaving a masonic lodge with friends. He
died in hospital shortly afterwards. He had served 10 years'
imprisonment after the death of Albert Cartledge who was
stabbed in the back in a Blairgowrie bar in July 1986.

In 2000 Edgar's wife, Carla, fell in love with Joseph Steele
who had been in prison with Edgar. She had seen a television documentary about the wars and become convinced that
Steele was innocent. For a short time, while he was on bail
pending the first abortive appeal, he had stayed with her.
According to her:

---

[10] *Sunday Mail*, 25 March 2001.

We slept together, but didn't have sex. We just had a kiss and a cuddle. Our relationship was more important than sex. Even though Joe had waited all those years, he said he respected me for wanting to wait a little longer.

Sadly, the relationship fizzled out when Steele decided to marry a Dolly Brennan.

Edgar was not missed by his neighbours, one of whom described him as 'a brutal, evil thug'. Others said he was involved in every crime in the area and had been linked to all the local gangs. People had almost been queuing up to kill him.[11]

Then in May 2000 another old-timer, Frank McPhee, went down. One explanation on offer was that he had fallen foul of former Northern Ireland terrorists who had moved into the drug trade. Apart from negotiating between dealers in the North and the rest of England he was thought to have been one of the powers behind a big dog-fighting ring, and in 1991 he had been fined £1,000 after being found at a fight. Another suggested reason for his death was that he had beaten up the son of another gangland figure. A third possible reason was that he had stabbed a member of another Glasgow gang whom he believed to be an informer. It was thought that a contract had been out on him for a year, and before his death he had been chased through Glasgow by a gunman.

This time he had almost reached the sanctuary of his home on the drug-riddled Maryhill estate which he ruled by terror,

[11] *Daily Record*, 29 December 1998.

itself only 400 yards from the police station, when he was shot by a sniper on his doorstep. The man escaped through the flats while paramedics tried to save McPhee as he died on the pavement.

Since 1978 McPhee had served a total of 18 years. First a 5-year sentence, followed by 8 years and then another 5. In 1992 he was acquitted of involvement in an armed robbery at the Dundee branch of the Royal Bank of Scotland. The next year came his 8-year sentence for dealing in drugs. He was alleged to have been the go-between acting as the linkman for a London-based dealer and another Glasgow baron. While he was serving this sentence he was accused of killing the murderer, William 'Worm' Toye, in Perth prison. Toye, who was serving a life sentence for axing Edward Marshall to death to stop him giving evidence at brother Gavin Toye's murder trial, had been involved in three fights with drug barons from the time when he was moved from 'D' to 'A' Hall. Now on 5 September he died in the third of them. McPhee was acquitted.

Three months after finishing his sentence McPhee was once again charged with murder. This time the victim was the milkman by trade, Christopher McGrory. Despite being unemployed, McGrory owned three houses in Ireland and was thought to be smuggling cocaine and heroin. McPhee had been an usher at McGrory's Dublin wedding only a fortnight previously. Now the groom was found strangled on a golf course near Milngavie. McPhee and Colin McKay were acquitted following non-proven verdicts.

A police officer offered as an epitaph:

He had been a dead man walking for years. For McPhee the end was always going to come like this.[12]

The drugs war which had broken out in 1995 in Paisley, 5 miles from Glasgow and, in Victorian times, a centre for manufacturing highly coloured shawls, continued. In the 1970s the mills closed and now lie derelict. Armed dealers moved in, taking advantage of the road, air and rail links in their battle for control of Glasgow's heroin and tranquilliser market, estimated to be worth £200 million annually. In early March 1995 there were five gun-related incidents in 24 hours, culminating in Andrew McLaughlin being shot on his doorstep in Linwood. The Chief Constable of Strathclyde, in whose area 85 per cent of all robberies took place, said that firearms could be rented for as little as £50 a day and that in the past year his force had recovered 790 weapons, many of which had been purchased simply to take them out of circulation. Much of the trouble came on the Ferguslie estate where a gang run by the later-imprisoned Stuart Gillespie fought off the predations by rival gangs. As the police have managed to catch various members of the factions, so the war has spilled over into the prisons at Shotts and Greenock where there has been a vast increase in the number of prisoner stabbings.

In December 1998 David Wingate was shot five times as he left a disco in what was known, because of its proliferation of bars and clubs, as the Little Soho area. As he left with a friend about 1 a.m. a masked man armed with a shotgun

[12] See Tony Thompson in the *Observer*, 13 August 2000.

opened fire. The friend ran for help and officers, helped by tracker dogs, sealed off the disco and the town centre, but the man had escaped. Neighbours paid tribute to Wingate, describing him as 'a smashing bloke'.

A year previously Wingate had been charged, along with two others, with the killing of the student plumber and small-time drug dealer Paul Hainey, who was found shot to death on a path near Houston, Renfrewshire.[13] The charges against the others were dropped at the Sheriff's Court but Wingate was sent for trial where he was found not guilty. Wingate was known to have been in America, where he was thought to have served a prison sentence, before returning to Scotland in 1996.

Not everyone echoed Wingate's neighbours' praise. One man described as an 'Underworld insider' put things in perspective:

> Wingate was into a lot of dirty dealing and he was involved in a killing which he got away with. I am not surprised someone caught up with him. He was a dealer and will not be missed.[14]

It was not until 1998 that Stuart Gillespie, another Scots drugs baron, failed in his High Court action to retrieve £9,000 found in the flat of his friend Robert Pickett. The seizure had followed a dispute between Gillespie and his

---

[13] This was not the only tragedy for the Hainey family. His brother David, on home leave from a young offenders' institution, had killed himself in a cemetery after strangling his girlfriend, Ann Smith.
[14] *Daily Record*, 15 December 1998.

team and the Rennie brothers. In October 1996 Gillespie was convicted of the murder of Mark Rennie, shot by a hooded man in broad daylight near his home in the unhealthy Ferguslie Park area of Paisley. Pickett was later jailed for 12 years for the attempted murder of three of Rennie's brothers and another man. It was during the inquiry into the Rennie killing that the police found £9,000 in cupboards and under the bed in Pickett's flat. He told them that he was minding it for a friend who used it to buy roofing stuff. Six months later he said that the friend was Gillespie, who then sued the Chief Constable of Strathclyde for the return of the money. In December 1998 the claim was dismissed after he had told Sheriff John McGowan that he needed the cash in hand to buy slates. His evidence did not appeal to the Sheriff, who said he could believe neither Gillespie nor Pickett.

Two rather younger men were linked to the Edinburgh drug scene in October 1999 when the charred bodies of 25-year-old John Nisbet and his friend William Lindsay, a year his senior, were found on a farm track in Elphinstone, near Tranent. Both had been shot in the head and body. It was thought they had been trying to muscle in on an Edinburgh baron's patch. The same day the body of 19-year-old David Ferguson was found dumped near a children's playground in Mossend, Bellshill. Nisbet and Lindsay had last been seen alive about 9 p.m. on 12 October in Hamilton. Nisbet was known to have been carrying around £20,000, but by the time their bodies were found the money had disappeared.

Nisbet came from Craigneuk, Lanarkshire, and was another with a long history of violence in both Scotland and

England. In 1994, along with two of his cousins, he was acquitted of the shooting of two men in Craigneuk in what was a long-running battle with members of the Murdoch family. John Murdoch was left paralysed in the attack. William Murdoch was later shot in the head at his scrapyard and a month later a grenade was thrown at his home. The same year there was an attempted shooting of Allan Murdoch which he survived, though an innocent bystander was killed. After that the Murdochs left the area.

Three years later Nisbet was charged with staging a £20,000 bank raid in Torquay, Devon, but was acquitted after his co-accused pleaded guilty. He was also suspected of masterminding an armed robbery in Kilwinning, Ayrshire, on 8 August 1996 in which a blonde 'woman' crashed her white Sierra car into a Securicor van. Nisbet was thought to have been the cross-dresser, while his hooded colleagues poured petrol on the guards and threatened to set them alight if they did not open the van. The men and the blonde left in a metallic-blue Mercedes with £900,000. Both the Sierra and the Mercedes had been stolen, the Sierra from a policeman in Hamilton, the Mercedes also from that town. Nisbet was arrested but released without charge. It was the money from the Kilwinning robbery which, it was believed, had enabled him to start his drugs empire. Two men were arrested in the January following the Nisbet and Lindsay murders but were never charged.

Another who died in 1999 was Gerald Rae who had been the main witness in a police perjury trial. He was found in his L-registration white Vauxhall in a Drysdale Street, Yoker, on 15 October when the seven accused officers were still on trial in Edinburgh. It was thought he had died of an overdose even though he was not a known addict. When his body was found he was clutching 'tenner deals' of heroin. Three rocks of diamorphine were also found.

Rae's criminal career had lasted over 20 years and he had convictions for drug offences, assault, housebreaking and robbery including tying up and beating an elderly Jewish couple for which he received 8 years. His real claim to fame, however, was the civil action he had brought against certain Strathclyde police officers, accusing them of beating him up after a raid on his home at 43 Cartside, Glasgow, on 30 November 1990. Rae was acquitted of charges following the incident and then began his civil action.

On 6 January 1998 Lord Marnoch gave his judgement in Rae's claim that drugs had been planted and that he had been assaulted with pick-axe handles and baseball bats, something the officers strenuously denied. His Lordship had not found Rae to be an impressive witness, referring to his almost incessant sniffing throughout the two days when he was giving evidence. The judge also found that Rae was quite prepared to tell lies to distance himself from the 'status symbol' of a drugs dealer. His Lordship dismissed the claim that the police had planted drugs but, on the balance of probabilities – the test for a civil claim – he found that Rae had been beaten up with at least one pick-axe handle. He went on to say that he felt:

> . . . quite unable to make any finding as to how many officers, if more than one, were directly involved in the beating which the pursuer received.

In that connection, it is, I suppose, possible that some of the officers who gave evidence were, in effect, covering up for other officers through some misplaced sense of loyalty. If that happened – and I only say if – then I cannot condemn too strongly that same misplaced sense of loyalty which has only resulted in yet further disgrace being brought on the Force.[15]

Damages in the event of a finding against the police had been agreed at £3,000. Now it was off to the criminal courts for the trial of seven officers for perjury, where the test for the prosecution was to prove 'beyond reasonable doubt'. The case against two of them was stopped at the end of the prosecution's case and, summing up, Lord Milligan told the jury that they had to be sure the officers were 'deliberately, clearly and unambiguously lying'. The jury returned verdicts of not guilty in less than two hours.

The chairman of the Strathclyde Police Federation commented, 'Complaints made maliciously by professional criminals can have horrendous consequences for innocent officers.'

The fallout in the destabilised Glasgow scene has not been helped by the sudden eruption of a triad battle with the newly arrived Tai Huen Chair, or the Big Circle Gang, attempting to take over the interests of the long-established Wo Shin Wo.

In the city, however, there seems to be another protection war at present. In the past the protection has generally been

---

[15] Opinion of Lord Marnoch in the case *Gerald Rae v The Chief Constable of Strathclyde Police*, p. 28.

of clubs and pubs and who shall have whose bouncers in place, but now the fight is over contracts for the security of building sites and schools.

By the end of 2001 there were suggestions that efforts were being made to set up an Apalachin-style peace conference[16] with senior Glasgow figures invited to attend. They would include McGraw, of course. His brother-in-law John Healy, jailed in 1998 for 10 years in the case in which 'The Licensee' was acquitted, has been released and there have been rumours that all is not well between the pair. Each is now said to be fearful of the other and Healy is alleged still to be controlling Glasgow's South Side from Castle Huntly prison near Dundee.[17] Others who would be invited if any such meeting did take place would be bound to include Gerry Carbin snr, recently released after serving 9 years in Spain for drug smuggling.

The suggestion of a meeting has been prompted by various shootings including the attempt on the life of Duncan McIntyre who was shot as he left a barber's shop in Springburn in June 2001. He was taken to hospital, while the gunman caught a No. 45 bus. McIntyre survived, just as he had survived a previous effort outside his home in the Gallowgate some years ago. Shortly before the attack on McIntyre, Tommy McGovern had been lured to the car park of the Talisman bar in Springburn and shot. He too survived.

---

[16] See James Morton, *Gangland International*.
[17] In the early summer of 2000 grandmother Irene Campbell, a close friend of Healy, was jailed for 7 years in Venezuela after being found with £500,000 of cocaine. She was arrested after taking three trips to that country in four months. She said she had financed them from bingo winnings.

Another McGovern brother, Tony, was shot in September 2000 outside the New Morven public house in Balornock. Despite wearing a £400 bulletproof vest he had not survived and, it was said, the secret of where he kept his money had died with him.

How did it all come on top? The McGoverns and the McIntyres – who at one time had rival enterprises in the Springburn area – were more recently thought to have been working in partnership but had again fallen out. The catalyst was the relationship which Tony McGovern had formed in 1997 with James Stevenson, the so-called 'Iceman' also known as 'The Bull'. It was not a relationship which appealed to Tommy McGovern and the pair suggested he had stolen £60,000 from them. They went looking for it and shortly afterwards Tommy McGovern was shot and run over by one of his own ice-cream vans. After that Tony McGovern and 'The Iceman' began to establish an empire based on drugs and money-lending. Meanwhile Tommy McGovern went to prison to serve a 4-year sentence for firearms and other offences. While there his elder brother, Joe, tried to broker a settlement between the brothers. Unfortunately the price demanded was that Tony dispose of 'The Iceman'. He was taken out to the country near Fintry but Tony botched the killing, merely grazing his neck; 'The Iceman' survived, running into woodlands. The next week Tony McGovern was shot in the shower of his home in Kenmure Crescent, Bishopbriggs. Amazingly only one bullet lodged and he also survived.

Attack and counter-attack followed. A garage in Springburn owned by 'The Iceman' was continually robbed.

In turn the Café Cini, a night-club in Greenock owned by former Celtic footballer Charlie Nicholas, was set alight. There is no suggestion that Nicholas knew anything of the feud which had engulfed him; it was simply a place which the McGoverns used.

By the summer of 2001, it was alleged that the Protestant Ulster Volunteer Force, along with some members of the Carbin, Madden and McIntyre families, was backing James Stevenson. Ranged with the McGoverns were the Catholic sympathisers, Frank Boyle, a schoolfriend of theirs, and McGraw. There was also Frank Carberry, who had been convicted in 1995 after throwing a horse's ear at a woman. James Milligan, who had an interest in the Café Cini, had disappeared in January 2001.

Jamie McGovern had previously been in the wars when he was shot in the face. His other brother, Paul McGovern, runs the thriving security firm M & M which has contracts with the Scottish Executive. The Carbins had been friends of both the Stevensons and the McGoverns. Caroline Stevenson was formerly married to Gerry Carbin snr, known as 'Cyclops' after a cataract left him blind in one eye. Tony McGovern was the best man at the James Stevenson–Caroline Carbin wedding. Carbin snr received a 9-year sentence in Spain for drug smuggling. Gerry Carbin jnr, in his early twenties, was given a bad beating by Tony McGovern shortly before the latter's death.

As for the McIntyres, they had also been friends of the McGoverns. The one-time head of that family, the now deceased Joe 'Fat Boy' McIntyre, was a career criminal. An ex-lawyer relative, James, went to prison in 1997 after the police found pistols and ammunition at his home in West Lothian.

In 1985 Charles Madden had been stabbed to death outside a club in Saracen, North Glasgow, allegedly by a man from the McGovern camp. He was acquitted, but since then the Maddens have aligned themselves with the Stevensons.[18]

On 24 August 2001 James Stevenson was charged with the murder of Tony McGovern, having been found in Blackpool the previous week and remanded in custody. It was expected that the committal for trial would be something of a formality, but then came a sensational development. Stevenson was released on the authority of the Procurator Fiscal, who then had a year in which to bring him to court again. In practice this has generally meant that, in the absence of further evidence, it is the end of the matter.

One man who would not be attending any peace meeting, and who said he was turning his back on crime, was Frank Carberry – one of the many who had worked for Arthur Thompson. In that capacity, at the age of 20 he was charged with taking out another gangster's eye but was found not guilty. Two years later he was acquitted of a £400,000 fraud but then served a sentence for assault. Now he ran a security company and was reported to be marrying a whisky heiress. He told reporters:

---

[18] For a full account of the feud and how the parties line up, see Russell Findlay, 'Revenge of the Iceman' in *Sunday Mail*, 24 September 2000, and David Leslie, 'Gang Wars' in *News of the World*, 8 July 2001.

I have promised that I will never again meet up with the gangsters I dealt with most of my life. I know I have to change. It is a last chance for me.[19]

Someone who is unlikely to be invited to the meeting is one of the senior Scots criminals who has led a charmed life in the past decade. Wattie Douglas is the former Glasgow milkman turned drug dealer, whose body was thought to have been found riddled with bullets in a canal in Amsterdam, the victim of a 1991 drugs war. It was not so. Using the traditional method of holding the day's newspaper, Douglas was photographed to show that he was alive and well and 'Look, no bullet holes.'

Then two years later it seemed that his luck had run out when in 1993 he was seized after a two-year probe by Interpol in an investigation which ran from Spain and Holland to Scotland. One boat, the *Britannia Gazelle*, was seized with a $60 million cargo of hashish. He was sentenced to 4 years in Holland in 1994 but was allowed bail when his lawyer appealed, alleging that the police had used unlawful phone taps to catch him. So it was off to Marbella to join the other refugees on the Costa del Crime – and it was there that he was found under the name of Terence Tomkins in May 1998. In fact Douglas could have been arrested two years earlier, but unfortunately the wrong house in Fuengirola had been raided. Nor were things to get any better for the authorities. In early September 1998 he was released after an application for extradition failed.

[19] *The Scotsman*, 13 July 2001.

However, it is just possible that another legendary Scots Underworld figure, who has been on the run for a decade following a drug deal with the Hell's Angels, may turn up. Billy Blackledge, now in his sixties and said, in the highest of criminal traditions, to run his empire from his luxury yacht, has been on his toes, so to speak, since being indicted by Grand Juries in America in 1990 and 1992. It was alleged that he had been using Angels' cash to buy drugs from the Cali cartel and then ship them to Canada, from where they would be smuggled into Europe. In recent years it has been suggested that he, another master of disguise, has been paying secret visits to Scotland.

Billy Blackledge was more fortunate than Paul Ferris who, after reports that he had been seen with a criminal, was returned to prison for breach of his parole. He had earlier been reported as having been involved in a fight with McGraw, something 'The Licensee' denied. He was now reported to be preparing to return to Tenerife.[20]

---

[20] *News of the World*, 12 May 2002; *Daily Record*, May 2002.

EUROPE

10

Ireland, Holland, Germany and Scandinavia

Ireland

The face of Irish crime itself changed irrevocably when on
18 August 1994 the gang-leader and robber known as 'The
General', Martin Cahill, was killed by the IRA in an ambush
in the Ranelagh area of Dublin.[1] The shooting took place
about half a mile from his home. Two men had lain in wait
for him, one sitting on a black motorcycle posing as a
council worker checking registration numbers. When
Cahill stopped his Renault 5 the man ran to him and fired
a single shot. The car went out of control and hit a pole.

---

[1] For his career see Paul Williams, *The General*.

The gunman then fired four more shots and escaped on the motorcycle.

From then on it might be hyperbole to say that the Liffey ran with blood, but it would not be all that much of an exaggeration. Eventually it led to the death of journalist Veronica Guerin, both as a revenge and for intimidatory purposes, probably only the second such killing in Western society in modern times.[2]

After Cahill's death a statement claiming responsibility was issued by the Irish National Liberation Army, with whom he was known to have links. Within a matter of hours, however, the IRA telephoned a Dublin radio station to say that a member had carried out the execution. The INLA then issued a statement saying the first claim was false. No arrests were made and within months a new leader of the Dublin north-side Underworld, Gerry Hutch from Clontarf, known as 'Mr Clean' or 'The Monk' because of his dislike of drugs and having something of a puritanical streak, emerged.

'The Monk', in his thirties, is thought to have been associated with a £1.4 (punts) million security van robbery in Marino in late 1987, but the police could not find evidence to link him to the crime. According to reports there were difficulties in trying to launder the money and some was lost. By 1996, of the three men allegedly involved in the robbery only 'The Monk' had survived. Married, with children who

---

[2] The other is Don Bolles in Phoenix, Arizona. The deaths of Chicago journalists Jake Lingle and Julius Rosenheim in the 1930s can be discounted as both were actively engaged in organised crime. On the other hand the death rate of journalists in Mexico is extremely high. One of the latest victims was Jesus Blancornelas, shot in Tijuana on 27 November 1997. He survived but his bodyguards were killed.

go to fee-paying schools, he generally avoided the publicity and the stunts which made 'The General' such a popular figure with the media.

The other new leaders in the struggle for power, and often a share of the drug trade, also seem either to have adopted or been given exotic soubriquets. After 'The General' and 'The Monk' came Derek Dunne, nicknamed 'Maradona' because he was once with St Patrick's Athletic, and George Mitchell, a drug dealer from Ballyfermot named 'The Penguin'. He is alleged to have had connections with Irish businessmen, including some with government links, who have laundered money on his behalf.

There are and have been many others given nicknames, according to Tony Gregory, the independent MP for Dublin Central, when he gave evidence to the Dail sub-committee on drugs. These have included 'The Warehouseman', 'The Coach', 'Pony', 'Psycho', and 'Cotton Eye'. He also named Tommy Mullen, a major heroin dealer in North Dublin and known as 'The Boxer'. On 15 January 1998 Mullen was sentenced to 18 years in London for conspiracy to import drugs. Also convicted with him was Turhan Mustafa from North London and Katherine Brooks who both admitted to conspiracy to export heroin.

Mustafa is a good example of the spread of the Turkish interest in the drugs trade. A middle-aged man with a butcher's shop in Tottenham, he was the front man for one of the number of Turkish syndicates operating in London at present. Katherine Brooks was one of the tragic pieces of flotsam who are washed up on the beaches and like drift-wood are then picked up, used and discarded. Originally she had come from a good background, and worked as a hotel receptionist before a boyfriend introduced her to drugs and she became a heroin addict, eventually supporting her addiction by prostitution. Through this she had met Mustafa.

In turn he persuaded her to give up prostitution and begin a relationship with him. He gave her clothes, paid for a flat and food. He supplemented these kindly gestures by supplying her with increasing amounts of heroin until she had moved from smoking to injecting and her habit, if she had been obliged to pay for the drug, would have cost her in the region of £1,500 a week. As Paul Williams points out in *Gangland*, his excellent account of Irish crime figures, Mustafa had effectively enslaved her. Soon he began to demand payment for the free heroin, and this consisted of working for Mullen. In 1996 she began work as a courier on the Holyhead to Dun Laoghaire route. Heroin was wrapped as a gift package and given to her. Once in Ireland she was to go to a car parked at the ferry terminal and leave the package in the glove compartment. She then booked into an hotel where she was given a shopping bag full of money.

It was soon after that Mullen was named first in the Dail and then by Veronica Guerin in the *Sunday Independent*. He left for Spain with his girlfriend, settling on the Costa del Sol from where he ran his business.

Katherine Brooks was arrested with a kilo of heroin on 12 June while on her way to London's City airport. In the loft of her flat another 3 kg were found. Both she and Mustafa were arrested. Once she had been in the detoxification unit at Holloway prison she made a statement. At her trial she received 3 years. Mullen was arrested more or less accidentally, trapped by *Operation Spiderweb* which was not looking for him at all but had its sights on a team of North London armed robbers. On 10 March 1997 he had returned to London and was seen going to a safe depository in Hampstead, and when he returned four days later he was stopped and searched. He was found to be carrying in excess of £100,000 and some false passports.

At his trial in September 1997 he explained everything. He had never been involved with drugs; in fact, the whole case was a conspiracy between the IRA and the Gardai. The money might, just *might*, have come from a series of robberies in Ireland. Katherine Brooks had given evidence against him but at the Snaresbrook Crown Court, where in recent years the prosecution has often struggled to obtain a guilty verdict, the jury disagreed. Four months later in January 1998 he was back in court. This time the jury returned a unanimous verdict of guilty in rather under four hours. He received 18 years after the judge was told that 'The Boxer' was the foremost trafficker of heroin in Ireland.

In early January 1995 a £3 million (punts) robbery took place near Dublin's airport at the Brinks-Allied security depot. The attack occurred minutes after the scheduled departure of the soldiers who had escorted the van, collecting cash from banks, through rural County Dublin. Thieves broke through two metal fences and constructed makeshift bridges over ditches, in an operation of which 'The General' (had he lived) would have been proud. As it was, 'The Monk' received the blame. He was released without charge after questioning.

'The Monk' was also thought to be behind the theft of valuable microchips which were stolen in August 1994, and involved in the theft of a Securicor vehicle in Limerick on

31 October the next year. His name was once again in the frame when in January 1996 a raid on the AIB cash depot at Waterford netted £2.8 million (punts). This time, however, one of the gang carried a machine gun or some other type of automatic weapon. The Gardai were not sure whether this meant that there was an IRA involvement or simply that the Dublin Underworld now had access to such weapons.

By the end of 1995 there was an escalating battle for the Dublin drugs trade. On the evening of Tuesday 5 December, Martin Foley, known as 'The Viper', and former right-hand man to 'The General', was shot as he left a block of flats in McCarthy's Terrace on Dublin's North Side. He was hit twice in the side but survived, staggering to another block of flats. 'It's the Provos,' he is said to have told the first detective who arrived at the scene.

One of the problems with Dublin in the 1990s was that there were no clear turf limits in which gangs could act without interruption by predators. On the edges of the city there may have been gangs such as the Tallaght in the south and the Ballyfermot in the west, but it was almost impossible to say that A has this piece of turf and B another.

Some killings, such as that of Christy Delaney – cabaret singer, ticket tout and schmutter designerwear salesman – on 24 November 1995, were simple gangland murders. He was killed on the orders of a Holland-based Irish dealer because he had siphoned off more than his share of money sent to be laundered. But there have also been tangential troubles with operations which may have had links to the IRA, taking a hand in meting out punishment to those it suspected of dealing. Delaney's murder followed immediately on the double killing of Eddie McCabe and Catherine Brennan; he was shot for selling Ecstasy to a girl who died of a drug overdose, she because she was a witness to the killing as they left a petrol station in Tallaght.

In February 1996 a hit list with 39 names of alleged drug dealers and criminals – not including that of 'The Monk' – was sent to a Dublin newspaper. The first on the list to go was Gerry Lee, said to be a close friend of 'The Monk' and a man who took part in the £3 million robbery the previous year. He was shot at 7 a.m. on 9 March when a hitman came to a party Lee had been holding for his birthday. Lee was also alleged to have been one of the men on the Marino robbery in 1987.[3]

By the end of March 1997 'The Monk' was said to be turning to drink as a result of the pressure being put on him. He is also said to have eschewed the drug trade, but those associated with him have not done so and he fears himself to be at risk because of their activities. However, there have been allegations that while he is not actively engaged in drug running he has financed some of the larger deals. The counter-argument is that by linking his name to drugs 'The Monk''s enemies are trying to undermine the support he has simply as an armed robber.

More serious than the robbery was the attack on crusading journalist Veronica Guerin by a man wearing motorcycling gear and a helmet, when she answered the door of her home on 30 January 1996. He pointed a handgun at her head

[3] The third alleged member of the gang on the Marino robbery, Patrick McDonald, was shot dead in 1992.

before he lowered the barrel and shot her in the right thigh. It was not the first time Ms Guerin had been threatened; in October 1994 shots had been fired at her home. She had previously profiled 'The Monk', whom she found to be cold and ruthless, but it was not 'The Monk' who was instrumental in her death. Indeed after her death, in a public disassociation from her killers, he went to the offices of Independent Newspapers on Middle Abbey Street to sign a book of condolence.

Veronica Guerin was killed on 26 June 1996 as she drove home from the Nass courthouse where she had just been fined for a speeding offence. She pulled up at the Clondalkin traffic light shortly before 1 p.m. and the rider of a white Kawasaki motorcycle bearing false 1969 Dublin plates shot her through the window. She had been on her mobile telephone to a Garda officer and the call, which had been taped, was interrupted in mid-sentence with a bang as she was shot.

A completely fearless woman, she had ignored the inherent threat when she was shot in the leg and a further attack made on her in her home. The previous week she had written about one of Dublin's most notorious drug dealers, labelling as 'King Scum' Tony Felloni, who had a conviction for living off immoral earnings and, apart from trying to poison his wife, had introduced his daughter to drugs. He had just been jailed for 20 years but, correctly, it was not thought that he was in any way responsible for Guerin's death.

Even with the glare of the world media on their city, the Dublin hardmen continued with their lives and deaths. Down on 8 December 1996 went one of the four Mr Bigs of Dublin, 'The Psycho', Peter Joseph Judge, shot as he sat in his car outside the Royal Oak public house in Finglas near his home. His was the fourteenth gang-related death since 'The General' had been shot.[4]

Judge was himself responsible for three of those deaths: Michael Godfrey, a money launderer, in 1991; William Corbally, who disappeared in February 1996 and whose body was never found; and Michael Brady, who was shot by the pillion passenger of a motorcyclist on the Quays in the September of 1996. Brady had previously been convicted of killing his wife, Julie, and his daughters said they were by no means sorry he had been shot.

Judge, once an armed robber, had stepped into the vacuum which followed the dismantling of a gang by the Gardai and a killing spree in November 1995 when four people died in a nine-day period. He had taken a large share of the drug business in Finglas and Ballymum, North Dublin. He was buried at St Canice's Church, Finglas, to the strains of 'I Will Always Love You' by Whitney Houston and 'The Rose' by Bette Midler. Amongst the mourners at the funeral was Ellen Hyland, the sister-in-law of Michael Brady.

Within days of Judge's death, on the night of 13 December his lieutenant, Mark Dwyer, was abducted from his girlfriend's flat at gunpoint by three masked men. He and another man were taken to Scribblestown Lane near Finglas, where both were beaten and Dwyer killed. It was thought that he might have been involved in the murder of Corbally, and now that Judge was dead reprisals could be taken.

Despite the inroads into at least one gang by the Gardai

---

[4] This includes the murder of Veronica Guerin.

in the wake of the Guerin killing, the flow of heroin into Dublin continued and prices remained stable. It was not thought that Judge's death would lead to anything much more than small skirmishes.

The killings continued sporadically throughout 1997 and included the death of Roberto Minotti, an Italian-born chip-shop owner who was suspected of being a key member of a major drug-smuggling syndicate and who had convictions for extortion and robbery. In September 1997 he was stabbed to death at the home of his former girlfriend. He had allowed his defences to slip, for he had the front and bedroom doors at his home in County Wicklow made of steel, and the lower windows of the house were bricked up.

Over the years the drug wars continued. In February 2000 two men were found dead in a Dublin canal and, at the end of April 2000, Thomas Byrne went down outside O'Neill's pub in Summerhill when a man walked up to him, shot him in the head and retired quickly. A relatively small-time drug dealer, his killing may have been part of the series which included the thwarting by the Gardai of an attempt to kill Seamus Hogan. In July a Dundalk publican, Stephen Connolly, was shot dead. It was thought that he had been killed on the orders of Nick O'Hare who was himself later murdered.

As the years went by the story of the killing of Veronica Guerin began to unravel and it revolved around 'The Warehouseman', John Gilligan, and his gang of drug and arms dealers. Gilligan had long been a thorn in the side of the Gardai.

For years the Gardai believed that he was leader of the

so-called Warehouse Gang operating, as all good thieves should, by specialising in identifying a ready market for a particular brand of stolen goods, whether it was animal drugs, videos, video games or children's clothes. The gang, which had operated almost unchecked for 10 years, would raid the target factory on a Friday night and by the time the loss was noticed the goods would have been distributed throughout Dublin. The items were then sold to small-time dealers or shops, and on occasions would be sold back to the losers.

On 2 January 1986, 850 new vacuum cleaners were stolen in an armed raid on a factory on the Cookstown estate. One of the team, David Weafer, in difficulties himself, passed information to the Gardai and Gilligan was trapped when seen unloading hardware goods from a lorry in the Walkinstown district. The case against him was dismissed over technicalities about proving ownership of the cleaners, but on Good Friday 1987 he was caught breaking into the Rose Confectionery warehouse on the inappropriately named Robin Hood estate. This time he was convicted and he received 18 months' imprisonment. On 7 November 1990 he went to Portaloise prison to begin a 4-year sentence for handling stolen goods. It was here that he would recruit the members of his second criminal empire.[5] Genuinely working for better conditions for the prisoners, he also began to plan his transition from warehouse-breaker to drug dealer. In Portaloise at the time were Brian Meehan, a getaway driver used by Cahill, and Paul Ward known as Hippo, a man with

---

[5] Aspects of Gilligan's career appear in many books on Irish crime, but undoubtedly the most thorough is by the investigative journalist, John Mooney, in *Gangster*.

25 convictions. Both would eventually become tried and trusted members of the Gilligan outfit.

Gilligan was released on 15 November 1993 after serving 3 years of his sentence. At a previous sentence hearing the 38-year-old former seaman had been described in court as having no other income than from crime. In 1988 he had been living on social security of £50 a week, from which he was maintaining three ponies at livery in a local riding school. By the time of his conviction in November 1990 he had acquired a house and the Jessbrook stables in County Meath, run by his wife Geraldine, buying up every acre on which he could lay his money. During the previous three years he had listened to the boasting of men such as Meehan about how much money could be made from drugs, and he was determined to establish his own operation.[6]

Now Gilligan turned to John Traynor, 'The Coach', womaniser, fraudsman, possible blackmailer and certainly retriever of a number of paintings from the Beit collection as well as some 145 files stolen by Cahill from the offices of the Director of Public Prosecutions. Gilligan had known Traynor since his days as a seaman and now 'The Coach' introduced him to Cahill. From then on it was gravy all the way. By the time Veronica Guerin started to investigate him Gilligan was making literally millions of pounds annually, principally from drugs but also from arms smuggling.

It is inconceivable that Gilligan did not believe that the

---

[6] Meehan had grown up in the Crumlin area and after a series of minor convictions graduated with a 6-year sentence imposed in 1989 for robbing Allied Irish Bank premises in Grafton Street.

shooting in broad daylight of a prominent Irish journalist would bring down the wrath not only of the police but also of the press on his head. He had threatened her and her son. He had then beaten her up and threatened to rape her son when she had visited him earlier, and she had not kow-towed. Instead she had reported the assault to the police. He now believed, alleged the prosecution at his later trial, that she would go ahead with the prosecution and if, as was almost certain, he was jailed, he would lose control of his empire.

Her death changed his life. Now he effectively became a fugitive, moving from place to place and, at the same time, shifting huge sums abroad. One effort to launder money in Holland through a casino had failed. Worse, there were defections from within the ranks.

At the end of 1998 Gilligan's armourer Charles Bowden, who was himself serving a 6-year sentence for drugs and arms dealing, turned informer and gave evidence against Paul Ward who was alleged to have disposed of the gun and the motorcycle used in the attack. On 18 January 1999 Ward was refused leave to appeal against his conviction for which he received a life sentence.

Now on 4 October Gilligan made a run from Heathrow to Amsterdam, checking in late with only hand luggage. He tried to repeat the same procedure two days later, but he had been noticed on the prior run and this time he was stopped and invited to open his suitcase. It contained £330,000 in various currencies. This was the last time he was free until his trial. During his period in custody he made spirited efforts in his defence – both legally with challenges to the extradition procedure and illegally with efforts to intimidate the witnesses against him. It was to no effect. He was finally extradited and in December 2000 he went on trial in Dublin for the murder of Veronica Guerin before three judges sitting without a jury at the special criminal court. Opening the case, Peter Charleton for the prosecution told the court:

> He committed this offence through his agents, his agents being members of a gang under his control who all the while acted according to his will.

Gilligan faced not only the murder charge but also a further 15 counts of smuggling drugs and firearms between 1994 and 1996. He had, said Charleton, told a Russell Warren to keep the journalist under surveillance after she left court following her speeding case. It was alleged that Brian Meehan had ridden the Kawasaki motorcycle with the gunman as pillion passenger. Meehan had been relegated to driver rather than shooter because of his inability to dispose of another victim, Martin Foley, on two occasions. Bowden and two other supergrasses gave evidence against him.

On 15 January 2001 John Gilligan received both good and bad news from the court. The good news was that the judges said that the witnesses were so unreliable that they would acquit him of Guerin's murder. The bad news was that he was sentenced to 28 years for running a drugs empire.

The writer John Mooney is by no means convinced that the result of the Gilligan trial was a success for the State:

There is no happy ending to this story. Gilligan is now appealing against his sentence and will probably succeed in having it reduced. If he behaves himself and the Court of Appeal rules in his favour he could be released much earlier than anyone expects. John Traynor, Shay Ward and Peter Mitchell are still on the run. The latest reports suggest they are running a drugs distribution business in Spain somewhere on the Costa del Sol. Brian Meehan and Paul Ward are appealing their cases. Patrick Eugene Holland vehemently denies carrying out Veronica's assassination. His 20-year sentence was reduced to 12 years by the Court of Criminal Appeal. He too is continuing to seek his freedom.

The three supergrasses are due for release and will be resettled, most likely in Canada, the United States or Australia. Geraldine Gilligan is still living in Jessbrook. The drug dealers Gilligan's cartel supplied are still out there pushing drugs. Few were charged and even fewer convicted.[7]

Things improved substantially for Paul Ward when, on 22 March 2002, his conviction was quashed. The Court of Appeal ruled that there was no corroboration of the evidence of Charles Bowden that Ward had disposed of the motorcycle and gun. Ward would, however, have to continue to serve a 12-year sentence imposed for taking part in a prison riot while on remand awaiting trial. It was thought that the successful appeal would increase the chances of appeal by Brian Meehan.[8]

---

[7] John Mooney, *Gangster*, p. 237. The book concludes with the verbatim judgement of the court delivered on 15 March 2001.
[8] *The Times*, 23 March 2002.

It was also thought that despite the inroads made by the Criminal Assets Bureau (CAB) into Gilligan's money, he was still worth in the region of £50 million.

Nevertheless, one of the great successes in the fight against organised crime in Ireland has undoubtedly been the Criminal Assets Bureau, established in 1996. Over the last seven years, one by one many of the major players have had their assets frozen with a view to confiscation. John Gilligan was forced to hand over three houses; Patrick 'Dutchy' Holland had his house confiscated when he was jailed for 20 years; Gerry 'The Monk' Hutch paid over nearly £2 million; and John 'The Coach' Traynor found himself facing a £500,000 tax bill and the loss of his Dublin home; he was arrested in Holland but released and went south to Spain where for a time he ran a bar not far from his long-time friend Mickey Greene. The CAB also removed £1.75 million from the vicelord Tom McConnell.

It was not all one-way traffic however. In August 2000 the CAB seized a nineteenth-century mansion along with its contents and an adjoining island near Sneem on the Ring of Kerry. It was thought to be worth £2.5 million, and belonged to the Dutch drug dealer Jan Hendrik Ijpelaar, who had been convicted back in 1992 of being the leader of a criminal gang and of possession and distribution of drugs. He had served 4 years of a 6-year sentence.

But where one door shuts on a criminal, another opens. Since 1998 a gang named the Westies by the *Sunday World* has been controlling the heroin trade and terrorising the Corduff estate in Blanchardstown in West Dublin, carrying out shootings, beatings and abductions over money owed after even relatively minor drug deals.[9] One of their leaders has been dubbed 'The New Psycho' and is alleged to have plotted to murder a senior Garda officer investigating the gang. Amongst their actual victims was their drug competitor, Pascal Boland.

Meanwhile in Limerick in 2001 there were more than 20 shootings which have resulted in nine murders, mainly in the drug wars. By the summer another inter-gang drug feud had broken out. One gang was said to have ex-Republican connections and another, which had access to assault rifles, operated in Galway and Manchester where it was thought to have a substantial hold on much of that city's drug trade.

One of the relatively more fortunate Limerick players is 27-year-old John Creamer who, on 11 October, survived a machine-gun attack. 'Relatively' is probably the correct word because a hail of bullets left him with part of his mouth shot away and a month later he was still unconscious. He takes over the dubious record of surviving the most bullets from Martin Foley, 'The Viper', who survived three gun attacks. Foley had fallen out with Brian Meehan who – the court was told at Meehan's trial for the killing of Veronica Guerin – first shot him in a bar and then opened fire with a sub-machine gun when he found him in the Liberties in January 1996.

Creamer's attacker is alleged to be a 19-year-old contract killer suspected of at least two more shootings. Creamer has

---

[9] See Paul Williams, 'They're out of control' in *Sunday World*, 11 November 2001. The original Westies were a long-running gang which controlled part of the West Side of New York in what was known as Hell's Kitchen and ran roughly from 8th Avenue to the Hudson River and between 40th and 50th, more or less from 1920 to 1980.

been no stranger to violence in his career. In 2000 a murder charge was dropped against him when a witness to the 1996 incident died. Two years ago he survived another serious attack but declined to name his attacker. It was thought he dealt with the matter himself.

Meanwhile 'The Viper' was awarded £120,000 by the High Court following the attack on him by Charles Bowden when Foley was shot in the back and also lost the tip of his finger. He may be in line for another payout because in September 2000 he survived another attempt on his life when he was shot in the legs as he left a Dublin swimming-pool.

Gerry Hutch continued his rehabilitation and in June 2001 he was given a licence to become a taxi-driver. Foley was, however, in more trouble in April 2002. He was shot as he left a swimming-pool at Terenure College, on Templeogue Road at about 9 p.m. It was the second attempt on his life within two months. The first had been stopped by uniformed Gardai.

One interesting feud in the area – which had been running between two families on and off for the better part of 20 years – resurfaced in September 2000 after a fight in a disco between two girls. A straightener was arranged for the following day in which, it is alleged, part of an ear went missing. The biter's mother was then captured and the letter 'S' carved on her face. Within a matter of days the younger children of each family were being taken to school in convoys. A gun was fired and on 12 November an Eddie Ryan was shot dead in a bar. Very much like the Tibbs–Nicholls war in London's East End in the 1960s,[10] violence escalated and

[10] See James Morton, *Gangland*.

a bomb was placed under a car. Throughout 2001 there were at least ten gun-related incidents, and Gardai investigations under the name *Operation Oileann* have resulted in arrests and the confiscation of guns.[11]

Earlier in June 2001 in Cork, Kieran O'Flynn was not as fortunate as Creamer. The 39-year-old O'Flynn had long been regarded as one of the leaders of the city's best established gangs. There had been some erosion in its membership over the years with a number of the gang being sent to prison and, seeing its weakened state, other gangs had thought to make inroads into its territory. There was some suggestion that O'Flynn had behaved unsportingly by disclosing information about his rivals to the Garda. This was not the first gangland death in the family. On 9 April 1995 his brother-in-law Michael Crinnon, who had failed to pay a debt to the Gilligan organisation, had been shot and killed.

The feuding in the Limerick area has continued unabated. From the beginning of the millennium there have been 17 homicides in the area. In January 2003 two young men, John Ryan and his brother Kieran, were apparently kidnapped at gunpoint. They turned up unharmed a week later. In their absence Kieran Keane was found shot dead with his hands tied behind his back. His nephew was taken to hospital with stab wounds. Keane, regarded as one of the drug barons of the area, had been suspected of the shooting of Eddie Ryan, the father of John and Kieran. Keane had survived an earlier attempt on his life when Eddie Ryan's gun jammed. In the last two years

---

[11] Jim Cusack, 'New ferocity to gang "wars" outside Dublin' in the *Irish Times*, 11 June 2001.

the police have retrieved over 160 firearms in the area. They included AK47s and Ingram sub-machine guns.[12]

Holland

In recent years Holland has become something of a second home for Irish criminals, who for one reason or another have found Dublin to be less and less to their liking. They have also found the relaxed attitude towards drugs in Holland makes it a far more congenial place from which to conduct their enterprises. However, there are signs – as many have discovered to their cost – that Holland may now be far more dangerous than in the relatively recent past. The policy of allowing coffee shops to sell a range of soft drugs including leaf marijuana, cannabis resin and magic mushrooms, on condition that under-18-year-olds are not admitted and that no hard drugs are on offer, has become almost impossible to control. A 1995 government policy of reducing the number of shops and the amount of drugs allowed to be sold has resulted in organised crime moving into the cities in a big way. Shops have had to buy from organised drug rings. The Dutch police now believe there are criminal gangs from up to 40 countries operating in the Netherlands. Death and arrest may not have gone hand in hand but they certainly have been bedfellows. Amsterdam and the other cities are places where it is easy to get into further trouble.

---

[12] For a full account of the Limerick troubles see *Sunday Tribune*, 2 February 2003.

In 1999 Brian Meehan, who after the murder of journalist Veronica Guerin was regarded for a time as perhaps the most wanted man by Ireland, was arrested when he met his girlfriend and the fleeing John Traynor at Amsterdam Central Station. He probably welcomed the arrest because he told the police that he thought they were rival criminals intent on killing him. Then in April 2000 Liam Fynes, a disc jockey who had hidden over 30,000 Ecstasy tablets in a child's buggy, was jailed for 3 years. Fynes had been a close friend of Sean O'Flynn from Cork – himself jailed in Utrecht in December 1998 for dealing in 25,000 of the tablets.

One way or another Ecstasy tablets and the Dutch Connection caused a good deal of trouble around that time. In 1999 Joseph Delaney was convicted of the 1996 murder of Mark Dwyer. This time some 40,000 of the tablets had disappeared en route from Amsterdam to Dublin, and Dwyer was tortured for several hours before finally being shot.

At the end of March 2000 the Dutch police seized Ecstasy tablets worth £14 million and two major Irish players. George Mitchell absented himself in something of a hurry. Mitchell had already spent some time in Dutch prisons and had been released in 1999 after serving a year out of a 3-year sentence for a £1.5 million computer parts theft.

Others who were not as quick off the mark included John Cunningham, who in days gone by had been a member of the team which kidnapped Jennifer Guinness. He had escaped from an open prison where he was serving the last few years of his 17-year sentence, and was thought to have been associating with people suspected of a series of hijacks of lorries both in Ireland and in Europe.[13]

One of the most horrific murders in Amsterdam in recent years also involved some Irishmen, even though the outcome was not quite as at first expected. Apartment 1058 on the fifth floor of a luxury block of flats on the beach at Scheveningen, a suburb of The Hague, was set on fire on Konninginnedag 2000. Neighbours called the fire brigade and when they reached the flat they found the bodies of Damien Monahan from Ennis and two brothers, Vincent and Morgan Costello, from Bansha. Their bodies – thought to have been there for six days – had been slashed repeatedly; one man had his throat cut and all three had been shot in the head.

This was also believed to have been another settling of drugs scores. Damien Monahan was known to be involved in the drug trade, if only on the fringes, and the previous year the flat had been raided. There were suggestions both that Colombians and Eastern European criminals may have had something to do with the killing, and also that he was a police informer. The killing had some of the hallmarks of the Colombian scattergun approach to witnesses.

In fact it turned out to be far more prosaic, the official verdict being that it had simply been the work of drug-crazed addicts. Mike Braxhoofden, known as Spike, received 18 years' imprisonment and his accomplice, Ronald van Bommel, was sentenced to 10 years. Braxhoofden's confession was an interesting one: the killings had been done because he feared that the Irishmen were going to kill him.

---

[13] See *The Mirror*, 5 May 2000.

I heard one whisper that we would be fed to the fishes. I felt very frightened and was sure they were plotting to kill us. There were a lot of weapons as well as drugs in the flat.

He continued:

It was excessive use of drugs that made me do it. Otherwise I wouldn't have shot my best friend – he was more than a brother to me – nor would I have killed the other two boys. Now I understand what the parents must be feeling. It is terrible for them and if I had been clean and sober I would never have done such a thing.

Braxhoofden had, he said, been involved in many drug deals with Damien and Vincent. At one time he had supplied 10,000 amphetamine pills and 25,000 Ecstasy tablets to Vincent, but the friendship cooled when Costello refused to pay.

There were also suggestions that Braxhoofden was an armed robber. He had been arrested in connection with the murder of his mother's boyfriend, but had been released. A spokeswoman for the prosecutor's office said the judges believed that 'these young men should be given another chance to show they can do better'.[14]

Then things took another turn for the worse with the death in his flat in the Singerstraat suburb of Amsterdam in early June 2000 of 'The Penguin''s protégé and son-in-law, Derek Dunne. The 27-year-old had left Dublin in 1996 after

[14] See *The Mirror*, 1 November 2000; *Irish Times*, 15 November 2000.

a public quarrel with the nephew of Gerry 'The Monk' Hutch to whom he had given a beating. Now, three men burst into the apartment and opened fire. Dunne died outside the flat and his children fled to a neighbour.

An earlier attempt to kill Dunne had been made after the battering he gave the teenager, and he left for Liverpool with a contract on his head. Then, following an unsuccessful prosecution for heroin dealing, he moved to the Continent. He was thought to have kept most of his fortune out of the clutches of the Criminal Assets Bureau (CAB). As for the contract, in 1998 George Mitchell had arranged a payment of £20,000 on Dunne's behalf for it to be withdrawn.

Once in Amsterdam Dunne had established himself as one of the biggest heroin suppliers to Dublin where there were an estimated 14,000 addicts. It was thought that he supplied 50 kg a week, and a further 1,000 kg of cannabis.

Dunne was selling high-purity heroin in batches of ½ kg upwards to Dublin-based dealers at a cost to them of £30,000, or £50,000 for a whole kilo. When cut on the streets this could fetch between £300,000 and £500,000. The drugs were transported in ½–2 kg consignments, so minimising the loss if a courier – some of whom were making weekly runs – was caught. Not all the batches made it safely to Dublin; one courier was watched and arrested after his fourth run with a kilo. A ½ kg seized at Dublin airport had been intended for a Ballyfermot dealer. The result of this loss was that two couriers, Darren Carey and Patrick Murray, were killed at the end of December 2000 and their bodies dumped in the Grand Canal. Their killer was thought to be a man from the Westies, the West Dublin gang, and the son of a former associate of Martin Cahill. It was also believed that he had killed Gerard Connolly back in 1995. Connolly had been a courier for a Ballyfermot gang and was suspected of passing information to the Gardai which led to a seizure of a quantity of drugs.

Two associates of Dunne were believed to have been at his home when he was shot. One managed his business, testing the purity of the heroin for which Dunne was highly regarded. The other was alleged to be a member of the gang which had shot Veronica Guerin. Neither was immediately visible, but they surfaced within a matter of hours to be treated for their injuries. Once more Dunne had been on the hit-list of a rival gang, and was thought to have paid another ransom of £20,000 shortly before his death to have his name removed. There were suggestions that he had been trading with Yugoslav gangs and the hit squad included one of their members.[15]

Dunne had been a close friend of Tommy 'The Boxer' Mullen who ran a heroin ring from his flat in Dominick Street, Dublin. Named in the Dail as a dealer, he had left to become an off-shore supplier following a march on his home by angry residents carrying a white coffin in December 1996. He was arrested in Manchester the following year and sentenced to 18 years' imprisonment. Another of Dunne's friends, Sean Comerford, had collected 12 years following a raid in November 1988 on his Manchester home where a consignment of heroin was found.

15 *Irish Times; The Mirror,* 5 May 2000.

Gangland Today

Holland also proved to be the nemesis for another major drug dealer in 2000. This time Mancunian Donovan Hardy was arrested after visiting a flat in Rotterdam. After he had left for England the premises were raided and 90 kg of cocaine was found in a false ceiling. Using a mobile telephone shop – Imperial Communications Centre in Cheetham Hill, Manchester – as a front, the 39-year-old Hardy had developed a drug-dealing business that allowed him to run a Porsche and a Honda Fireblade as well as to order a custom-built speedboat. He had paid for the boat in cash instalments, using high-denomination banknotes which were later found to have been contaminated with cocaine.

Taking a leaf out of Curtis Warren's book, he also had cut out the middlemen and dealt directly with the Colombians. Couriers with sports bags containing up to £30,000 in used notes would go to Panama. Cocaine would then come back in cargo ships bound for Holland and Spain. There the drug would be divided in safe houses and brought in through Dover in 5 lb packages. From there it would be distributed throughout the North West.

Hardy's downfall came about through an American Customs agent who had infiltrated the cartel with whom Hardy was dealing. He was asked whether he had a British connection and Hardy's name was mentioned. British Customs were informed, and a second undercover officer introduced as a middleman arranged to meet Hardy and Delroy Bailey, Hardy's first lieutenant, at a London hotel. The pair were then under surveillance as they moved £300,000 in briefcases to South America via Panama and the Cayman Islands. Hardy received 25 years and Bailey 14 at Manchester

Crown Court in March 2001. Two other men who had run the courier network received 20 years each.

Nor was Holland necessarily that much safer for criminals from other countries. By 2001 at least five gangland networks were fighting for a share of the country's illegal trade worth an estimated 6 billion guilders, much of it coming through the sale of firearms rather than the traditional sex and drugs. Now hotels, restaurants, night-clubs and pubs in the red light district in Amsterdam are thought to be owned by 16 specific criminal groups, and the Turkish infrastructure dominates the Spijker district of Arnhem.

Amsterdam has become one of the places to arrange the acquisition of Kalashnikovs and anti-tank guns. In 2000 the gangland murder rate was initially down from the previous year when five had died. In 1998 it had totalled 26 involving Turkish and Yugoslav gangs alone. Nineteen people thought to be helping the police had either been killed (11) or injured. Then on 25 September Jan Femer, head of one of the cartels, was shot dead as he sat in his car, and within weeks Sam Klepper, a leading Hell's Angel and the so-called Godfather of Dutch crime, was shot at 5 p.m. in the middle of a crowded shopping precinct. Shortly after, a Turkish gangster was shot and killed in broad daylight almost opposite a police station. Worse was to come. In November a man wearing a gorilla mask walked into the Kobe restaurant, a Japanese sushi bar near Dam Square, Amsterdam, and shot three customers dead. Two of them were Yugoslavs, one a known criminal.

Organised crime has been mushrooming in the Netherlands since the 1970s. Two early features were the

kidnapping of Caransa[16] and the hold-ups by the Thinkers
from the working-class neighbourhood of Kinkerburt who
were involved in the drug trade, car and lorry theft, robbery
and extortion and illegal gin mills. In the 1980s Group F, a
team of about five men, took part in a number of hold-ups
in the Netherlands and Belgium.

A decade ago the drug trade in Amsterdam was led by
Klass Bruinsma with an inner circle of about 10 men. He
was thought to have killed three rivals and had attempted
to kill three others before he was murdered in 1991 by an
ex-police officer who was associated with a gang from former
Yugoslavia.

Early drug smuggling came from a contact on the coast
of Dubai between Dutch ships on hydraulic engineering projects and Pakistanis wishing to trade in heroin. Several Dutch
Kampers, a small gipsy community some of whose members
carry a tradition of violence, funded large shipments of
hashish and when they had not sufficient funds to pay for
larger imports then a bank took over. Later a driver could
get between 20,000 and 50,000 guilders for a successful
hashish delivery from Morocco, and up to a maximum of
150,000 guilders for a big run. Sentences for drug dealers
have been low in comparison with those imposed in Britain,
but in February 1997 Johan Verhoek, 'The Stutterer', received
6 years after the dismantling of the so-called Octopus Gang
and his conviction for dealing in large amounts of hashish.
The conviction was the first on evidence by others in a criminal syndicate when a Pakistani supplier cut a deal with the

[16] See p. 200 and Mark Bles and Robert Low, *The Kidnap Business*, Chapter 9.

prosecution. The syndicate had been operating since the 1980s. Five ships had sailed between Pakistan, the Netherlands and Canada delivering an estimated 200 tons of cannabis resin to the world market.

The triads have been largely displaced from the top of the tree on which they sat in the great days of the 1960s[17] and now in Holland, for a number of reasons, liquidations are highest in the Turkish heroin trade. The first reason is the political struggles with the Grey Wolves; the second is that the Turkish are arms-bearing, and the third is their tradition of feuds. A dispute between an organised Rotterdam crime family and newcomers cost 11 lives in 1992.

In recent times the Hell's Angels have been on the receiving end of Underworld attacks. On 22 February 2000 four Hell's Angels were found dead in the Sex Club Esther in Haarlem. Fifteen hundred people including 400 bikers attended the funeral of one of the Angels known as Fakko. Another 1,200 were present for a funeral mass for one of the others, a member of the Kamper community. The club, one of three similar sex clubs in the north of Haarlem, had changed hands shortly before the killing and had become an Underworld hangout. A local reporter, Jon Oomkes of *Haarlems Dagblad*, said he believed the killings were part of a power struggle or were drug or prostitution related. The Hell's Angels have controlled a large part of the trade in cocaine, amphetamines and Ecstasy in the Netherlands and have close links with the Kampers, one of whose leaders was connected to the Cali cartel.

[17] See James Morton, *Gangland International*; Maurice Punch, *Conduct Unbecoming*.

With rewards increasing, the present struggle seems set fair to continue and, while substantial criminal assets including a hotel were seized in 1999, the police want more powers to seize the assets of suspected and not merely convicted criminals.

Meanwhile Franz Meijer, the so-called Ronnie Biggs of the Netherlands, was another who came home in 2001. He had been absent from Holland since 1985 when he escaped from custody following arrest for his part in the kidnapping of the Dutch lager king Alfred Heineken. In 1995 he had been traced by Dutch journalist Peter de Vries to Paraguay, where he was the owner of a small restaurant and was now married with three children. The restaurant had been financed, in part at least, by some of the £2.5 million which had never been recovered.

The Heineken kidnap was only the fourth kidnap-for-ransom case in Dutch criminal history. The first, back in 1974, was an amateur affair – the kidnapping and murder of five-year-old Caroline Peters by a factory worker, Eddie van Laar, who demanded a ransom of £17,000 from Caroline's cigar-merchant father. After making the demand he panicked, killed the child and buried her body in a field. He received a 20-year sentence.

The second, three years later, was more of an international affair with the snatching of a millionaire property speculator, Maurits Caransa, from outside his bridge club in Amsterdam. On his release five days later, after the payment of £2.3 million, he said he had been relatively well treated. Although chained to a pipe he had not been physically attacked and had been allowed to sleep on a bed.

The basic arrangements had been undertaken by locals who provided safe houses and cars, the actual snatch being done by foreign criminals. Two Italians were arrested on the Italian–Swiss border and served 4-year sentences in Italy. One unusual feature of the case was that the ransom demand specified that payment should be made in 1,000-guilder notes. An Argentinian was alleged to have changed some of the money in Los Angeles, but the Dutch authorities were never able to extradite him. However $200,000 was confiscated from an account in his name in a Lugano bank.

The third kidnapping, in 1982, was also one of international co-operation. Antonia van der Valk – who, with her husband, had a chain of restaurants in Holland and Belgium – was kidnapped from her own home on 27 November 1982. The ransom money was paid in Swiss francs, marks and guilders in Benelux countries and Germany. Twenty days after her capture she was released. In total 11 people were arrested including four women. £1 million was recovered from a bank in Zurich. The police had been monitoring the situation but, to protect Mrs van der Valk, did not move before her release.

Heineken's kidnap took place on 9 November 1983 when three armed men held the magnate, a man with immense social and political connections, and his chauffeur at gunpoint. The kidnapping caused an immediate uproar. The ransom note left at the scene demanded that £8 million be paid in guilders, marks, French francs and American dollars. With the kidnappers simply playing tapes of Heineken repeating their demands, there was considerable concern as to whether the hostages were still alive. Photographs of the men holding daily newspapers were eventually provided, and a series of messages was placed in *De Telegraaf* by both sides. Only one police officer was allowed to take the money on the drop and was finally instructed to stop the car on a bridge where an eight-lane motorway crossed a minor road. A hole had been cut in the metal grating and the officer dropped the five sacks containing £8 million straight on to the back of a waiting pick-up truck. There was no chance of following the truck because there was not another turn-off on the motorway for 20 kilometres.

The police had, in fact, been partially successful in identifying some of the kidnappers. After a member of the public had given details of five men he thought were behaving suspiciously, they were followed and one was seen to obtain a Chinese takeaway meal for two. A raid on buildings in a woodyard seemed to show no trace of the hostages; but a second showed a crack in the wall of one of them, behind which were two cells. Both Heineken and his chauffeur were found unharmed.

Thirty-three people were arrested, two of whom each had about £700,000 on them. Jan Boellard, the owner of the woodyard, received 12 years and the man who was seen fetching the Chinese meals, Martin Erkamps, 10 years. For the moment the leader of the team, Frans Meijer, escaped arrest and for the next few weeks he wrote a series of letters to the newspaper *Het Parool* saying how he regretted his actions and how he wished to commit suicide on Christmas Day. At the end of December he surrendered and, pleading insanity, was sent for examination to a psychiatric clinic from which he escaped.

Following his identification in Paraguay, Meijer fought a

long and debilitating battle against his extradition. He was released in 1995 after a judge ruled that the correct arrest procedure had not been followed. He was not then arrested again until January 1998, and in May 2001 an appeal court finally upheld the Dutch government's application for extradition.

The end came for one of the other kidnappers, Cor van Hout, in January 2003 when he was shot dead. He had a traditional funeral with his coffin drawn through Amsterdam by eight Friesian horses.

As for Heineken, since his ordeal he has been protected by two bodyguards. Apparently, this has not stopped one of the other gang members periodically seeking him out and abusing him in the street.

Germany

Germany has always had some difficulty in accepting that there is organised crime in the country.[18] Two large-scale investigations, the first in 1985 and the second five years later, concluded that there were no wide-ranging structures in place. However, things speeded up with the fall of the Berlin Wall and by the early 1990s there were Polish gangs dealing in stolen cars. Showrooms were ram-raided and entire fleets of vehicles removed. In 1993, 27,000 cars stolen in Saxony went to Kiev and Moscow. In May 1994 the Mercedes belonging to Berlin Police Chief Hagen Saberschinsky was stolen while his driver had gone into a department store,

[18] For a view see Wilfried Kuper and Jurgen Welp, *Beitrage zur Rechtswissenschaft.*

apparently to use the lavatory. The car was found in Podolsk, south of Moscow, stripped of two-way radio, cellular telephone and radio but otherwise in good order. The minimal extra mileage on the odometer indicated that it had been flown to Russia, probably aboard an aircraft formerly used for Soviet military equipment when the Red Army left East Germany.

Yugoslavian gangs were running prostitution and illegal gambling and there was a healthy market in icons stolen in Russia. There was also a thriving banking system organising money laundering. In 1991 a Munich-based Yugoslavian explained at his trial how he had laundered £175.4 million drug money in Germany in the previous five years through a string of fake businesses. Frankfurt has long been regarded as a capital of crime, and even in the early 1990s there were gun battles near the railway station between Albanian, Yugoslav and Polish criminals battling for territory.

Now, in the last 10 years, again things have changed enormously and it is increasingly the case that indigenous German criminals are linking with or fighting off a variety of organised crime gangs including the Hell's Angels, Italians, Russians, Albanians, Turks and Vietnamese. The Russians and Italians alone are said to account for an annual revenue of DM 35 million.

The Italian Mafia – notably the Camorra, the *Cosa Nostra* and the *Sacra Corona Unita* – are all present. The Camorra is particularly strong in Munich and has been extending its interests into Leipzig, Dresden and Erfurt. One Italian who worked in Saarland managed to obtain work as a translator for the police. Much revenue comes through the use of

Schwartzarbeiter, workers in the black economy, on building sites in Berlin from which money is laundered. Munich has also been targeted by small groups of Polish housebreakers who have crossed the border and then returned home. In turn, they have been the victims of the Polish mafia acting as thieves' ponces.

As with England, there is a belief that the Russian *mafiya* has not as yet made the inroads that might have been expected, but it is actively recruiting young German criminals. In recent years about a million Germans have returned from Russia and Eastern Europe. Parents will speak German, but the children do not. Over the years they have been truly displaced. In Russia they will have been regarded as German and in Germany they are now regarded as Russian. Many do extremely poorly in the education system and, once they are in a cycle of petty crime and are in youth prisons, they are drawn into the gangs. Prominent recruiters are the very dangerous Solentsevskaya group, thought to have well over 5,000 members.

At present the centres for Russian criminal activity are Berlin, Dusseldorf and Frankfurt and the principal interests are in money laundering, extortion and prostitution. Girls are brought from Moscow and Kiev, the plumper ones being shipped off to the East and the prettier, thinner ones sent to the West. It is not a life which a great many manage to leave. They are taken to blocks of flats and their passports are confiscated. At the start of their careers the prettiest can earn several hundred dollars an hour for their employers, but as they get older and more worn they are traded down-market or sent to Asia. If they try to escape, often they are killed.

One was tied to a car bumper and dragged at high speed; she did not survive. Russian criminals in Germany favour not the single bullet in the back of the head but what is known as total killing. As an example, when in 1993 the bodies of two racketeers – Jurij Bulgakow, known as 'The Fat One', and Russlan Beretschetov – were found in a Berlin suburb, their throats had been slit, their lungs crushed and their skulls shattered. Some gangs, however, have been positively soft-hearted, with the Ukranian group, Jibu, really only specialising in muggings.

Until recently the Vietnamese have controlled the illegal cigarette trade in a bloody internecine war in which, by the middle 1990s, 32 had been killed with the Quang Binh Gang from central Vietnam finally getting the upper hand.[19] Now there are signs that other Eastern crime groups, particularly the Chechen group, the Obshina, have moved in on their former monopoly.

With its Reeperbahn, Hamburg has always been regarded as the German capital of prostitution and new laws now allow the women to claim for social benefits and sue in the courts if a client refuses to pay. Nevertheless, of the estimated 3,700 prostitutes in Hamburg the majority are believed to be 'illegals' controlled by the gangs, principally Albanian, which have brought them to the country. In the city, members of the Trinitas group have recently been prosecuted for organising prostitution. It is thought they had in excess of 200

---

[19] In May 1996 7 bodies were found in a flat in Berlin's Marzahn district. All had been shot in the head and their hands and feet were tied. This was regarded as a typical Quang Binh execution.

girls working for them. The Hell's Angels are also involved in a very heavy drug trial which began at the end of 2001.

By the beginning of the new millennium, Hamburg had taken over from Zurich as Europe's open market drug city. Asylum seekers on moored ships in the harbour, many from Ghana and Burkina Faso, some of whom have thrown away their passports to avoid deportation and 'claiming to be younger than they are', says an observer, sell crack. When approached the young men swallow the drugs. The authorities, once thwarted by waiting for the drugs to travel through the system, now use emetics to obtain a speedier result.

Scandinavia

Just as the Montreal war between the Hell's Angels and the Bandidos was punctuated by truces in an effort to stave off legislation and pacify an increasingly hostile press, so their Scandinavian counterparts did the same. The wars began in 1994 and reached their peak with the grenade attack on a Hell's Angels' compound in 1996 which killed two and wounded 19. A truce was declared in 1997 and the next year a Bandido was sentenced to life imprisonment.

Other biker gangs have feuded with both the Bandidos and the Angels. One of them, the Brotherhood (Brodraskapet) also known as the Wolfpack, was led by Danny Fitzpatrick, 'Danny the Hood', a Briton born in Kenya. Over the years he had served 8 years for armed robbery and was also suspected of being involved in more robberies, extortion and drug smuggling. On his release from prison in 1995 he founded the Brotherhood and began a string of battles with both the numerically superior and more powerful gangs. In June 1998 he ended his career at a roundabout in the centre of Stockholm when he was gunned down. One of the other founding members of the gang was allowed out of prison for the funeral. The police thought, and no doubt hoped, that the Brotherhood would die with him.

Sporadic killings occurred, each bringing the possibility of a war. One of the most curious, in its execution, was the death of Claud Bork Hansen, one-time leader of the Bandidos in Denmark, in the spring of 2001. Hansen was shot 19 times by a single pistol on the pavement outside his home. What made the killing so curious was that the forensic investigation showed that he was being shot at by at least another four gunmen at the same time. Seven other bullets hit him. A social worker initially charged with supplying the weapons was released, and a man with links to organised crime was later charged with the murder.

So far as the Angels were concerned, things had quietened down in England over the years. As with their American counterparts, there had been efforts to change their perceived image of bearded and tattooed monsters forcing old-age pensioners to have oral sex on the backs of their machines in supermarket car parks. Nevertheless there have been outbreaks of violence, one of which involved Ronald Wait – known, on account of his size, as Gut – the vice-president of the Angels' Essex chapter, in turn known as the Hatchet Crew.

A hatchet, said the prosecution at Wait's trial at the Old Bailey, was exactly what he had been wielding in January 1998 at a Rockers Reunion concert at the Battersea Arts

Centre when Malcolm St Clair and David Armstrong died. The attack on the Outcasts, said the prosecution, was part of a campaign to become the leading bikers' group in Britain. Wait and two others were acquitted of murder, the jury having disagreed after a four-day retirement in a case in which a number of witnesses had refused to make statements. However, Wait was jailed for 15 years for conspiracy to cause grievous bodily harm.

11

France

Three-twenty in the afternoon of 27 September 2000 saw the end of one of the dominant figures of the *milieu* when, in the basement of l'Artois Club, in the street of the same name just off the Champs Elysées, in front of the television screen showing the afternoon's racing from Saint-Cloud, Francis Vanverberghe, 'François le Belge', said to have been the mastermind of the French Connection, was shot nine times – seven bullets in the body followed by two in the head. He had on him at the time approximately £20,000 in francs. Another person in the club was also wounded. He was probably following one of the traditional ways of laundering money made, in his case, from slot machines, prostitution and drugs. He would buy a winning PMU ticket from a gambler and, being able to show he had been paid out, so clean the money. The 54-year-old Vanverberghe, half Belgian and half Spanish, born on 3 March 1946 in the Belle-de-Mai quarter of Marseilles, had been a top and ruthless player on the Côte d'Azur and in Paris for nearly a quarter of a century.

He began his documented criminal career at the age of 16 with an arrest for the theft of a caravan and then, three years later, he was into prostitution. At the age of 22 it was into the big time. This was the age of Gaetan 'Tony' Zampa and Jacky 'Le Mat' Imbert[1] warring from their Pigalle hangout, the Equipe des Trois Canards, with the then all-powerful brothers Guerini. Vanverberghe joined in enthusiastically.

Zampa took out six Belle-de-Mai men in a six-month period and on 31 March 1973 reprisals came at the Tanagra, a bar in the old port, when four of his men were shot at cocktail time. Zampa escaped, but the next month Vanverberghe was caught by the police in bed with a starlet in Paris. Brought before a judge and questioned about the social qualities of her lover, she commented, 'When I have a fine boy like the Belgian in my bed I don't ask for his police file.'

But in Vanverberghe's hideaway, the flat of his official girl-friend and one of the women he had on the street, the police found false papers and three guns hidden behind the bath. He received 30 months, during which time Zampa reinforced his position in Marseilles. Vanverberghe had been out for only a few days in 1975 before he was back to prison. This time he was betrayed by an American over his part in the French Connection drug-smuggling ring. Fourteen years. Now Vanverberghe blamed his former ally Zampa for his misfortunes and sided with Imbert.

[1] 'The Fool'.

On 1 February 1977 Imbert was ambushed as he drove his Alfa Romeo to his home at Cassis. Years later a Parisian gunman who had been present told the newspaper *Libération*:

> The Chief gave an order to the men. 'Don't finish him off. Leave him whimpering like a dog.' He then lifted his hood and said to The Fool, 'Cunt, look at who has killed you.' It was Gaetan Zampa. Only The Fool survived.[2]

He did survive, but with eight bullets in his body and a paralysed right arm. From then on, along with Vanverberghe and the Lebanese Hoareau brothers, he waged an all-out war against Zampa in which an estimated 28 men were killed.

In 1984 Vanverberghe was again betrayed, this time by François Scapula, another informer from the days of the French Connection who at the time was serving a 20-year sentence over the exportation of some 20 kg of heroin from Asia to the United States. That year he and Zampa were in the same prison after his arch rival and his wife had been arrested on tax-evasion charges. Zampa took the responsibility and he and Vanverberghe found themselves in Les Baumettes prison. Both were clients of the same lawyer, Jean-Louis Pelletier, who maintained the splendid balancing act of visiting each of them every Saturday. A month after Vanverberghe's release Zampa hanged himself in his cell, and the war between the remainder of his men and the Hoareaus intensified.

---

[2] Patricia Tourancheau, 'Neuf Balles au bout de la route du Belge' in *Libération*, 30 September/1 October 2000. See also Patricia Tourancheau, 'François le Belge, un mort bien nettoyé' in *Libération*, 14/15 October 2000.

Vanverberghe served four years before his conviction was quashed. Later he was awarded £11,000 for wrongful imprisonment. He promptly announced that he was donating all the winnings to the 81-year-old Abbé Pierre's Emmaus movement of self-supporting communities for outcasts and dropouts; but, despite the Abbé saying that the gangster had a good heart, he rejected this kindly act. Nevertheless, by this gesture Vanverberghe took another step up the ladder towards folk hero.

Vanverberghe's death followed the increasingly popular pattern first used by the Colombian drug gangs with two helmeted men on a motorcycle. One kept the engine revving and the other pulled the trigger. There were thoughts that Vanverberghe had been slipping. Arrested for running prostitutes from a bar in the rue François 1er in March 2000, he had been sentenced to two months' imprisonment. This was regarded as a downward step in his career.

Worse, perhaps, the killing of his godson François Boglietto in Aix-en-Provence on 28 February the previous year had passed without reaction. When Vanverberghe's brother, José, had been shot 10 years earlier his killers had not lasted four days. Although he had consistently said that after his brother's death he expected to be killed, over the years Vanverberghe took no great precautions. He generally went without bodyguards and for that reason no one was particularly keen to sit next to him in public.

Why was he shot? The reason lay almost certainly in the continuing war over the highly lucrative gaming machines. He was thought to have owned about 150 of these *machines à sous* which provided him with an income of some 3 to 4.5

million francs a month.[3] Additionally he had interests in girly bars and night-clubs. He declared an income of around £500,000, claiming it was due to his success at gambling on horse-racing. If he was killed over slot machines, then he would not have been the first to go down in recent times. On 9 January 2000 Roger Spanu, once a lieutenant to Imbert, and known as 'Roger Specs' or 'Petit Roger', was shot in the neck after leaving pizzeria in Marseilles. Marc Monge, the so-called Godfather of the Vaucluse, and another man with known interests in machines had strayed into the Paris *banlieu* and were killed in the 8th *arrondissement*, near the Champs Elysées, on 8 January.[4]

In 1999, although said to be in semi-retirement, Vanverberghe – along with his two heavies, Joel the Turk and Philippe the SS – had attended a meeting with the three powerful Hornec brothers – described as sedentary gipsies, who run Champs Elysées night bars and who are said to have been involved in bank robberies, smuggling and drug dealing – and their associates, Ihmed Mohieddine, known as 'La Gelée' because of the supposed state of his brains, and

[3] *Le Figaro*, 26 July 2001.
[4] Monge, who had a long criminal career, was also politically connected. In May 1983 he was arrested and released after Daniel Scotti and Jean Chicin were killed in a car bombing the previous March near the main synagogue in Marseilles. In fact the bombing seems to have had no anti-Semitic connections; the inept pair were intending to blow up a bar on the rue du Dragon. Monge's criminal career nearly came to an end when he fell through a window and was partially paralysed during a 1986 robbery. He made his way to Belgium where in September 1989 he was shot while working with Frédéric Godfroid, an ex-policeman, in a series of hold-ups. After his release it was back to drugs in Marseilles and hashish in Spain where he was imprisoned in 1993. He was shot again in the summer of 1997. One of the men questioned and released, Paul Faruggia ('Petit Paul'), was himself killed in an 'account settling' on 1 October 1999.

Nordine Mansouri. Other friends include the gipsies Michel and Serge Lepage, a father and son who are alleged to run the south *banlieu*.

One report suggested that the meeting had been called to arrange for the division of spoils between former rivals and that an agreement had been reached. Another scenario is that the brothers reneged on the agreement and sent youths from the *banlieu* to kill Vanverberghe.

Reprisals were relatively swift and one of the suspected killers, Boualem Talata, an associate of another of Vanverberghe's rivals, Dijali Zitouni, was shot dead in Paris within the month. Talata, originally from Dreux, had been steadily climbing the ladder.

Zitouni, himself a known police informer, lasted less than a year. On 22 July 2001 he was shot in the head, neck and shoulders when his Mercedes was ambushed near his home in Gennevilliers, Hauts-de-Seine. Cartridges from a .9 and a 7-65 littered the pavement. He died two hours later. He had been playing cards. Like so many others, Zitouni had owned a share in a night-club on the Champs Elysées.

Another who died shortly after François le Belge was the Portuguese Antonio Lages, from Montreuil, killed as he drove his Mercedes (loaned him by a garage, suggested his lawyer Karim Achoui) to a car park off the Champs Elysées. Lages had been something of a petty criminal in French terms, although on one occasion he and another man had been found hooded and gloved with a sawn-off shotgun. He was, however, a known associate of 'La Gelée'. Lages, who had been out of prison only a few weeks, had spent the day with his father who had cancer and then gone to a meeting near

L' Etoile. As he was parking his car a hooded man opened the passenger door and shot him twice in the head. Lages' passenger was hit in the hand. The bullets fired were of a type normally used to kill wild boar. It was never quite clear whether this was a revenge killing for Le Belge or the settling of a different account.

Yet another who died was Farid Sanaa, shot at the place des Tenes on 19 October 1999. Sanaa had tried to muscle in on the protection afforded to the Japan Bar near the Champs Elysées and was known to have quarrelled with friends of Mohieddine, but it certainly could have had nothing to do with 'La Gelée' because he was in Oran looking after his export business at the time.

The Frères Hornec – of whom the youngest, Marc, was said to be the most formidable – had come to power with their elimination of the Clan Genova in a brief but bloody war in 1994. Claude Genova, 'Le Gros', from Villemobile, and his friends had taken over from the retired or dead Zemour brothers and for a time had a stranglehold on the *milieu*.[5] But then they faced a challenge from the gipsies. Genova was noted for the tattoo of a butterfly on what the papers described as a 'sensitive part of his anatomy'. Apparently at moments of passion it flapped its wings.

The serious trouble started when Eric Pasquet, Genova's right-hand man, foolishly kidnapped 'La Gelée' and tortured him to reveal the whereabouts of his savings. The Clan Genova paid heavily. Petit Riquet and Christophe Tizzo were

---

[5] For the rise and fall of the Zemours who ran the *milieu* in the 1980s, see James Morton, *Gangland International*.

trapped when Riquet left his revolver in the boot of his car
and were killed in the rue de Charonne. After this bodies
fell on both sides until the war ended when Genova, on a
temporary release from prison, was shot on 22 August 1994
as he left a bar at the Concorde-Lafayette near Porte Maillot.[6]

The last few years had not been entirely happy for
members of the Marseilles *milieu*. Jean Toci, one of the last
of the Marseilles Godfathers with a link to the French
Connection, was shot and killed in a supermarket car park
on 7 May 1997.[7] There were also signs that Russian organised-
crime groups had established a base and the *milieu* might be
under threat. In Grasse that year six members of a Georgian
clan were sent for trial on charges of kidnapping, fraud and
money laundering. In Italy there were thought to be around
fifty Russian gangs. One Georgian group, headed by a man
who lived in Cannes, was thought to be planning to make
a move on the Brooklyn empire of Vyacheslav Ivankov after
his arrest.

Then following an attack on a Brinks armoured car on 18
July 1998 at Codoux, Aix-en-Provence, the members of the
team of robbers had fallen out in true *film noir* fashion. The
first to go was probably Jean-Claude Zamudio who had been
employed at the Le Mas disco near Aix-en-Provence on the
night of 12 November. His death may not have been as a

[6] Some of Genova's men continued operations in one way or another. Two, the
son and ex-chauffeur of one of the fallen clan, were found dead in December
2000. They had been masterminding 12 prostitutes in the forest of Armainvilliers
who had been serving lorry drivers. The scheme had been run with some give
and take; in return for their earnings the girls were provided with social security when ill and a five-week annual holiday.
[7] Toci was a half-brother to Zampa. It was estimated that there had been probably 40 killings over the slot-machine war. *Le Figaro*, 15 September 2000.

result of the robbery but because of his connections to 'François le Belge'. He was followed by Raphael Liminana, in the car park of a hotel in Viltrolles on 21 November, along with his alleged lieutenant, Abdel Djendoubi. Both were shot and their cars burned with Molotov cocktails.

Next was Henri Tournel, who had a 1997 conviction for drug trafficking and who was killed in the same way at the beginning of December, but this time in Puy-Sainte-Reparade (Bouches-du-Rhône). The next down was a man whose identity was never discovered; his body had been completely burned along with a stolen car at Saint-Cannat (Aix-en-Provence) on 13 December. Then Michel Datena, who had been an agent for slot machines, was shot at Septèmes-les-Vallons (Bouches-du-Rhône) on 6 March.

In early June 2001 eight men were arrested and questioned, held for three weeks and released. They were all members of the team once headed by the late and lamented Marc Monge. On 19 June Lamaine Adrar, one of Tournel's supposed killers, was committed by an examining magistrate. If the police thought that was an end to matters they were wrong. On 30 June two men were found dead in a burned-out car. One, who had a conviction for pimping, had been involved in a pinball machine company at Port de Bouc, near Marseilles, which had been in compulsory liquidation for some two years. The other was not known to have a criminal record and may just have been in the wrong car at the wrong time.[8]

---

[8] See 'Guerre des Gangs dans le grand sud: déjà huit cadavres' in *Midi Libre*, 8 July 2001.

Back in parts of the *banlieu*, such as the depressed
Aubervilliers, a weapon of choice would now seem to be a
monkey which has replaced the pit-bull. The monkeys are
the powerful Barbary apes and are imported illegally from
Gibraltar, Morocco and Algeria through Spain. They can be
bought in North Africa at around £30 each and retail for
£300 in Paris. Good biters with powerful limbs, strong teeth
and short tempers, their favourite method of attack is to hurl
themselves at their target's head. An increasing illegal sport
is that of monkey fighting.[9]

Rather more serious was the use by Saphir Bghouia – a
petty drug dealer shot dead by the police in Béziers on 2
September 2001 – of a rocket launcher with which he
managed to hit two police cars. Having killed Jean Farret,
an aide to the town's mayor, the previous evening, he had
then challenged the police to a face-to-face duel. The
confrontation had developed from a fight on an estate
between North African immigrants and Romanies. Now it
was feared that, monkeys apart, arsenals of assault rifles,
grenades and anti-tank rockets were available to the estate
ghettos. Kalashnikov rifles were selling at the equivalent of
£200 compared with ten times the price in 1999. Rocket
launchers were available for a few hundred pounds more.

On 17 September 2001, in a routine search of what turned
out to be a stolen Citröen Xantia in the 19th *arrondissement*,
the police found two RPG 64 rocket-launchers in the boot.
The arrested man David S., a 20-year-old of Jewish–Tunisian
origin from the Côte d'Ivoire, said he had been given 5,000

[9] *Guardian*, 27 September 2000.

francs (£500) to drive the car between the Porte de Montreuil and la place de Fêtes.[10]

A search of his home produced 100,000 francs, 400 grams of hashish and a .22 long rifle. In a second home the police found *un jeu de plaques minéralogiques allemandes*. In the Underworld the rockets, which were of Russian design and made under licence in Serbia, would fetch 25,000 francs each.

However, this was nothing to do with terrorism but rather with straightforward armed robbery, and it was by no means the first such seizure. In May 2000, in a warehouse in rue de La Croix-Miret in the 15th, eleven such launchers had been found wrapped in linen. And the next month four more turned up in an hotel at Vajours; these had come from Yugoslavia.

'At a time when it is learned that a series of lightly armoured security wagons is transporting astronomic quantities of Euros in Paris and the suburbs, the increasing number of these heavy arms in the possession of the *milieu*'s gangs hardly reassures us,' said the newspapers.

On 29 December 2000, the day after a spectacular attack on two armoured cars at Gentilly, six men were found in their hideout at Paray-Vielle-Poste (Essonne) with over 34 thousand millions of stolen francs along with 15 machine guns and grenades. Said a spokesman:

The difference with drug trafficking is that there one doesn't need a stock of arms. However the increasing

[10] 'Prolifération de lance-roquettes avant l'Euro' in *Le Figaro*, 20 September 2001.

number of incidents offers us the chance to make some
interesting recoveries.

The launchers were being stored for possible attacks on security vans delivering the new Euros. In turn Germany had its first Euro robbery when an armoured car was attacked in early September 2001. In fact, attacks on security vehicles were becoming the crime of choice. During the night of 22 September thieves broke into the postal depository in Bari on Italy's south-eastern coast. In addition to carrying Kalashnikovs, pump-action shotguns and pistols and wearing body armour, the gang of ten had a wrecking ball and a chain of tyre-piercing spikes. They were largely thwarted in their efforts, managing to steal only 5,000 Euros, which were awaiting distribution throughout the Puglia region, because they had failed to deal with an alarm. They fled when guards surprised them. It was thought that the work was that of the *Sacra Corona Unita*.

In the middle of September gold was stolen from a security van in Zurich. On 27 September five men were arrested after a caravan containing bullion, guns and £25,000 cash was stopped at 3 a.m. at Dover docks for a routine search. An infra-red detonator was also discovered, sparking a five-hour bomb search. The men, who had South African passports, were thought – rather like a number of the alleged 11 September terrorists – to have stayed in England before going to the Continent for the raid.

Raids on armoured cars have long been the stock-in-trade of serious French gangsters. Teams with names such as SS and the China Tea were eclipsed by the so-called Dream

Team which was put together in the south by the grandly named Michel 'Mad Dog' Crutel in 1995. The former para-trooper, described as possessing the dress sense of a Marseilles pimp, brought together a number of serious players including Jean-Jacques Naudo (known as 'Mimi') and Karim Maloum, 'Le Grand Karim', both of whom had played for the Perpignan rugby club in their younger days. A year later Crutel recruited the brains of the outfit, Daniel 'Pretty Boy' Bellanger, who a decade earlier had been linked to the hold-up of the Saint Nazaire branch of the Banque de France which had liberated some £10 million. He also had thwarted aspirations for the stage. Under Bellanger's guidance the Dream Team became real professionals. No job under £750,000 would be considered, and there was a minimum annual target.

In 1996 the Team stormed an Air Inter jet at Perpignan, netting over £1 million when the gang dressed as ground crew and holding Kalashnikovs also held up a banner telling the pilot to stop his engines. From then on they produced a series of stunning raids which drew grudging admiration from Commissaire Yves Castano, the head of the French equivalent of the Flying Squad:

> You can spend a whole career as a police officer and maybe see one truly brilliant criminal operation. These people did it time and time again. They had it all: the discipline, the imagination, the equipment. I think they are the best there has ever been.[11]

---

[11] William Langley, 'The Parisian Job' in the *Sunday Telegraph*, 10 June 2001.

It was thought that their raids on security vans and deposit vaults cleared something in the region of £20 million between 1996 and the end of 2000. In fact 1998 was not a wholly successful year. A January attack at Orly airport failed when the expected delivery was rescheduled and, in the May, Daniel Merlini and Maloum were arrested over an attempted security van raid at the Gare du Nord. They were, however, released in July. On the plus side were successful raids in Luxembourg and Brussels.

Crutel was killed in Algeciras in May 1999 on something of an indiscreet expedition; Bellanger had arranged the relief of 700 lb of hashish from a Spanish team. Crutel's head was shot off and his body left in the back of a van. Now, although Bellanger took full charge of further operations, he was by no means the flavour of the month. It was thought that attacks on rival gangs merely led to unnecessary trouble. Things were better by the August when a raid on a Malaga warehouse collected nearly £3 million in jewels and cash.

The final appearance of the Dream Team was made on Boxing Day 2000 when an attempt to rob two Brinks-Mat security vans on the roundabout at the Porte de Gentilly went seriously wrong. Initially things were in place. The vans were blocked in by a Cherokee Jeep, a breakdown truck, a Renault Espace and a Volkswagen Golf; also present was an Audi estate with a police light and siren which would be used to escort the fleeing robbers. The usual method of the Dream Team was to put wheel clamps on the vehicles they were attacking but, on this occasion, the first Brinks-Mat van made a break for it, smashing into the Cherokee.

Under a burst of machine-gun fire it reached the round-about and set off in the direction of the A3 to Lille. It was unfortunate for the Team that a police car with four officers who had been on traffic patrol also turned up. The robbers were told to lay down their arms and responded with a burst of automatic fire. The police car overturned, the robbers blew a hole in the side of the second Brinks van and, with the raid over in 90 seconds, were on their way with £3.4 million.

Unfortunately, as they went through Rungis, the Espace cut up a man in a Renault and the passenger gave him the traditional French one-fingered gesture of contempt. The man set off after the Espace, following it to Paray-Vieille-Poste with a view to explaining the finer points of road courtesy to the driver. When he saw three men get out in avenue Alsace-Lorraine he decided that discretion was the better part of valour and drove off. That evening he watched an amateur video of the raid on television and went to the police.

The house in avenue Alsace-Lorraine was surrounded and Merlini, Maloum, Naudo and two other men were found asleep in a garden shed. Another man was arrested in a nearby flat. Bellanger was arrested at his home in Sitges. On this occasion there was no honour amongst thieves and Merlini and the others explained to the police the role of Bellanger since the death of Crutel. Bellanger may have had more brains than the paratrooper, but he did not command that man's respect and loyalty.

Meanwhile back in Marseilles, with the death of Vanverberghe the old order had been changing and now one of the more senior *caïds* was Raymond Mihière, described in the French press as a putative Godfather and known, because of his looks, as 'The Chinaman'. He had been involved in the 1980s war for control of the night-clubs in both Marseilles and Aix-en-Provence, and also involved in gambling machines again in Marseilles and Barcelona. He was thought to have interests in hotels, casinos and brothels in North Africa when he fell from grace in January 2001 and, more importantly, again in May of the same year.

Before that his career had been studded with acquittals dating from 1986, including one for fraud. In 1996 he had also been investigated over the death of a bar owner on the Costa Brava the previous year. However, in September 1999 he appeared in Avignon charged with associating with criminals, and on 19 January 2001 he was sentenced to 6 years' imprisonment. Matters did not end there, however. He was bailed pending an appeal and on Friday 24 April he was arrested in a villa at Bouc-Bel-Air in a raid in which the police retrieved some £66,000, a machine pistol and 50 kg of hashish thought to have been brought into France through Spain from Morocco.

The *Affaire Yann Piat* had been concluded rather unsatis-factorily with the convictions of low-level players, but thoughts that those who had contracted the shooting had gone undisturbed. The MP and estranged god-daughter of the right-wing leader Jean-Marie Le Pen had been shot in her chauffeur-driven car by a motorbike hit-squad on a lonely road near her home at Mont-les-Oiseux on the outskirts of Hyères in February 1994. Before her death she had written that if she were to die mysteriously certain people should be questioned.[12]

The official version of the death of Piat was that the 44-year-old mother of two was gunned down because she had threatened to smash the local banditry if she was elected mayor of Hyères. However, in 1993 the Toulon Underworld leader Jean-Louis Fargette, nicknamed 'Bar of Soap' because of his ability to slip through the fingers of the police, had been assassinated. Many politicians turned out at his funeral at which the priest in his homily said, 'He forgot certain moral values but I know he would never touch drugs or prostitution out of respect for his mother.' A counter-suggestion was that the killing of Yann Piat might have been tied to his death.

Initially two local gangsters were arrested and charged with her killing. They were released early in the investigation and confessions were then obtained from other small-time crooks. One retracted, claiming police intimidation, but a name put about as the organiser of the contract was that of the owner of the Macama (a local restaurant), Gerard Finale, who was arrested, charged and has continued to protest his innocence from prison. Even he was not thought to be anything more than the middleman and the word in the summer of 1995 was that the orders for her murder came from Paris.

---

[12] The Var province is notorious for the high casualty rate amongst government officials. In a 10-year period, 12 were either shot or had their cars blown up. The speciality is the motorcycle assassination. Professional killers often hired from Italy use a stolen motorcycle and a .38 revolver; one bullet for the victim's stomach, the second for the face.

The trial of seven men accused of various degrees of complicity in her killing began near Nice on 4 May 1998. One, Marco di Caro, admitted he was the rider of the motorcycle from which the shots had been fired, and he received 20 years. Finale, accused of masterminding the assassination, still denied his involvement. It did him little good for on 16 June he was found guilty and received a life sentence – as did Lucien Ferri, who was found to have fired the shots. During the trial Ferri refused to say who had ordered the killing, maintaining that his family would be in danger if he did so.

That still left such well-known faces as André Cermolacce (known as 'Gros Dédé') from Marseilles, who had interests in slot machines, night-clubs and prostitution. In November 2000 he had been sentenced to a term of imprisonment for trying to buy a local policeman through the good offices of a journalist, Christian Rodat – once with the *Provençal* newspaper and Europe 1 radio station – but had been released on bail. Cermolacce along with Richard Laaban had, said the prosecution, tried to bribe Axel Grot, a newly arrived member of the Brigade de Répression du Banditism, a rough equivalent to the National Crime Squad. The officer had been given a bundle of 500-franc notes, but had passed them to his superiors and been told to play along with the trio. Rodat, who had been made redundant, had gambled away his £70,000 cheque in casinos at Cassis and Bandol. When he was arrested the police found a dossier of the Mafia clans of the coast. Rodat had managed to deposit some £75,000 in his account which the prosecution alleged came from dealings with 'Gros Dédé'. He claimed that the money represented expenses in connection with his journalism. At his trial he admitted he had given the money to Grot, but claimed that it was only money given to a friend with financial troubles.

Then there was Roland Cassone, the one-time bodyguard of Jacky Imbert, and Souhal Hanna Elias, nicknamed 'Joel le Libanais', also involved in the *machines à sous*. The Perlettos, Pascal and Frank, both well connected and who had been enemies of Fargette, were arrested in May 1998 in *Operation Topaze*, an investigation into the importation of cocaine and Moroccan cannabis. Others scooped up included Antoine Cossu, 'Tony the Eel', who had been Vanverberghe's right-hand man and was now alleged to be the king of the south-east of the French *milieu*.

Another 'Chinaman', this time Jean-Claude Bonnal, moved into the limelight towards the end of 2001 – not that he had really been out of it. Born in Vietnam to a Breton father and Vietnamese mother, Bonnal, 'Le Chinois', started his career back in 1973 when he murdered an elderly woman. He then took up bank robbery and from 1979 he collected nearly 30 years in sentences though serving, with remission, only 18 years. In November 1998 he was part of a team involved in a hold-up at a Paris *bureau de change* which left 10 people injured. Arrested, he was in custody until December 2000 when an appeal court overturned the decision of a magistrate that he should remain in prison. The thinking was based on a series of measures by the Justice Minister, Elisabeth Guigou, which were designed to speed up the judicial process from arrest to trial.

On 6 October 2001 a gang raided Le Fontenoy, a bar-tabac in the suburb of Athis-Mons. Only £1,000 was stolen but the owner, his wife, a waitress and a cleaner were each shot in the head with a single bullet. On 16 October a gang broke into the house of a hospital consultant in the Plessis-Trevise and took the family hostage. A niece taking a shower telephoned the police, and when they arrived two officers were shot dead. One of the gang was injured but the remainder escaped. Bonnal, who was said to have been identified by DNA as a member of the tabac killing, was arrested three days later.

At least one hostage-taker was sent down that month: Omar Zemmiri, one of a team of bank and supermarket robbers in Belgium and Northern France. In March 1996 a car bomb was discovered outside police headquarters in Roubaix. Four of the team were killed but Zemmiri and Christopher Caze, probably the leader of the gang, fled across the Belgian border where Caze was shot dead by frontier guards. Zemmiri was wounded in the shooting but broke into a house in Kortrijk where he held two women hostage for seven hours before surrendering. On 30 January 1997 he was sentenced to the maximum term of 13 years. Subsequently extradited he ran the defence that his robberies had been politically and religiously motivated, but it was not a story which appealed to the prosecution: 'L' Islam n'a été qu'un alibi culturel.' Nor did it appeal to the judges. Zemmiri, who 'remained blank faced', this time received 28 years while his surviving companions Mouloud Bourgelane and Hochine Benadaouli picked up 20 and 18 years respectively.[13]

[13] *Le Monde*, 19 October 2001.

One thing at which the French criminals excel is escape from prison by helicopter. This first happened back in 1981, but in 2001 the escapes multiplied. First there was an escape on 24 March, followed by a foiled attempt on 27 May when one guard was badly injured. Then on 25 June 2001 Louis Carboni, alleged to be a major drugs baron, escaped from Borgo prison in Corsica when yet another helicopter was used. This was the thirteenth attempt over the past 20 years and the fourth since March. On this occasion the pilot and co-pilot were taken hostage and forced to fly the helicopter on to the prison roof from where the hijackers lowered a ladder to Carboni out on the sports fields. Within minutes the hijackers and Carboni were dropped off in the village of Furiani where a car was waiting. He survived on the outside until January 2002 when he was found in Figueras, Spain.

On 12 October 2001 Frédéric Impocco and Pascal Payet were both lifted from Fleury-Merogis. In March 1997 Impocco had kidnapped and killed the 69-year-old Jean-Claude Spillaert in Cannes in a ransom operation which failed. Spillaert's body was found in a refrigerator. He had been strangled and then left in the boot of a car with his head in a dustbin bag. Payet was suspected of being the leader of a gang of bank robbers and had been involved in a raid in November 1997 in Provence when a Banque de France guard was killed.

Early 2003 saw the end of life on the run for 37-year-old Corsican Joseph Menconi, another major figure, thought to be close to the Bastia-based Brise de Mer gang, who escaped from the Borgo prison in November 1998. Captured unarmed and without a struggle in Rocquencourt (Yvelines) on 3 January, over the coming months he would be questioned

abut what he could say of an April 1997 attack on an
armoured car at Saint Laurent-du-Var which cleared over 10
million francs; a double murder in Bastia in August 2001;
the shooting of Christophe Montigny, also in Bastia, in a
cyber café the following month; and the destruction of the
François Santoni-led Armata Corse.[14]

Violent crime is now seen as endemic in France. Saint-
Ouen, one of the poorer suburbs north of Paris, has been
described as Bronx-sur-Seine, and in November 2001 police
throughout the country decided to march through Paris
protesting about the number of attacks and ambushes by
armed criminals. This followed an incident on 7 November
when two officers were injured in Saint-Ouen. Seven officers
had been killed during the year, although that aspect of the
problem does not seem to lie with professional criminals but
rather with youth gangs. In Strasbourg more than 1,500 cars
were set on fire in the first ten months of the year, and on
Bastille Day 130 cars were torched in Aulnay outside Paris
by rioting youths.

Back with tradition. A great embarrassment came to the
French when it was announced that corruption investigations
were being conducted at eight of its embassies, including one
which was alleged to have sold tens of thousands of visas to
prostitutes. The trade was also being carried on at the
embassies in Africa. The trade at one was of a rather higher
class; there, places at the International Lycée were on sale.

The scams came to light when police in eastern France
and Belgium noticed an unnaturally high proportion of young

Bulgarian prostitutes on the street. When questioned they produced legitimate visas allowing them to work for companies in France for a limited period. On checking it was found that these had been obtained with false supporting documents. French visas issued in Sofia had doubled to 60,000 and blank visa forms were being sold through tourist agencies at up to £300 each. It was thought that up to 30,000 visas had been issued in the scam.[15]

Just as England has troubles with the theft of mobile phones, so has France where 20,000 mobile telephones were snatched in Paris alone in the year to the end of October 2001. There have also been problems on the Côte d'Azur which echo those in Johannesburg. Drivers now keep the doors of their cars locked and, if necessary, will jump red lights to avoid thieves or car-jackers.[16] Some mayors have imposed 11 p.m. to 6 a.m. summer curfews on 13-year-olds. More seriously, 26 bazookas were seized along with 16 anti-tank weapons up to the end of October. Today's young innocent rioters are tomorrow's professional criminals.

---

[15] *Guardian*, 28 August 2001.
[16] At the end of December 2001 a British family was kidnapped and held hostage near the village of Vétheuil, north-west of Paris. Their car was stopped by two men and the younger members of the family were put in the boot while two others were taken at gunpoint to cash machines where they were forced to withdraw £1,000. When they were returned to their own car the gunmen slashed the tyres. *Daily Mail*, 1 January 2002.

There was a spate of car-jackings of luxury cars in Brussels in 1997–8. Social Affairs Commissioner to NATO Padraig Flynn had his Mercedes taken away at gunpoint and Chawki Arnali, the Palestinian envoy, lost a new BMW in similar circumstances. The Mercedes of the German ambassador to NATO survived an attack when gunmen were forced to flee. Diplomats were not the only losers. Other owners of expensive cars also had them hijacked. The cars were presumed to have been sold behind the old Iron Curtain. *The Times*, 8 January 1998.

12

Spain

The coastline around Marbella began to receive career criminals from England in the 1970s when people such as Ronnie Knight, Freddie Foreman, Clifford Saxe and Charlie Wilson, the latter from the Great Train Robbery, moved to the sun, sand and safety – at any rate from the authorities, if not from other criminal gangs. At the time there was no extradition treaty between Spain and Britain and, for the most part, they and others lived relatively peaceful lives, opening bars, clubs and restaurants and cutting up touches with visiting faces. It was an almost idyllic existence except, said one expatriate, for the absence of Walls' sausages. Visitors were required to carry not guns but bangers in their hand luggage.

Another later semi-permanent resident was Joe Wilkins who had the distinction of escaping from prison, being re-arrested, and pushing off again. As journalist Paul Foot wrote,

'To lose one Wilkins might be an accident; to lose two seems like carelessness.'[1] Wilkins had led an interesting criminal career. A man with a penchant for good-looking women and champagne and a career which variously embraced fraud and living off immoral earnings, this long-time working associate of Frank Fraser had been serving a 10-year sentence for drug smuggling. On 17 August 1987 he had been found sunbathing on *The Danny Boy*, a boat carrying £1.5 million of cannabis. He did not do his old friend Fraser any favours, naming him as one of the drug kings of the Costa del Sol. Wilkins also claimed he was acting as an undercover agent for the Spanish police. Scotland Yard was not well pleased by Wilkins' arrest, they having hoped to follow the drugs through to their expected arrival in South London.[2]

While in Maidstone prison Wilkins had made a long state-ment to the *Sunday Times* in relation to the alleged shooting by the SAS of three unarmed members of the IRA in Gibraltar. His sister, Coral Edgar, had received £2,000 and, shortly after, Wilkins was moved to the more relaxed open prison at Ford, near Arundel, from which he absconded to the Costa del Sol. He was recaptured when he returned to England in August 1991 and was sent to Highpoint, another low-security prison near Newmarket. From there it was back over to Spain once more. Over the years, seemingly no one has been that interested in retrieving him.

There were, of course, hiccups. Fraser, visiting Marbella

[1] *Daily Mirror*, 9 October 1992.
[2] For an account of Wilkins' career see James Morton, *Gangland*, and for a more personal account see Frank Fraser, *Mad Frank*.

to retrieve some money after a property deal had fallen through, was arrested and held for a couple of weeks before being released after a visit by his lawyer, John Blackburn Gittings, the future Attorney General of Gibraltar. Fraser seems to have forgiven Wilkins for naming him as a drugs mastermind because they spent some time together drinking champagne.

Just as the Heineken kidnapping was broken when one of the men involved was seen with Chinese takeaways, so the November 1987 kidnapping near Marbella of the daughter of former London club owner and gold smuggler, Raymond Nash, was ended after one of the men dropped his wallet with the ransom note. It was found by a woman who handed it to her priest to give to the police.

Raymond Nash, who had been the partner of the property dealer Peter Rachman,[3] was refused re-admission to Britain after he had been convicted in Tokyo and fined £23,760, with 18 months' hard labour in default of payment, over smuggled gold in 1965. Nash had owned the fashionable Le Condor Club in Wardour Street. The club went bust after Rachman took it over and Nash reopened it as La Discothèque. It was alleged – something which Nash constantly denied – that La Discothèque and its sister club of the same name in Streatham were the centre of the Purple

---

[3] Peter Rachman, a slum landlord who gave his name to Rachmanism, was a friend of both Christine Keeler and Mandy Rice-Davies. He came to Britain after the Second World War and a period in a Russian labour camp. At the time of his death in 1982 he had built up a property empire of some 500 houses and flats mainly in the Paddington area. He specialised in the eviction and bullying of tenants, using ex-wrestlers. In one case he dealt with recalcitrant tenants by having the roof taken off the house.

Hearts trade. He had led an interesting life at the time; not long before his arrest he had been shot at by Chinese gunmen in the Hong Kong Hilton.

Nash then lived in Marbella with his new wife, the Korean opera singer Princess Kimera. Their daughter was snatched from outside the school she attended near Mijas and a ransom of £8 million was demanded. Negotiations began and it was then that one of the kidnappers dropped his wallet with a new demand note. In a police raid on the apartment in San Pedro, near Gibraltar, where the child was held, a Frenchman, Constant Georgoux, trying to use her as a shield, was shot in the throat.

Some, however, experienced more permanent indigestion. John Moriarty, a supergrass and regarded by some as more involved in the so-called Epping Torso murder than he would have cared to admit, was killed. So also was Charlie Mitchell, extortionist, fraudsman and horse doper, who had turned against the Kray Twins at the end of the 1960s and so saved himself from a lengthy spell inside. Neither was greatly missed, but Charlie Wilson was. Like one or two other members of the Great Train Robbery team, he was thought to have been dealing in drugs and he was shot by the swimming-pool at his villa on 24 April 1990.

Initially it was reported that Wilson had been killed with a single karate blow, but the autopsy showed he had been shot in the side of the neck and the bullet had lodged there. As the bullet passed through the larynx it would have caused heavy bleeding, and as he inhaled blood he would have been unable to cry out.

The inquest was told by Detective Superintendent Alec

Edwards that although there was no direct evidence to link Wilson with drug dealing there was much circumstantial evidence, such as his lifestyle and his visits to Morocco. A verdict that he had been shot by persons unknown was recorded.

After his release from prison in 1978 – he was the last of the Great Train Robbers to be freed – Wilson led something of a charmed life so far as the courts were concerned. In 1982 he was one of seven men charged in a £2 million VAT fraud involving the melting down of £16 million gold Krugerrands. Charges against him were dropped after the jury had disagreed twice, and he paid £400,000 to Customs and Excise. In 1984 he spent four months in custody awaiting trial for the alleged armed robbery of a security van before he was freed.[4]

The gunman, or at least the lookout, in the Wilson killing was the South London villain Danny Roff. Retribution caught up with him later when he was shot in the Passport Club in New Cross; on 10 February 1996 a gunman opened fire, spraying the crowded bar with bullets. At the time of the Wilson killing Roff had been on the run after escaping while serving a 13-year sentence for robbery. By 1996 there were extradition procedures in place between Spain and Britain and the Spanish police were trying to retrieve Roff, who had at one time been arrested in Holland. Roff survived the shooting but was left crippled. Just over a year later, on 24 March 1997, he was shot and killed as he got out of his car

---

[4] For an account of the circumstances and immediate fallout from the death of Wilson, see Duncan Campbell, *The Underworld*; James Morton, *Gangland*.

in the driveway at his home in Bromley, Kent. At the time
of the first shooting a senior detective was reported as saying,
'It looks like the debt has finally been collected for Charlie.'[5]

By and large, however, there was peace and quiet on the
coast in those early days. After his acquittal in the cannabis
trial, Patrick Adams had taken a house in Sierrazuela on the
outskirts of Fuengirola and could be found in Gilligan's, a
drinking club in Mijas which had live racing via satellite television. Breakfast as mother made it was always on offer on
the coast, and there was an English bookshop for those who
could read.

But, as with so many Gardens of Eden, it was not to last.
For a start a much more unruly British element arrived,
bringing with it serious drug dealing. There were reports of
gang warfare and a Moroccan suspected of drug dealing was
found with an axe in his head. Shortly after that in the spring
of 1993 Ronnie Knight's club – R Knights, in Fuengirola –
was closed after it was alleged that a gun and drugs had been
found in the lavatory.[6] There was no suggestion that Knight
was near the premises at the time.

However, these were small-time incidents. Then came an
influx of gangs from Amsterdam, Hamburg, Marseilles and
Naples as well as a whole host of fugitive Irish criminals.
Shortly afterwards, the Russians arrived. In 1994 there were
some 3,000 Russian visitors and by 1997 there were 28,000
coming annually. In the previous five years 23,000 had estab-

---

[5] *Sun*, 13 February 1996.
[6] It was reopened as the Moonbar by a group of Moroccans and was closed in
1998 amidst allegations of drug dealing and money laundering.

lished homes. Many had paid cash and some arrived with suitcases stuffed with dollars to pay for the houses, the yachts and the expensive motor cars. With them they brought crime. A Russian couple and their small daughter were killed in their villa in Nueva Andalucia, just west of Malaga, in a settling of scores. Their bodies were found half-buried in Casares. Ivan Ivanov received three 28-year sentences for their killings. In 1995 Roman Frumson, said to be one of the Godfathers of the Coast, was found shot dead. Shortly before that another Russian had paid cash for a Porsche, but had never collected it for the simple reason that he fled after Frumson's killing. The Costa del Sol became the Costa del Plomo.

Now there was a huge Russian statue, the 'Victory', over the entrance to the marina and casino complex at Puerto Banus. Just who paid for it and what it was doing there was the subject of endless speculation. In theory it was meant to be a gift from the people of Moscow to thank the town for its kindness in taking the money from their visitors. However, shortly after the statue was in place, along came a bill for 141 million pesetas (around £560,000) for transport and Customs charges. Originally the mayor of Marbella, Jesus Gil y Gil, proposed settling this by the gift of three prime sites to the mayor of Moscow. His proposal caused so much dissent that it was dropped.

Gil y Gil – one-time president of Atletico de Madrid, Spain's third largest football club but now languishing in the second division – also proposed a floating casino off Banus. He has had a long and interesting career. One of his election promises was that he would clear the town of street crime so that he could leave a jewellery box on the back seat of his Rolls-Rolls convertible in the knowledge that it would be there when he got back. To this extent Gil was successful; he doubled the local police force and drove out street crime. But there is always a price, and there were allegations of brutality and suggestions that transvestite prostitutes had been offered one-way tickets to the destination of their choice provided they promised never to return. There were also suggestions that while low-level crime had been tackled, the same was certainly not the case with organised crime which had taken something of a stranglehold.

There were now thought to be 16 organised crime gangs of various nationalities working on the coast. In 1996, in *Operation Papagallo*, the police seized 13 tons of hashish, arresting Colombian, Dutch, Argentinian, Bosnian and Spanish nationals in the swoop. That year the Spanish seized 152 tons of cannabis resin. It was the tip of the crop, however. The estimation was that 93 per cent of hashish smuggled from Morocco came through undetected. The method of choice was no longer swallowing packets by so-called *culeros*. X-ray machines had done for that. Now the hashish was smuggled in lorries or crop-spraying planes. Another favoured method was sending the drug over on rubber dinghies to be collected from the deserted beaches north of Tarifa. Barbate was thought to be a landing-stage, with the drug being transferred to warehouses in Seville. The trade was believed to be in the hands of Dutch and British gangs.

In October that year, members of a French Algerian drugs ring were thought to be behind the killing of Jacques Grangeon (also known as Lambert), shot 27 times, and his pregnant girlfriend, Catherine Castagna. The pair had been running marijuana and cocaine from Morocco to France. They were said to belong to the same ring as their killers, who broke into their house in the smart area of Las Lomas de Marbella and opened fire. Castagna's 18-year-old daughter, Rebecca, escaped by hiding but Jean-Pierre Bruno, who was also in the house, was hit in the chest, arms, leg and head.

Earlier in the month, police inspector Juan Alameda had been shot and killed when he stopped a Dutch national suspected of drug trafficking in what should have been a routine search. A second officer escaped when a bullet lodged in a bundle of warrants he had in his breast pocket.

Worse was to come for the resort's reputation when Francisco Bocanegra, a 38-year-old tax consultant, was found in the bedroom of his home, bound hand and foot and battered to death. His brother Ricardo, a lawyer with a substantial number of foreign clients, accepted that he had worked for criminals (mainly British ones) in the past, but had not realised their profession until he saw their names in the newspapers. A Bulgarian, part of a homosexual prostitution ring, was sentenced to 17 years' imprisonment.

Up the coast in Benidorm, Roy Davies, said to be the head of a 16-strong gang of smugglers of hashish from Morocco to Benidorm and then on to England, was questioned in May 1997 over the death of a Briton, Yuri Slavinkas, who had been stabbed to death at his home. His mother, who was also attacked, said her son had been working with Davies who had a business installing satellite dishes. Davies was arrested in a raid on a warehouse at Villajoyosa near Benidorm, when a ton of hashish was seized.

Murder was not confined to the mainland. In November 1997 Manfred Meisel, the self-styled King of Beer who ran the Bier K:nig Palace in Majorca, was found executed at his home. His 8-year-old son, Patrick, had been shot twice through the head and the child's nanny, Claudia Liestein, had also been killed. She had been bound with her hands behind her back in Meisel's office, where both she and the beer king were shot. It seems she had been pushed to the floor and a pillow placed over her head. Unusually the killings, which otherwise had the hallmark of the professional, had been done with small-calibre 6.35 bullets.

Meisel had popularised the cheap drunken night out, catering for German tourists of whom it was estimated 4,000 could go through his palace in an evening. But he had made enemies and in the week of his death should have been in court after a complaint by a local that he had received a beating when he parked his car in front of the Bier K:nig. Meisel had been hospitalised the previous year after fighting with an Argentinian and, because of his habit of carrying his takings in a cardboard box, had been mugged on several occasions. He also might have fallen foul of one of the gangs of enforcers amongst the 28,000 German residents on the island. The following week, the villa of Majorca's 'car king', Hasso Schuetendorf, was set alight. He was reported as saying that he had been threatened the previous year.[7]

The next year 15 people were held in Madrid as part of a Bulgarian ring which stole expensive cars and exported them to Eastern Europe and Northern Africa. A Russian and

[7] *Guardian*, 22 November 1997.

three Poles were arrested in Denia charged with the attempted kidnapping of a Russian multimillionaire. Three more Poles were arrested in Madrid, charged with shooting their 'boss' in the face while he was asleep.

On occasions, Spain could be just as dangerous for travelling Irishmen. On 10 August 2000, Michael McGuinness from Limvady, County Derry – or rather his rotting remains – were found in the boot of a Range Rover parked at Malaga airport where the temperature was 35°C. Initially the police thought it might be a booby-trap planted by the Basque organisation ETA, but it was only McGuinness, his hands cuffed behind his back and his head in a black plastic bag.

Not a great deal of information was forthcoming about his death, but he had rented a flat in Puebla Aida just outside Mijas. At 2 o'clock on the previous Monday morning two men were let in by him through the gate security, seemingly to collect money. An argument followed and he was taken away at gunpoint. His girlfriend was unable to give any real description of the men and has since disappeared. One suggestion is that McGuinness had been money laundering on behalf of a major Dublin criminal and the accounting procedures had gone awry in his favour. The death of McGuinness was the fifth on the Costa in 2000 which could reasonably be attributed to gangland crime. The previous week a Frenchman was shot and killed in San Pedro. Two other victims were Arabs who were shot at close range as they sat in their vehicles near Marbella.

One unsuccessful kidnap at the beginning of 2001 was that of the Spanish international football player, Iván de la Peña, on 31 January. He was driving to his apartment in

Barcelona after finishing some physiotherapy at the Nou Camp stadium. As he went down the ramp, the would-be kidnappers followed him through the security barrier. He parked and, as he was getting out of his Porsche, he saw the men putting on balaclavas. He jumped back into his car and drove out, opening the security gate by remote control. He turned down a side street and as the kidnappers drove past he wrote down the licence number. Their vehicle had been stolen in a car-jacking at Castellefels two days earlier.

In a chase by the police the car overturned at a roundabout and, as Santiago Canton was wrestled to the ground, he shot a policeman in the stomach. He had previously escaped and was on the run from the Mondelo prison in Barcelona where he was serving a 17-year sentence for robbery with violence.

Prostitution was, as always, a major source of revenue. In March 1998 the police arrested 14 people in the Bilbao region suspected of belonging to a prostitution ring organised by the Russian *mafiya*. This time the women had been offered fake jobs in show business and child-minding. There has been an increase in the trafficking in teenagers from Eastern Europe, Africa and Asia who were being smuggled into Western Europe to work in the sex industry. In Italy social workers estimated that 16–30 per cent of the prostitutes they assisted were under age.

The standard techniques employed to persuade young women away from their homes were the age-old ones, the five countries whose women were the most exploited being Thailand, Brazil, the Philippines, Colombia and the

Dominican Republic. Viviana,[8] one of a number of women lured from Cali after her home town Tulua became the focal point for the country's civil war, described her experiences:

> It began when a neighbour told me I was pretty and could work in a casino in Spain and make good money. She said I could earn $1,000 a week. It seemed like the only way I could buy a house for my son. So I said yes.

She was provided with a visa and plane tickets and enough money to persuade the immigration authorities that she was a tourist. Once in Asturias, Spain, she realised that she would not be working in a casino but in a brothel. She was told about charges for condoms, sheets, towels and that she owed $4,000.

A woman from Chile, also working in the brothel, took pity on her and arranged for a man to pose as a client willing to pay extra to take her out for the evening. He then gave her $100 to travel to Madrid where she took refuge in a convent, which was already housing two other women who had escaped from brothels. With the help of the Hope Foundation she then returned to Colombia where threats were made to kidnap her five-year-old son.

In the first half of 2000 the Colombian police broke up six networks of traffickers in women, arresting 1,200 people. The crime is now punishable by 6–8 years in prison, coupled with a fine of up to $15,000.[9]

[8] A pseudonym.
[9] Timothy Pratt, 'Escape from Sex Slavery' in *San Francisco Chronicle*, 26 February 2001.

Back in 1998 there were now allegations of corruption floating around Gil y Gil and his seven years as mayor of Marbella. The complaints about the 'Victory' statue resurfaced and it was suggested that £1.8 million from the town had gone into Atletico de Madrid. Some 80 claims over his business dealings had been lodged. Nor had Gil pleased the citizens by putting a bronze of General Franco in the town hall foyer.

In fact Gil had very good reason to pay homage to the General. Born in 1933 in El Burgo de Osma, a small town north of Madrid, he had shown his entrepreneurial talents at an early age. At the age of 17 he was said to have been paying his rent in a boarding-house, in which the other occupants were 19 prostitutes and a priest, by keeping the books. Later he mended trucks, bought and sold them and then moved on to property. In 1969 he built an apartment block in Segovia. It had neither plans nor architect, and hardly was the building up when it collapsed, killing 58 people. He received a 5-year sentence but was pardoned by Franco after 18 months. He then borrowed money and once more was up and running. In the early 1980s he transferred his attention to the burgeoning Marbella and was made a *persona non grata* because of his disregard for local planning regulations. He then formed his own political party, Grupo Independiente Liberal (GIL), and won the 1991 elections in a landslide.

On 30 October 2000 the Spanish authorities finally managed to capture a man considered to be one of the most powerful of the Spanish drug barons in Galicia. Laureano Oubia – known as 'El Barajito' or 'Little Bird', because of his ability to fly away from trouble – was arrested on the Greek island of Halkida where he had spent the previous three months. He had been gone just over a year, following the arrest of his wife Esther Lago and 16 helpmates when a boat flying the Honduran flag had been captured off Morocco carrying 15 tons of hashish. A call on a mobile telephone to the restaurant where he was dining had been sufficient to send him across the border into Portugal and then on across Europe.

He had been in the eye of the authorities from 1990 when a prosecution for drug smuggling failed and, instead, he received a mere four months for tax fraud. It was not until 4 October 1999 that, *in absentia*, he was charged with drug trafficking and sentenced to 4 years' imprisonment coupled with an £8 million fine for an abortive attempt to move 6 tons of hashish from Vigo to Holland two years earlier.

Oubia had begun his career as a lorry driver and was first charged and acquitted back in 1983. On this occasion the substance was tobacco. He had then been married with eight children but after meeting Lago, who worked as a bingo caller at Villagarcia de Arosa, he deserted them. Together he and Lago built an empire which included an estate at Baion producing Albarino, the local wine. Although renovations were never completed it had been Lago's ambition to include a replica of the Mannekin Pis from the Grand Place in Brussels, urinating Albarino. The estate was confiscated by the courts back in 1994 and the production of the wine taken over by the well-known Freixenet group.[10]

Another drug baron had flown however. Carlos Ruiz

[10] See *Independent on Sunday*, 3 December 2000.

Santamaria, known as 'El Negro' and regarded as the head of one of Spain's leading drug gangs, had been charged with smuggling 11 tons of cocaine into the country using Spanish fishing boats. He had been held in Madrid's Valdemoro prison where a psychiatrist diagnosed him as suffering from extreme depression. Well, he might have been. The prosecution was demanding a 60-year sentence and fines and confiscation orders of £280 million. The psychiatrist also considered Santamaria to be a suicide risk. To the surprise of many and the horror of the prosecution, an appeal to the equivalent of the High Court resulted in his being bailed on an £18,000 bond on 22 December. The Spanish newspapers were convinced he would abscond and they were right. Due to begin his trial on 14 January, he disappeared, possibly to South America.

The summer of 2001 was a reasonably good one for the Spanish authorities when 3 tons of cocaine – worth £115 million on the street and designed for tourist resorts in the south of the country – was seized when it was found under false floors in a vessel in the Basque port of Santurce. Better still was the arrest of Oded Tuito in May. Tuito, alleged to be a global dealer who marketed Ecstasy tablets stamped with the Star of David and the Tweety Pie cartoon bird, was arrested near Barcelona in the seaside town of Castelldefels. His arrest did not apparently stop his activities, and he is alleged to have continued organising matters from his cell in the Soto del Real prison in Madrid.

However at the end of July, worldwide police co-operation saw the arrest of up to three dozen of his alleged associates – in Spain where his principal lieutenants were arrested in

Barcelona, and also in Los Angeles and Australia. The arrests made inroads into a gang said to be trafficking also in cannabis and cocaine as well as having links with a gang of Israeli armed robbers who had been carrying out a series of raids on jewellers in Barcelona.

Tuito was alleged to have been buying up the entire production of pills from clandestine laboratories in Holland at around 50c each which, after they had been moved through Spain, Belgium, France and Germany, were then couriered to America by a variety of agents including pensioners, teenagers and strippers, where they fetched £19 each. Young Hassidic Jews were also recruited on the basis that their clothing and general demeanour would make them less liable to be searched.[11] There was also another line of distribution to Latin America via Panama and a third to Asia via Thailand.

In February 2001 Spanish police arrested one of Russia's most wanted men, Sergei Butorin, the reputed head of the Orekhovo group. Butorin, who was wanted in Moscow for his alleged involvement in the deaths of 29 people including six policemen and a prosecutor, was found along with Marat Poliansky, said to be his right-hand man, in a night-club in Castelldefels. Both were said to have been disarmed before they were able to draw their pistols. At the house where they were living the police discovered two sub-machine guns. It was thought that efforts would be made to extradite them to Russia.

---

[11] *Guardian*, 21 August 2001. This was a ruse which could backfire. When two members of the Red *mafiya* dressed as Hassidic Jews were endeavouring to avoid arrest they made the mistake of travelling on the Day of Atonement. Pensioners in Britain have been introduced to a life of crime, particularly in cigarette smuggling. One reported that he would return from the Continent with some 10,000 and make a profit of £400 a trip. *The Times*, 1 May 2001.

There was, however, continuing trouble in Madrid where guns were out between Colombian cartels. On 21 September three Colombian women were shot dead in a flat in the city in a settling of arguments over the drug trade; they had each been shot once in the head. Eight days later three men were killed and a fourth seriously injured in a shoot-out in a public telephone and fax centre used principally by immigrants to call home. Colombians do not require visas to enter Spain and it is thought that there may be as many as 60,000 in the country.

Meanwhile, in the summer of 2001 things were looking up for Jesus Gil y Gil, now charged with fraud in the Marbella court, when 13 of the prosecution's files disappeared. The anti-fraud prosecution department said that, while it would be difficult and costly to replace them, it was not giving up. The disappearance of original documents would now make it impossible to carry out certain handwriting tests. 'If it was so easy to replace the documents, nobody would have bothered to steal them,' said anti-fraud prosecutor, Carlos Castresana. He went on to add that security in the building was not a problem; it was an inside job.[12]

It certainly seems to have been so because, on 3 October, Francisco Calero, a prime suspect, was arrested and driven back to his home on the fourth floor of a block of flats above the San Francisco café in Marbella. Within minutes there was a thud outside the café and Calero's body lay on the pavement. He had apparently escaped from police custody and jumped.

[12] *Sur in English*, 31 August 2001.

'Why would I wish to delay the trial?' asked Gil rhetorically. The answer was simple. He was approaching the age of 70, after which Spanish justice in its wisdom and mercy cannot imprison anyone. And, as most professional criminals will tell you, anything other than an immediate prison sentence is as good as an acquittal. But in April 2002 Gil y Gil was sentenced to six months' imprisonment and disqualified from holding public office for 28 years. He had been found guilty of corruption and perverting the course of justice by diverting funds to the football club Atletico de Madrid.

13

Italy

The Mafia is Dead: Long Live the Mafia

On 18 April 2000 Valerio Viccei was shot dead after he and another man were stopped in a routine patrol as they were driving along a road frequented by prostitutes in Termo, 100 miles east of Rome. He had been returned to Italy from Britain to complete a sentence imposed 13 years earlier.

1987 was the year of Viccei's inside job which surpassed, on paper at least, even the Brinks-Mat robbery. In July of that year the Knightsbridge Safe Deposit Box Centre, opposite Harrods, was robbed of £40 million by him along with American antiques dealer Eric Rubin and the manager of the deposit company, Parvez Latif, the black sheep of a wealthy

Pakistani family who had been promised a third share of the proceeds.

Latif, then in serious financial difficulties, agreed to let Rubin and Viccei into the building. The guards were tied up and threatened and the 120 safety deposit boxes were stripped. Once again it was a grass who brought about the team's downfall and Rubin, a shadowy man who held neither bank account nor credit cards and who commuted from New York for the robbery, received a 12-year sentence. Valerio Viccei had links with neo-Fascist terror groups in Italy going back to his teens. Since then he had lived the life of a playboy with expensive tastes in women, Gucci shoes, fast cars and cocaine, not necessarily in that order. He was wanted in Italy for a series of bank robberies.

In January 1987 Viccei and Rubin had teamed up to rob Coutts Bank in Cavendish Square, the first time in its 300-year history that Coutts had been robbed. To make things even cosier amongst the conspirators, Viccei was also sleeping with Latif's girlfriend, Pamela Seamarks. Viccei, whose fingerprint was left at the scene – some police think deliberately, when he cut himself – had intended to go to Colombia, taking with him his black Ferrari Testarossa. But he had difficulties in obtaining an export licence, delayed his departure and was arrested. He received 22 years, while Latif received 16. Steve Mann, the member of the gang who turned Queen's Evidence and so put them all away, had the now almost statutory 5 years.

Back home Viccei had been benefiting from the lax rules of the Italian prison system. Described as an exemplary prisoner, he would have been eligible for parole from 2003 and had been given a release date of 2007. In the meantime he was only required to sleep at the prison, with a 10.30 p.m. curfew.

On 18 April 2000 the police patrol leader, Enzo Baldini, approached Viccei only to be met with handgun fire and was wounded. He went down and Viccei approached the wounded officer intending to shoot him again. A second policeman, Franco Di Giannatale, fired some fifteen shots, killing Viccei. By this time his companion had run off into the woods, where he was arrested. It was thought that the pair were in the relatively early stages of preparing a bank raid; carnival masks were found in the car, a stolen Lancia.

In the long tradition of the media reporting that gangsters had 'died yellow', one newspaper heading described Viccei as dying 'a miserable nobody'. He did, however, have a new Ferrari which he parked every night at the prison, saying it was the safest car park in Pescara. Many, not so fortunate as to own a new Ferrari, might think that he had gone out in some style to which they could only aspire.[1]

Another rather older robber, and this time a press favourite, died on Christmas Eve 2001. Horst Fantazzini had a heart attack in the Dozza prison in Bologna where he was on remand for yet another robbery. He had begun his career with the Red Brigade of the 1970s and graduated from stealing bicycles and mopeds to cars. He first came to the public notice when, after stealing a Fiat 600, he outdrove the chasing *carabinieri* in Alfa Romeos. From there it was on to bank robberies where, according to legend, he would wait his turn in the queue before holding up the cashier. He would

[1] *The Times*, 19 April 2000.

claim he had a pistol, but he never produced one.

Over his years in prison he took part in an escape attempt from Fossano, when he took two warders hostage and wounded three others before being captured. During the attempt he suffered severe injuries. He was also a leader in a protest against conditions in the Badu e Carros prison in Sardinia.

On his release Fantazzini returned to Germany where he had been born, and robbed banks there as well as commuting to Bologna and Milan for raids on Italian ones. At the time of his last arrest he was on day release, like Viccei, but things turned full circle. He could not stop working and was caught trying to pedal away on a bicycle after robbing a bank in the suburbs of Bologna.

His 40-year career was lovingly followed in *Il Resto del Carlino*, and Enzo Monteleone made a film of his life, *Ormai è Fatta!* (*Now It's Done!*), starring Stefano Accorsi.[2]

Viccei and Fantazzini were one-off romantic figures. The Mafia still retained much of its romance for the readers if not its victims. However, there had been serious attempts to reel the old figures in.

Eventually things catch up and old age is not necessarily a defence. In March 2001, 83-year-old money launderer Vito Palazzolo, already serving a sentence for Mafia-related crimes, was sentenced to a further 30 years for ordering the 1978 killing of Giuseppe Impastato. Palazzolo was one of the leaders in the seaside town of Cinisi when, as a teenager, Impastato began to speak openly against the organisation.

[2] *The Times*, 27 December 2001.

Later, after he appeared on local radio to do the same, his body was found on the railway outside the town. He had been dynamited. His story was made into the very successful film, *I Cento Passi* (*The Hundred Steps*).

On trial separately was Gaetano Badalamenti, convicted in New York in 1987 for his part in the so-called Pizza Connection heroin ring, and currently serving 30 years. He was said to have been the boss of Cinisi, and had lived across the street from the Impastato family.[3]

One of the younger generation had also been arrested. Vito Vitale, then aged 39 and described with some hyperbole as 'the most dangerous *mafioso* still at large', was arrested in April 1998 when he was ambushed by police outside Palermo. Wanted for questioning about several killings, he was widely alleged to have supplied the acid bath into which Giuseppe Santino, the unfortunate son of an informer father, was thrown after being strangled by Giovanni Brusca, 'The Pig' or 'The Slaughterer'.[4]

The one who did remain at large was 'The Tractor', or Uncle Binu, Bernardo Provenzano. Back on 24 June 1995 the capture of his henchman, Leoluca Baragella, had led to speculation that Provenzano might also be arrested soon. He was believed to be suffering from cancer and had been receiving treatment in a Palermo clinic, running a police gauntlet to keep his appointments. His wife was not wanted by the police and had returned with their children to

---

[3] See Shana Alexander, *The Pizza Connection*.

[4] See James Morton, *Gangland International*, Chapter 35. In March 2000 it was announced that Brusca had been granted witness-protection status and a monthly payment of $250 as a *pentito*. In a prison memoir he had confessed to killing Giovanni Falcone and also a hundred more killings.

Corleone, which fuelled suspicion that Provenzano might actually have died, but this was denied. One difficulty in tracing him has been the lack of any recent photograph of him on the police files. The last one was taken over thirty years earlier, showing him with a teddy-boy hair-style.

But nothing came of that particular piece of action and his wife took the opportunity of insisting that she was proud of the family name and that her husband, who had had a hoe in his hand since he was a child, was being persecuted. He was not a serial killer, she told *La Repubblica*.

One significant triumph, however, was the arrest of Gaetano Scotto in Chivari, near Genoa. He had been convicted in his absence of plotting to kill the anti-Mafia judge Paolo Borsellino and his five bodyguards on 19 July 1992, when the judge was visiting his mother. Scotto, who was finally arrested on 7 August 2001, had also been sentenced to 16 years for drug trafficking.

However, it was not entirely clear whether the war against the Mafia was being won. Conflicting reports were coming from a United Nations summit meeting held in Palermo to adopt a new convention on measures designed to deal with Italian, Russian and American organised crime. The murders in Sicily had dropped, said Pietro Grasso, chief prosecutor in Palermo, from 200 a year in the 1980s down to 10 a year, but it would be irresponsible to underestimate the Octopus's reach. He believed there were still more than 5,000 *mafiosi* on the island divided amongst some 190 families. Under the overall aegis of Provenzano, Palermo, by far the largest with 89 clans; Trapanzi, in the north west, mustering 20 clans; Messina in the north east, but thought to have a total membership of less than 20. In the centre of the island came Enna, with 40 members divided between six clans, and Caltanissetta, having 17 clans and about 270 members. In the south west of the island was Agrigento with nearly 500 members. In Syracuse on the south eastern end of the island there were believed to be two clans, one of which had two members. Slightly larger were the clans in Catania which had 135 members.

There had been some progress against the Mafia, particularly in Palermo, where properties owned by alleged *mafiosi* had been confiscated and converted into schools. One villa was now the headquarters of the *carabinieri*.

Unfortunately, at the time of the conference one report alleged that some 390 politicians, law-enforcement officials and businessmen were aiding and abetting the clans. The bad news was compounded by other reports that the Mafia was moving into the Balkans.

Then for a time, as far as Provenzano was concerned, it seemed as though the authorities had made progress. In February 2001 the same story was trundled out when Vincenzo Virga – said to have been one of the 10 most wanted criminals in Italy, and the business brain behind Provenzano – was captured in a house in Trapani. It was now only a matter of days.

It seemed that Provenzano had nearly been cornered the previous month when the police captured another of his lieutenants, Benedetto Spero, along with Vincenzo Di Noto, a doctor who had been treating both him and 'The Tractor'. Provenzano was thought to have been in a neighbouring house, but the raid was alleged to have been ruined by professional rivalry between the *carabinieri* and a paramilitary force.

Once again it was only a matter of time before the net closed on the elusive 'Tractor'. Virga faced charges of murdering a judge, a journalist and a prison guard who refused to help jailed *mafiosi*. As for Provenzano – who over the years had given the lie to the taunt that, even if he shot like an angel, he had the brains of a chicken – he was thought to have last seen his wife, Saverina, nine years earlier. Letters written to the Godfather in the township of Mezzojuso were intercepted and found to contain advice from his wife on how best to wash his socks in cold water. Since she and her son ran a laundry no doubt the advice was worthwhile. The letter said she was also sending the fleecy jacket and snow trousers he had requested and immediately the hills near Agrigento were searched.

But, as the months passed and despite suggestions that other old men, held under the harsh so-called Bis 41 regulations, might be tempted to inform and secure more comfort for themselves, this elderly and apparently ailing wraith still flitted over the Sicilian hills eluding his pursuers. Perhaps it is the fear that the comfort might only be temporary which has held them back.[5]

There were also signs of what has been described as the *Cosa Nuovo*, a hi-tech arm of the old *Cosa Nostra*, with an emphasis on low-key behaviour and building networks rather than making enemies. One who failed to go along with the trend was Giuseppe Di Maggio, a man known for his flamboyance and trouble-making. On 21 September 2000 his

[5] See Frances Kennedy, 'The Last Godfather' in the *Independent*, 9 August 2000.

body was found in a plastic bag afloat in the Gulf of Palermo. He had suffered *incaprettamento*, 'goat-choking', a classic Mafia killing in which hands and feet are bound with a single rope which is then tied in a noose around the neck. The more the victim struggles, the tighter the noose becomes until he strangles himself. He had been thrown in the sea and the gases from his body had created a balloon effect.

The *Cosa Nuovo* may have been building a Mafia archipelago stretching from the Atlantic to the South China Sea, but some old and tried rackets were once again finding favour. One of these was dog-fighting, which until the 1980s was confined mainly to Sicily and Naples but which, in any event, is having something of a resurgence worldwide. In Italy, it is now regarded as a $500 million business. Dogs from about 40 different breeds, with pit-bulls and Rottweilers particularly favoured, are bred and trained in time-honoured fashion, often by women and children, for money, prestige or a combination of both.

The dogs are placed in a sack and then beaten before the neck is opened and they are allowed to see a cat or small dog. In this way they may get a taste for blood. They are then given sparring partners, either older dogs who have survived the fights – which can last from a quarter of an hour to two hours until one is exhausted, dead or too badly injured to continue – or stolen pets. To strengthen their neck muscles, dogs have to pull weighted sledges towards food and water. Probably around 5,000 dogs die each year in Italian pits. The attraction for the Mafia is the betting, which can range from $250 up to $5,000 per person per match.

The new and improved Mafia seemed also to be taking a

lesson from their Indian counterparts and putting the bite on Italian film-makers for protection money from films made in Sicily. For example, when Giuseppe Tornatore shot the film *Malena* in 1999 it was beset by difficulties. A fire badly damaged scenery and the production company's offices were broken into and disks with the names of extras were stolen. In another incident costumes were damaged. Tactics used with other film-makers who have not paid up include infiltrating an extra who, as soon as the director calls 'Shoot', starts screaming or falls over.

Another example of the new Mafia's work was the scam, this time run by the Naples Camorra, which came to an end in July 2000. Thirty people were arrested in a series of raids which uncovered a network of Mafia-controlled companies making fake butter using chemicals, oils and laboratory-produced substances. In the past three years over 16,000 tons had been churned out in the Naples area and sold to firms in Belgium, France and Italy for use in baking and ice-cream. In one raid in Belgium the butter seized had no trace at all of milk or dairy products. Of the £30 million grossed, half had come from EU subsidies.

The Mafia has also turned its attention to Pompeii, where a number of opportunities have arisen in recent years. One-third of the site remains unexcavated for fears that once the treasures have surfaced they will be swiftly removed by thieves, aided and abetted by some corrupt staff members. The principal predators are the Camorra, who meanwhile collect protection money from the stallholders and restaurants.

Across the water in previously unsullied Capri, local

councillor Antonio Cioffi, of the right-wing Forza Italia party, was arrested over a £20,000 bribe he had received for awarding the Camorra a contract to build an aqueduct. When the police raided his home they found not only the money but an airline ticket for Cuba along with the telephone numbers of Cuban hostesses from escort agencies. He was given a two-year suspended sentence in return for becoming a *pentito*. Others on the island were not so fortunate. Giuseppe Marchione, fearful of being implicated, slashed his wrists in the lavatory of his home. His son broke down the door and rushed him to hospital. However, the father was steadfast: he jumped to his death from a hospital window.

There are few pies too small for organised crime to take a slice. Another scandal broke out, this time in Sicily when in October 2000 30 people were arrested at the University of Messina on the north-east coast of the island. A long-running scam had started – it was thought back in 1984 – with small bribes to the teaching staff to pass examinations, but it soon developed into a business. A bachelor's degree in economics and commerce cost £2,500, while the price for a medical degree was £3,100. It was not long before organised crime in the form of the 'Ndrangheta organisation in the person of Giuseppe Morabito turned up. The staff then underwent tutorials on how to move into the drug market, either by investing or selling drugs stolen from the university's laboratories.

Things began to get out of hand in 1998 when Professor Amadeo Bottari was murdered to stop him going to the authorities. Then in 1999 his colleague, Giuseppe Longo, was arrested. His ring had basically bribed professors, controlled the administration of the university and managed the local drug trade.

This was not the Mafia's only recent foray into culture, however. In March 2001, 14 people were arrested and accused of helping it to take over Italy's National Institute for Ancient Drama and, in the process, turning a £163,000 annual profit into an £11 million loss. The takeover by the Urso-Bottaro family was modest at first, with the car-park, usher service and the renting of cushions coming under their control in 1994. It was not long before they had complete financial control, rigging contracts and falsifying the books. Amongst those arrested was the Institute's artistic director.

It is always helpful to the defence to find a sympathetic juror in the court, but the Sicilian authorities took the view that having the mistress of a man on the run from a sentence of life imprisonment was too much. The 34-year-old woman, only identified as Sonia, had been the mistress of Francesco Nangano, convicted of murder and extortion. It was thought that six trials of alleged *mafiosi* would have to be abandoned. Sonia was reported to be mystified about the fuss.

There was both good and bad news for the Riina family in 2001. In Palermo, Giovanni Riina, now 24, was sentenced to life imprisonment for four murders he had committed when he was 18. Previously convicted of Mafia association, he had been in prison since 1997. Two of Riina jnr's victims were husband and wife, shot in front of their young children.

The good news for his father came earlier in the year when in March he was allowed out of solitary confinement for a limited time each day, having been in isolation since his arrest in January 1993. Even that pleasure must have tasted bitter when, in the November, he was given another life sentence to add to the 15 he was already serving. Riina, who had survived many years on the run, was convicted on the evidence of the Mafia supergrass Tomasso Buschetta who, against the odds, survived in a United States witness protection programme until his death from natural causes in April 2000. Bernardo Provenzano picked up another life sentence in his absence.

What was clear, however, was that giant strides were being taken by the wives and daughters of senior imprisoned Mafia figures in their efforts to continue the good work. Perhaps this followed the publication of a study, *Come Cambio la Mafia*, which set out the causes of the decline of the traditional Don. It was a blueprint for organised crime worldwide.

Problems were caused by peer pressure at school. Drugs were being taken rather than made and sold. Society was offering role models which were at odds with traditional Mafia thinking. There were fears that the old heroes were dying, being arrested, collaborating with the state and becoming afraid. They were, however, trying to ensure the continuity of their lineage and breed sons who would carry on the vendettas against their betrayers and enemies. In 1998 two Mafia wives gave birth even though their husbands had been in high-security prisons for four years. Foresight, said their lawyer; they had the sense to have sperm frozen in advance. A blind eye to conjugal visits, said the less techno-minded.[6]

Whatever the reasons, the women were definitely coming into their own. The trend was set in Naples, where the authorities discovered numbers of women taking a pro-active part in the running of Camorra clans and activities – the reason being that they were the wives, sisters or mistresses of clan bosses in prison. Therefore, at least temporarily, they had risen above their more customary status as messengers and dealers. Elvira Palumbo, for example, was recorded in the Poggioreale prison visiting-room giving advice to her lover, Enzo Romano, on who to use in a contract shooting. Romano had been the lieutenant of the clan boss Ciro Mariano of Naples' Spanish Quarter. Her lover's original choice did not, Elvira said, have the necessary ability to perform the job adequately.

Another, Rosetta Cutolo (known as 'Ice Eyes'), was arrested in a villa in Ottaviano near Naples on 8 February 1993 after what was said to be 13 years on the run. By then she was 57 and headed the 5,000-strong New Camorra Organisation, said to have been founded by her brother Raffaele who had been in custody for most of the previous 20 years.

---

[6] In fact, fathering children in prison is now not all that uncommon. In December 2000 two former guards in the federal prison at Allenwood in White Deer, Pennsylvania, were charged with bribery. They had, it was alleged, accepted thousands of dollars to smuggle out sperm to impregnate the inmates' girlfriends. One of the men had fallen foul of an undercover agent, posing as a girlfriend, who had paid him $5,000 to smuggle out a cryogenic sperm kit. It was reported that five New York mobsters had fathered children in this way. The investigation began in 1998 when Kevin Granato, a convicted Colombian hitman, was seen showing off a young child to whom he referred as 'my son'. Granato had been in prison for the previous 10 years.

Rather as the Corleonesi had carried out a war in the early 1980s so, it was alleged, Rosetta Cutolo waged war against Raffaele's enemies including the deputy chief of the Poggioreale prison. Guided by her brother from behind bars, she ran the family business until she disappeared from official view in 1980, and was believed to have spent long periods in Brazil and Venezuela and, for a time, in a convent. According to the authorities, this did not stop her trying to organise a daring prison escape for her brother – she had sworn not to marry but to devote herself to his interests – in 1978 when a wall was dynamited. She was also alleged to have ordered the contract killing of Vincenzo Casillo in a car-bomb attack which also crippled his second-in-command, Mario Cuomo, because she thought they were both traitors. Later, Cuomo was killed in his wheelchair.

According to reports Rosetta burst into tears when she was arrested in 1993, saying she had been contemplating giving herself up but feared assassination. She wanted, she said, to have an isolated cell.[7] She was released in 1999.

Although claiming to be a simple housewife, also in a position of power would seem to be Carmela Giulana whose husband Luigi, along with two of her children, were under house arrest. Luigi Giulana had come to power in the war with the Cutolo family, but later served a 10-year sentence. The family lives in a heavily fortified house in Naples.

Sicily's first *mafiosa* was Maria Felippa Messina, arrested in 1995 after conversations regarding the murder of members

---

[7] Clare Pedrick, 'Italian police arrest woman said to head Naples Mafia' in *Washington Post*, 9 February 1993.

of a rival clan were overheard. She had taken over in 1993 when her husband was jailed for murder. Another *mafiosa* arrested by the Sicilian police was Concetta Scalisi in April 1999. On the run for the previous six months and accused of organising the killing of three members of her clan who were thought to have gone astray, she had taken over the reins on the death of her brother who was killed in 1987, five years after the death of their father, Antonio. In theory two nephews were the heads of the family, but it was she who ran things, certainly after their arrest in 1997. The family had interests in loan-sharking, drugs, extortion and that fine source of revenue, the control of public works contracts. She was arrested as she was having breakfast at a friend's flat near Catania. Immediately, she smashed a glass and slashed her wrists and stomach in the hope of being sent to hospital rather than prison. In this she was unsuccessful.

As they stepped out of the shadows of their husbands and brothers, the women became targets in their own right. In 1997 Santa Puglisi was killed at the age of 23 when visiting her husband's tomb. Rivals feared that she had taken over her dead husband's business. Later her nephew Stefano was also killed, probably because he had witnessed his aunt's execution.

By the middle of December 2000 the police had rounded up a good proportion of a Mafia family from the rather shabby Graziella quarter of Syracuse, said to be run by women. In all, 12 women were arrested along with 12 men, but curiously the latter were regarded as being subservient to the women members of the clan. The Urso sisters, Maria, Irene and Mirella, all in their early to mid-thirties, were considered as having key roles along with Rosetta Di Luciano and Floridia Urso, the 37-year-old ex-wife of Sebastiano Urso. Another in the round-up was a second Irene, Sebastiano's mistress.[8]

---

[8] For an account of the growing influence of women *mafiosi*, see Clare Longrigg, *Mafia Women*.

14

Greece, Turkey and Albania

It came as something of a surprise when 49-year-old London-born Susan Aris (her Anglicised name) was blown up in her white BMW in Athens on 3 May 2001. At first it was thought that she had fallen victim to another attack by the November 17 terrorist group which had killed the British military attaché, Brigadier Stephen Saunders, in June the previous year. Further investigation showed that it was very likely that the accidental killer of Mrs Aristides (her Greek name) was her Rottweiler dog.

As a young girl she emigrated to Australia with her mother, but at the age of 18 had married Spyros Aristides, settling in Voula, south of Athens. They had two children and she worked in the half-world of her husband's night-clubs which were protected by the local Mob. For some time all went well. Then in the middle 1990s, after moving into the more lucrative strip-club business, Aristides disappeared with a Russian entertainer. There were conflicting stories that he had been killed or had simply returned to Australia. One son was badly injured in a car accident and the other, Paul, who at one time had a night-club, left for the United States.

It was then that she became involved with Vassillis Grigorakos, alleged to be one of the kings of the drug trade, and his son Niko. Grigorakos had been a protector of Spyros Aristides and had taken an interest in Paul's night-club venture. Now Susan became the godmother of one of Niko's children. Unfortunately, Vassillis Grigorakos was at the time involved in a losing battle for control of the city, and after surviving a bomb attack he was shot to death in the summer of 2000. The police now closed in on the family and Theodoros Grigorakos, another of his sons, was convicted of racketeering along with a number of cousins and uncles. Nor did their rivals fare much better, losing men to both the police and bullets.

It seems that Aris now became a hitwoman, albeit not a completely successful one. On 3 May 2001 she had packed her ears with cotton-wool and was on her way to bomb a rival gang member's home. It is possible that the dog knocked the remote control panel which she had in a separate bag; in any event the nail-bomb exploded and killed both Susan Aris and the dog. At her home the police found the kitchen had become a bomb factory with grenades, masonry nails and switches. It was thought that the bomb which killed her had only been intended as a warning to the rival family.

'Maybe she was bored and wanted some excitement in her life,' said an acquaintance.[1]

Unsurprisingly Italian racketeers are powerful in Greece, with contraband cigarettes producing something in the region of $50 million annually. Russian gangs are involved in the flesh trade.

By the end of the last millennium there were fears of serious problems in Cyprus arising from what was described as a Pontian problem. Russian Greeks, who were given Greek passports after the collapse of the Soviet bloc, had created a ghetto, settling in blocks of flats along the two main streets in the middle of Paphos, the tourist resort at the west of the island. About 7,000 Pontians had arrived since 1993, and were alleged to have been responsible for a variety of crimes including organised prostitution and maintaining links with their colleagues in the former Soviet Union. There were reported clashes between rival gangs of Ukranian and Georgian Pontians, though the police claimed the problems were more cultural than criminal.

Before the arrival of the Pontians there had been a relatively low-level war between rival gangs in Limassol and Larnaca, with car bombings the principal sport. During the 1990s, there was also a period of what was described as score-settling between Russian and Eastern European gangsters, but in time this had cooled down. Cyprus has become not only a smuggling but also a money-laundering haven. Of some 24,000 companies registered, only 1,100 have a physical presence.

As for the Turkish mafia, in June 1999 that notorious

---

[1] *Evening Standard*, 4 May 2001; *Sunday Times*, 6 May 2001.

Turkish Underworld figure Alattin Cakici, a former leader of the Grey Wolf organisation, wanted to go home. He claimed he had been the subject of racist and inhuman treatment while held in prison in Marseilles, fighting extradition for the alleged murder of his wife, Ugur, and attacks on a bank director and journalist. He had been arrested on a false diplomatic passport supplied to him by a member of the Turkish Intelligence Service.

Cakici had graduated from the Ulkucus, or Grey Wolves, the youth wing of the Turkish Nationalist party. Throughout the 1970s, a time of serious political unrest, the group had been active in universities, schools and in the police force. During this time they had been responsible for the deaths of a number of left-wing activists, their most startling coup being the 1978 massacre of seven left-wing students in Behcilevler. In time the Grey Wolves, like so many quasi-political groups, had moved into organised crime. One of their then leaders, Abdullah Catli, had been killed in a 1996 car crash with a police chief and a leading Turkish politician.

Now Cakici – who claimed that, 'In France, the so-called cradle of civilisation and human rights, I have been imprisoned in a Nazi camp for 10 months' – was said to be Turkey's most wanted man and also to have been involved in drug running and extortion.

He probably did well to avoid the trouble which broke out in the Bayrampasa prison in Istanbul in September that year, when a member of his group was shot dead in his cell. Fighting which then broke out left a further six people dead. All in all it was not a good year for the Cakicis. In August the patriarch of the family, Dundar Kilic, described as a leading member of the Underworld, died; then in early December Alattin Cakici's brother, Gencay, was shot. Worse, the attack had been arranged or possibly even carried out by Alattin's 16-year-old stepson, Ismail Onur Ozbizerdik, in revenge for the murder of his own mother who had been shot dead while on holiday at a winter resort in 1995.

Ozbizerdik's driver surrendered at the police station, saying that it was he who had shot Gencay Cakici and a woman with him on the boy's orders. However, eye-witnesses said that the shooter fitted the description of Ozbizerdik himself.

By December 2000 Alattin Cakici's wish had been granted and he had been extradited on the basis that he would not face the death penalty. Now he was back in Istanbul, where during the following year the charges against him mounted. First, he stood trial for establishing and leading a criminal gang and ordering the assassination of a journalist. For this crop he received 8 years. He would soon face charges of inciting murder. Prosecutors were asking for a sentence in the nature of 300 years.[2]

Another riot in Bayrampasa in June 2000 left two prisoners dead and a further eight, including two warders, injured. It was thought to be a revenge attack for the previous year's violence.

Reports of Cakici's rivals, Nuri and Vedat Ergin, leaders

---

[2] The longest sentence ever imposed seems to have been in Madrid when, on 19 April 1967, Crespo Ruiz received 6,616 years, six months and one day for the sale of non-existent flats on the Costa Brava. His sentences were made to run consecutively.

of the so-called Karagumruk Gang, were that they were living in something approaching luxury in Usak prison near Izmir in Western Turkey, which they effectively controlled. A Turkish newspaper *Hurriyet* published a photograph showing their gang members on a canopy-bed surrounded by carpets, while talking on their cellular telephones. The photograph had been discovered in the prison at the beginning of November after five inmates were killed in riots when Nuri Ergin's supporters took 28 hostages, tortured eight prisoners and threw three out of the windows. Five inmates had died in the rioting which, said Ergin, awaiting trial for kidnapping and extortion, began after members of a rival gang entered the prison to try to kill him. *Milliyet*, another paper, showed a picture of the brothers, together with Nuri Ergin's son, posing behind the governor's desk. Another riot alleged to have been led by the Karagumruk Gang took place in the Usak prison in November 2000. This time one dead inmate and four injured prisoners were thrown from a prison window after 26 prison officials and guards had been held hostage; the injured prisoners died in hospital. The trial for kidnapping and other offences began in April 2001 but was adjourned because of what was described as 'deficiencies in the file'.[3]

Along with other Balkan gangs, the Albanian gangs came on to the international scene following the break-up of Yugoslavia, and by the middle of the 1990s they had established themselves as some of the most serious players. Initially working for others, at the end of the 1980s they moved into

[3] *Turkish Daily News*, 20 November 2000; 7 April 2001.

independent operations establishing a network across Western Europe as well as in the United States. They are regarded as mirroring the original Sicilian Mafia with a high code of *besa*, or honour, based, some historians claim, on the Canun of Lek Dukagjeni.[4] Their activities, naturally, include all the time-tested and more modern crimes – kidnapping, burglary and contract killing as well as drug, arms and refugee-smuggling.

A number of reasons have been suggested to account for the dramatic rise in the scale of Albanian criminal activity.[5] The first is the breaking in 1986 in the United States of the so-called Pizza Connection whereby the Sicilian Mafia delivered heroin to a chain of pizzerias – franchised through Louis Piancone from Carato Bari – to American crime families such as the Gambinos.[6] The subsequent trial may not have seriously damaged the Mafia's overall position, but it dealt something of a blow to the Tri-State area's income. It was followed by the assassination of Paul Castellano and even further disruption. Before then the Albanians in organised crime had been employed at a relatively low level by the Gambino, Genovese and Lucchese Families. Now they had the opportunity to buy into the pizzerias, which were often converted into Albanian social clubs.

In Albania itself, by early 1992 prostitution, drug running

<hr/>

[4] Albanians fled to Southern Italy in the fifteenth century after the Ottoman invasion. See Misha Glenny, *The Rebirth of History*.
[5] Gus Xhudo, 'Men of Purpose: The Growth of Albanian Criminal Activity' in *Transnational Organised Crime*, Spring 1996.
[6] For an account of the establishment and breaking of the Pizza Connection see Claire Sterling, *Octopus*; Shana Alexander, *The Pizza Connection* and Joe Pistone, *Donnie Brasco*.

and extortion were crimes of choice, with the population observing a self-imposed dusk curfew. The solution of putting more police on the streets was not the hoped-for remedy. What were once individual acts had become co-ordinated, and it became easier to buy former state-owned businesses, often financed through land frauds, many of which were then used as fronts. Travel also became easier and so links were established between émigrés in Paris and New York.[7] In the first week of March 1991 over 20,000 refugees arrived at Italian ports, with more than 4,000 being allowed to remain. In the middle 1990s it was estimated that between 600 and 1,500 Albanians were entering Greece daily and, as with any immigrant community, many were criminals before they entered their new country. Many of those who were not subsequently turned to petty crime and became mules and enforcers for the Sicilian Mafia. At a higher level the breakdown of the communist regime left the old state intelligence agency, the Sigurimi, out of power. As with the Stasi from former East Germany who assisted the Russian *mafiya*, members now without pensions offered their services to organised crime groups. By the middle 1990s there was also some evidence that some members of the Albanian Intelligence Service, either independently or acting on orders, were involved in arms and drug trafficking.[8]

Gus Xhudo suggests that the outbreak of civil war in Yugoslavia disrupted some 60 per cent of Western Europe's

[7] See Gus Xhudo, *ibid.*; Liam McDowall, 'Albania learns the art of wrecking' in *New Statesman and Society*, 13 December 1991.
[8] Marko Milivijevic, 'The Drug Threat from Eastern Europe' in *Jane's Intelligence Review*, November 1995.

heroin trade. The country had been part of the conduit for many years; Albanian criminals were keen to offer an alternative route for drugs, arms, medical supplies, foodstuffs and other goods, as well as refugees for the latter parts of the journey. The route would be through Turkey to Greece and then to Macedonia where Albanian gangs with cheaply purchased trucks – sold to them by the government sometimes for as little as £125 – would move the drugs or other commodities through Elbasan to the ports of Vlor, Durrs and Sarande. There they would be loaded on to small craft which would then sail for the Dalmatian coast or across to Italy with the consent and co-operation of the *Sacra Corona Unita* of Puglia.[9] By 1995 it was suggested that Albanian criminal elements controlled 70 per cent of all the illegal heroin trade to Germany and Switzerland, where there are a number of ethnic communities able to launder the profits.

As to the composition of the Balkan gangs, many insist on their members being of Albanian origin at the very least, others concentrating on the family and close friends as another hedge against betrayal. Blood relatives would attain higher positions than those in the family through marriage.

---

[9] Dating from the early 1980s, the *Sacra Corona Unita* (or the New Holy United Crown from Puglia) has seen the opportunity to divert smuggling from its traditional home in Naples to its own eastern coast which faces Albania. Like the Mafia but unlike the Camorra, it has a pyramidic structure with soldiers, enforcers, *trequartino* as middle-management and *crimine* at the top. Along with the smuggling has come the distribution of heroin as well as alien-smuggling. As a result enforced labour and prostitution for the refugees who have to work off their fares has followed. While adapting the kidnapping of the 'Ndrangheta and the drug-running of the Sicilians it has, however, operated in a way foreign to the more traditional organised crime fronts in Italy. In many ways it has set up what appears to be a direct challenge to the state. See James Morton, *Gangland International*, Chapter 35.

Again the role model is the traditional Sicilian Mafia with oaths of allegiance and secrecy. As with other communities Kosovars smuggled to European cities such as Brussels were in the same trap as the Chinese taken to America. They were now in the power of their benefactors. With false papers they were at risk of betrayal, and in any event the papers had to be paid for. Many were ideal targets for recruitment.

Despite the adherence to the Mafia structure it seems that the Albanian gangs have borrowed from the Russian *mafiya* in adopting a looser chain of command devolving through a Leadership Council which may (but does not necessarily) issue instructions to area units. Each family will be headed by an executive committee, or *bajrack*, of which the head, or *krye*, will appoint the underbosses, or *kryetar*, who in many cases will be blood relatives. The *bajrack* will provide the resources, possibly including training for day-to-day operations such as drug smuggling or high-class burglaries which can be organised on quasi-military lines and may be assisted by the ex-members of the Sigurimi.

One such operation took place in America in 1994–5 when four men – Ardjan Bujaj, Sokol Nukaj, Nikolin Prelaj and Engjell Rezaj – were finally arrested in August 1995 and charged with a series of burglaries of cash machines, supermarkets and restaurants. They were found to be in possession of high-quality surveillance equipment and cutting tools. There was also some suspicion that the Albanian gangs were now sophisticated enough to establish counter-surveillance networks, and that when the authorities called off their own surveillance the various enterprises went ahead.[10] There was some evidence that the Albanians carried out robberies on two levels. The first, or so called A-team, was highly sophisticated, with metal drill rods capable of reaching temperatures between 9,000 and 10,000 degrees F; while the B-teams, armed with sledgehammers and crowbars, operated on a more physical level. To an Albanian used to severe punishment if caught by the Serbs, an American prison with a bed and food represented something more in the way of a holiday camp. The position is mirrored in Europe. In 1999 there were nearly 2,000 Albanians held in prisons in Switzerland charged with a variety of offences including smuggling guns and narcotics, but the code of silence has to a great extent remained in place.[11] In early 1996 two regional leaders, Mirsan Pjitrovic and Vucksan 'Ranko' Mickovic, were arrested. Now it was hoped that this might be the beginning of the destruction of the gangs but, Hydra-like, if anything they improved their position, operating from the cafés and clubs such as the Besa and Gurra in the Bronx.[12]

What was clear was that the Albanians had linked up with the New York Families at an early stage in their development. Abedin 'Dino' Kolbiba went to America in the early 1960s and, settling in the Fordham district of the Bronx, worked with the Gambinos. He also worked as a contract killer for

[10] See the *New Jersey Star Ledger*, 16 August 1995. For a full account of the composition and organisation of Albanian gangs in New York see Gus Xhudo, *ibid.*
[11] See e.g. *Chicago Tribune*, 3 November 1993; *Washington Post*, 4 January 1995; *Philadelphia Inquirer*, 23 March 1995. See also Mark Galeotti, 'Albania Organised Crime: Europe's latest threat' in *Cross Border Control*, 1999.
[12] *New York Post*, 11 January 1996.

the Lucchese Family before branching out on his own working
for Albanian families in the Tri-State area who wished their
vendettas to be settled. In time he took on other Albanians,
such as Anton Spaci – now in his late forties or early fifties
– who had also settled in the Bronx. The pair worked in partnership until the mid-1990s when Kolbiba went to Greece
and disappeared. Anton Spaci disappeared when either his
son or nephew, Andreja Spaci, fled to Italy. He had hidden
in Milan for two years before being arrested and extradited.

Another of the Albanian mafia operating in New York was
Zef Mustafa, also known as Mustafa Korca – another who
began his rise to power as a chauffeur, this time for Frank
Locascio, the Gambino *consiglieri*.[13] He had also worked as
a hitman and it was thought that Locascio had helped Mustafa
to avoid a conviction following a murder in the Bronx in
1985. From that relatively humble beginning he was believed
to have graduated to an investment fraud in Pocradec in
1993, and was also thought to have a considerable interest
in the drugs trade in Boston, Chicago and Detroit where there
are substantial Albanian communities.

In Europe, notables have included Basri Bajrami who, after
two years on the loose, was arrested in 1995 for his part in
the kidnapping of the former Belgian Prime Minister Paul
Boeyenants. He had escaped from St Jules prison and gone
to Macedonia where, quite openly, he started a series of

[13] On 23 June 1992 Locascio was sentenced, along with John Gotti snr, to life
without the possibility of parole, and ordered to pay $250,000 costs after being
found guilty of a variety of charges including involvement in the murder of the
former Gambino Don, Paul Castellano. At the sentencing Locascio maintained
that the only crime he had committed was that of being a friend of Gotti.

boutiques which the authorities thought were fronts for a drug-smuggling operation. He was also suspected of being a member of the Patrick Haemers gang which had specialised in the robbery of armoured cars.

There have been growing signs that the Albanian gangs are working on an international basis and one man who has been regarded as a Godfather is Daut Kadriovski, who has allegedly organised a drug ring in the Albanian communities in Sydney and Brisbane. He was wanted by the police after attempting to obtain a new passport from the Australian Embassy in Athens. Thought to have serious contacts in the United States and reputed to have links with the Grey Wolves, he vanished into Germany. Gashi Agim, arrested for dealing in drugs by the Italian police, had houses in Hungary and Germany as well as a perfume boutique in London. Prince Dobros (also known as Dobroshi), arrested in Prague in March 1999, was alleged to be the leader of a drug-running operation in Norway.

After working initially in Italy with the *Sacra Corona Unita* and *La Rosa*, the Albanian gangs have established links with other gangs such as the Calabrian 'Ndrangheta.[14] They have also branched out on their own and been engaged in a battle for control of the trade in drugs and prostitution in Milan,

---

[14] The word probably comes from the Greek *andragathia* meaning manliness. The 'Ndrangheta in the late nineteenth century was also known as the Fibbia. As with the Sicilians, at first it was a rural organisation before moving into towns and the lucrative building industry. For decades the 'Ndrangheta had been regarded as little more than a local operation in Calabria, specifically in the area around the Aspromonte mountains, dealing principally in extortion. When the 'Ndrangheta branched out it was into more general protection and the sale of heroin from Turkey. From there it has been a short step into legitimate business and the development of the Calabrian coast.

continues

eliminating local Arab and North African interests. In Germany, where the heroin trade has provided the framework for a multi-ethnic criminal empire and 75 per cent of the drug trade is in Albanian hands, most of the street-level distribution work is undertaken by ethnic Croats. In recent years in Madrid, the Albanian gangs operated an international robbery ring which was estimated to have carried out over 1,000 break-ins.

By 2001 Albanian gangs were regarded as having established a very substantial base in London, where it was estimated that they controlled nearly 80 per cent of the vice trade in a more or less amiable relationship with the traditional East End and Maltese enterprises. It was thought that up to 14,000 Albanian women were in the vice trade throughout Europe, principally in Italy and Greece but also in France, Britain, the Netherlands and Austria. Some working in Soho are said to have to pay up to £420 per night to their owners. Failure to do so results in a beating.[15]

Serbian gangs who once made their livelihood smuggling were reported to be turning their hands to kidnapping. In April 2001 Miroslav Miskovic, reputedly one of former Yugoslavia's wealthiest businessmen, was kidnapped. He was

---

On 19 March 1995 Guiseppe Ninta, aged 82, under house arrest after his conviction and kingpin of the 'Ndrangheta, was shot to death at his home in Binaco. He had been due in the Italian criminal appeal court the next day and his death was thought to be to prevent him making a statement. It was he who had transformed the 'Ndrangheta into a drug-trafficking operation with worldwide activities. Today the most powerful of the 'Ndrangheta is the Siderno Group headed by Cosimo Commisso (known as 'The Quail') with branches in Canada, the United States and Australia. For a fuller account see James Morton, *Gangland International*, Chapter 35.

[15] *The Economist*, 23 June 2001.

taken from his own vehicle near his company's headquarters in New Belgrade and put in the boot of the gangsters' Audi before being driven away and held for 24 hours until a ransom, said to be £1.65 million, was paid.

15

The Red *Mafiya*

Just how powerful and dangerous have the Russian gangs become in Britain and the world? As always the answer will depend upon the viewpoint of whoever is giving the answer. Not that dangerous, considered the NCIS report of 2000, while admitting that there were 18 crime gangs principally from Lithuania, Russia and the Ukraine running counterfeiting, money laundering, prostitution and people-smuggling rackets in this country. They were also involved in selling sex on the Internet, excise fraud and drug smuggling and were thought to be making £70 million from cigarette smuggling alone. Nevertheless NCIS thought that the position of the so-called Red *mafiya* has been exaggerated and that, compared with Turkish and Colombian organised gangs, the players were still struggling to make their presence felt in mainstream crime.[1] Others abroad, for example in the United States, might feel that the Red *mafiya* has more than made its presence felt and that its members are rapidly climbing the table of successful criminal enterprises.

In the United Kingdom, *Project Dynamo* was set up in July 1999 as a monitor to provide a critical and balanced assessment of the threat. It found that shipments of heroin, cocaine and cannabis, intended for the Western European market, were beginning to come through the post-Soviet republics. One route was from Dushanbe to the Russian port of Astrakan on the Caspian Sea, a three-day train journey. In 2001 120 kg was found under the floorboards, but more often the smugglers are the mules used by any major organisation and the drugs are hidden in the usual orifices. Once again the payment, given the risk of arrest or death, is pitiful – £140.[2]

The report was keen to avoid lumping numerous small groups and even individuals into an amorphous Red *mafiya* or assuming that post-Soviet nationals were masterminds instead of the minor players the evidence suggested. In America, Russian-speaking organised crime is the politically correct, preferred way of describing them.[3] However, this was not a view shared by journalists who saw some of the Russian groups – and this was another lumping together of which the report specifically disapproved – as providing the fastest

[1] *Project Dynamo, Organised Crime from the Post-Soviet Republics: Impact on and Threat to the UK*, 2000.
[2] There is also a story that camels addicted to opium could be trained to cross the desert alone until they reached their next fix, finally arriving at slaughter-houses in Iran. Guy Dinmore, 'General declares war on desert traffickers' in *Financial Times*, 10 January 2000.
[3] P. J. O'Rourke, 'The Godfather Decade; organised crime in Russia during the 1990s'.

growing criminal organisations currently in the game.

Times are changing. Journalists in the Western world have generally been regarded as immune from attacks by organised crime gangs, but this is certainly no longer the case in Russia where politics and organised crime are entwined. In the autumn of 2000, after the headless body of Georgi Gongadze was discovered, high political figures were accused of involvement. On 7 July 2001 President Kuchma of the Ukraine came under renewed pressure to resign after Ihor Aleksandrov, a journalist who had crusaded against corruption and organised crime, was attacked and killed in his offices in the eastern town of Slavyansk. An attempt in 1998 to silence Aleksandrov by imprisoning him for two years and banning him from working for a further five had failed when he took his case to the European Court of Human Rights in Strasbourg.[4]

The killing and harassment of journalists in the former Eastern bloc countries has continued apace. In early June 2001 Milan Pantic, who had been investigating industrial crime for his paper *Vecernje Novosti*, was attacked as he went into his block of flats in Jagodina, central Serbia. He died from his injuries. By the middle of August there had been no arrests, and threats are being made to reporters weekly if not daily. Although the threats are reported to the police, journalists believe that little investigation is being made into the complaints from people seen as traditional enemies of the police. Again in June, the police stood back when protesters beat journalists at rallies held by the Socialist and

[4] *The Times*, 9 July 2001.

Serbian Radical parties protesting against Slobodan Milosevic's extradition to The Hague.

Nor, it seems, were the authorities in Western countries always that much more protective. Robert Friedman, who wrote investigative articles for *Village Voice, Details* and *New York*, was threatened by the Russian organised crime figure Vyacheslav Ivankov, known because of his looks as 'Yaponchick', 'The Little Japanese'.

At the time of the threats to Friedman, Ivankov was supposedly out of harm's way serving a sentence for extortion in a federal penitentiary. In fact he had continued to control his empire from his cell in the Ray Brook Correctional Institution in upstate New York from which he sent Friedman a handwritten death threat including his cell block unit and prison number. Friedman reported the matter to the FBI and agreed to give evidence against Ivankov, but no proceedings were ever brought. It was not until after Friedman approached the New York-based Committee to Protect Journalists and an article appeared in the *Metro* section of the *New York Times* that Ivankov was transferred to the maximum security prison at Lewisburg, Pennsylvania.[5] Friedman told the *New York Times*, 'I want him to know that I am behind this punishment. And I want him to know that he cannot threaten the American press the same way the *mafiya* does in Russia.' Ivankov is due for release in 2005.

Ivankov's was one of the great success stories of the immigrant criminal. When he came to New York in 1992, he was given $1.5 million in cash by friends on his arrival at Kennedy

[5] Blaine Harden, *New York Times*, 5 March 1999.

airport. From then he took over control of organised crime in Brighton Beach in Brooklyn and developed it into a business of which he could be proud, linking with members of New York's Five Families. On 29 January 1997 he was sentenced to 9 years and 7 months for extortion.[6] By this time the growth of Russian-speaking crime in America had been exponential. There were thought to be 30 distinct criminal cartels located principally in New York, Miami and on the West Coast, with smaller syndicates in traditional organised crime cities such as Boston and Philadelphia as well as Denver and Baltimore.

One of the problems for the authorities in America has been that, as with the Yardies here, for some time the *mafiya* was dismissed as less worthy of attention compared with more established crime groups. By the time its force was realised it had become ineradicable. Another serious problem is that the middle and upper echelons of the *mafiya* are not dumb; they are often highly educated, speaking up to five languages.

The Red *mafiya* is regarded as having one of the best developed structures in the world. There is a boss, or *pakhan*, and four cells with a brigadier intermediary. One cell heads direction, another security, and there are two working cells.

Certainly in the intelligence category comes Semion Mogilevich, known as 'The Brainy Don' and holding an economics degree from Lvov University. He was originally involved with the Solntzevo crime gang, and one version of

---

[6] For an account of Ivankov's early upwardly mobile career see William Kleinknecht, *The New Ethnic Mobs*.

his early days is that he sold fish in a street market in Kiev. He served two sentences in Russia, both for illegal currency dealing. The first, for which he received a short term, he describes as buying a gold coin for a girlfriend. The second, 'helping a friend', attracted 4 years. Much of his early money was made swindling Jews emigrating to Israel; he would buy their assets and then fail to pay them in the hard currency he had promised. He was also said to have bought weapons from Russian generals when they left East Germany, which he then sold on to Syria, Iraq and Iran.

In 1990 Mogilevich went to Israel, but a year later he moved his operations to Budapest where his situation was described by a senior American official as, 'There is nothing he does not control there from prostitution up – extortion, drugs, everything.' In 1994 British intelligence had him 'organising all the blackmailers from the former Soviet republics through the Czech republic. This includes deals involving weapons, including heavy weapons, drugs and precious stones.' The operations also extended to Vienna, Prague, Moscow, the United Kingdom and Israel. His group is regarded as having one of the best structures and is still involved in prostitution, laundering, drugs, precious stones and now nuclear material. It also has links to the Camorra.

He was alleged – despite his consistent denials – to have been involved in a company named Benex through which, along with its brother companies, millions of dollars was laundered. The scheme involved a London lawyer, Lucy Edwards, born Ludmilla Pritsker in St Petersburg, and her husband, Peter Berlin.

The scheme was designed by Russian bankers and operated

through a chain of banks and companies in Nauru and America. Nauru is an eight-square-mile area of coral covered with guano which has provided fertilisation for Australian and New Zealand farms for nearly a century. Now, with the deposits likely to dry up, so to speak, the island metamorphosed into one of the world's best banking systems for organised crime. In 1998 it was estimated that £49 billion was laundered through Nauruan banks. The process, which could be undertaken on the Internet, cost around £25,000. The island billed itself as offering improved social status as the owner of a bank, at the same time protecting one's assets from inquiring wives and ex-wives. At a recent count there were 400 offshore banks, one for every 25 Nauruans.[7]

Two established banks, Sobinbank and MDM, opened Depozitarno-Kiliringovy Bank (DKB) and Flamingo Bank, put funds through these new banks and then into a shell in Nauru called Sinex, founded by Aleksey Volkov who worked with Edwards and Berlin. Sinex opened a correspondence account with the Commerical Bank of San Francisco and payments were made to a series of shell firms including Benex International which in turn opened accounts with the Bank of New York. Much of the operation was conducted by Edwards and Berlin from offices at 118–121 Queens' Boulevard in Queens, and in three years £7 million was cleaned. It might still be in business had not some of the $300,000 ransom for Russian businessman Edouard Olevinsky gone through the Benex pipeline and attracted FBI attention. Benex, which was registered in New Jersey, had filed no accounts and indeed had no telephone, but had done business with YBM Magnex, controlled by Mogilevich.

In February 2000 Edwards and Berlin pleaded guilty to money-laundering charges in New York and they began co-operating with the FBI. Questioned about Benex, Mogilevich was reasonably jovial when he was interviewed in Russia. The jowly man, weighing around 300 lbs, going bald and with a faint moustache, would tell everything. 'The size of my underwear in 1972, what I had for breakfast, how much time it takes for my lovemaking.' He was the most popular man in the world, he said, and as such he had a deal to offer Proctor and Gamble, one which would make everyone vast amounts of money. He would manufacture a soap. 'The name will be "Mogilevich".' There was to be an advertising slogan: 'Mogilevich guarantees that this washes everything from underwear to money.'

As for Sergei Mikhailov, acquitted in Geneva in 1999 and said, along with Victor Averine, to be in control of the powerful Vienna-based Solentsevskaya, named after a Moscow suburb – well, he had met him in the sauna and at one time they had apartments in the same building but nothing closer. As for allegations that he had a contract out on Friedman, nothing could be further from the truth.[8] In the autumn of 1999 the FBI asked the Hungarian authorities to charge Mogilevich with money laundering.

With much gangland crime, who did what to whom can be fairly easily established, if not proved, but the labyrinthine

---

[8] See Raymond Bonner, 'Umbrage' in *New York Times*, 11 September 1999. For the Benex laundering scheme see 'The Billion Dollar Shack' in *New York Times Magazine*, 10 December 2000.

machinations of the Cyrillic Underworld make explanations open to question. What is without doubt is that in January 2000, Tomas Vida, alleged chief of the south Slovak Underworld, was killed in Dunajska Streda, south-west Slovakia, shot in his car. What was also not in dispute was that he had been an associate of Mogilevich, maintaining close ties with him. Vida had been absent from the Slovakia scene, returning only after the massacre in March 1999 in the Fontana Bar (also on Dunajska Streda) when, in something resembling the St Valentine's Day Massacre, ten people including the then heads of the south Slovak Underworld, the Papay Gang, were killed. One explanation on offer is that Vida's killing was a reprisal for that shooting.

At the beginning of the decade one-time Mogilevich henchman Monya Elson was also having serious, if not fatal, troubles. He was awaiting trial in New York on a variety of charges including murder, having been extradited from Italy. When in 1978 he arrived in America via transit camps in Vienna and Rome he started as a petty thief, moved into armed robbery (mainly of Russian–Jewish jewellers) and then into murder. It was he and a friend who had been arrested, dressed as Hassidic Jews, travelling on the Day of Atonement. He admitted he had killed approximately 100 people. He is being defended by James LaPietra, the partner of the old-time lawyer for the mob, Aronne.

Other outstanding Russian-organised crime groups are thought to be Mazurska, said to be headed by Anatoly Roxmann (also known as Anton) and by Alexei Petrov. The group is based, as the name suggests, in Poland, specialising in kidnapping, stolen art, drugs, robbery, stolen vehicles and money laundering. In Cologne there is Taiwanchik headed by Alimzhan Tochtachunov known as an associate of Otar Kvantrishvili who was killed in 1994. Tochtachunov (nicknamed 'Taiwanchik') was extradited to Israel in June 1995. There is also the Brandwain/Nayfeld group based in Antwerp with sections in Vilnius, Berlin, St Petersburg and Moscow as well as in Israel and New York.

Initially the Russians teamed up with the Italian Mafia in America. 'It's a marriage of convenience,' says FBI agent Raymond Kerr. 'They don't have the contacts to do some of the things. So they need the Italians. The Italians need them for the overseas access.'[9] Now, not only have the Russians made gigantic strides in integrating with the Five Families, they have also linked with the Colombian cartels. Meetings have been held in the Caribbean with Colombian cartels in Aruba, St Vincent and Antigua over sales of AK-47s in exchange for cocaine and the delivery of a helicopter and a submarine. By 1997 nine offshore banks had been established in Antigua by Russian companies.[10] Perhaps even more important are the bases in and ties with Israel.

Although there are signs that in Germany the traditional organised crime groups in Berlin are now seriously involved with the Red *mafiya*, it is perhaps in America that it has made the biggest progress in the West. There, in the middle of 2001, the FBI was predicting that since the dissolution of the Soviet Union, criminal organisations had stolen more than one million credit account numbers and were poised

---

[9] Pat Milton, 'Russian mob seeks money and power in America and overseas' in *Associated Press*, 18 June 2000.

[10] See 'Russian–Colombian crime groups join hands' in *Dawn*, 1 October 1997.

to trigger a cybercrime explosion. While the United States was seen as a major target, nearly every major city world-wide with the possible exception of those in Africa had an Eastern bloc criminal organisation operating in it. What is staggering is the progress that the *mafiya* has made in such a short period of time.

16

Israel

Only in the last two decades have indigenous Israeli gangs reached out across their own borders and become an international force. Much of this has been due to the break-up of the former Soviet Union and the thousands of Georgian Jews who emigrated to Israel from the mid-1970s. However, over the years there have been plenty of indigenous gangs. Throughout the 1990s they fought each other over control of night-clubs and illegal gambling, with the Alperon brothers from Givat Shmuel, regarded as the 'Israeli Corleones', in pole position but also suffering the most casualties. Of course, this may be because there were so many of them.

In 1992 Nissim Alperon and a number of his family including a sister, Shoshana, were put on trial for planning to murder a wide selection of dignitaries including a judge, a rabbi, Assistant District Attorneys and senior police officers. Such evidence as there was against them – a disgruntled night-club owner whose business they had absorbed – was discredited and they were duly acquitted, but over the years Nissim was convicted of counterfeiting, illegal gambling, extortion, arson and drug dealing.

Throughout the years they have battled, mostly successfully, with others such as Pinhas Buhbut, killed in September 1999 in his hospital bed in Tel Hashomet, *à la Bullitt*, the Steve McQueen film, by two gunmen masquerading as police officers. The real police denied that they had been warned of the impending attack. This time the Alperons were not to blame. It was thought Buhbut had fallen foul of the Pardess Katz mob who were alleged to have been involved in seven murders over the previous two years.

Back on 24 February 1993 Iraqi immigrant Yehezkel Aslan, now a Tel Aviv kingpin, was shot outside a restaurant. Years after his death, despite the fact that he had introduced heroin on to the streets, he was still a local hero in the poor Hatikva Quarter where he grew up. People spoke of how he would help others in trouble and of his 'big heart'. Like so many other criminals he financed the local football team.[1]

---

[1] Other folk heroes of Israeli crime of the period included Ronni Lebowitz who, before his arrest in October 1990, carried out a string of one-man bank raids, shooting into the ceiling to gain attention. He was released in 1998. Another was Yitzhak Drori, 'The Brain', who in 1985 robbed the safe-deposit boxes at a branch of the Bank Hapoalim in Jerusalem. In prison he wrote *Hamoah* (*The Brain*); the book is still in print. The murderer Herzl Avitan is yet another. He gained a good deal of public support when he escaped from prison in 1990. Sara, the wife of his partner Smhaya Angel, was acquitted of the 1984 double murder charge. She was then jailed for attempting to smuggle a gun into prison for her husband. He had, she claimed, demanded this small service as the price of a divorce. She also sold drugs, because (she said) she had to pay her lawyer on the gun charge. She later had a newspaper column and appeared on numerous television programmes whose presenters wanted to know, but were never told, whether she was actually guilty.

Aslan served only one three-year sentence in Israel after having been found with a single gram of cocaine in his room at the Ramada Continental. He had been arrested for car theft at the age of 16, and in 1971 was arrested at the airport in New York when he was found trying to import 50 kg of hashish. He served a one-year sentence and was returned to Israel where, included in the List of 11 – a catalogue of the country's leading crime figures – he was suspected of being involved in the killing of his own brother, Shimon. His reputation was sealed when in 1982 he was shot eight times outside his home and survived.

However, he did not survive the attack in 1993. He had just left a Tel Aviv fish restaurant with a young woman and was sitting in his black Mercedes when he was shot through the window. Ze'ev Rosenstein was held over the killing for 30 days before being released. Whoever killed Aslan, the reason was thought to be a battle for control over drugs and gambling. In turn Rosenstein was shot on 2 June 1996, but was able to drive himself to hospital.

On 2 November 1996 Gad 'Shatz' Plum, newly returned from serving 13 years of a sentence for the murder of an Israeli drug dealer in Germany, was killed outside a bar in the same city. His companion at the time, Yehuda Hazan, was shot in the leg and survived. Plum who, on his return from abroad, maintained he had given up his life of crime, was regarded as a singularly dangerous person. He was feared, said the police, by other criminals. Hazan was alleged to manage the Allenby Street territory on behalf of Plum, dealing in drugs and looking after small casinos.

In August 1994 Amnon Bahashian, alleged to be the leader

of the Israeli mafia in the United States, was killed outside a Tel Aviv steakhouse. In the early hours of 14 January 1995, 42-year-old Moshe 'Mussa' Alperon lost his left leg in an attack after a bomb was planted under the seat of his purple Honda Civic which had been parked outside his girlfriend's home in Ramat Gan. Mussa had earlier served a year for his part in an attempt to print counterfeit dollars. According to reports he remained conscious and upright – sending away his 23-year-old girlfriend, Keren Mazar, who had survived unscathed, so that she would not see the damage done to him. He then asked for a blanket to cover him before photographers arrived. He was taken to Tel Aviv's Ichilov Hospital, where Godfather-like the Alperon brothers hired private guards to patrol the hospital corridor.

Unlike his brother Nissim, Mussa Alperon had endeavoured to clean drug dealers from his neighbourhood. Shortly before the attack he had become a partner in a gaming club fronted by a snooker club in a red light district near the Ramat Gan diamond exchange, where brothels are advertised as health centres.

Then three days later Illa Aslan took a call on his mobile telephone at his snooker club in what had been the city's central bus station. He left the club and was shot in the neck. Within hours he was on the same hospital corridor as Alperon. Illa Aslan was regarded as more involved in illegal gambling. In August 1993 he had been arrested and released over the attempted murder of a bouncer in a slot-machine arcade in Jaffa.

Now the soft-spoken and highly intelligent Ya'acov became the leader of the Alperon family. It was after this that Plum was shot. Ya'acov had run a debt collection agency, Alperon Management and Business Promotion, and, said the *Jerusalem Post*, 'Usually the name Alperon was sufficient for debtors to empty their children's savings accounts.' One defaulter, a midget, was allegedly tied upside down to a tree and beaten. As a *procès d'impressment* with clients, Ya'acov was reputed to clean his fingernails with an axe which he kept in his office along with a baseball bat.

Over the years in Israeli organised crime, bombings have been a favourite method of attack and on 14 May 2000 Ya'acov Alperon was injured, followed up by an attack on brother Nissim on 18 September 2000. Ya'acov was injured when a stolen scooter blew up outside his house.[2] Nissim, who had served an 8½-year sentence for drugs and assault charges, had been released early from prison despite objections from the state that he had twice been given early release and had gone straight back into crime. There were indications that he was yet another mobster who continued to organise matters from his cell. Now the Parole Board released him on the grounds that his children should get to know their father.

Ya'acov Alperon also had his troubles with the Parole Board. Beginning in 1975, he had served five prison terms by 1996. Now he was again applying for parole, despite having received it on three of the first four occasions and violated the conditions each time. Nevertheless, in July 1996 the Parole Board decided once more that he should have

---

[2] See *Jerusalem Post*, 2 June 1996, 14 May 2000, and Heidi J. Gleit, 'Who are the Alperon Brothers?' 18 September 2000. The Aslans and Alperons were not, of course, the only warring factions. Gangs in Bnei Brak, the Pardess Gang and the Ramat Amidar Gang had been involved in a long-running dispute in which 'honour killings' were exchanged.

parole, citing the Prison Board's report that he had behaved well and their view that he had a sincere desire to rehabilitate himself. This did not exactly correspond with the police views that he was another who had also continued to run things from his cell. The parole decision was overturned.

On 31 October 1999 Zalman Alperon was arrested on charges of blackmailing a family of property developers. This was the second time in two years. On the previous occasion he was suspected of a series of arson attacks on properties belonging to Benjamin and Shalom Sharbat. The allegation was that Alperon had been working for Eli Ziv, owner of the Mireli construction company, who was in dispute with the Sharbats over alleged late payments which had caused him financial problems. The brothers' cars had been set on fire, a prefab caravan had been set alight and a hand grenade had been thrown into one of their houses. Alperon was released when one of the defendants – Moshe Shriki, who had been expected to turn state's evidence – declined to testify against him. A year later Shriki had reconsidered things.

Zalman Alperon had led an energetic life. He had been accused of involvement in blackmail in 1994 and of drug trafficking a year later. With the imprisonment of his brothers he had taken over the running of the business. That year he had climbed a 30-metre crane in Kfar Shalem and threatened to jump because two of his brothers, then in prison, had not been allowed to visit their father in hospital.

On the plus side, however, there were reports that Shoshana Alperon, along with Mussa's wife and a former debt collector for the brothers, Yossi Hayman, had become 'religiously observant'.

In its way the infiltration of Russian crime into Israel has been a microcosm of all development of organised crime. The main injection in Israeli crime came with the thousands of Jews who emigrated to Israel from the Republic of Georgia (Gruzia) in the mid-1970s. Within a decade the police discovered that the Georgian Jews included what were seen as special types of criminals engaged in 'big and serious' crimes, practising the trades they had learned in Georgia. They specialised in the use of violence and controlled the carting and haulage services at air- and seaports. This resulted in the large-scale theft of passengers' luggage as well as major thefts from cargo planes and ships at anchor.[3] There were now sophisticated frauds involving religious objects, and extensive counterfeiting of driving licences and professional degrees to go with the longer-term operations.

Between 1988 and 1995 some 650,000 immigrants arrived from Russia and other states of the former Soviet Union. Apart from the burgeoning needs for forged papers, the influx brought with it shoplifting, fraud and money-lending. The forgeries were false Jewish status documents which ensured preferential treatment, and professional status documents as well as driving licences. There was an increase in controlled prostitution, with the old Russian criminal gangs forging ties with locals, and also an increase in the rise of the number of Russian youth gangs.

[3] What happened in London in the 1960s was being replicated. It is an example of how crime can flourish if countries do not learn from other people's lessons. London's Heathrow airport was known as Thiefrow because of the major pillage of cargo and luggage. See James Morton, *Gangland* 2, pp. 32–3.

The Knesset Commission of Inquiry into Trafficking in Women found that there were between 2–3,000 prostitutes operating in the Tel Aviv area. A high proportion were women smuggled across the Egyptian border by the Bedouin. In August 2000 a woman told the court that she had been kidnapped, raped and robbed and forced into working as a prostitute by a Beersheba gang who had then sold her. Apparently she and another woman had agreed a double date in a Tel Aviv hotel. Two men had arrived to say the meeting was off and as the women walked through the car-park from the hotel entrance, they were seized and bundled into a vehicle. She had then been sold to a brothel. Auctions of women, some of whom were smuggled in from the Ukraine, were quite common. In Ramle, Boris Yasser went on trial accused of selling women to a brothel at $3,000 a time.[4] Usually the women were kept in prison by the authorities for up to six months before they gave evidence against their pimps and kidnappers, as a reward for which they were deported.

Professor Amir, of the Hebrew University of Jerusalem, now sees three types of Russian immigrant organised crime. The first is what he calls 'natural crime' with individuals and the Russian *mafiya* joining together in forgery, illegal gambling, thefts, drug dealing, money-lending and extortion. The second is 'local international crime' in which the local Russian groups have their operations overseen by groups in Moscow, St Petersburg and cities in the Caucasian and Muslim republics as well as by such internationalists as Mogilevich. Now organised prostitution in the form of brothels and

[4] *Jerusalem Post*, 2 August 2000.

massage parlours comes into play, with part of the revenue being returned to Russia. 'Soldiers' are recruited to oversee operations and assist in the infiltration of local illegal casinos whose current owners can be persuaded to enter into partnerships. There is also a scam defrauding innocent immigrants of their 'absorption package' which, at between $50,000 and $70,000, is well worth diverting.

The third 'high' type of Russian immigrants is the white-collar end with concentration in investments on a large scale in Israeli banks, property and other businesses with mainly illegal but some legitimate money. There are few controls on bank investment, and it is estimated that between $2.5 and $4 billion has been invested in banks and $600 million in real estate. Anti-money-laundering laws have been lax in the extreme, and although legislation is now in place it remains to be seen if and how it will be enforced.[5]

Nor is it wholly a question of importation. Israeli gangs have developed the traffic in Ecstasy, and in April 2001 Jacob Orgad pleaded guilty to being responsible for the sale and distribution of millions of pills in the United States from 1998. Orgad, who had become a naturalised United States citizen but maintained links with Israeli organised crime, was the largest Ecstasy trafficker to be convicted in the States.

---

[5] I am very grateful to Professor Menachem Amir for allowing me to use his paper 'Organized Crime in Israel' (August 1996), The Hebrew University of Israel. See also A. Buchner, *Organized Criminality in Israel: A Police Internal Committee Report* (1986), Israeli Police.

AMERICA

17

New York

As with England, much of the interest in American organised crime lies in what the old folks have been doing to integrate with or fight off the younger generations and the police. As might be expected, some have been more successful than others. By the end of the last millennium some Families had suffered serious predations; some were thriving; and the deaths of some of them, such as the Californian and Detroit Mafia, had been widely reported. In Boston the old Winter Hill Mob was locked in combat with the courts, and in Philadelphia there were signs that Skinny Joe Merlino, the present Don of the Family, was under siege from rivals and defectors. In New York the Gambinos, with the loss of Gotti *père et fils*, were particularly under siege.

By the spring of 2001 the father, John J. Gotti, was said to be suffering from advanced stages of cancer and had been confined to a wheelchair in the federal prison in Springfield, Mo. A cancerous growth had been removed from his neck in 1998. Throughout the summer there was an ongoing interest in his health. Would the Church allow a mass? After all, the family of Paul Castellano – gunned down on Gotti's orders outside Sparks' Steakhouse at 210 E 46 in 1985 – had been refused a public funeral mass. There was also something of a local sport of Gotti relative-spotting, with Springfield locals noticing that his family had been visiting Bijan's, Gilardi's Ristorante and Mudhouse, whose owner admitted to being a *Sopranos* fan.

The intention was that Gotti would be buried in St John's Cemetery in Middle Village, Queens, near the graves of his father and his son Frank, killed 20 years ago at the age of 12 when he was struck by a neighbour's car. Shortly afterwards the neighbour had disappeared.

Obsequies have long been of intense interest for Mafia watchers. Decisions about public masses for mobsters are taken on a case-by-case basis. Frank DeCicco, a Gotti underboss who had helped arrange Castellano's murder, was denied a funeral mass when he died in a car bombing outside a Brooklyn social club four months after Castellano's death. Prior to that, Carmine Galante was also refused a mass after being shot in a Brooklyn restaurant. However, a priest recited prayers at a funeral home service for Galante.[1]

---

[1] For those interested in the final resting places of *mafiosi*, Lucky Luciano has a marble crypt in St John's Cemetery. Near him lies his great rival Frank Costello. Others buried there include Joseph Colombo. In St John's Cloisters, a five-storey mausoleum, can be found Carlo Gambino, the founder of the Family, and one of the Family's underbosses, Aniello Dellacroce, Carmino Galante, Vito Genovese and the founder of the city's Five Families, Salvatore Maranzano.

Not so fortunate was Gotti's son-in-law, Carmine Agnello, who was caught in another police sting. This time he had tried to take over a rival scrapyard through extortion and arson. As part of his plea agreement to federal racketeering and tax fraud charges in August 2001, he agreed to serve 9 years and was ordered to forfeit $10 million. 'Mr Agnello has accepted responsibility for his crimes,' said his lawyer, the noted Benjamin Brafman. 'He is eager to complete his sentence and be reunited with his children.' Really he did not have very much alternative. When he turned up at the Stadium Scrapyard to demand crushed cars at a bargain rate, he was unaware that the yard was police-operated. Unsurprisingly the police did not co-operate and a John Roberts, armed with gas-filled bottles, was despatched with instructions to burn the place. It was not a happy period for Mr Agnello who, despite having a perfectly good business, had demanded that as the husband of Gotti's second daughter, the writer Victoria Gotti, he should be made a member of the Gambino Family. Roberts tried to fire the scrapyard three times and failed on each occasion before he was arrested and rolled over.

Mr Gotti had not regarded his son-in-law too highly. He was overheard on tapes describing him as an imbecile and asking rhetorically, 'Does he get in the back of a car and think someone has stolen the steering wheel?' Victoria Gotti was believed to have issued a divorce petition.

Before his incarceration in the harsh conditions at Springfield, Mr Gotti was thought to have been conducting his family's business from his cell. It was certainly a possibility. Salvatore Avellino of the Lucchese Family had been doing just that for the four years from 1993 while in the federal prison at Schuykill, Pa. In March 2001 he entered into a plea bargain to conspiracy to commit extortion and accepted a further 5 years on top of the 10½ he was serving. He also agreed to forfeit $6.5 million of the $20 million made from the sale of his carting firms in 1997, and to pay a further $1 million in back taxes.

When visited by his son Michael, he had given instructions on how to threaten and deal with rivals and carters who did not wish to do business with the Avellino-controlled garbage station in Holtsville. In 1989 two carters who had refused to co-operate, Robert Kubecka and Donald Barstow, had been killed in their East Northport office. The gunman was alleged to be Frank Federico, who was still wanted and thought now to be in Italy. Avellino had pleaded guilty to murder-conspiracy in 1993, and five years later Kubecka's and Barstow's families received $10.8 million in a settlement from the state. Both Avellino's son Michael and his son-in-law pleaded guilty to the 2001 racketeering charges.

In what was regarded as possibly one of the last trials of its kind, down went 70-year-old Anthony Spero, one-time acting boss of the Bonanno Family, convicted in April 2001 of ordering three murders. Spero was regarded as being near the top of the list of the old-timers who had not been dealt with. Like Marlon Brando in *On the Waterfront*, he bred racing pigeons and preferred cooking on his Staten Island home barbecue to the tonier restaurants favoured by John Gotti snr and other Dons of recent years.

The victims were an eclectic group. One was a petty thief who had burgled the home of Spero's daughter, another was an over-ambitious member of his own crew who was plotting against him. The third was Louis J. Tuzzio, who had helped a fugitive mobster avoid arrest during a manhunt for the killer of Everett Hatcher, a federal drug agent shot in 1989.

Of the three, Tuzzio had been shot eight times in the head when his body was found slumped across the wheel of his Chevrolet Camaro in Borough Park in January 1990. The thief was Vincent Bickelman from Bath Beach, Brooklyn, who had made off with a necklace that spelled the name of Spero's daughter, Jill, in diamonds. He had been killed on 15 September 1991, allegedly by one of Spero's lieutenants, Paul Gulino of the so-called Bath Avenue Crew.[2] According to the indictment, membership of the Crew required numerals to be tattooed on an ankle to demonstrate unity and solidarity. Gulino – the victim of his own success – was murdered in his kitchen in Bensonhurst in July 1993, allegedly on Spero's orders.

The evidence against Spero could perhaps be described as thin and was seemingly the common mixture of informers and turncoats. There were no wire-taps and of the ten co-operating witnesses only three who were called said they had heard him speaking about the killings. The investigation against him had begun in the middle 1990s when the Drug Enforcement Agency was investigating a crack-cocaine ring

---

[2] Burgling houses of or near high-placed *mafiosi* has always been a dangerous sport. On 15 May 1962 the bodies of two young burglars, Billy McCarthy and Jimmy Miraglia, were found in the boot of a car in south-west Chicago. They had been tortured and their throats cut. Their crime had been to rob and shoot three businessmen in Elmwood Park, a smart Chicago suburb favoured by top figures in organised crime and consequently a no-go area for the rank and file.

in Bath Beach where, at the time, Spero was running a social club. By the end of the investigation a number of gangland turncoats had come forward and the social club had become the offices of a pet-cremation home. Gerald Shargel, Spero's lawyer, commented, 'It makes me think that in cases like this the presumption of innocence is just words on a page.' James Walden of the United States' Attorney's Office was predictably happier with the result: 'The jury saw the realistic fact. It's difficult to catch people on wire-taps when the whole organization is designed to avoid just that – Mr Spero, in particular, being a master.'[3]

It was almost as though the authorities felt they had broken the first ranks of the Five Families and were now concentrating on the second division. Singled out for interest were the DeCavalcante Family, not always regarded as major league but nevertheless with close ties to the Gambinos. The founder-father was Sam DeCavalcante, known as 'Sam the Plumber', who had been early on the field in the more sophisticated labour racketeering schemes.

As it was, the imprisoned boss Giovanni 'John' Riggi – in jail since 1989 – had a hard time obtaining permission to attend his wife's funeral. Sarah Riggi, who had been suffering from cancer for years, died two days before Christmas. No, said the federal prosecutors. Yet another to be running the family from his cell, he had ordered two hits on gangsters. Riggi went to the courts and a compromise was worked out by District Judge Michael Mukasey in Manhattan. Marshals were to take him to the funeral home on Boxing Day for a 15-minute visit.

[3] *New York Times*, 4 June 2001.

There had been a concerted attack on them, with three indictments since December 1999. Now, in the spring of 2001, came the fourth and possibly the most crippling. The first attack had been on Vincent Palermo, described as the Family's acting boss who, along with 30 others, was arrested after the Family had been infiltrated. The next year it appears that Palermo himself was co-operating and a dozen more Family and friends were indicted.

In the September came the unhappy news for the Family that someone who was certainly co-operating was Sean J. Richard, Riggi's daughter Sara's husband. He had been an unknown labourer until in 1996 he was taken to see Riggi in jail where he met the great man in khaki prison overalls and he had 'seemed Presidential'. It was marriage to Sara after that, and Richard threw himself wholeheartedly into the Family business.

However, things and he came apart in the summer of 2000 when a raid was made on one of Richard's companies and he rolled over. He was another to speak disparagingly of his peers. Emmanuel Riggi, John's brother, was 'so fat he breaks chairs at every family function'. His father-in-law ought to 'thank me for feeding his useless kids' who 'you wouldn't take miniature golfing'. For his part he said, 'If I drop dead tomorrow, I lived, baby, I lived,' which is rather like writing your own epitaph. As for the DeCavalcantes themselves, they were reported to have regarded themselves as the models for the Sopranos.

Richard had become very much the part. He ate oysters and steaks in the Oak Room and visited the Paradise Club near the Empire State Building where he lavished money on Lola, a stripper with whom he eventually went into hiding.

Now, quite apart from labour racketeering, the Family had moved into stock fraud which featured in the third set of indictments. The latest collection was simply more of the same. There were now two additional murder counts, along with a further eight murder conspiracies facing the family. It seemed that the DeCavalcante Family had been taking lessons from the Colombians who were said, when pressed, to kill even the family goldfish. Francesco Polizzi was accused of ordering the murder of the wife and children of a suspected informer.

Also accused was Philip Abramo, regarded as one of the Mob's best scholars in security frauds. He had served a one-year sentence in Fort Dix following a plea to tax evasion in 1996. Now he, Riggi and Frank Scarabino (known as 'Franky the Beast') were accused of the murder of Frederick Weiss, undertaken on behalf of John Gotti who feared that Weiss was co-operating in an investigation into the Gambino ties to a waste corporation.

All this, said Barry W. Mawn, an assistant director of the FBI's New York office, showed that the DeCavalcantes were far from being the loveable rogues of Hollywood.[4]

Certainly no loveable rogue, in July 2001 Jersey City former boxer Elvis Irizarry acquired a full house of convictions including

---

[4] Sam DeCavalcante was one of those who warned Angelo Bruno about the weakening of his Philadelphia Family by the induction of Anthony 'Tony Bananas' Caponigro. Caponigro may well have been behind the assassination of Bruno on 21 April 1980. He was shot to death and his naked body discovered near the Staten Island expressway on 17 April that year. See *New York Times*, 18 April 2001.

five counts of murder, robbery, arson, conspiracy to distribute cocaine, extortion and illegal use of a firearm. Described as a murder machine for hire, the former freelance hitman faced a total of five life sentences plus 240 years in prison.

One of the long-time favourite manoeuvres of the authorities has been the cat-and-mouse trick. The defendant serves almost all his or her sentence and then, just when there is a sight of the prison gate, is re-arrested. It was worked twice in a week in January 2001. First, Joseph Watts was arrested shortly before he completed his 6-year sentence for conspiracy.

Watts was regarded as one of John Gotti's most loyal soldiers and a man said to have been the back-up shooter for the killing of former Gambino Don, Paul Castellano. His 1996 trial had been eagerly awaited. Defending him was the celebrated F. Lee Bailey who would be pitched against the one-time underboss of the Gambinos, Sammy 'The Bull' Gravano, who was busy informing on all his former colleagues. In fact the prospect of an entertaining trial collapsed when Watts pleaded guilty, and so both sides avoided serious problems; for the prosecution the possible discrediting of their star witness Gravano, and for Watts a seriously long sentence.

Now Watts, who had also been a liaison officer between the Gambinos and the formidable Irish gang, the Westies,[5] faced an indictment containing counts alleging murder and money laundering.

---

[5] Until the gentrification of the district, the Westies had run the notorious Hell's Kitchen area of New York located between 8th and 9th Avenues.

The cat-and-mouse manoeuvre was successfully repeated the next week when Alphonse Persico (known as 'Allie Boy'), said to be the acting boss of the Colombo Family, thinking that he could enjoy the sunlight following a 15-month sentence, was charged with racketeering and money laundering. There was also the suggestion of a conspiracy to murder a member of the Colombo Family, William Cutolo, who disappeared in 1989. Along with Persico were John J. Deross and nine others. All pleaded not guilty.

It was thought that the main witness would be the former Miami night-club owner, Chris Paciello, which would explain his plea of guilty the previous October to part of the indictment against Anthony Spero to committing a robbery-murder on behalf of the Bonanno Family.

Paciello had been a media favourite, a friend of Madonna and other celebrities, and had dated supermodels. His real name was Ludwigsen and his brother George was part of the Bonanno Family's Bath Avenue Crew. In August 2000 George was charged in a 34-count federal racketeering indictment detailing a seven-year-long bank robbery operation running from New York to Florida. According to prosecutors, Paciello had begun his career with the Family in the early 1990s when he worked for Spero. The crew specialised in armed robberies on banks, shops, pet stores and homes.

So far as could be seen from court papers, the only time Paciello met Persico had been in 1999 while Persico was on bail in a gun case in Florida. They had lunched together in Shooters, a fashionable Miami Beach restaurant said to be a favourite with holidaying New York crime figures. In the event, possibly the threat of Paciello's evidence was enough.

At the end of December 2001 Persico decided to plead guilty to federal racketeering and money laundering. If the plea was accepted he would be sentenced to 13 years and be fined $1 million. The bones of the case were that, in 1996, a search of Persico's briefcase had produced records of loan-shark transactions, and three years later a search of his flat on Fifth Avenue had found another set of records including a list of members of Cutolo's crew. Persico had moved with the technological times as well. A computer disk hidden in a stove contained more financial information about the missing Cutolo.[6]

Paciello's name also surfaced in the investigation into the killing of Konstantinos 'Gus' Boulis. On 6 February 2001, Boulis, founder of fast food Miami Subs – once owner of the casino boat *SunCruz* which sailed the Intracoastal Waterway, and another 10 floating casinos – was shot and killed by a team of hitmen. Driving home he was the victim of a traditional hit, boxed in between two cars and shot three times. Having managed to drive a few blocks before crashing, he died in hospital within the hour and rewards of $100,000 for information were posted. Despite dozens of calls, not everyone was convinced these would lead to arrests. 'They'll never catch 'em. Couple of guys come in from Detroit. Then boom, they're gone,' said a *SunCruz* passenger.

For some time Boulis had been embroiled with the federal and state authorities, as well as being involved in a long-running and bitter divorce suit. He was also the driving force

[6] *New York Times*, 21 December 2001.

behind Florida's maritime casinos which had sailed into endless controversies. Casinos are banned in Florida, but once the boats are outside the three-mile limit the tables are opened and the machines unlocked.

In September 2000 Boulis had sold his fleet to a group of Washington-based entrepreneurs who paid $23 million cash and a further $124 million in promissory notes and acquired loans. Boulis had managed to conceal that he was under a legal obligation to sell his fleet until four days before his death. He was also under a court order restraining him from going within 500 feet of any property owned by SunCruz Casinos. The order had been obtained following a row in Washington in December 2000 between Boulis and Adam Kidan, a 36-year-old disbarred lawyer whose mother, Judy Shemtov, had been murdered at her Richmond Hill home in 1993 by associates of the Bonanno Family; it was on this occasion that Paciello was the driver. Apparently, when she answered the door one of the crew accidentally shot her. It had been hoped that the raid would produce some $200,000.

When, after the takeover, Kidan had told Boulis that all but one of the present staff were to be replaced, Boulis stabbed him with a pen. Kidan told a local newspaper that the attack had brought back unhappy memories of his mother's death.

As for the requirement that he dispose of his fleet, Boulis had been charged with concealing ownership of his boats. Part of the settlement of the action, in which he paid $1.5 million, was that he should dispose of the company and relinquish any interests in maritime gambling. Now there were allegations that he had not been completely frank with Kidan over the transaction.[7]

In fact, when it came to it the prosecution of Watts was not an unqualified success. In August 2001 he was convicted of tax evasion, but the jury could not agree on the question of laundering $2 million acquired by loan-sharking. The tax charge carried a maximum of 5 years and the laundering 45 years. The prosecution indicated that new charges would be filed against Watts.

The Gambinos and the Colombos were not the only members of the Five Families in difficulties. On 16 April 2001, 300 federal agents and police officers arrested 45 men in New York, New Jersey and Miami following the taping of thousands of hours by a Mafia turncoat. The resulting charges ran the gamut of the penal code from the murder of John Borelli, a Gambino Family associate, down to stock fraud and extortion from the owners of delicatessens. The defendants were said to be members and associates of the Genovese Family and included Frank Serpico, a former acting boss but no relation to the celebrated police officer from the Knapp Commission days, and two retired police officers.

The Gambinos had some further problems with the fallout from *Operation Taylormade*, designed to bring down Taylor Breton. From one viewpoint until he was blacklisted in the spring of 2001 he was a high-rolling dice player who could attract credit of up to $1 million in the casinos on Atlantic City's Boardwalk. The Queens County District Attorney

[7] Sean Gardiner, 'Finding Mob's Traces in Murder' in *Newsday*, 15 July 2001; *Miami Herald*, 8 February 2001; *Globe and Mail*, 17 February 2001.

preferred to see him as a bookmaker with Mob connections who ran a $25 million money-laundering operation from New York to Central America. Worse, it was claimed that he was an associate of the Gambino Family, something his lawyer denied on his behalf:

> Once they stick 'associate' on the jacket of someone, it stays there for a lifetime. I don't see anyone slapping a label on anyone for associating with priests and rabbis.[8]

Breton maintained that he ran a legal offshore Internet sports book, but it was claimed that the only bets he took were over the telephone. According to investigators, Breton had been seen in the company of several well-established Mob figures including Anthony 'Bruno' Indelicato, Anthony Megale and Vincent 'Vinnie Gorgeous' Basciano, alleged to be a soldier with the Bonanno Family.

Indelicato had achieved fame nearly a quarter of a century previously when he was one of the men suspected of the killing of the ruthless and dangerous Carmine 'Cigar' Galante who had been pressuring the other New York Families to follow his leadership in his war with the Gambinos. Galante had been planning a trip to Italy and on 12 July 1970 he was paying a farewell visit to Joe and Mary's restaurant in Brooklyn. He had gone out to the patio, where he was killed with his cousin Giuseppe Turano and his bodyguard Leonardo 'Nina' Coppolla. Indelicato, the son of Alphonse 'Sonny Red' Indelicato, survived an attempted hit in 1981

---

[8] Lawyer Kenneth Hense quoted in *The Star-Ledger*, 23 July 2001.

which killed his father, and then went into hiding.[9] Now he was charged with violating his parole granted in 1998.

Megale was alleged to be a made member of the Gambino Family and Basciano, a known gambler, was reputed to be a soldier of the Bonanno Family and a gambling associate of Breton. There is no doubt that Breton was a high-roller. In Atlantic City's 12 casinos he purchased $82.4 million worth of chips in the years 1999 to 2000, earning for himself $5 million in comps (complimentaries). The question to be decided is whether it was all his own money he was playing with or if he was merely laundering. When he was bailed on $150,000, Basciano did the leg-work in rounding up the money and one of the casinos is alleged to have sent a limousine to the Essex County jail so that Breton could travel home in style. Breton had earlier had a slight problem with the casino regulators when in 1994 he was seen eating at Foxwoods, the Indian reservation casino in Connecticut, with John Gotti jnr. He was subsequently banned from that casino, but was still allowed to play in Atlantic City and his name did not go into the notorious Black Book in Las Vegas.

The Gambinos also featured in one of the more entertaining trials that took place during the summer of 2001. Steve Kaplan, alleged to have connections with the Family, and certainly the owner of the very high-profile strip club in Atlanta, the Gold Club, went on trial in that city on 42 charges of racketeering, money laundering, credit card frauds and loan-sharking. Most of the fun was reading about who

---

[9] Alphonse Indelicato led the faction in the Bonanno Family which opposed a takeover by Philip Rastelli. He was killed along with Dominick Trinchera and Philip Giacone on 5 May 1981.

had been there and what took place in what a hundred years earlier, if it was true, would have been called a brothel. Sexual favours were said to have been on offer to a variety of baseball, football and basketball stars. The presence of famous names and faces had drawn the run-of-the-mill punters and boosted Kaplan's profits and, in turn, boosted those of the Gambinos. On conviction he faced a sentence of up to 195 years.

In fact it all fizzled out when, in a plea bargain which did not require him to co-operate with the prosecution, he received a prison term of 16 months, a $5 million fine, was required to surrender his club and make restitution of $300,000 to Delta Airlines and customers. Four of the other six defendants also threw in their towels, pleading to minor counts. Seasoned observers were rather disappointed because the prosecution's case was generally regarded by the *cognoscenti* as a weak one. Judge Willis Hunt apparently thought that as well, saying that the prosecutors had been 'relatively unsuccessful' in linking Kaplan to organised crime. Two defendants, however, including former Atlanta police officer Reginald Burney and an alleged Gambino man, Michael 'Mikey Scars' DiLeonardo, refused to plead.

The new year did not start well for a former Gambino associate. On 3 January 2002, a matter of weeks after being released from a 2–6-year sentence imposed in 1996, Martin Bosshart was found shot once in the back of the head at 155th Avenue, near Lahn Street, itself near the Belt Parkway in Queens. Prior to his arrest he had been running one of the top stolen automobile parts operations in New York, overseeing a warehouse that covered an entire block in Queens.

Profits were shared with a member of the Gambinos. However Bosshart, now in his early thirties, was suspected of being much more than a dealer in stolen spare parts. He had been the subject of a Grand Jury credit card fraud investigation in Fort Lauderdale, and he was wanted for questioning in Florida over three killings in 1995. His list of arrests rather than convictions included robbery, assault, forgery, drug dealing and attempted murder. While his former lawyer expressed surprise at Bosshart's death, the police took a more pragmatic view, saying that the list of people who might want him dead was a lengthy one.[10]

There was no question that the Mafia were behaving merely as colourful rogues after the 11 September 2001 attack on the World Trade Center. In fact they were behaving extremely badly. While souvenir hunters took away pieces of the rubble and shops were looted, the Mafia were alleged to have been involved in stealing 250 tons of scrap from the ruins. Following tip-offs, the police found 75 tons of mainly steel girders in a scrapyard in Deer Park, Long Island, and another 180 tons in a New Jersey yard. A Grand Jury investigation was launched, and now trucks were given an escort on their way to an FBI-controlled dump on Staten Island.

One of the greatest police undercover operations of recent years ended in December 2001 with the arrests of 73 alleged members of the Genovese Family, the oldest and largest of New York's Five Families. Since the conviction of Vincente 'The Chin' Gigante in 1997, the Family had flourished. Gigante had roamed the streets of Greenwich Village,

[10] *New York Times*, 4 January 2002.

unshaven and in a dressing-gown, in an unsuccessful attempt to persuade the court that he was unfit to stand trial, but had received a 12-year sentence. The 73-year-old was yet another alleged to be running the Family business from his cell. Attention then turned to the fortunes of John Gotti jnr and the Gambinos, and as a result the Genoveses prospered.

In April 2001, in raids in New York, Florida and Nevada, 33 reputed Genovese members were part of a round-up of 45 people. Now it emerged that a detective known as Big Frankie had emulated the celebrated infiltration of Donnie Brasco into the Bonanno Family in the 1970s. Big Frankie had gone undercover for two years, posing as the owner of a Virginia haulage firm involved in cigarette smuggling and the disposal of stolen cars.[11] He had been introduced to

---

[11] Detective Joe Pistone was originally part of a relatively minor FBI operation in Tampa in 1975, working on a ring of car and lorry thieves. How the FBI came to be involved is yet another example of how an informant is born. A teenage boy had been arrested on an unrelated charge and his father volunteered, in return for a non-custodial sentence for his son, to blow the whistle on the team which was operating all over the south-eastern United States, stealing bulldozers, Lincolns, Cadillacs and occasionally aeroplanes. In February 1976 the entire ring, consisting of thirty people, was arrested. From there Pistone became part of the Truck and Hijack Squad in New York and it was only a short, but large, step to take to become Donnie Brasco, jewel thief, looking to hang-out with the Mafia.

It took him several months of frequenting a local bar, offering to sell stolen jewellery to the barman, before he was gradually accepted into the milieu. He moved on to a knock-out shop, dealing in stolen clothing, and from there was taken up by rival mobsters. In the end he was more or less selected by Benjamin 'Lefty Guns' Ruggiero, connected to the Bonanno Family, and groomed by him, if not for stardom then at least as high as an outsider could rise in the Mafia.

After he left and testified against leading lights in the organisation, a contract of $500,000 was put on his head. The people to whom he was closest in the organisation were also under threat. Tony Mirra, who had at one time wanted to use him on a more permanent basis, was murdered in New York in 1982, six months before Brasco began to testify. Sonny Black was found, handless, in a hospital body bag in the Mariner's Harbor section of Staten Island, some five months into the trials of other *mafiosi*. See Joe Pistone, *Donnie Brasco*.

Joseph Savarese, a former police officer and associate of the Genovese crew allegedly run by Pasquale 'Patsy' Parrello from his restaurant, Patsy's Rigoletto, in the Italian section of the Bronx. He was next introduced to Parrello's brother, Neil, before meeting the great man himself. Much of Big Frankie's time had been spent in the Rigoletto and he was said to have put on several pounds in weight as a result.

Patsy Parrello was said to have been so security conscious that he regarded the old-fashion pat-down in the lavatory as passé. Instead he carried an electronic device designed to detect hidden tape recorders. But, as time went by and Big Frankie proved such a good earner, his guard slipped. Frankie, a single man unlike Brasco, recorded the insurance frauds, handlings and robberies planned and sometimes executed, which had produced, so the prosecution alleged, $14 million. These included the planned snatch of the $5 million payroll from the *New York Times'* printing plant in Queens. Frankie's cover was so secure that he was invited to birthday parties and weddings and, according to reports, was offered the opportunity to become a made member of the crime Family.

The operation was not without its dangers. Frankie had been obliged to sell his house on Staten Island and also move his parents after running into some of the Genoveses while off-duty.

Now Patsy Parrello was accused of embezzling over $1 million from the benefit funds of the United Brotherhood of Carpenters and Joiners, Locals 11 and 964, and Joseph Savarese was accused with Anthony Cappanelli of planning the *Times* raid. Others faced charges of extortion, bank fraud and embezzlement.

In January 2001 came an echo of the Buddy Boys, an earlier great police corruption scandal of the 77th Precinct in Bedford-Stuyvesant, New York. This time, in the same precinct, Anthony Trotman admitted that he, along with his partner Jamil Jordan, was part of a robbery gang and that he had fed them information from police computers. He had also plotted to kill Detective Michael Paul because by chance Paul had exposed a lie Trotman had told over an arrest. In 1994 he had shot and killed Keith Richardson who, he said, had a BB gun which looked like the real thing. A bystander was also killed, but the shooting was ruled to be justified.

By the end of January Trotman was in court in the witness box, sobbing as he recounted his alternative lifestyle. Giving evidence against an alleged gang member, James Woodard, who was charged with an armed robbery on a jeweller in Garden City, Trotman began crying so hard that he was handed a wad of tissues by the usher. Amongst his admitted crimes was the theft by him and another officer of $200 from a woman they had been sent to escort home to Atlantic Avenue in Brooklyn. A third officer had taken a large sum of money from a crime scene. Now he admitted that in addition to Paul, Federal Prosecutor Dan Alonso had also been in his sights.

Trotman went on to tell the court how he had been committing crimes for nearly the whole ten years of his service. Once he had kidnapped a drug dealer in the Bronx and beaten him senseless; on another occasion he had hand-cuffed another dealer to the steering-wheel of his car and robbed him. A network of informers would tell him when such and such a man was to be carrying a large amount of money,

In March Jamil Jordan was in court pleading guilty to his part in the string of robberies as well as the plot to kill Michael Paul.

Back with the families an era ended on 11 May 2002 when Joseph Bonanno died at the age of 97. He had been living in Arizona in retirement after he had, apparently, twice been kidnapped before he had faced a Grand Jury in 1964. Hailed as the inventor of the double coffin in which a *mafioso* was buried by the funeral director along with a genuine client, he had also written his autobiography, *A Man of Honour*, in which he represented himself as a venture capitalist. He was widely regarded as having been the prototype for Don Corleone in *The Godfather*.[12]

The dapper Don, John Gotti snr, died on 10 June 2002 only a few days after his brother Peter, a retired sanitation worker, was charged with having taken over control of the Gambino family.

The Gotti funeral was suitably impressive. His bronze coffin led a motorcade of over 100 cars pausing at his favourite Bergin Hunt and Fish Club, in Ozone Park, Queens, the scene, when it came to it, of so many troubles for him and others. Victoria Gotti, his widow, was accompanied by his children Angela, Peter and the popular novelist, Victoria who, after describing her father as 'truly the wind beneath my wings', went on to add:

[12] See Joseph Bonanno, *A Man of Honour* and James Morton, *Gangland International*.

His roar will never go unheard, his courage will never be ignored, his legend will live on in the memory of those fortunate enough to have been touched by his kindness and generosity.

Peter Gotti, his brother, spent a good part of the autumn of 2002 in solitary confinement following an allegation that there had been a plot to kill the warden of the Springfield federal prison hospital in Montana, where John died. Eventually his talented lawyer Gerald Shargel obtained an order that he be brought back into the mainstream of the prison, but not before there had been threats to imprison the warden for contempt. Peter Gotti's trial, along with that of six others, on a 67-count indictment, began in January 2003. There was some immediate success when Judge Frederic Block refused to allow Michael D'Urso, a former Genovese crime family associate, to give evidence on Gotti's role, if any, in the family. D'Urso had apparently tired of family life after his cousin, Sabatino Lombardi, was shot and killed and he himself was shot in the head. Gotti's trial ended in tears when on 17 March 2003 he was convicted of racketeering, conspiracy and money laundering. Richard V. Gotti was also convicted as was his son Richard G. Gotti. Defence lawyers said they would appeal.

It is not clear who will now assume control of the Gambino Family. Keeping up the tradition of chauffeurs who rise to boss, Joseph 'Jo Jo' Corozzo, once the late John Gotti's driver, is believed to be the heir apparent to the Gambino Family's top spot. There have been reports that he had been elevated to *consiglieri* behind Peter Gotti and Arnold Squitieri. But

Salvatore 'Sammy the Bull' Gravano, whose co-operation resulted in the conviction of Mafia boss John Gotti – *Associated Press, ABC, INC*

Salvatore Gravano's son Gerard has his handcuffs removed before testifying at a hearing in The Superior Court in Phoenix – *Popperfoto*

Freddie Foreman and Tony Lambrianou, ex-Kray associates turned fashion models — *Popperfoto*

Kenneth Noye returns to England to face trial in the M25 road rage killing — *Popperfoto*

John Palmer, timeshare
fraudster, arrives for his trial
at the Old Bailey – *Popperfoto*

Peter Ryan, English-born former
commissioner for police in NSW
– *Popperfoto*

Crusading Irish journalist
Veronica Guerin –
Popperfoto

Police tape off the area
after she was shot in a
contract killing – *Popperfoto*

Paul Ferris, Scottish crime baron, now returned to prison following breach of his licence – *Topham Picturepoint*

Jesus Gil y Gil displays a local football shirt – it was another club that brought his downfall – *Popperfoto*

People Left Side All is Well	Latin Kings	Vice Lords	P-Stones	Insane Unknowns	P.R. Stones (Puerto Rican)	Other
						Bloods
Makeup	Puerto Rican Mexican Few Whites	Black (Few White)	Black	Puerto Rican (Few Mexicans & White)	Puerto Rican (Some White)	Black
Colors	Black/Gold	Red/Black Yellow/Black	Black Green/Red	White/Black	Black/Orange	Red
Clothing Trends	L.A. Kings/ L.A. Raiders Hat/Jacket	Mirror Dice Playboy Jewelry		Gym Shoes (Black & White Laces)		Red Bandanas
Criminal Activities	Narcotics Drive-Bys Intimidation	Narcotics Prostitution	Narcotics Burglary Theft	Narcotics Drive-Bys	Narcotics Drive-Bys	Narcotics Drive-Bys
Areas of Influence	Chicago/ Suburbs Nation Wide Fed Prison	Chicago/ Suburbs Multi-State	Chicago/ Suburbs	Chicago/ Suburbs Milwaukee	Chicago/ Suburbs	California Nationwide
Symbols/ Graffitti					P STONES	Bloods Pirus C/K

Folks Right Side All is One	Black Gangster Disciple Nation	Maniac Latin Disciples	Satan Disciples	Spanish Cobras	Ambrose	Other
						Crips
Makeup	Black	Mexican Puerto Rican (Some White)	Mexican Puerto Rican (Some White)	Puerto Rican (Few White and Black)	Mexican Puerto Rican (Some White)	Black
Colors	Blue/Black	Black/Blue	Black/Yellow	Green/Black	Lite Blue/Black	Blue
Clothing Trends	NWA Hats	Georgetown Sportswear	NWA Hats		Oakland A's Sportswear	Blue Bandanas B/K Shoes
Criminal Activities	Narcotics Drive-Bys	Narcotics Drive-Bys	Narcotics Drive-Bys	Narcotics Drive-By	Narcotics Drive-Bys	Narcotics Drive-Bys
Areas of Influence	Chicago/ Suburbs Nationwide Fed Prisons	Chicago/ Suburbs Multi-State	Chicago/ Suburbs	Chicago	Chicago/ Suburbs	California Nationwide
Symbol/ Graffitti						Cuz Crips B/K

Chicago street-gang symbols

The Artois Club of the Champs Elysées, scene of the killing of François le Belge – *James Morton*

India's bandit queen, now turned politician, Phoolan Devi, addresses an election campaign meeting – *Popperfoto*

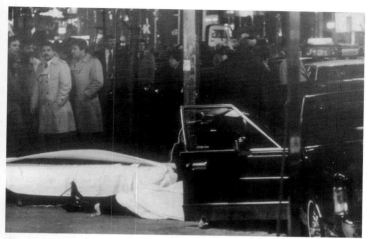

The body of American criminal Paul Castellano, covered with a sheet after he was gunned down – *New York Times Co./Ruby Washington/Hulton Archive*

Vincent 'the Chin' Gigante – feigning insanity in New York – *Frank Spooner Pictures*

Protection for the dapper Don John Gotti Senior, who died 10th June 2002 after a long illness – *Associated Press*

Joey 'Skinny Joey' Merlino leaves the Criminal Justice Center in Philadelphia – *Associated Press, H. Rumph Jr., Stringer*

with Gotti in custody, another brother Gene serving 50 years for heroin trafficking, John Gotti's son John jnr doing a more manageable 6 years and Squitieri on parole and barred from meeting with reputed criminals, *de facto* control may have passed to Corozzo. He may have been a chauffeur but his pedigree is faultless. His elder brother Nicky was tried along with Gotti for the murder of former boss Paul Castellano.

At the beginning of 2003 Joseph Massino, the alleged head of the Bonanno Family, was charged with the murder of Dominick Napolitano, who had unwittingly introduced the undercover agent Joe Pistone, known as Donnie Brasco, into the family, something which had alarming repercussions. Napolitano was found with a gunshot wound in the head. His body, with its hands cut off, was dumped in a swamp on Staten Island. It was thought that possibly another six men were executed after the Brasco fiasco. This, thought the authorities, brought down the last of New York's Mafia chiefs. Time will tell.

There has been something of a change in direction in smuggling by the so-called Red *mafiya*. Caviar has proved just as profitable as cocaine and with far less risk. The methods are the same tried and tested ones, with mules picking up suitcases in Warsaw and then awaiting collection in New York, Miami and Los Angeles. The trade has become profitable because of the United Nations' Convention on the International Trade in Endangered Species (Cities) ban on trade in Beluga meat and caviar. This means no licences are being issued for the legal export of the top grade of Beluga caviar. And where there is a vacuum, organised crime will fill it.

18

Boston

It is perhaps an over-simplification, but organised crime in Boston has always been seen as divided into two camps. The players have been the *Cosa Nostra* which from time to time have sparred, joined and split with their sometime rivals, sometime friends, the Irish Mob from South Boston, which in turn has feuded amongst itself. On the touchline and increasingly involved on the pitch has been the FBI, whose avowed aim has been to bring down the city's Italian Mafia almost regardless of the cost. The cost was to turn something of a blind eye to the activities of Stephen 'The Rifleman' Flemmi, James 'Whitey' Bulger (brother of the politician Bill Bulger) and their friends. Over the years the involvement of the FBI on the playing pitch had been hinted at, but it was not until the trial of Flemmi, the now absent 'Whitey' Bulger and a host of other players, big and small, that it became clear exactly what some of its agents had been doing.[1]

After the destruction of Howie Winter's Winter Hill Mob – named after the district in Boston, not the seemingly eponymous Mr Winter – with indictments in February 1979, their interests were taken over by Flemmi and Bulger. Winter and his partner, Anthony 'Fat Tony' Ciulla, had bribed jockeys along the East Coast at tracks such as Suffolk Downs, Garden State and Atlantic City. It started when a jockey, who had been paid $800 to throw the third race one afternoon at Suffolk Downs, preferred the fleeting thrill of riding a winner. Hauled up by Winter, he got himself off the hook by agreeing to involve other jockeys.[2]

Flemmi, an Italian-born former paratrooper in Korea, who had preferred the relative independence of the Winter Hill Mob rather than the more structured format of the Mafia, had nevertheless worked closely with the Family's Larry Zannino. What was not realised was that he had been a fully paid-up FBI informant for years. Operating out of the Marconi Club, described as 'a combination bookie joint, massage parlour and brothel', he had been recruited in the mid-1960s and worked under FBI agent Paul Rico.

A suspect in the murders of the Bennett brothers and the bombing of the Boston lawyer John Harrison, who lost part of a leg, Flemmi had been tipped off by Rico and gone on the run in Canada, returning only when a witness changed his evidence. He was regarded as 'Whitey' Bulger's front man, acting as both collector and frightener.

---

[1] Scott Lehigh, 'How much does Bill Bulger know?' in *Boston Globe*, 30 May 2001.
[2] For a full account of Ciulla's activities as a race fixer see *Sports Illustrated*, 6 November 1978.

James Bulger, known as 'Whitey' from his yellow hair, had grown up in the Irish immigrant quarter of South Boston, 'Southie', where he had been friendly with John Connolly who went on to carve out a career in the FBI. Bulger's brother, William, ran for public office in 1960 when Connolly was one of his campaign workers. Qualified as a lawyer, Bill Bulger maintained a small practice and moved up from the House of Representatives to the Senate in 1970. By the end of the decade he was firmly in control, a position in which he has remained.

As with many a good *film noir*, his brother took an opposite path. At the age of 13 'Whitey' Bulger was charged with theft, and from then on it was a steadily upward path of assault and robbery, working with the Shamrocks who had taken over what remained of the Gustin Gang after their disastrous encounter with the Italians.[3] At the age of 27, in 1956 he was doing 9 years for bank robbery in a chain of federal prisons from Alcatraz to Leavenworth and then home via Lewisburg. Given a job as a janitor on his release, he was soon back working as an enforcer and debt collector for Donald Killeen, then the best known of the South Boston bookmakers. Bulger became his bodyguard and defected when he thought there would be trouble from the Mullin Gang. There was – and Killeen was killed as he left his son's

---

[3] Frank Gustin, a red-haired former boxer also known as Wallace, had led the Gustin Gang successfully over a period of years, enforcing his interests in bootlegging and hijacking the shipments of his rival Italian interests. At 1.30 p.m. on 22 December 1931, he, along with Barney Walsh and Tim Coffey, had gone to the then head of the Italians Joe Lombardi's offices at C. F. Importers in Boston's North End, either lured there to discuss a treaty, or as extortionists. He and Walsh were killed; Coffey survived. In short order the Irish retreated to South Boston.

fourth birthday party. His killer was alleged to be Bulger, although he was never charged. Nor, for that matter, was anyone else.

After the compulsory retirement of Howard Winter, from then on it was onwards and upwards for Flemmi and 'Whitey' Bulger along with their friends and helpers such as 'Cadillac' Frank Salemme and his younger brother by six years, Jack 'Action Jackson' Salemme. And all the time, it turned out, as they robbed and murdered they were protected by Connolly and another FBI agent, John Morris.

In 1990, after a fifteen-month investigation, 51 people were arrested as being part of a South Boston-based drugs ring. All pleaded guilty and Ed MacKenzie, a kick-boxer who ran Connolly's Corner Café, rolled over. Even then, though he provided good evidence against a Los Angeles group with contacts in Boston, he had nothing to say about the home talent. His employer, the eponymous Timothy Connolly (no relation to FBI agent John) did have something to say. He turned informant, telling the authorities he had been making weekly payments to a Bulger associate and, when he did not keep up his payments, had been threatened and 'fined' $50,000. He ran to the welcoming arms of the United States Attorney.

Then 'Whitey' Bulger apparently won $14 million on the Mass Millions lottery and now, with an apparently legitimate income of $80,000 a year, he bought a condominium in Florida and, after acquiring an EU passport thanks to an Irish grandparent, began to travel extensively. In fact, alleged the US Attorney's office, the whole thing was a scam. Bulger had offered the real winner $2 million if he would name him and two others as the joint winners. With Bulger on the run, it was suggested that the prosecution might not be too unhappy if he continued to elude his pursuers. If caught, it was thought that he would cause considerable embarrassment by running the same defence as Jackie Presser, the former Teamsters' President, who had claimed that his illegal activities were sanctioned by the FBI. In 1995 the FBI took Bulger's annual lottery cheque and claimed it was money involved in a money-laundering conspiracy.[4]

In the winter of 1994, when it was decided that arrests should be made, the idea of the FBI was that the first to be pulled in would be 'Cadillac' Frank Salemme. But the US Attorney's office had other ideas; they wanted Flemmi and Bulger, initially on charges of extortion. Flemmi and a young woman were picked up as they left Schooner's restaurant. Detectives took away Flemmi's gun. The young woman declined to go to the police station with them.

Salemme, who avoided arrest for 18 months, was found sporting a sun-tan and looking fit and well in West Palm Beach, Florida, in August 1996. He agreed to return to Massachusetts without the need for extradition. His son, Frank jnr, had died earlier in the year and although he did not attend the funeral 'Cadillac' Frank's girlfriend, Donna Wolf, did so. From that moment it had been only a question of time before the fish was reeled in. Of Bulger there was no sign.

But by then the cards in the prosecution's hands were not looking quite so strong. It was thought that the bookmakers who had been lined up to give evidence against 'The Rifleman'

[4] *Sun-Sentinel*, 15 August 1995.

and Salemme might be more prepared to face the wrath of a federal judge by refusing to give evidence, than that of the new Winter Hill Mob, however weakened it might appear to be on paper.

At the end of 1996 Bulger was still loose, said to have been alerted to the possibility of a trap in New York and so successfully trotting around it. The FBI had been watching a car for days to no avail. Neither had they done too well with their advertisement in *USA Today*, nor with posting his picture on the Internet. Bulger was regarded as a master in the evasion of electronic surveillance. Back in 1980 he had learned that a police state bug had been placed in the garage he was using as headquarters and nothing more was heard from him from that source. In 1984 agents were forced to retrieve a bug from his car after he had learned of its presence.

The beginning of the trial of Frank Salemme, Stephen Flemmi and the still absent 'Whitey' Bulger got off to a slow start in January 1998. First, former FBI agent Nicholas Gianturco admitted he had exchanged Christmas presents with Bulger and Flemmi. The defence to the indictment was that the FBI knew about and allowed Flemmi and Bulger's criminal activities, so there could be no criminal conspiracy. In other words they had been long-term informers. Then Judge Mark L. Wolf thought he might have to recuse himself since he had been party to some of the documentation in the case when working in the District Attorney's department in February 1983. It was now thought that the still absent Bulger, head of the Irish Mob in the 1980s, had essentially been the equal of the Italians' Jerry Angiulo.

During the trial it also became apparent that Peter Limone

had been wrongly convicted of murder 33 years previously as part of an effort to bring down the Mafia. Four of those years he had spent on Death Row. Limone and four others including Louis Greco had been convicted of the killing of a small-time criminal, Edward 'Teddy' Deegan in 1965, shot to death in an alley in Chelsea. Also accused was Joseph Salvati, who at the time had made the mistake of being in debt to Joseph Barboza, 'The Animal', to the tune of $400. When Barboza's men came to collect payment Salvati acted with far less humility than he should have shown in the circumstances. Limone, who at the time ran some small-time illegal gambling, had in happier days offered to sponsor Stephen Flemmi for the Family.[5] Later he had fallen foul of 'The Rifleman's' brother, Vincent (known confusingly as Jimmy the Bear) whom he had evicted from his card club.

Much of the evidence against Limone, Greco and Salvati came from Barboza, who became an FBI witness and who later admitted that he had fabricated a good part of it. As the Flemmi trial went on it became obvious that Barboza, who was killed in February 1976, had been offered many inducements to give evidence in the Limone trial.[6] There was

[5] Dick Lehr and Gerard O'Neill, *Black Mass*. Their book is a comprehensive account of the activities of Flemmi, 'Whitey' Bulger and FBI agents, including John Connolly and John Morris, over a 20-year period.

[6] Barboza was a man of uncertain temperament who, while possessing great ability with a rifle at both stationary and moving targets, had few other admirable qualities. Never a made member of the Mafia, he was used by them on a regular basis after his parole from a robbery sentence in 1958. By 1966 Barboza was almost out of control. He received six months for assaulting a police officer and, worse, he had offended the New England leader Jerry Angiulo by trying to extort money from a club owner. Now Barboza was being left to sweat in custody and, as a result, began to listen to the siren songs of FBI agents who visited him.

continues

also internal FBI evidence from informants that Deegan was likely to be killed and the killers had been named. They did not include Greco or Limone. Nor did their names appear on another agency list of the likely killers. It appeared that the FBI had been protecting its own informants at the expense of Limone and Greco. Joseph Salvati, released in 1997 when the Massachusetts governor commuted his sentence, was also cleared. The fourth man, Henry Tameleo, died in prison; he had been regarded as a major Mafia figure.

As the months went by Stephen Flemmi must have wished he had fled, courtesy once more of the FBI, in the days before the indictment. In 1988 he had failed in an application to Judge Mark L. Wolf to claim immunity by reason of the FBI's conduct.

Things changed inexorably and, by May 2001, 'The Rifleman' found himself more and more isolated. True, the evidence of the FBI agent John J. Connolly jnr had been effectively destroyed. Slowly but irrevocably during the trial it became clear that, far from running Flemmi and Bulger as informants, they were running him. Connolly was now indicted with Flemmi but, set against that, 'Cadillac' Frank Salemme had defected.

During the summer Flemmi's lawyers negotiated a deal by which he pleaded guilty to obstructing justice, extortion and money laundering in return for a sentence of 10 years.

He pleaded guilty to conspiracy to murder and received a one-year sentence concurrent to the 5 years he was then serving. He was paroled in 1969 on condition that he left Massachusetts. On 11 February 1976, as he left a friend's flat in California, he was killed by four blasts from a shotgun. For an account of the New England Mafia and Barboza's exploits see James Morton, *Gangland International*.

Flemmi accepted that he had extorted money from five book-makers and a drug dealer between 1978 and 1992 and he had laundered money over a 13-year period from 1984. On the face of it the deal, which included the dismissal of four murder charges, looked a good one. Because Flemmi had been in prison for something like 6½ years waiting for and during the trial, he would have to serve very little actual sentence. However, there were still serious clouds on his horizon.

The judge had some harsh words to say about the conduct of the FBI:

> The evidence in this and other reported cases indicated that the FBI's relationship with Bulger and Flemmi was not an isolated, aberrant occurrence attributable to anybody's South Boston roots. Rather, while hopefully extreme in degree, it may have been typical of the relationship that the FBI had with a number of its top echelon informants. If Mr Flemmi has committed any of the crimes with which he remains charged, he was able to do so because of the protection of the Federal Bureau of Investigation.

In August 2000 Kevin Weeks, who had once said he would face hard time rather than say a word against Bulger, became another to roll over. Charged with racketeering, he suspected it would be only a matter of time before he was charged with murder. On 14 January 2000, under directions from Weeks, who was anxious to show good faith, the body of John McIntyre was exhumed from an embankment off the Southeast Expressway. He had disappeared in 1984 when it was feared he was an informant. In the same grave was the body of Arthur Barrett who had disappeared around the same time.

By late September 2000, thanks to the evidence of Kevin Weeks' five bodies had been uncovered. They included Paul McGonagle, from the rival Mullin Gang, and Tommy King who had warred with Bulger. There was also the body of Flemmi's stepdaughter, Deborah Hussey, found in an unmarked grave in Dorchester. Flemmi was alleged to have ordered the hit.

In an indictment of 28 September 2001, Flemmi was charged with 10 murders and Bulger with 18. If that was not sufficient there were further troubles for Flemmi. State prosecutors in Tulsa and Miami filed murder charges against him and the absent Bulger over the killing of Roger Wheeler – president of the Florida-based World Jai Alai[7] Association – in his car in Tulsa after completing a round of golf on 27 May 1981; he had been shot through his car window. His death was because he believed that the Irish Mob was skimming money from the company. His killers were Edward Brian Halloran, once a respected henchman of Bulger but now an alienated cocaine addict, and John Martorano who had originally been an associate of Howie Winter.

The second in the trio of deaths concerning the World Jai Alai was Halloran, who had effectively signed his own death warrant by telling the FBI that Bulger, Flemmi and accountant

---

[7] Jai Alai, or pelota or fronton, is a game usually played either as singles or doubles with *cestas*, or curved racquets, in which the ball is caught and then thrown against a stone wall. It is an attractive medium for betting on teams and scores, and bets can be placed throughout the game.

John B. Callaghan had wanted him to kill Wheeler. He might have saved himself because there was talk of his giving evidence against Bulger and Flemmi but, when he refused to wear a wire, it was decided that the chances of obtaining a conviction on his more or less uncorroborated evidence was remote. He was left on the street. Halloran was killed, shot with 12 bullets from two guns on 11 May 1982; he had been ambushed while driving his Datsun.

A search was now mounted for Callaghan, a man who spoke Chinese and had a fondness for cigars and Dom Perignon. In the early 1970s, when the Winter Hill Mob were intent on taking over World Jai Alai and Callaghan's involvement with Flemmi and Bulger was about to be made public, he resigned. Later he tried to purchase the company. Now his Mob connections were threatening the possibility of getting a licence for a fronton in Hartford, Conn.

On 31 July 1982 Callaghan arrived at Fort Lauderdale airport and was killed the next day. His body, stripped of identification and jewellery, was later found in the boot of a silver Fleetwood Cadillac at Miami airport. He had been shot twice in the head and a dime had been placed on his body, the traditional indication of an informer. In 2000 John Martorano pleaded guilty to the murder. He admitted to a total of 19 Mob hits and, with one eye on the gas chamber or a lethal injection, rolled over.

Then in October 2000, after further weeks of digging, the police found the body of 26-year-old Debra Davis, Flemmi's girlfriend of seven years who had disappeared on 17 September 1981. She had vanished shortly after announcing that the relationship was coming to an end. Olga Davis,

Debra's mother, said she had reported the disappearance of her daughter to the local Randolph Street police who had passed the matter to the FBI. Digging was also continuing under the Neponset River railroad trestles for yet another body. Efforts to find the corpses of Walter and Edward 'Wimpey' Bennett, bookmakers and loan-sharkers who disappeared on 3 April 1967, were unsuccessful. At the time of Walter Bennett's disappearance Flemmi was alleged to have told FBI agent Paul Rico that there was no point in looking for the body. He was later charged with the 23 December 1967 murder of William Bennett, shot and dumped on a snowbank from a moving car in Dorchester, but was acquitted when witnesses changed their evidence. It was on that occasion that Flemmi fled to Canada, from where he had kept in contact with Rico.

As the search was called off Barbara Bennett – aged 9 at the time of the disappearance of her father, Walter – dropped a note on to the ground near where it had been hoped to find his body.

As a little girl you were taken from me, something I may never understand. Daddy, I am a grown woman now, you would be proud of me. All the pain over the years now needs to come to a stop . . . I can no longer hold on to you; it is time for me to say goodbye.

On 13 June 2001 Flemmi's brother, Michael, a retired police officer who had served 32 years on the Boston force, was indicted with using a dealer to sell stolen jewellery for $40,000 to another Boston gems merchant. The indictment alleged that he had maintained 'an illicit relationship'.

Meanwhile, 'Whitey' Bulger had been placed on the FBI's 'Ten Most Wanted Fugitives' list, with up to $250,000 on offer for information leading to his capture. Described as between 5 ft 7 inches and 5 ft 9 inches, Caucasian male aged 70, his weight was given at between 150 and 160 lbs, blue eyes, silver/white hair with no scars or tattoos. Just the man to stand out in a crowd of old-age pensioners snowbirding in Miami or Palm Springs! There was also a suggestion that he had gone to Canada, whence Flemmi had fled decades before.

Despite the offer of rewards, by the end of 2001 Bulger was still leading the pursuers a merry dance and had been reported as being sighted in (apart from Canada and in alphabetical order) Alabama, Florida, Iowa, Ireland, Italy, Louisiana, and even Southie itself. Regular sightings were also reported in Southern California, including two at a beauty salon where it was thought Catherine Greig, Bulger's girlfriend, might have had her hair done. On the other hand, Stephen Flemmi was awaiting further trials in the maximum security MCI-Cedar Junction in Walpole. His request to be transferred to a lower-security prison had been rejected.

As for John Connolly, he was indicted on charges of obstructing the course of justice, bribery and associating with Bulger's Winter Hill Mob. After leaving the FBI he had joined Boston Edison, but by the end of February 2001 he had left amidst speculation as to the reason. As for the Italians, they were busy trying to have their old convictions overturned.

There were fears that the problems of the FBI in Boston might have been replicated on the West Coast with the Bureau allowing a plot to kill a Latino gangster, Chuey Martinez, to go unimpeded for seven months in 1997–8. During this period he was shot and wounded, another who was known to have been threatened was killed and various associates of Martinez were attacked in prison.[8]

The Boston FBI fiasco moved a small step nearer to its ending when, on 16 September 2002, the former agent John Connolly received the maximum 10 years after being convicted of helping organised crime figures such as Bulger and Flemmi.

In January 2003 came the news that James Bulger had spent some of his time on the run in Britain and Ireland. Police in Dublin found a safety deposit box which was opened with a key that had been found a week earlier in a raid on another box, this time in London. He was also known to have rented property in Brighton. But of the man himself there was still no sign and one thought was that he might be hiding with the help of the IRA. Back in Boston, Bulger's brother, the politician William, took the Fifth Amendment when he appeared before the Government Reform Committee.

[8] *New York Times*, July 2001.

19

Chicago

Yet again, to misquote Mark Twain, the reports of the death of the Outfit – as the Chicago *Cosa Nostra* is known – are also greatly exaggerated. The general public may think that the Outfit is finished but, as is so often the case, they are wrong.

Probably, however, both the police and the Outfit have reason to be pleased with themselves. The police say that while there have been any number of killings by and amongst street gangs and drug dealers, there has been only one killing amongst members of the Outfit in recent years. The Outfit itself will be pleased because, to all intents and purposes, it has followed the path towards becoming legitimate taken by the Godfather, Michael Corleone, in Mario Puzo's novels. Well, legitimate is probably not quite the correct word, but they have metamorphosed into businessmen even if they have quite dirty white collars. Their transformation, however, does not mean they have been anything less than active; just not so publicly active.

The Chicago Crime Commission may now be a shadow of its former self as it was in the days when it could force Al Capone out of the city and into the suburbs, but it still keeps an informed and close eye on Mob movements.

> The Chicago Mob of 1997, like generations before them, is like a serpent that sheds its skin. Its present appearance may be different but, beneath the surface, it is the same dangerous beast. The Mob is more flexible and adaptable than ever before. Its power and wealth has never been more sound and difficult to permeate.[1]

A roll-call of honoured figures from the early 1990s shows the depredations the Mob has suffered. Amongst the dead, mainly of illness and old age, are Tony Accardo, Sam 'Wings' Carlisi, James LaPietra and Jackie 'The Lackey' Cerone. In prison remain Albert Tocco and Gus Alex, along with the fearsome Harry Aleman who was retried and convicted of the murder of Teamsters' official William Logan in 1977. The judge in the first case, Frank Wilson, who was said to have accepted $10,000 in a bench trial – that is one without a jury – committed suicide in Arizona during inquiries into the case. In prison or on parole

---

[1] Chicago Crime Commission, *The New Faces of Organized Crime*, p. 9. My thanks are particularly due to the Commission for allowing me to quote extensively from this and other reports.

remain another two dozen figures prominent from that time.[2]

At the turn of the century the Commission believed that the Chicago Outfit was still headed by John 'No Nose' DiFronzo, who acquired his nickname in 1949 after part of his proboscis was shot by the police as he was caught holding up a clothing store in Michigan Avenue. He was next in view when in 1952 he was suspected of (but never charged with) involvement in the murder of the West Side politician, Charles Gross. After that he was arrested, together with two former police officers, as a ringleader in a juice loan racket. Since then, apart from the hiccup of a conviction in 1993 for federal extortion-related offences, he has remained out of the limelight, first running the West Side on the instructions of Joseph Aiuppa who had taken over from Joseph Ferriola, and then assuming overall control. He received 37 months, reduced on appeal, after allegations that he and other senior members of the Outfit had tried to overrun a Native American casino belonging to the Rincon tribe in San Diego County. Convicted with him was the mathematical genius Donald 'The Wizard of Odds' Angelini. Sam Carlisi was acquitted.

Joint second-in-command was alleged to be Joey 'The Clown' Lombardo, who on 13 December 1992 completed his sentence in what was known as the Pendorf case in which Alan Dorfman, the Teamster official in control of the Pension

[2] In 1990 Albert Tocco was convicted of the 1980 killing of a chop-shop owner and his wife as they left a Joliet courthouse. Sam Carlisi was convicted in 1994 of extortion and the attempted murder of an informer. Gus Alex was convicted of operating an extortion ring in 1993 on the evidence of Lenny Patrick, a former member of the North Side Crew. For more of the history of the Chicago Mob see James Morton, *Gangland International*, Chapter 5.

Fund, became for a while the Mob's plaything.

On 11 December 1992, shortly before his release from prison, Lombardo inserted an advertisement in the Chicago *News*. It read:

> I am Joe Lombardo. I have been released on parole from Federal Prison. I never took a secret oath with guns and daggers, pricked my finger, drew blood or burned paper to join a criminal organization. If anyone hears my name used in connection with any criminal activity please notify the FBI, local police and my parole officer, Ron Kumke.[3]

No one ever did; or if they did, no notice was taken because, six years later, the Crime Commission named Lombardo as still being actively involved with the Outfit as an adviser along with Angelo LaPietra.

Over the years 'The Clown' has belied his nickname. In his younger days he was believed to have been the boss of the street crew which controlled the Chicago Mob killings, and at one time was ranked fourth in Outfit hierarchy behind Joseph Aiuppa, Jackie 'The Lackey' Cerone and Tony Accardo.

In 1963 he was acquitted of kidnapping. Then in 1974 he was acquitted along with Dorfman of stealing $1.4 million from the Teamsters' Union's pension fund. The case effectively collapsed when the main prosecution witness, Daniel Seifert, was shot to death in September 1974 in front of his wife.

In 1982 Lombardo and Dorfman were once again in court

[3] Chicago *News*, 11 December 1992.

together, this time charged with extorting $800,000 from a builder, Robert Kendler, and – with Roy L. Williams, the Teamsters' then President – attempting to bribe Senator Howard W. Cannon of Nevada. In the meantime Lombardo's name had been linked to the deaths of Robert Harder, killed in 1974, Sam Annerino three years later and Raymond Ryan the same year.

Harder was a pornographer who had helped the police to solve the murder of a brother officer. Annerino was prominent in a car theft gang and Ryan was believed to have been killed for his evidence in the case which led to the conviction of longtime Chicago and Las Vegas hardman, Marshall Caifano.

The next year, while still awaiting trial, Dorfman was shot and killed on 20 January 1983 in a hotel parking lot because it was feared he would become a prosecution witness. In August 1985 Lombardo received a sentence of 15 years on the bribery charge. Williams was sentenced to 10 years, but he later gave evidence against Lombardo, Aiuppa, Cerone, Angelo LaPietra and Milton Rockman for concealing the true ownership of the Stardust Hotel in Las Vegas and conspiring to skim over $2 million from the Stardust casino in the period 1974 to 1978. Lombardo received a concurrent sentence of 10 years.

On the other hand, LaPietra has maintained a much lower profile than his co-counsellor. Since the heady days of Accardo there certainly have been changes. On ground level, what were seven street crews have been consolidated into three, of which the West Side and DuPage County were under the control of Anthony Centracchio; the Southside and North West Indiana under the reign of John Monteleone. Joe 'Joe the Builder' Andriacchi, Lombardo's cousin, was running the

North Side, Elmwood Park and Lakewood County. Monteleone had at one time been in charge of the 26th Street Crew, a team which dealt in organised gambling, chop-shops and freight car thefts from the depots on the Southside.

Nor did a job in the Outfit seem to be pensionable. On 11 January 2000 Gloria Granata pleaded guilty to assisting her late husband Frank, a former associate of Joseph Ferriola, the short-time leader who died in 1989 while awaiting trial. Frank Granata had been laundering money in the mid-1990s and after his death in 1995 she continued taking 10 per cent of the money cleaned. Unfortunately for the widow she was caught in an undercover operation.

One vacancy recently occurred high up in the structure when on 6 August 2001 the 71-year-old Anthony Centracchio died. He had been suffering from cancer and was also awaiting trial on federal racketeering charges with his right-hand man, the former Stone Park police officer Thomas Tucker, and the ex-mayor of Stone Park, Robert Natale. In March 2002 Natale received 18 months' imprisonment when he pleaded guilty to accepting bribes from the Outfit. 'It looked pretty much like he was going to be taken down at trial, but the good Lord did it first,' Wayne Johnson of The Crime Commission remarked sympathetically of Centracchio. In May 2002 Thomas Tucker was sentenced to over 4 years' imprisonment and ordered to pay fines and forfeits of $15,000 after admitting being the bagman for Centracchio.

Centracchio could have been regarded as one of the New Mob with interests in everything from an abortion clinic where he maintained an office, to carpeting, bug extermination and the adult entertainment business. He was also regarded as being, for a good part of his career, a very successful fence, buying from a string of thieves including the noted Paul 'Peanuts' Panczko.

The previous October 'The Wizard of Odds', Donald Angelini, had died. Like Dutch Schultz's financial genius Oscar 'Abbaabba' Berman in the 1920s, he had been able to run the numbers game so that payouts were kept to a minimum. Shortly before his death he, Robert Cechini and Lawrence Scialabba were banned, in the Illinois version of the Las Vegas Black Book, from gambling on the riverboats. Angelini was another to receive 3 years in the Rincon tribe case. Wayne Johnson paid another oblique tribute, saying that, while he did not like to admit it, Angelini had been one of the great minds in organised crime.[4]

As to the hits, while there had been over 1,100 since the Crime Commission began counting back in 1919, there had only been a bare half-dozen since 1990. Included, since the arrest was made in 1997, was one of the strangest of Mob killings, which happened on 2 July 1988 with the death of William Benham who had defaulted on a $100,000 Mob loan. The prosecution alleged that James DiForti, a Laborers' Union official, had been sent to collect the debt and had shot and killed Benham, who in turn had shot DiForti. It was not until 1997 that an FBI informer named DiForti as the killer and DNA technology was used to match blood found at the scene.

Earlier, receiver Edward Pedote was found beaten and shot at a furniture resale store on South Cicero on 6 November

---

[4] Chicago *Tribune*, 24 October 2000.

1991. He had received 5 years' probation in 1985 and was regarded as an informer. On 23 November 1991 Wallace Lieberman, the associate of Robert Bellavia of Ernest Infelice's Lakewood County Crew, was shot in the neck. His body was found in a Cicero alley at 6000 West 31st. Bellavia's wife worked as a secretary for Lieberman. The next year, on 5 November, Sam Taglia was found in the boot of his own car; he had been shot twice in the head and had his throat cut. His criminal record showed some 40 arrests for robbery as well as drug offences. Albert Vena, allegedly a member of Vincent J. Cozzo's Grand Avenue Crew, was charged with the murder and found not guilty.

Giuseppe Vicari, said to have been involved with a Bari, Italy, faction, was found beaten and shot in the head at his restaurant, La Casa de Caffe, in N. Harlem, Chicago, on 5 November 1994. He was then on bail in DuPage County for illegal gambling.

The last in the accredited line was the killing of Ronald Jarrett, the Bridgeport mobster, shot near his home on 23 December 1999. He never recovered consciousness and died on 24 January 2000 in Cook County Hospital. He had been on his way to the Orland Park funeral home to pay his respects to his friend and Mob turncoat, Charles 'Guy' Bills. He was known to have been involved in acrimonious squabbles with other top Bridgeport mobsters, one of which concerned the division of gambling profits.

What did come out of the investigation into his death were charges in November 2000 against 15 people alleged to be part of a major Midwestern cocaine ring based in the Southside. Wire-taps had been authorised in an effort known as *Operation Vendetta* to trace Jarrett's killer. In turn it became *Operation Vendetta II*. Chris Marcotte and Peter Frigo, associates or members of the Mob's Bridgeport Crew, were hauled in during the sweep. Marcotte had only just been released from a sentence imposed in 1992 for second-degree murder. It was alleged that, along with Southside's Satan's Disciples, they had been taking in excess of 2 lbs of cocaine to the Upper Peninsula of Michigan every month. Two reputed leaders of the Disciples, Richard Velasquez snr and his son, Richard jnr, were also netted.[5]

There was an aftermath to the Jarrett killing when, on 25 July 2001, Vince Kirsch – the 35-year-old son of the dead Mob figure – watched his van blow up as he left his grandmother's flat in Bridgeport. It was thought that somebody might be sending him a message.

One death which curiously was discarded as being a Mob killing was that in 1998 of Donald M. Schemel who had run a water-taxi business on the Chicago River. Traditionally, control of the boats had been in the hands of the old First Ward, the political arm of the Outfit. Schemel's operating tactics annoyed other boat-owners and what was described as a slew of citations and complaints followed. It was suggested that he made disparaging remarks when a passenger had either fallen or jumped from the boat of a rival concern, a report of which appeared in a newspaper: he had copies of the page printed up and circulated. He was also accused of having more than two people soliciting for customers, and of being

[5] Satan's Disciples, whose colours are canary-yellow and black, owe overall allegiance to the Folks. Their symbols are a pitchfork, devil and, appropriately enough, the Folks logo.

wrong to boast that his was the only 1½-hour trip in operation. Executed on the 1900 block on South Lumber Street
only a few yards from the river, where his truck had been
obliged to stop for a train, his killer had shot him as he waited.

'I've got a question. Who killed Donald Schemel and why?'
wrote journalist John Kass of the *Tribune*, suggesting that
Schemel's death was an organised crime hit. 'If you know,
pick up the phone and let me know.'[6]

While Johnson may have failed to link Lombardo to the
administration, he had one major triumph when he thwarted
the granting of a gambling licence to a proposed casino in
Rosemont – something which, until he spoke up, was
regarded as a mere formality.

On 30 January 2001 he attended the Gaming Board to
voice the Commission's objection. Allegedly, a business
partner of the mayor has been William Daddano jnr, who
has himself appeared on three charts produced by the
Commission and is the son of the late North Side Outfit
boss, Willie 'Potatoes' Daddano. Johnson claimed that the
father of another business associate of the mayor had been
the victim of a Mob hit and that one Rosemont employee,
Anthony 'Jeeps' Daddino, had a conviction for extortion but
that the mayor had written to the judge praising him. Peter
DiFronzo, a brother of John 'No Nose' DiFronzo, was a beneficiary of no-bid contracts from Rosemont and a contributor
to the mayor's political campaign. Johnson also alleged that
in the past, the great boss Sam Giancana had business
dealings with the mayor; something which Giancana's

[6] Chicago *Tribune*, 14 August 2000.

daughter supports. To a great deal of surprise the board refused the licence by a 4–1 decision – the board's administrator, Sergio Acosta, saying that its investigation showed 'organised crime elements associated with this proposed project that cannot be ignored'. Writs began to fly.

Then, in October 2001, came the interesting and wholly unexpected report that there had been a major shake-up in the Outfit's hierarchy. The new boss was said to be James J. 'Jimmy the Man' Marcello. This was somewhat surprising because the 59-year-old Marcello was living out of Chicago in Milan, near Ann Arbor, Michigan, where he was finishing a 12-year sentence for racketeering. On his release he was expected to return home to Lombard where he was alleged to have once run a DuPage County criminal enterprise. Over the years of Mafia history, former chauffeurs have gone on to higher things and Marcello had once been chauffeur and bodyguard for the old-time boss Sam 'Wings' Carlisi, who had himself been the chauffeur to boss Joseph Aiuppa. Carlisi, convicted of an attempt to take over the Rincon Indians' gambling hall near San Diego, had received 12½ years' imprisonment in December 1993 and died on New Year's Day 1997 following a heart attack. He had been suffering from throat cancer.

Second-in-command of the new and possibly improved operation was thought to be Anthony 'Little Tony' Zizzo of Melrose Park, on home confinement after serving a term. Demotion may have been the price paid by 'No Nose' DiFronzo for the Rosemont fiasco. Now after Anthony Ciaramonti, who once reported to DiFronzo, had been released from a prison sentence there was a suggestion that he might be trying to carve out a career at a higher echelon.

If so, it came to an abrupt end when Ciaramonti was shot to death on 22 November 2001.

Ciaramonti, a great friend of Carlisi and described by a Mob watcher as a 'violent, nasty, son-of-a-bitch his entire life', had a reputation as a distinctly unpleasant man with whom to deal. Said to have 'punctuated his point' by jabbing a fork in a man's chin, he had also picked up a trucker by the throat. Unfortunately, as the court heard, the trucker was wearing a body mike at the time. On another occasion Ciaramonti pushed a restaurant owner, unable to repay his loan, face down on his own hot griddle. It was thought that his death might cause problems for the boss-elect Marcello.

The Mob itself may not have been involved in many public killings, but the same could not be said for the street gangs. In 1993 the death toll was 116, up 13 from the previous year. The next year the Chicago total of murders had reached a staggering 930, of which a third were reported to be gang killings. Most of the deaths arose from disputes over territory and the distribution of drugs.[7] Street gangs influential in the Chicago area and sheltering under the Folks' umbrella included Black Gangster Disciple Nation, Maniac Latin Disciples, Satan's Disciples, Spanish Cobras, and Ambrose. Under the rival the People's banner came the Latin Kings, Vice Lords, P-Stones, Insane Unknowns and the P. R. Stones. All dealt in drugs, and all the Folks in drive-bys.

Of the People's collection, in addition the Vice Lords traded in prostitution while the P-Stones had added burglary and theft to their repertoire. All the others had drive-bys in their curricula,

[7] Chicago Crime Commission, *Gangs*, p. 17.

while the Latin Kings also had a sideline in intimidation and were strongly represented in gangs in the prison system.

On 12 December 2001, after a 2½-year investigation, 20 gang members were arrested in a federal sweep. Amongst them were Hugh Rogers, also known as Ardell, who was alleged to hold the rank of General in the Black P Stone Nation and who was the head of sales and distribution of cocaine and crack in the Southside and in the South suburbs. Half a million dollars' worth of luxury goods were seized. FBI Special Agent Thomas K. Kneir, announcing the arrests, commented, 'Groups such as the Black P Stone Nation are the domestic equivalent of terrorists, bringing violence and destruction to America's inner-city.'

The Outfit and the street gangs do not have a monopoly on crime in Chicago any more than they do in other major American cities. Other heads have poked out of the ground in recent years and have established a presence and formed alliances. Apart from the Asian gangs, notable amongst the relative newcomers are the Eastern European Organised Criminal Travellers (EEOCT). According to the Crime Commission, while both groups have their origins in Poland, Romania and Yugoslavia, deriving from a sub-culture originating in India and Iran, the European travellers operate in both America and Europe while the American counterparts work North America only. They are involved in all types of crime but specialise in confidence tricks and financial offences. They are literally travellers, being on the move for between 40 and 70 per cent of their time.

When at home in the Chicago area they can be found in the city itself, Morton Grove, Niles and Lincolnwood. They are regarded as producing more victims than any other single criminal organisation. It is estimated that up to 95 per cent of EEOCT are illiterate. As the years have gone by they have become more violent, the European groups marrying into the Hispanic community and linking with street gangs. The structure of the EEOCT closely resembles that of a traditional Mob outfit, with the Rom Baro, or boss, assisted by Kris Romas, or *consiglieri*. Under the boss is the underboss, or Vista Chief, who rules over Baros, or *caporegimi*.

Although they operate separately, both groups share similar beliefs and habits and are extremely superstitious, with a fear of the night. Consequently, most of their crimes are committed during daylight hours. Breaking a window to effect a burglary is regarded as bad luck and they rely on tricks, such as asking for water for their children or saying the landlord has sent them to do repair work, to gain entry. Many of the scams operated are standard well-tried con tricks such as the pigeon drop, the 'lost' wallet, and insurance frauds. They are, however, increasingly involved in home invasions and the younger generation has been aligning itself with street gangs in drug operations. The women members of the gangs are taught to be fortune-tellers. As with the pimps who control street prostitution, the Rom Baros will allocate the women specific areas in which they are to work.[8]

[8] Other cities experience similar troubles with fortune-tellers and in 1999, under *Operation Crystal Ball*, there was a crackdown in New York. One woman was arrested after allegedly having taken $50,000 from a client to remove a curse. Another victim paid $2,000 for the psychic to go to the Middle East to obtain a special root. The victim, an insurance agent, told the police, 'I'm not naïve or unintelligent.' Many women operate under pseudonyms, including the less than Romany-sounding Helen Uwanawich. *New York Times*, 30 June 1999.

Nevertheless, there are a number of differences. The Rom Baro of the European groups will fly in to meet the team, whereas the American group Rom Baro will travel with them. The Europeans use four-door cars registered to empty parking lots or fictitious addresses. The Americans use pick-up trucks, often with a false magnetic company sign on the vehicle door designed to instil confidence in the potential victims.[9]

Insurance frauds are stock in trade, but a particularly interesting one was played against Disney World when two sisters and a brother staged a mock rape at a Disney hotel. An hour before calling the police, to add authenticity, the 'victim' had intercourse with a friend. She rehearsed her emergency call to the police and then her brother bound and beat her. A leading hotel chain agreed to an out-of-court settlement of $1.4 million but, on the day when payment was due, the 'victim's' sister claimed that the cheque should be made out to her because she did not trust her siblings. The hotel chain refused and the sister went to the police to tell them the whole story. The 'victim' received 3 years' imprisonment.

The EEOCT links with the Outfit have included using the latter to fence stolen jewellery. Nevertheless, they would seem to have something left to learn about both business relationships and levels of violence. On one occasion a Rom Baro decided to cut out an Outfit enforcer who had been allowing the EEOCT leader to fence merchandise in return for a

[9] Another group of travellers are the so-called Irish Travellers based in Murphy Village, North Augusta, South Carolina, who share the same characteristics as the EEOCT but do not mix with them. Inter-marriage is common and again they are on the road for half to three-quarters of the year, travelling in groups of 25 or more, speaking a language known as Shelta, and earning up to $100,000 per crew member.

percentage. The enforcer invaded the leader's home and placed a shotgun in the mouth of one of his children before making off with the stolen merchandise and personal jewellery. Once an apology was received the personal jewellery, but not the stolen goods, was returned.

Nigerian gangs have also established bases in America, notably in Chicago, where they are regarded as:

extremely organised, well-educated and highly adaptable. The organisation is so highly disciplined, it can be compared with an elite military special forces group. They are helped by the fact that while members speak fluent English and may speak several other languages their accents may well sound as if they come from Haiti or the British Virgin Islands.[10]

Apart from the celebrated 419 frauds – from the section of the Nigerian penal code – the principal crimes committed are dealing in drugs, money laundering, dealing in stolen credit cards, counterfeiting, producing false credit cards, mail order and telemarketing frauds. This last is the standard telephone call to say that a prize of a holiday has been won and a smallish sum (usually under $50) must be forwarded to qualify. This may be charged to a major credit card.

A female-led Nigerian heroin smuggling operation was broken in October 1996. Based in a clothing store on Northside, it began operating in 1992 and controlled a minimum of 80 per cent of all the white heroin brought into Chicago. Single white, black and Asian women were hired

[10] Chicago Crime Commission, *The New Faces of Organised Crime*, p. 71.

to bring the drug from Thailand via Europe or Mexico. The owner of the boutique then oversaw the distribution of the drug throughout the United States, using wire transfers and Federal Express to remit funds to the original suppliers. Thirty-two people were arrested in the States.

A second major bust of Nigerian organised criminals took place two months later when 15 individuals were charged in a 32-country conspiracy indictment. This time the heroin had come from Thailand and West Africa and was sold in the Chicago suburbs and in northern Indiana. Profits were channelled into cars and jewellery. Rather over $3 million cash was confiscated or forfeited.

At the beginning of 2002 Chicago's police superintendent Terry Hillard announced that the department would be taking aggressive steps to deal with the rising number of murders which had reached 666, the highest in the United States, in 2001.

20

Detroit

Nor was the Detroit Mafia in much greater repair. Until the arrests of more or less everyone who was anybody in 1996, theirs had been a stable Family for something approaching 70 years since the battles for control in the 1930s ousted the old Purple Gang.[1]

Now the first-ever split in the ranks of the Detroit Mafia came when Nove Tocco, described as a street soldier but nevertheless a cousin of the Don, Jack Tocco, and the nephew of Anthony Zerilli, imprisoned in 1998 for racketeering, conspiracy, extortion and weapons violation, rolled over during the trial.

He and his partner, Paul Corrado, had been caught on tape as they discussed the day-to-day routines – both their

[1] See Paul R. Kavieff, *The Purple Gang*; James Morton, *Gangland International*.

own and, worse, those of their elders and betters whom they resented for trying to keep some control on them. 'It was like listening to a bad version of *The Sopranos*. They're morons, but they're scary morons,' says a Detroit reporter.

The roll-over came with the re-sentencing of the boss, Jack Tocco, who, to the wrath of the FBI, received only a year's sentence from District Judge John Corbett O'Meara for his leading part in the racketeering conspiracy. The apparent leniency was explained by some as a reflection of the wasted efforts and enormous amount of money spent over something like 30 years to bring the Family to its knees, when in the end no murders could be laid at its door, only conspiracies. It was felt by some observers that many senior men in the FBI were coming to the end of their careers and that it was better to go out with a win even if it was far short of the Championship pennant, let alone the World Series. If that was all that could be produced, then the sentencing of an old man could reflect it.

Wrong, said the appellate court, and re-sentencing was ordered. Now in March 2000 into the box stepped the very penitent and, for that matter, still very overweight Nove Tocco to tell how Cousin Jack and the others ran things. One thing he did not say, but which has always been alleged against the Family, is that their series of inter-marriages – together with their habit of having children born around the same time and then naming them identically – has been done deliberately to confuse the authorities.

In turn Jack Tocco's lawyers spoke of his wife Marie as a cancer sufferer beset by anxiety, nightmares, stomach pains and headaches. The judge heard from Tocco's podiatrist, Dr

Peter Torrice, of his client's ingrown toenails, open sores on his feet and nail fungus. He had such poor circulation that he had to wear two pairs of woollen socks. It was also said that he had been a substantial contributor to a home for mentally challenged children and adults in Chelsea. It was an uphill struggle, however. The prosecutor wanted to know the Pope's position on the Mafia, and whether donations from racketeering proceeds were tainted in the eyes of His Holiness.

Nove Tocco was rewarded for his efforts when, on 20 November 2000, he also appeared for re-sentencing – but this time it would be down rather than up. In a carefully prepared speech he spoke of the sadness he had caused to his extended family, and how in the past two years he had had time to reflect on his mistakes – the most serious of which might yet turn out to be his defection. His brother had been assaulted and threatened. His wife, he said, had been obliged to leave Michigan and to sell her condominium in Arizona; she, like him, would probably end up in the witness programme. His grandchildren had been mewling, 'When are you coming home, Poppa?' Now he had learned that his father had been correct when he said that even if there was only bread and onions to eat, it did not matter if they could be eaten with the family. 'I ask you sir, to return me to them, if only to eat bread and onions.' And the kindly judge – telling Nove Tocco, 'I hope you take care of yourself. And your father is still here, and he needs to take care of himself too' – reduced his sentence to one of 50 months, which in effect would mean a very early release.

Someone who did not take care of himself sufficiently was

the son of another of the defendants, John Jarjosa jnr, who was in busy traffic on Eight Mile in his Corvette a little after lunchtime on 19 June 2001 when he was followed by two men driving a Trans Am. When he pulled into a turnaround to head back west, the car pulled across him, blocking his escape. The passenger stepped out and fired several shots in his head and neck. Jarjosa jnr was dead on arrival at hospital.

Jarjosa jnr, whose father was serving 18 months for his part in the Tocco affair, had interests in City Heat, a topless bar at 20771 W. Eight Mile, and had borrowed the Corvette from a disc jockey. The club had recently been raided by the police. There had been a number of incidents involving Jarjosa jnr before his death. Angela Dover, a former dancer, was awarded $5,600 after she claimed that he had thrown her from the club, injuring her foot. There was also an incident in the Motor City Casino which resulted in Ramsey Rayis suing Jarjosa jnr for assault, and in turn Jarjosa suing the casino for not providing adequate security.

Initially the police received a number of leads over the killing, but these tailed off after it was announced that Jarjosa jnr's family would be putting up $25,000 reward for information. Cynics point out that this is a standard way of announcing a bounty.

In the meantime Tony Jack Giacolone, whom many thought should be able to say far more about the disappearance of Teamster leader Jimmy Hoffa than he ever did, died in St John Hospital, Detroit, in February 2001. He was 82 and, because of his health, never stood trial for his part in the conspiracy. Giacolone, described as 'impeccably dressed and icy-eyed' by Joe Swickard of the *Detroit Free*

Press and as 'the most dignified man I ever met' by Detroit lawyer N. C. Deday LaRene, had been suffering from heart problems and failing kidneys.

He began his adult life selling vegetables from his father's horse-drawn wagon in Detroit's fashionable Indian Village in the 1920s, but moved up through the organisation. The horse which drew the wagon was, in later years, replaced by Cadillacs and Tennessee walking horses. His home had 'the most beautiful lawn in the complex'.

'May the angels lead you into paradise, Anthony,' said Father Jackson at the conclusion of the mass held for Giacolone at St Michael Catholic Church, Sterling Heights.

Perhaps the disappearance of Hoffa was the Detroit Mafia's finest or worst hour. They had striven for years to do the sensible thing and keep themselves well out of public sight, but here they were absolutely in the spotlight.

James Riddle 'Jimmy' Hoffa, the 62-year-old one-time leader of the Teamsters' Union, disappeared on the afternoon of 30 July 1975. By then he had been out of prison for 3½ years.[2]

He was at his home on Square Lane between Pontiac and Holly, Michigan, when he received a call from a New York Teamster locale. Although technically, because of a court ban, he had nothing to do with the Union he kept in touch with senior members. This did not please everyone. One former colleague, Charles 'Chuckie' O'Brien, who had been so close to Hoffa that he called him 'Dad' and was effectively an adopted son, and had a plane fly a 'Happy Birthday' banner

---

[2] There are many accounts of Hoffa's career. See, for example, Dan Moldea, *The Hoffa War*.

over the jail every year during Hoffa's sentence, had almost completely fallen out with him. Hoffa believed O'Brien was in debt to Giacolone and saw him lining up with Frank Fitzsimmons, the International Union president, whom Hoffa wished to challenge for control of the Union.[3] It was also alleged that O'Brien was upset because he had not been getting sufficiently good jobs in the Union. While his adopted father was in prison he had been promoted to international organiser and had become far closer to Giacolone, whom he referred to as Uncle Jack.

Hoffa told his wife, Josephine, that he had a 2 o'clock appointment with Union members as well as Tony Giacalone and Tony Provenzano, a New Jersey Teamster boss, in the Manchus Red Fox restaurant in out-town Detroit. There had been problems between Hoffa and Provenzano after they served part of their sentences in the same prison, the federal penitentiary in Lewisburg. Provenzano had gone down for racketeering and extortion. The quarrel came about because Hoffa blamed Provenzano for the problems caused to the Teamsters' Union by federal authorities.

The meeting had been cancelled on previous occasions but, according to James Hoffa jnr, his father had already met Anthony Giacolone and his brother Vito on 15 May at James jnr's office, as a preliminary move in the effort to settle the quarrel. Hoffa had told his wife he would be home by 4 p.m. to barbecue steaks for dinner.

---

[3] O'Brien had a curious sense of humour. After there had been anti-Hoffa articles in the paper, he borrowed a human head from a local medical school, propped its eyes open with toothpicks and sent it to Martin Hayden, then editor of the *Detroit News*.

On the way to the meeting Hoffa stopped at Airport Service Lines, an airport limousine service in which he was a sleeping and hidden partner with Louis 'The Pope' Linteau,[4] and told employees about the meeting. He then telephoned his wife at around 2.20 p.m. complaining that no one had arrived. He was last seen in the parking lot of the restaurant getting into a car at about 2.45 p.m. Louis Linteau said he had a call from Hoffa at 3.30 p.m. saying that Tony Jack had set up the meeting and then failed to keep the appointment. The next morning Hoffa's green Pontiac was found unlocked at the restaurant car park. Of Hoffa there was never again a sign.[5]

Giacalone was able to produce a cast-iron alibi. First, he had been to a barber who remembered him well, and then he had been with his lawyer, Bernard Humphrey. He was also seen somewhat 'uncharacteristically glad-handing his way around the Southfield Athletic Club'.[6] Provenzano had been playing kalooki at his union hall in New Jersey. He too denied there was to be a meeting with Hoffa at the Manchus Red Fox. The police kept a detailed surveillance on both the Giacolones during the next month, but were completely unable to link either of them to Hoffa's disappearance.

However, on 5 November of that year, Teamster Ralph

---

[4] The nickname came not from any religious habit but because he always seemed to be everywhere at once.

[5] There had been troubles in Detroit, seemingly related to the Teamsters, earlier in the summer when the car of Local 299 vice-president Richard Fitzsimmons was bombed in full daylight outside Nemo's, a bar near Tiger Stadium. Jack Kresnack and Joe Swickard in the *Detroit News* and *Free Press*, 19 December 1992.

[6] For a short account of Giacalone's career see *Detroit Free Press*, 24 February 2001.

Picardo contacted FBI agents from prison, where he was serving a murder sentence, to say that when he had been visited by Stephen and Thomas Andretta, friends of Provenzano, Stephen had let slip that he had provided the alibi for Tony. This brought the expected rush of activity, a series of police line-ups and a Grand Jury hearing involving Gabriel and Salvatore 'Sally Bugs' Briguglio, two of Provenzano's closest associates. In the event nothing much came of the hearing. Lawyers for witnesses are not permitted to be present during the evidence but can be conferred with outside. Stephen Andretta left the Grand Jury hearing over 1,000 times to confer with his lawyer, William Bufalino snr. On the 1,000th occasion Bufalino handed out autographed footballs. Stephen Andretta earned himself a prison sentence for contempt and continued to refuse to testify even after he had been offered immunity from prosecution.

On 12 August James Hoffa jnr received a ransom note signed 'Queen Liz' demanding $1 million in small bills:

> If law is around, good-bye James Riddle Hoffa. We send back nuts, not ears. He is already wounded we had to cut him up a bit.

The money was to be delivered to the 711 Bar on Michigan in downtown Detroit. Only the police attended the proposed rendezvous.

The reason for Hoffa's death was almost certainly to do with Union politicking. One version is that he was murdered to stop him regaining power, something which his Mafia friends could not countenance; a second opinion is that he was killed to prevent him blowing the whistle on the control which organised crime figures still had in the Union; yet a third is that he died because he had too much knowledge of the John Kennedy assassination.

As to the death itself, there is speculation that Hoffa was garrotted in the car in which he left the restaurant; bits of his hair and some blood could be traced to the back seat. Various methods of disposal have been suggested, including the use of a fat-rendering plant. A Mob executioner, Charles Allen, said that Hoffa had indeed been garrotted by Salvatore Briguglio but that the killing had taken place in a syndicate hide-out. Hoffa's body had then been processed at a meat-grinding plant and the pieces thrown into a swamp in Florida. A further version is that his body was dumped in the Gulf of Mexico in a 55-gallon drum filled with wet concrete.

At a senate hearing in 1988 the then FBI director, William Sessions, said that he believed the men responsible for Hoffa's death were now in prison after being sentenced for other crimes.[7] 'Chuckie' O'Brien, who came under considerable suspicion, maintained that the government killed Hoffa as an excuse to investigate the Teamsters again and had left him as the fall guy. He claimed that on the afternoon of Hoffa's death he had been helping the Teamsters' vice-president's wife cut up salmon. He then took the car for petrol and had

[7] Tony Giacalone was later sentenced to 10 years for tax fraud. Tony Provenzano died while serving a life sentence for the murder of Anthony Castellito in 1961; he had been convicted in 1978. The body of Castellito – who had been secretary treasurer of Local 560 – was never found, but it was said he had been garrotted with piano wire. On 21 March 1978, Salvatore 'Sally Bugs' Briguglio was shot to death outside a Little Italy, New York, restaurant; he had been indicted in the Castellito killing. Louis Linteau died of natural causes in 1978 aged 64.

taken the opportunity to clean fish blood off the back seat.

In 1974 he went down to live in Hallandale, Florida, where in October 1990 an attempt was made to remove him from the Teamsters there on the grounds that he was 'acquainted with, or a friend of leading members of the Detroit Mafia'. It was alleged that he had violated the union constitution and had brought 'reproach' to the union by being convicted of making a false statement for a bank loan and accepting a car from an employer who had a contract with the union. He was also said to have used an American Express card to embezzle $12,000 of union funds, chartering a LearJet to fly to Texas for a concert. O'Brien said he had repaid half the money and intended to reimburse the rest. He admitted knowing Jack Tocco 'as a personal friend'. At one hearing he said he had not seen him for a couple of years, and on another occasion that it had been 'over 12 maybe 13'.[8]

Hoffa was legally declared dead in 1982. Then in 1989 contract killer Donald 'Tony the Greek' Frankos told *Playboy* that Jimmy Coonan had shot Hoffa. 'Mad Dog' Sullivan had dismembered the body and kept the parts in a freezer for five months before burying them in an oil-drum in the end zone of Giants Stadium, in New Jersey.[9] A New York court judge and former prosecutor of Sullivan said, 'There is no doubt he is capable of it.' The end zone was never excavated.[10]

The story was revived with the approaching death of

[8] *Detroit Free Press*, 21 December 1992.
[9] *Playboy*, 20 September 1989 and D. Frankos, *Contract Killer*.
[10] There is a fairly detailed if anecdotal account of Sullivan's life in D. Frankos, *Contract Killer*.

Giacolone who, it was hoped, might leave some tantalising clues or at least comments behind him, but he said nothing. Then in the autumn of 2001 came the announcement that the FBI had some DNA evidence which apparently proved the original police suspicions that Hoffa had been driven from the Red Fox by O'Brien. James Burdick, O'Brien's lawyer from the time of the investigation, was sceptical, saying his client was a notorious big mouth who could not possibly have kept his mouth shut. 'If he knew anything about it, he'd be deader than a doughnut 25 years ago,' he said.[11]

So just where did the death of Giacolone and the defection of Nove Tocco leave the Detroit Mob? There was a suggestion that the Red *mafiya* would take an interest, but it was felt that since the Mob's principal illegitimate business in recent years had been beating up illegal bookmakers there was no real likelihood of a war. Over drugs perhaps; illegal bookmaking, no. The probable answer to the question is that the Mob has crumbled in a crumbling, boarded-up city. It is doubtful if it will ever be a force again. While the economy has been good, the inner city has never recovered from the riots of the 1970s followed by looting of shops by youth gangs. As a result shopkeepers moved to safer and more salubrious areas such as Oakland – on the borders of which, incidentally, young Jarjosa was killed.

Since the days of the Carter brothers and the Young Boys Inc. (YBI) who dealt in cocaine and heroin respectively, there has been no new drug which needed to be marketed aggressively. The crack epidemic in the city has waned. As a result

---

[11] *Sunday Telegraph*, 9 September 2001.

no new powerful gang has emerged. An attempt by Asian
youth gangs came to nothing; the Asian community in Detroit
is both small and closely knit and, at the first sign of intimidation, the leaders simply went to the police. Similarly,
although there have been Russian stirrings in the area, again
that community is small and the pickings consequently poor.

However, one figure from the past, Milton 'Butch' Jones,
of Young Boys Inc., has resurfaced. He was last heard of
facing murder charges, of which he was acquitted when the
judge ruled that the prosecution had delayed too long in
bringing the case of a 1982 murder to court in 1988; they
had been in possession of the crucial witness since 1985.
Back went Jones to jail to serve out his sentence for drug
trafficking, with a couple of years tagged on for being an
accessory after the fact in the murder of drug dealer Herman
Amos. Of him a Detroit detective commented, 'Watching
Jones could be instructive just like watching a traffic accident.' On his release he wrote his memoirs, copies of which
he presented to homicide officers, and announced that his
new aim in life was to redeem youth.

Jones had what could be described as an interesting career.
According to his memoirs, at the age of 14 he killed his first
man, someone he described as Stick-Up Mike who was threatening the drug-dealing operation of Jones's brother-in-law Dr
Bombay.[12] Jones then switched allegiance to a man he calls
Black Joe and began to take on contract arson – which meant
a petrol bomb in a supermarket at $500 a throw.

His first murder contract found him hiding in a dump-

---

[12] Milton David 'Butch' Jones, *YBI: Young Boys Inc.*

ster until the victim came, as he did regularly, at 7 a.m. to trash the garbage. Jones leaped out and the man tried to run away in terror before Jones shot him in the back. The killing was regarded as a great success and Jones now moved up a rank from contract arsonist to contract killer.

It was a career which could not last. His brother was killed on 31 January 1974, the day Jones's son Moe Moe was born, and just over a year later, on 22 March 1975, he received a 7½–15-year sentence for manslaughter. Released in 1978, he had devoted his not inconsiderable talents to setting up Young Boys Inc., a drug-dealing syndicate which controlled some 80 per cent of the marketing of heroin in the city and suburbs. Competition from the Pony Down Gang was brushed aside.

One of the greatest assets in Jones's survival was the lawyer W. Otis Culpepper whom Jones had rescued from the depths of the Public Defender Office. The Young Boys provided him with sufficient work to begin a career in private practice which would lead to him becoming one of the most sought after criminal defence lawyers in the city. Jones was so enamoured of him that he promised him a Rolls-Royce if Culpepper could obtain an acquittal on a murder charge, something the lawyer accomplished.

But even Culpepper could do nothing when, after years of trying, the authorities arrested 41 Young Boys (and girls for that matter) in 1982. Jones had saved the estimated sum of $5 million and bought himself a modest spread in Arizona. Now his bail was set at $10 million, the same figure as that of John DeLorean who was later acquitted of fraud following a spectacular trial. Jones had secretly hoped it would be higher. Down he went, along with most of the others, in sentences ranging well into double figures. An exception was Raymond Peoples who received a modest 18 months. He might have been better off with longer, for it was believed that he had rolled over and he was shot to death in 1984.

Jones took up chess in prison and for a time thought of living off social security, which would enable him to play in tournaments around America. He had, he says, almost reached Master status.

Unfortunately the Jones redemption mission was put on hold, if only temporarily, when in the summer of 2001 he found himself in custody awaiting trial, indicted in a cocaine conspiracy along with State Senator Keith Stallworth. The Senator had been having something of a torrid time in 2001. Before this case he had been arrested for obtaining a false driver's licence while allegedly trying to disguise his financial involvement in the sale of a topless bar, something for which he faced a $5,000 fine and 5 years' imprisonment. Now he was charged in an indictment with another 13 people with a variety of crimes including murder. The allegation against Stallworth was that he received $20,000 from drug sales in 1998.

Kidnapping as a means of enforcement is popular in Detroit and two cases provide good examples.[13] In the first, in 1996, Gena LaShawn Wright was found shot dead in an alleyway. A popular girl, who had been a junior varsity basketball coach, she had the misfortune to associate with Lamaah Carter and it probably cost her her life. At first the police

[13] Angelo B. Henderson, 'Detroit Kidnapping Casts a Grim Light on a Shifting Crime' in *Wall Street Journal*, 18 April 2001.

thought her death was a result of a robbery, but it appeared that she had been kidnapped and forced to make a series of withdrawals from cash machines. Claude Daniel was charged with and acquitted of an inside robbery. Allegedly it had been set up by Lamaah and his brother Jermaine, who was found dead with what the police said was a self-inflicted gunshot wound. It was the same weapon which had been used to kill Gena.

When an armed raid took place at the Coney Island Diner in run-down East Detroit in June 1999, it was assumed that the target was robbery. In fact David 'Skip' Watson, armed with an AK-47, and Rynell Davis were looking for Carl 'Bart' Simpson who, until their arrival, had been playing a video machine and was now pulled from under a table. He was dragged outside and thrown in the boot of the waiting car.

Watson and Davis believed that Simpson had broken into an abandoned home at 763 Philip Street where they were holding a cache of guns and drugs, and had stolen them. One of the guns was a particular favourite of Watson's, a Calico, a semi-automatic 86 centimetres long, half of it barrel, capable of holding 100 rounds, and which he called his 'bitch'. Davis, who pleaded guilty, said that he had discovered the theft, contacted Watson on his mobile and had been told that he (Rynell), had to get the gun back. Watson did not care if he had to kill someone to do so.

In fact Rynell had shown the gun to Simpson a few days earlier and the boy and Juan Dawonne, who lived with Simpson's cousin, were suspected. According to Dawonne's evidence, Watson appeared and pushed the AK-47 in his chest demanding the return of the 'bitch'. When Dawonne said he knew nothing of the gun he was shown Simpson in the boot of the car. Watson said he would kill the whole family if either he did not get his gun back, or they called the police, or both, and drove off. There followed a week of calls, with Watson threatening the family and Simpson pleading for help down the line. Now, said Davis, at this point he had dropped out. Unsurprisingly Simpson was not well by this time and he was kept in a disused apartment block where he was bound foot and mouth with duct tape and left in a kitchen where the temperature was over 100 degrees. When two or three days later Watson returned, he found Simpson in an appalling state, poured some cold water in his mouth and fed him a piece of festering Vienna sausage. He then left him and called the family, again demanding the gun. Apparently he next went back some eleven days later and, he said, found Simpson gone; he thought he might have been taken by a crackhead. Simpson's body was found in a burned-out Buick Riviera on Detroit's west side on 28 June.

In return for a second-degree murder plea and giving evidence against Watson, Rynell Davis received 15–25 years. Watson, who made a full confession which included an apology, was tried in October 2000. His confession was ruled inadmissible because he had been detained over the permitted period, and the jury disagreed. He was retried in April 2001 and sentenced to life imprisonment. The Calico was never found.

Detroit is still a big numbers town with several major players, such as Eddie Martin who ran the game at automobile plants around the city, grossing over $1 million weekly. Unfortunately he attempted to launder the proceeds be lending money to University of Michigan basketball players in the hope of a pay-off if and when they became stars in the professional National Basketball Association. In May 2002 Martin pleaded guilty and faced up to 30 months' imprisonment, depending on how much he co-operated with the authorities in a government inquiry. It never came to that. He died in a Detroit hospital of a suspected pulmonary embolism on 14 February 2003. Meanwhile his son, Carlton, received 18 months' imprisonment. The University of Michigan imposed sanctions on itself by forfeiting 113 victories from the early 1990s, imposing bans on the men's team and returning $442,000 won in tournaments when ineligible players were fielded.

The manner of Jarjosa's death seems to epitomise what Joe Swickard of the *Detroit Free Press* calls a 'brash unsophisticated approach which the elders worked so hard to tamp down. The strength of the old Detroit Dons was that it was a business. Something like this is inevitably bad for business.'

One possible scenario which will benefit the town's criminal element is that Canada, five minutes away through the Windsor Tunnel, will legalise marijuana – and then it will be back to the 1920s, the good old days of the Purple Gang and their rivals the Little Jewish Navy. 'There is still hope that the Lord will provide,' says Swickard.

[14] Betting in many American sports is not on the winner, which in, say, college football is often almost pre-ordained, but by how many points a team will win. Point shaving is keeping the score out of a betting pattern, e.g. University of Michigan to win by 10+ points. Spread betting is now becoming increasingly popular in British sport.

21

Philadelphia

The trials and tribulations of the alleged boss of South Philadelphia, Skinny Joe Merlino, continued throughout 2001 with his former associate, Ralph Natale, playing the Sammy 'The Bull' Gravano role.

The Philadelphia Outfit had fallen on hard times. Once said to have had Albert Dimes – the right-hand man of Billy Hill, King of the London Underworld of the 1950s – as its tried and trusted British representative, its street credibility plunged when on 10 October 1988 Thomas Del Giorno gave a new twist to the Mafia induction ceremony. The hitman turned informer told the court that:

> Then they bring out a gun and knife and he asks you if you would use the gun to help anyone in this room. Then he chooses a guy to prick your [trigger] finger. And they burn

a tissue and you say, 'May I burn like the saints if I betray anyone in this room.' Then you kiss him on both cheeks.

This referred to the picture of the saint which is set alight in the hand of an inductee who should say, 'May I burn like the saint in this picture . . .' Del Giorno had already undergone some troubles of his own, particularly when he survived an assassination attempt.

Many of the troubles of the Philadelphia Mafia were of their own making. Angelo Bruno, regarded as the quiet Don and the friend of Dimes and Hill, had been assassinated on 21 March 1980. From then on there has been something approaching a twenty-year war with the police picking off survivors from the sidelines. In the first four years alone 30 people were killed in the war of succession. With the approval of the New York Families, the leadership initially passed to Phil Testa, but he lasted less than a year and was killed on 15 March 1981 by a bomb hidden in his porch which was detonated while he was on the roof. Since (correctly) the underboss Pete Casella was suspected of the killing, the leadership passed to the *consiglieri*, Nicodemo 'Little Nicky' Scarfo. In 1989 he was convicted following the murder of Frank 'Frankie Flowers' D'Alfonso but retained control in prison until in 1991 John Stanfa, who had been present at the killing of Bruno, became the head of the Family. Although he was Sicilian and seemingly of impeccable pedigree, his appointment did not suit a group of Young Turks.[1]

---

[1] For a fuller account of the Philadelphia Mafia and the wars following the death of Bruno to the arrival on the scene of Skinny Joe Merlino, see James Morton, *Gangland International*. For a detailed account of the Scarfo years and the downfall of John Stanfa, see George Anastasia, *Blood and Honour*, *Mobfather* and *The Goodfella Tapes*.

On 5 August 1993 the leader of this faction, Skinny Joe Merlino, was hit in the buttocks and his friend, Michael Ciancaglini, was killed in a drive-by shooting in South Philadelphia. The killers pulled up in a white car, jumped out and fired 10–15 shots before fleeing. The getaway car, found burning shortly afterwards, was traced to Battaglia Motors in Hammonton. Curiously, two hours before the hit Sergio Battaglia and Herbert Keller had been arrested in possession of a semi-automatic shotgun, two 9 mm pistols, Teflon-coated bullets that could pierce a bullet-proof vest, rubber gloves and ski masks. They could not have been involved in the shooting because they were then held in custody on bail of $100,000, reduced four days later to $7,500 when they were released. Both were described as 'significant associates' of the Stanfa Family.

If, as the police suspected, these were attacks by the Stanfa faction, reprisals were not long in coming. On Tuesday 31 August 23-year-old Joseph, son of John Stanfa, was hit in an ambush as he rode with his father to work. The attackers had lain in wait in a white van with portholes near the Schuykill Expressway during the morning rush hour. One bullet shattered the back window, hitting Joseph Stanfa in the jaw.

Now it was thought that the pro-Merlino faction had over-reached itself. Quite apart from Stanfa's connections he was regarded as having a far greater operational strength than Merlino. But when it came to it Merlino survived. In March 1994 John Veasey, described as 'a slugger, a guy who looks like a bouncer, a wannabe, who Stanfa gave a chance to get into the big time',[2] was shot three times in the head when

---

[2] Frederick T. Martens quoted in the *New York Times*, 6 October 1995.

he was caught unguarded in a flat over a meat store. He had slashed his way out of immediate danger and by the time he had thought things through he defected into police custody. Now he appeared before a Grand Jury to say how he had been ordered to kill both Merlino and Ciancaglini. On 17 March the police swooped, arresting Stanfa and eleven of the Family in a cross-Philadelphia and New Jersey raid.

Stanfa was charged with attempting to kill Skinny Joe Merlino as well as with the murders of Michael Ciancaglini and Frank Baldino, the latter killed as he left the Melrose Diner in South Philadelphia on 17 September 1993. Described by a neighbour as 'a nice guy. I knew him a long time', Baldino was a low-level soldier who collected street taxes for Merlino. This killing was supposedly in revenge for the failed murder by men in ski masks of Leon Lanzilotti and Michael Forte on 15 September. That pair had been poaching taxes from Merlino-owned men on the street.

Three days earlier Joseph Merlino snr, Skinny Joe's father, had been released from prison and was now said to be poised to take control of the Philadelphia Underworld. Since his own shooting Skinny Joe had been back inside, jailed for 3 years for violation of probation and a court order not to mix with LCN figures. While under the order he had been formally inducted into the Philadelphia Family. He was paroled in May 1992 after serving 2 of a 4-year sentence for an armoured-truck robbery which had netted more than $352,000.

Perhaps Veasey should have thought twice and then again about his defection. His 36-year-old brother Billy was shot dead in his greenish-blue Jeep in Bouvier Street in a hail of bullets at 6.45 a.m. on the morning when John Veasey was due to give evidence.

A week later Veasey gave evidence to say that his instructions were, 'Just kill anybody aligned with Merlino', adding, 'After I killed two people, I got a tattoo on my back . . . it had two bullets on it.' After the second killing he received a pay rise from $300 a week to $500. The tattoo was later embellished with 'Loyal and Faithful to John' in Chinese characters. He accepted that he had been on anti-depressants: 'I was having nightmares from the shooting and my family not being in the program.'

In November 1995, after a 30-hour deliberation over six days, the jury returned verdicts against Stanfa in 33 of the 35 counts against him and seven other men.

If that was not enough for the Family, hardly had the ink dried on Stanfa's certificate of conviction when law-enforcement authorities announced that they were focusing on Ralph Natale and Joseph Merlino. The inquiry would, they said, feature the failed shooting of Joseph Ciancaglini at his Gray's Ferry restaurant on 2 March 1993 and the successful shooting of Rod Colombo in Audubon. Colombo, a former professional bodybuilder, came to South Philadelphia in September 1992 after working as an enforcer for a Los Angeles-based Mob. He was found shot twice in the back of the head and was suspected of holding back contributions he had collected on behalf of his boss.

The law officers did not regard the once mighty and stable Bruno Family as now being much more than a disorganised rabble. They had little faith in the ability of Joey Merlino to raise the Family much above the level of a street gang. During the Stanfa trial he had apparently been seen rolling dice in the hallways – not what is expected of a potentially great Don.

However, it may be that, as Mark Twain wrote: 'The report of my death was an exaggeration.' In the middle of 1996 Stanfa was actively pursuing a series of appeals on a variety of legal grounds. He argued that his conviction should be reversed on the same grounds as that of Oliver North, that the prosecutors had illegally used secret testimony given before a Grand Jury.

Meanwhile Skinny Joe Merlino, described as having dark good looks, flashy clothes and a beautiful wife, now alleged along with Ralph Natale to be the boss of Philadelphia, had assumed the mantle of defender of the poor. He threw his first Thanksgiving-cum-Christmas bash for poor children in South Philadelphia on the day John Stanfa and his associates were convicted of racketeering. Merlino said he hoped that this event would be an annual one. He planned to make it 'like the Jerry Lewis telethon'. 'Why do it?' he was asked. 'It's something nice for people who don't have nothing,' he replied. 'If you didn't have nothing to eat, I'd invite you in,' he said.[3] Over the years he sensibly continued the annual parties complete with turkeys, Santa Claus and presents for the kids.

An interesting event took place on 18 March 1998 when Anthony Turra was murdered on the steps of his South Philadelphia home. He was the father of the Philly drug lord Louis Turra who had himself been killed the previous

---

[3] *Organized Crime Digest*, 4 December 1996.

year. It was never quite clear what Anthony Turra's killing was all about. Neither he nor his son were actually part of the Philadelphia Mob, but at the time of his death Anthony was on trial for conspiring to kill Merlino, something which he denied. It could have been a message to Anthony Turra's brother Rocco to stay out of things. As might be hoped, Rocco Turra had sprung to his brother's defence saying that while he might be a drug dealer he 'couldn't hurt a fly' and had certainly not planned to kill Merlino. Two arrests of Merlino supporters were made, but the men were released and it was never clear whether Anthony Turra's killing was a reprisal, a warning or something completely unconnected – although that last was probably not the way to bet.

By 2001 all was definitely not well with Merlino. The prosecution's threats to go after him and Natale were carried out and he was arrested in 1999, to be followed by a Federal Grand Jury indictment in March the next year. Now in the dock with Merlino were his *consigliere* George Borgesi, Steven Mazzone (said to be the underboss) and four others. And there in the witness box was the 69-year-old Natale, claiming he had been the real boss and telling more or less all against Skinny Joe. Natale had the expectation of a lighter sentence at the end of the day and here he was paying off his debt.

> Whenever I wanted something done on the street, whether it was an extortion, a beating or a murder I would pass the order on to Joey Merlino, and then he would have to go find the men within our family to go ahead and do it.

Natale also shed some light on the death of Billy Veasey. One of the defendants, John Ciancaglini, had asked his permission to carry it out, he said. When it came to it Ciancaglini was able to call three witnesses to say that he had been at his mother-in-law's at the time of the hit.

Natale had been recorded in prison conversations speaking in less than respectful terms about his boss and former friends. On 29 October 1999 the tape picked up Natale calling Borgesi 'panicky' and a 'homosexual'. His own uncle, Joseph Ligambi, was 'a freak'. Martin 'Marty' Angelina was a 'fat drunk' who 'looks like a penguin'. Predictably most of the wrath was aimed at Skinny Joe who was, said Natale to his associate Daniel D'Ambrosio, 'a combination of Nicky Scarfo and John Gotti'.

In his role as penitent Natale had already caused problems for Milton Milan, the Mayor of Camden which was regarded as the poorest city in New Jersey, who had followed two of the previous four incumbents of the mayoralty into the dock.[4] Natale gave evidence that he had channelled between $30,000 and $50,000 to Milan over a two-year period to get the mayor in his pocket so that he could direct contracts to Mob-backed businesses. Natale had paid for the mayor's celebratory dinner on the night he was sworn in, and also for a holiday he had taken in

[4] Angelo Errichetti, the Mayor of the Borough of Camden, New Jersey, who for a $25,000 bribe offered to make introductions, was the first down. According to conman Mel Weinberg, who worked undercover for the FBI in return for the dropping of an indictment for fraud, he also '. . . offered us the Port of Camden for drugs. I mean, he was – he was a nice guy. I mean anything crooked he'd do.' Errichetti later served 3 years. His successor, former school superintendent Arnold Webster, and Milan's predecessor, pleaded guilty to accepting $20,000 in school district funds.

Florida with his girlfriend. It was at this trial that Natale
made his claim to leadership, and he went on to give
chapter and verse for some of his killings. Included were
the 1970 murder of George Feeney, shot twice in the face
for insulting him, and the Christmas Day 1973 killing of
Joel McGreal, shot in the back of the head because he
wanted control of a bartenders' union. 'I gave my whole
life to La Cosa Nostra. I did enough,' Natale told the court,
adding that if he had any life left he wanted to spend it
in peace with his wife and children. Natale's evidence was
backed by the drug dealer José Rivera who said that he
had given or lent $65,000. The mayor had been around
him so much, said Rivera, 'People thought he was my bodyguard.'

Much of the defence case in the Merlino trial was devoted
to an interesting, if high-risk, strategy. Being the boss was all
in Natale's mind, ran the argument. If so, then the defendants could not be convicted of crimes in a racketeering
enterprise. The aim of this was to offset Natale's boast that
he was the former boss of the 'Philadelphia–South Jersey La
Cosa Nostra'.

In support of the theory Bruce Cutler, John Gotti's one-
time lawyer who was now appearing for Borgesi, examined
Natale's parole hearing. He had violated the terms of his
parole and stiff penalties seemed likely until, on 8 December
1999, the government department wrote saying that 'Mr
Natale is the first boss of the La Cosa Nostra Family to co-
operate.' It added that this uniqueness 'shall make him a
target for the rest of his life'. Natale had earlier written that,
'I considered myself boss from the day I came home from

Allenwood Low' (a federal prison in north-eastern Pennsylvania).[5]

Another strand of the argument was that as Natale did not behave in accordance with the accepted traditions of a *mafioso*, therefore he could not be one. Cutler's suggestions of un-Mafia-like behaviour included both the slapping of a 70-year-old, partially blind man in a restaurant and openly carrying on an affair with a 30-year-old woman who had once been a friend of his own daughter. If he behaved like this, he certainly couldn't be a Mafia leader.

Mazzone's lawyer, Stephen Patrizio, suggested that Natale had fallen out with his client because of his failure to show proper respect to the girl and because his wife had refused to go out in company with her. Certainly parts of his evidence were true. As sometimes happens with older men he had spent thousands on the girl, including paying her rent for both a condo and a summer home and buying a car. Not accepted was the suggestion that somehow Natale had conned Merlino and others out of $400,000 in part to support this lifestyle; loans he never intended to repay. He had, he admitted, discussed legitimate business deals, but these were not cons and were only part of conversations relating to Mob business including several hits. The last of the prosecution witnesses, bookmaker Michael Casolaro, was very nearly just that. The authorities claimed that a plot to kill him after he had given evidence had been foiled.

In the end everybody could claim something out of the

[5] For reports of the case see *The Inquirer* and the Philadelphia *Daily News* including Kitty Caparella, 'Cutler stages unusual defense', 20 April 2001.

trial, but probably Skinny Joe Merlino was the outright winner. The jurors had been out for a week in the four-month trial when they returned a verdict finding him guilty on 20 counts of extortion, bookmaking and receiving stolen property, but crucially not guilty of the one murder charge he faced. 'In a nutshell, the jury rejected the government's case,' said Merlino's lawyer, Edwin Jacobs jnr. The *Philadelphia Inquirer* described the verdicts as 'a stunning rebuke to federal prosecutors and the FBI'. 'We came out winners,' said Kathy Ciancaglini, wife of soldier John. The defendants appear to have owed much of their good fortune to one juror who held out against any convictions for much of the six-day retire-ment. He was joined by two others on the charges of murder and violence. One juror commented, 'In general, I would say 11 of the 12 thought these people did all the murders. But there was enough gray area.'[6]

In many ways it was not surprising that some of the jury could not bring themselves to convict on the evidence of such men as Peter 'Pete the Crumb' Caprio and Philip 'Philly Phil' Casale. The first took his name, he said, because as a child he always ate the crumbs but not the cake. It was he who had dug the grave of Butchie – a local low-level wiseguy, shot in 1975 for skimming gambling profits – in the base-ment floor of his club. The burial caused difficulties because when the City of Newark later bought the premises for rede-velopment, Caprio and a friend had to exhume Butchie. Sadly, portions of him were stuck in the mud. They 'removed several leg bones but the remainder of the body was left. More acid

---

[6] *The Inquirer*, 21, 23, 24 July 2001.

was poured on the body and the hole was cemented over again.' The leg bones were buried in a local garbage dump.[7]

Speaking of Caprio, George Fresolone, who had known him in the 1970s and 1980s, gave the lie to the cake story:

> He had a social club on Hudson Street, kind of a dump in a real bad neighbourhood. And a lot of times he would sleep on a cot in a back room. He also dressed like a slob, that's why we called him 'The Crumb'. He used to wear a toupee that cost, like 18 bucks. Real cheap. That was his lifestyle. That's why he was 'The Crumb'. If he offered you a sandwich or a coffee, you wouldn't take it. It was just a filthy, filthy place.[8]

Casale was known as a hitman whose *modus operandi* was close-range work and who fed himself on potato crisps while waiting for victims to appear. Once when waiting for a victim in 1991, he had finished his fourth bag before there was any sign of the man. When he called Caprio for instructions he was told simply, 'Eat more chips.' Afterwards the packets became a code joke between the pair: 'Tonight's potato chip night' and 'I think it's potato chip time'. Casale cut himself a deal in 1999 and Caprio, who admitted involvement in four murders, rolled over on his arrest in March the following year. Casale, whose record boasted an attack and sexual molestation of a 10-year-old girl back in 1977, had been working with the North Jersey branch of the Philly Mafia.

[7] FBI quoted in George Anastasia, 'Witnesses offer an underworld diary of hits and hidden bodies' in *The Inquirer*, 13 March 2001.
[8] Quoted by Jerry Capeci, 'A Crumb Bum' in *This Week in Gangland, The Online Column*, 12 July 2001.

He admitted carrying out five murders, usually while sitting next to his victim in a car.

In his confession 'The Crumb' admitted that after Merlino's arrest he was plotting to take over the Family and eliminate the top men, killing Joseph Ligambi, Borgesi and Steven Mazzone by luring them to a meeting in New Jersey.

Juries simply do not like this sort of witness and the prosecution tends to try to shift the blame for having to call men such as Caprio on to the defence. They point out that the only witnesses to a criminal conspiracy are participating criminals. However, their metaphor 'Swans don't swim in sewers' does not always appeal to juries, and clearly it did not do so in the Merlino trial.

There was, of course, the sentencing aspect still to come, but again the defendants did not seem overly displeased. Skinny Joe Merlino collected 14 years and would be released in nine. The federal prosecutors, describing him as a 'confirmed enemy of civilised society' whose crimes were 'deliberate, premeditated and systemic', had sought a term in excess of 24 years. His father, now serving 45 years, would probably be out before him. George Borgesi, seen as No. 3 in the hierarchy, received 14 years. Martin Angelina collected 78 months and John Ciancaglini, whose brother Michael had been killed in the attack on Merlino and whose other brother had been crippled in the 1993 war, drew 9 years. 'Fat Ange' Lutz, also known as Buddha because of his 400 lbs weight, not a made member and in some ill-health, collected the same.

But all was not over for Merlino on the charge of having murdered racketeer Joseph Sodano, allegedly killed for showing a lack of respect, in 1996. Now in an indictment unsealed on 20 August 2001 in Newark, N. J., the prosecution decided to have a second go, alleging that he and Vincent 'Beeps' Centorio had been involved in Sodano's death. The allegation was that Caprio had received orders from Merlino and Natale to kill Sodano. The actual murder, it said, had been carried out in a parking lot by Casale. The Philadelphia jury had only found the case 'not proven'. Naturally the defence raised the double jeopardy issue, but on 17 October Judge Dickinson R. Debevoise rejected the defence motion. Merlino was to face another trial.

In early 2002 it was rewards time again. This time the lucky man was Fred Angelucci, who had recorded 40 conversations talking about $1 million-plus cargo thefts in South Philadelphia. The recordings ended when his machine fell out of his pocket. Now he pleaded that he should be allowed to look after his severely disabled son rather than go to prison. He was sentenced to 5 years' probation. It was the second time he had given evidence and been admitted to the witness programme. In the late 1970s he had given evidence in a counterfeit currency scam and, in return, had been let off a number of outstanding theft cases.

There was another attack on the crumbling empire when in December 1999 the police raided three sports bars and 20 homes during *Monday Night Football*. Charges were a long time in filtering through but, when they did, in the dock were Joseph 'Mousie' Massimino, alleged to be a Merlino soldier, and Edward 'Pop' Parisi. The investigators said that the gambling ring of which the pair were said to be leaders netted in the region of $30 million. Also indicted was a local councilman, William 'Porky' Samploski.

It would be a mistake to completely write off the Philly Mafia, however. A city lawyer said that the new man on the block would probably be Joseph Ligambi, uncle of the defecting Natale,[9] who had survived the Caprio plot. But, 'Now, he may be simply keeping the seat warm.' The lawyer was yet another who regretted the passing of the good old days of the Mafia:

> When I was living in the old Mafia area you didn't need to lock your door. When I went to mass on a Sunday the men would be outside a grocery store and they would tip their hats. Now, the new generation simply stands and stares.

On the domestic front all may not be well with the post-conviction Merlino household either. At 7.15 a.m. on 6 December 2001 the one-legged William 'Billy' Rinick, a convicted sex offender and under a drug investigation, was found hiding under a bed in the Merlino house on Sydenham Street near Hulseman. Within hours he was reported to be frantically trying to establish contact with Merlino to explain what he was doing.

Deborah L. Wells Merlino, in her nightclothes, had been ordered to open the door in a raid by state drug agents.[10]

---

[9] Conversation with the author, August 2001. Defection by relations does not appear to be an impediment to leading Mob figures. Skinny Joe Merlino's uncle, 55-year-old Lawrence 'Yogi' Merlino, a former *capo* who had been living under a new identity in the federal witness protection programme, died from cancer in November 2001. He had been an informant in the trial of Nicky Scarfo.

[10] Thirty-three-year-old Deborah Merlino was born in Korea when her father was in the army. A stylish woman, she lived in Texas, Florida, New York and New Jersey before settling in Philadelphia where she took a job at Saloon, a South Philadelphia restaurant on 7th Street where she met Merlino. Said to favour Versace clothes, she has a licence to sell real estate.

Documents and a quantity of money were seized. Rinick was also being investigated over the 31 October death of drug dealer Adam Finelli, known as Adam Silver, who owned Nick's Charcoal Pit on Snyder Street. Explanations as to the presence of Rinick, who had lost his leg in a motor accident, included his acting as Mrs Merlino's bodyguard in the absence of her husband; he had already guarded her on a trip to Maryland. Edwin Jacobs, the lawyer for both Merlino and Rinick, told reporters that Billy was a friend of the family. However, there were suggestions that Rinick's life expectancy might not be great.[11] But after she had given evidence before a Grand Jury in January 2002, Deborah Merlino's lawyer said, 'Some people confused friendship with infidelity.' Merlino was said to be '100 per cent behind his wife'.

Rinick seems to have been quite capable of taking care of himself in hand-to-hand combat at least. He was next arrested for smashing the face of Salvatore 'Sammy Boy' Abbruzzese inside Gigolo's men's shop on 23 December. The pair had become involved in an argument and Abbruzzese later underwent two operations to reconstruct the bones in his cheek; he had two metal plates and nine screws inserted in his face.

Then at the beginning of 2002 another old figure showed signs of frailty. The 74-year-old Raymond 'Long John' Martorano was shot while driving to an appointment at Pennsylvania Hospital on 17 January.

Back in December 1980, Martorano, who had owned the Cous Little Italy, was involved in the killing of Roofers' Union

[11] *Daily News*, 8, 10 December 2001.

boss, John McCullough, who simply would not go along with the Philadelphia Mob. Convicted in 1984, the conviction was overturned because of prosecutorial misconduct. Nevertheless, he served 17 years in prison on drug charges before his release in 1999. While in prison he had reputedly turned against Nicky Scarfo, both because of the loss of his loan-sharking operation and also because he thought more could have been done for his son, George 'Cowboy' Martorano, who had received a life sentence for drug trafficking also in 1984. At one time he had been thought strong enough to be a potential leader of the Mob, but questions were now asked as to whether he had the friends to shoot back. Clearly somebody thought he was sufficiently dangerous and powerful to be worth trying to kill. Indeed they succeeded. The tough old Martorano initially survived, but infection set in and he died in February 2002. Gang observers thought that he had been more powerful than at first believed, and that he could have been making a play for the top spot in Philadelphia.

22

Las Vegas and Los Angeles

In the late 1980s there were conflicting reports as to whether Mafia-controlled crime in Los Angeles was actually flourishing. Reputedly the head of the local Family was an ex-Clevelander, now the 61-year-old Westlake Village businessman Peter John Milano, whose wife ran a bail bond business. His brother, disbarred lawyer Carmin Milano and allegedly the underboss – something he denied – was, according to an interview he gave, then living in a modest home in Tarzana watching a little television and tucked up in bed by 9 p.m. He had been disbarred following his handling of fraudulent workers' compensation claims, had moved back to California and, it was alleged, lived with and under the guidance of Luigi Gelfuso jnr, then said to be a *caporegime*.[1]

[1] Kim Murphy, 'Not entrenched like Eastern Families,' in *Los Angeles Times*, 29 June 1987.

Things became slightly clearer towards the end of the twentieth century. The California Mafia, despite rumours of its death, was still breathing a little fire. The great days of Jack Dragna and Mickey Cohen might have gone, but there was still a little work about. The California Mob had also turned their thoughts towards Las Vegas, always an open city but one which in recent years had been under the guidance (if not in the grasp) of the Outfit. Now Anthony 'The Ant' Spilotro was dead, were there any pickings about?

For example it turned out that Carmen Milano had been doing more than simply watching a little television before a good night's sleep. In 1998 he had been named in indictments alleging he had participated in a series of racketeering and money-laundering schemes including heading a fraudulent diamond racket. This was simply one of the good old-fashioned tried and tested cons. Victims were to be offered a genuine diamond which was then switched after the sale had been made. Later Milano would tell the court that the scheme had never in fact been carried out, though he did accept that one of the money-laundering schemes had involved dealing in fraudulent food stamps in Los Angeles.

Milano also cleared up the question of his being an under-boss, in 1998 admitting that he had indeed held that position. He had turned himself in to the FBI on 3 February that year, the day the indictment against him was unsealed. 'Rubbish,' he said of it initially. Unfortunately he had been behaving in a wholly Sammy Gravano-like way. Although when indicted he claimed that he had been framed and was the victim of a government conspiracy, saying the Los Angeles Family had been dead for a decade, it appeared that he had been debriefed by the FBI at a Primm hotel-casino in May the previous year. Later he would claim that the report of the conversations in which he talked about his brother Peter was inaccurate, but critics would question what he was doing giving the FBI the time of day in the first place. It was difficult to think other than that he had initially stayed out of custody on the money-laundering charges in return for his co-operation.

Now he named names and became a co-operative witness and, in return for his penitence, in July 2000 he received the minimum sentence of 21 months. This would be followed by 3 years' parole with a condition that he did not associate with any Mafia figures. Happily there would be no possibility of that. When questioned by reporters about his criminal activities he replied, 'That's a past life. I'm here to retire.'

He was certainly more fortunate than his former partner, 'Fat' Herbie Blitzstein. At the end of 1996 had come the news that his was to be a new name in the notorious Las Vegas Black Book which listed those banned from the city's casinos. Blitzstein, once a close associate of Anthony Spilotro, came into the frame when Ted Binion, son of Benny and an executive of the Horseshoe Club, admitted being with him over two dozen times in the past year. Although suspended from casino work, Ted Binion was alleged to have been cashing insurance cheques totalling around $11,000 for Blitzstein. John Momot, Blitzstein's lawyer, said he would challenge the listing. He claimed that since Blitzstein's release from prison in 1991 when he had served a term for fraud charges, he had only been a 'struggling small businessman'.

In the end the efforts to list him proved premature or

possibly fatal. The man who had once been a Mob enforcer and was now a used-car salesman and who, because of two heart bypass operations, was no longer fat, was found shot dead in his townhouse in Las Vegas, killed shortly after Milano's confession. The finder, so to speak, was his business partner, Joe DeLuca.

Blitzstein's lawyer paid his 63-year-old former client tribute:

> Herbie was the last of a breed. He was not going to hurt anyone. This was the type of guy who was never going to give testimony against anyone. If he's convicted of a crime he goes away and does the time. He's not a rat.

In fact Blitzstein's career had been much more upmarket than that of a mere struggling small businessman. When in 1967 Arthur 'Boodie' Cowan, a bookmaker and one of Blitzstein's associates, was found in the trunk of his car shot in the head, it was thought that he had been withholding 'street tax'. When another bookmaker, Henry Kushner, went to prison Blitzstein took over both his and Cowan's customers.

Anthony 'The Ant' Spilotro was sent to Las Vegas to master-mind Chicagoan interests and Blitzstein, who had long been a Spilotro man, then weighing 300 lbs, came with him as muscle, or fat as the case may be. Either way he was an imposing sight. At the time he lived with his third wife on the far north-west side of the city. He drove a white Cadillac Eldorado and was known as a snappy dresser. It was here that he learned the art of receiving, working with Spilotro's brother John at the Gold Rush, a combination jewellery store and electronics factory where many of the top thieves in America, particularly from the west, sold their stolen goods.

Later Blitzstein became a member of Tony Spilotro's burglary ring, the Hole in the Wall Gang, which until it was closed by the FBI on 4 July 1981 existed through the generosity of corrupt members of the Clark County Sheriff's Organized Crime Unit. The trial in early 1986 was declared a mistrial after two jurors were heard allegedly discussing bribes, and Tony Spilotro was shot and killed before the re-trial. Now, in 1987 Blitzstein pleaded guilty to a variety of charges including receiving and using counterfeit credit cards. He received 8 years, during which his health deteriorated; he underwent two heart bypass operations and, suffering from diabetes, had several toes removed from his right foot.

Blitzstein's killing happened almost immediately after Carmen Milano's confession, which might not have earned the underboss a similar encomium. When it came to it the authorities did think the killing was to do with organised crime. In April, eight arrests were made. Two of those indicted, Peter Caruso and Alfredo Mauriello, were named as being involved in the murder, said to have been because of Blitzstein's reluctance to allow the Californian Crime Family to muscle in on his Any Auto Repair business.

Even more interesting than Blitzstein's death was that of his friend, 55-year-old Ted Binion. The legendary casino operator was found dead at his Las Vegas home on 17 September 1998 apparently having taken an overdose of sedatives, what one might call a Prozac end for such a flam-boyant character. In fact the drugs were lethal doses of Xanax – which was a prescribed sedative – and heroin which was not. Born in 1942, as a boy Binion had come to Las Vegas with his father Benny, who had experienced some trouble in Dallas where he was wanted at least for questioning over several murders arising from gambling. The killings were later deemed to be self-defence. The legend is that Benny Binion arrived in town with two suitcases containing $1 million. What is not legend is that he would take bets in his Horseshoe Club which other casinos would decline. Ted Binion gambled all his life and under his control the Horseshoe prospered and the casino also became the home of the Poker World Championships.[2] He bought a 160,000-acre ranch in Montana and another in Pahrump, Nevada, near the brothel. He also began to collect silver bars.

Unfortunately, as the years went by and the various Mob interests were seemingly eliminated from the casinos, Ted Binion failed to shake himself loose of the undesirable elements. In 1986 he was arrested for heroin trafficking and in 1989 he was fined $1 million over some doubtful cash movements. In 1990 he and seven others were charged by the FBI with robbery, kidnapping and beating 'undesirable patrons', many of whom happened to be black. The case never came to trial, but then he failed a drugs test and the Nevada Gaming Commission banned him from his own casino. His appeal was refused in 1997. A few months before his death there had been a shooting at his home.

After the loss of his licence he consoled himself at the Pahrump ranch with his girlfriend Sandy 'The Irish Venus'

---

[2] For a highly entertaining account of Benny Binion, the Horseshoe Casino and the World Poker Championships see Anthony Holden, *Big Deal*.

Murphy, a topless dancer. Ms Murphy had once worked in a bar, the Cheetah Lounge, earning money to pay off a $20,000 gambling debt. This was where Binion had seen her and had liked what he saw. Eventually she had become the *soi-disant* Mrs Binion. He was also smoking rather than eating heroin and becoming increasingly fearful that he might be killed. Guns were kept unloaded in the house and, rather ambiguously, rearview mirrors were attached to beds to warn of intruders. Life with Ms Murphy seems to have been something of a switchback. He gave her a cellphone and a credit card on which she ran up $5,000 a month. He gave her a Mercedes. He also gave her a beating up and made her a beneficiary of his will, leaving her $300,000 and his house.

It was there that he decided to preserve his now considerable collection of silver – estimates of its worth varied up to a maximum of $8 million – by burying it on the edge of his land so that if anyone were to dig it up, they would be seen.

In that respect at least he had a good sense of security because, within 24 hours of his death, Rick Tabish (a builder friend) and two others were arrested. They had taken a mechanical digger to the site and were found removing an estimated $4 million-worth. The builder explained that he had been merely fulfilling Ted's last wish by returning the silver to his Las Vegas home. There was a great deal of urgency because the excavations were halted by the police at 3 a.m. Sandy Murphy then disappeared. It was thought that she had been romantically involved with the builder and had told him the location of the silver.

Two days before his death Binion had written Ms Murphy

out of his will, saying he feared she was going to kill him. A fortnight after his death the police were convinced that there was no question of murder: it was suicide or an accident. Binion's sister was unconvinced. But now there were suggestions that perhaps his death was neither an accident nor suicide. A private detective was hired by the family.

The tributes at and after the funeral, at which there was no Ms Murphy present, were suitably moving. Judge Claiborne was happy to explain Binion's Mob associations as a charitable act of taking pity on an old hood down on his luck. Doyle Brunson, a member of the Horseshoe's Poker Hall of Fame, said of him:

> He had the whole package, the personality, the looks, the talent, the guts and the money. He had some problems but he was one of a kind.

When 'The Irish Venus' finally appeared, she was represented by the legendary Oscar Goodman, whose client list read like a Roll of Honour of Nevadan and other *mafiosi*, and who the next year would go on to become the city's Mayor. She declined to answer some 200 questions put by Richard Wright, representing the Binion estate, including whether she and Tabish had had what was coyly described as a romantic relationship.

At a little after 7 a.m. on 22 February 1999 a search warrant was executed at the two-bedroom Unit 5014 on the Bella Vista apartment complex at 251 S Green Valley Parkway. There the police found both 'The Irish Venus' and Mr Tabish. Soon on the scene was Mr Goodman, who denied on behalf of his clients that there was any kind of tryst. Tabish's business records for the previous two years were found and, more intriguingly, so were a pair of Gucci pants, an Armani shirt, a Wilke Rodriguez top and two pairs of boots that Ms Murphy was said to have purchased for Tabish. From there it was then a relatively short step to their arrest for Binion's murder at the end of June.

It was a story which kept the tabloids and the public happy over the months. In the November Sandra Murphy's lawyer made an application for the return of her black panties which, he said, had been illegally seized to conduct tests for bodily fluids. There was also the question of how the panties had disappeared while in the custody of the detention centre. The motion, perhaps predictably, asked the court to get to the bottom of the matter. This was followed by allegations in the February of 2000 that alibi witnesses for Rick Tabish had been paid. Tabish had claimed that when Binion ingested the fatal drugs he had been at the All Star Transit Mix in Las Vegas. A counter-allegation was that the authorities had instructed a prisoner to steal Tabish's legal notes. The inmate in question, David Gomez, declined to answer questions, citing his constitutional right not to make self-incriminating statements. The following month Ms Murphy, who had been granted bail, was back in custody. She had gone shopping without permission, so violating the terms of her bail.

In fact, although the press and public galleries were a third empty when the trial started in late March 2000 it was of course a several-week wonder. In words which may yet find their way into a Country and Western song, John Momot, representing Murphy, told the jury, 'That's what happens when you love your drugs more than your woman.' Two pictures of Binion were shown during the prosecution's opening speech on an oversized screen. One showed a jovial Ted, the other had him in what was described as the 'mortuary position'. 'There is no murder here,' said Louis Palazzo for Tabish.

As the jury retired Tabish and Murphy joked with reporters as to where they would take their celebratory acquittal dinner. They had misread their peers, however. At the end of eight days, with 4 of the 9 women jurors obtaining permission to wear dark glasses in court, verdicts of guilty were returned.

The pair had become close in the summer of 1998, spending weekends at Mr Binion's expense in Beverly Hills. Like so many others who have plotted murder, Ms Murphy seems to have been unable to keep her mouth shut. Her manicurist told the court that 'The Irish Venus' had been able to predict Binion's death from an overdose.[3]

Asked how, had he been alive, her brother would have reacted to the convictions, Becky Binion Behnen commented, 'He'd be saying, "The bitch got what she deserved and she's the most evil, devious, deceptive person I've ever met".'[4]

On 24 May both were sentenced to life imprisonment with the possibility of parole after 20 years. The jurors had heard how 'The Irish Venus' had been raped at the age of 14, and again 8 years later. She had, her mother said, grown up as

[3] One who talked her way to the gallows was the Blackpool murderess Louisa Merrifield who in 1953, shortly before the death of her employer from Rodine rat poison, was able to predict that she would soon come into money.
[4] For full reports and later developments on the case see the Las Vegas *Sun* and the Las Vegas *Review-Journal* 1998–2001, in particular 20 and 25 May 2000; *The Times*, 2 October 1998; *Newsweek*, 12 July 1999; *Independent*, 22 May 2000.

part of a close-knit South Californian family where she played sports and worked with the handicapped. Neither of the defendants admitted any part in the killing. In July 2003 the Nevada Supreme Court quashed the murder and theft convictions against the pair saying there should be a retrial but upheld the kidnapping and extortion charges against Tabish.

Meanwhile the trial of those accused over the death of 'Fat' Herbie Blitzstein was progressing in an unsatisfactory and unscheduled way. The reasoning behind the death was now thought to be not only his automobile business as such but rather his loan-sharking interests. Caruso wanted Blitzstein dead so that he could take over his street rackets and hired Mauriello to make it happen. In turn there was a conspiracy charge against Toni Davi and Richard Friedman who was alleged to have pulled the trigger.

The prosecution then decided to seek the death penalty and, as a result, all sorts of scurrying for cover occurred. DeLuca was now in the frame. He had, said the prosecution, set up a fake burglary under cover of which the killing took place. DeLuca named names.

Into the frame came the 60-year-old Steve Cino, regarded as a long-standing Buffalo-born crime figure, and Bobby Panaro also from Buffalo, a man with no criminal convictions but also linked by the police to the Todaro Family. They were alleged to have given approval for the killing. Now the FBI was forced to reveal that it had been conducting a long-standing investigation – known as *Operation Button-down* – into organised crime in Nevada.

The FBI had hundreds of hours on tape with two informants, Tony Angioletti and John Branco. The immediate problem was that nowhere was either Cino or Panaro mentioned.

On 31 July 1999 Mauriello was sentenced to 15 years' imprisonment after pleading guilty to accepting $10,000 from Caruso for Blitzstein's murder. He also admitted paying Davi and Friedman to kill 'Fat' Herbie. Davi pleaded guilty and agreed to give evidence in return for a 20-year sentence. Then Caruso and DeLuca pleaded guilty to the burglary of Blitzstein's home. Caruso was sentenced to 2 years' imprisonment and, because he was in debt to the tune of $250,000, was not required to pay restitution. DeLuca was ordered to pay $9,000 and received 18 months. Caruso had written piteously:

> I allowed my desire to continue to play the part of a Las Vegas big-shot to overcome my better judgement. This was a mistake for which I have already paid dearly and which will follow me for the rest of my life. I regret it deeply.

Then, sadly, Caruso died in his cell following a heart attack. His wife told reporters:

> My husband had no real Underworld connections. He was a wannabe, but he could never be because he didn't have no heart [for violence].

Friedman took the offer of 25 years, instead of the risk of a life sentence, by pleading guilty. He accepted that he had received money for participating in the crime but continued to deny that he was the actual killer.

That left only Cino and Panaro in the dock who, after a

four-week trial, were found not guilty of Blitzstein's murder but guilty of conspiracy to extort from him. It was hardly a satisfactory result so far as the prosecution was concerned. Louis Palazzo, who appeared in the trial for Cino, commented, 'The government paid $1 million in "rat-snitch" fees and this is the return on your money when you go out and buy their testimony.'[5]

All of which went to show that perhaps organised crime had not been cleared out of Las Vegas after all, and that there had been more life in the admittedly disorganised Californian Mafia than people had credited.

In fact it was not only Californian interests which had been looking at Las Vegas. The Gambino Family were also said to have been paying undue attention, this time to the adult entertainment business. The allegation is that members of the Family were pressuring a computer expert to divert telephone calls intended for call-out nude-dancing services to competitors. Although prostitution is illegal in Las Vegas its barely distinguishable sister, nude dancing in hotel rooms, is not. The FBI investigation arose as a result of an action brought by Hilda Brauer, owner of the Perfect Bodies and the Young and Sexy Bodies nude-dancing services, against a telephone company and a publisher, alleging they had conspired to divert telephone calls from her business. She lost the action, but the publicity had intrigued the FBI. There

[5] In recent years Las Vegas juries have gained something of a reputation for refusing to convict on the evidence of informants. For an account of Blitzstein's life with Spilotro, see William Roemer, *The Enforcer*. Both the Las Vegas *Sun* and *Review-Journal* carried a full account of the Blitzstein murder case and sentencing. For comments on Carmine Milano and the Los Angeles crime family see the Las Vegas *Sun*, 7 February, 1 September 1998.

were suggestions that the problem had extended beyond the adult entertainment business.[6]

The names in the Nevada Black Book have changed in the 40 years since its pages were first opened in 1960. In 1976 the name itself was changed to The List of Excluded Persons because a black citizen claimed it was a racial slur. At first, it was a looseleaf binder with names and photographs of 11 men who were thought to be 'notorious or [of] unsavoury reputation'. Casino operators had to keep them from their doors or face the revocation of their licences. Despite the change of name the book, which now has a silver cover, has never been known as anything but the Black Book.

Nominated and entered into this dubious Hall of Fame on 13 June 1960 were, in alphabetical order:

John Louis Battaglia
Marshall Caifano
Carl James Civella
Nicholas Civella
Michael Coppola
Louis Tom Dragna
Robert L. Garcia
Sam Giancana
Motel Grzebienacy
Murray Llewellyn Humphreys
Joseph Sica

Four years later the names of Ruby Kolod, Felix Alderisio and William Alderman were added, to be followed 10 years later by two Hawaiians involved in the gambling junket business, Alvin Kaohu and Wilford Kalaauala Pulawa, along with Anthony Giordano, Michael Santo Polizzi and Anthony Joseph Zerilli. Three years after them, in 1978, Anthony Spilotro joined the ranks to complete the first 20 names.

The first to challenge the Black Book had been Californian Louis Tom Dragna, nephew of Jack. Accompanied by civil rights lawyers and trailed by gaming agents, he toured the Strip, refusing to leave and visiting the Tropicana, Stardust and the Dunes.[7] After leaving the next day he filed an action asking the Federal Court to declare that the Black Book was illegal. He was unsuccessful.

Marshall Caifano then took on the Gaming Board, head on. After his exclusion, he visited hotels on the Strip. First, he stayed in the Tropicana and then when told there was no accommodation available, he took a room in a motel without a gaming licence. Finally he asked the Tropicana for a room for the Sunday night. Throughout his stay he toured the casinos on the Strip. The Gaming Control Board struck back, confiscating dice and cards from the casinos Marshall had visited. He too began an action, this time against Governor

---

[7] Regarded in its heyday as the jewel of the Strip, the Dunes was closed by its new owner, Steve Wynn, in January 1993 and was imploded to provide room for a 14-acre lake resort. It had run into hard times and in 1974 was cited for comping Kansas City organised crime boss, Nick Civella. He had stayed under a false name. The Dunes was fined $10,000 despite the defence that the State had not specified the procedure to be followed in dealing with a person listed in the Black Book. In 1975 Morris Shenker, a St Louis lawyer who represented Jimmy Hoffa, bought an interest. In 1987 it was sold to a Japanese businessman who later sold it to Wynn.

Grant Sawyer. He lost, with the Federal Appeals Court ruling that the state's classification of who was, or was not, 'notorious' was reasonable, reinforcing the state's position that entry to casinos in Nevada was a privilege and not a right.[8]

Forty years later Caifano and Dragna still headed the list, followed by the Hawaiians Kaohu and Pulawa. They were the only surviving members from before 1975. Gone were such celebrated names as Sam Giancana and the Civellas, although Anthony 'Tony Ripe' Civella had been added in 1997.[9] The most recent additions since 1999 were Peter Joseph 'PJ' Ribaste, Fred Pascente, Michael Joseph Balsamo and Peter Jay Lenz.

Fred Pascente, a former police officer who in 1997 was named by the Chicago Crime Commission as an associate of the Outfit, went on the list in November 1998. He had served a 20-month sentence after a conviction in 1995 involving him in a 61-count mail fraud.

Balsamo, a native of Las Vegas, was a six-time-convicted slot-machine cheat (Clark County, 4; Douglas County, 1; Atlantic City, 1) who on 22 July 1999 was named when nine of his associates were arrested in an alleged nationwide conspiracy to defraud the casinos of $6 million. He had previously been arrested in Atlantic City on money-laundering charges and had been released.

Peter Jay Lenz followed on 27 January 2000 after being convicted on bookmaking charges and federal charges of

---

[8] *Marshall v Sawyer*, 301 F.2d 105.
[9] Civella was part of the Family which had headed Kansas City over the years, inheriting the leadership from his father, also Anthony but known as Cork because of his temper. Anthony 'Tony Ripe' Civella served a 4½-year sentence for fraud beginning in 1992.

making false statements on a passport application, a far cry from the great crimes of Caifano. Overall Lenz was the fifty-first name to be placed on the list. In 2001 35 were still alive, including Frank Rosenthal.

Rosenthal, one of the more colourful characters on the list who had been linked to Tony Spilotro, now had his own web site. In 1962 he had pleaded guilty to attempting to bribe a New York University basketball player in the NYU v West Virginia game. There were also suggestions that he had tried to bribe an Oregon football player. In 1976 Rosenthal was refused a licence as a key employee at a casino. He later succeeded in obtaining a licence following an application to Judge Joseph Pavlikowski, who had been given a write-off of $2,800 – the cost of his daughter's wedding two years earlier – at the same hotel where Rosenthal then worked as a publicity director. Rosenthal survived an attempt on his life when his Cadillac was blown up in 1982. An effort to have him included in the Black Book in 1988 was temporarily thwarted by Judge Pavlikowski, but his decision was overruled and Rosenthal became the thirtieth entry on 30 November 1988.

Another killing initially thought to have organised crime implications was that of author Susan Berman, whose best-known book is perhaps *Easy Street*. Her body was found on Christmas Eve 2000 in Beverly Hills. She had been shot at least two days earlier by a single bullet to the head.

She was the daughter of David Berman who, on the death of Bugsy Siegel, picked up points in the trail-blazing Flamingo Hotel. Berman, who had served time for kidnapping and been a long-time friend of Siegel, was one of the mobsters called to a meeting to divide ownership of the hotel, the day after the shooting of Siegel on 20 June 1947. Other buyers included the engagingly named 'Ice Pick' Willie Alderman. Berman also acted as the personal muscle for the eventual manager Gus Greenbaum.[10] Said to be so hard he could kill a man with one hand tied behind his back, Berman died of natural causes when Susan was 12. Her mother killed herself the next year.

Susan Berman had led a secluded life over the years, bringing up two children from a long-standing relationship. At the time of her death apparently she was considering a number of projects which would involve Las Vegas and the Mafia, possibly of a tell-all variety. One suggestion was that, because of her childhood, she knew too much about too many people and people feared to read more about themselves. Others, loyally and almost certainly correctly, suggested that the killing had been designed to look like a Mafia hit.

Then a rather curious thing happened. The Westchester, New York, police announced that they had been wanting to speak with her regarding the disappearance of the 29-year-old Kathleen A. Durst who had vanished nearly 20 years earlier. She had been the wife of the wealthy property owner Robert Durst, and they had spent a weekend at their country home near Salem. Kathleen was attending medical school and had apparently telephoned to say she felt ill and would not be able to attend class. She was never seen again. Susan Berman had been a long-standing friend of Durst who, after

---

[10] For a full account of the building of the Flamingo and the career and death of Siegel, see Ed Reid and O. Demaris, *The Green Felt Jungle*. For a shorter account of organised crime in Las Vegas, see James Morton, *Gangland International*.

his wife's disappearance, went to live in California. Durst now vanished.

More or less the next page in the story told of his arrest. In the autumn of 2001 a young boy opened a black plastic bag washed up near Galveston, in which were various body parts; other sacks contained other pieces of Morris Black, a former neighbour of Durst who had been renting an apartment in the city. He had been living in drag under the name of Dorothy Ciner. It transpired that he had been weaving his way across the States for the better part of nine months, appearing sometimes in cocktail lounges in Manhattan, sometimes in diners in New Orleans, but usually as a woman. As a change from this he pretended to be a deaf-mute. Durst was granted bail in the relatively modest sum, given his wealth, of $215,000. It was promptly lodged by Debrah Lee Charatan whom he had married in the autumn of 2001, a marriage which apparently caused something of a rift with Berman. And off he went again.

On 30 November 2001 he was arrested once more. It appears that he pulled up at a Wegmans supermarket in Bethlehem in a dilapidated car in the boot of which was around $37,000. He then went into the supermarket and put a $7 sandwich and a newspaper inside his coat; as he made to leave he was stopped by staff. He then announced that he would not fight an extradition to Texas, where it was thought he might enter an insanity plea to the murder of Black. According to the magazine *Talk*, shortly before her death Susan Berman said Durst had confessed to her that he killed his first wife.

Meanwhile in Arizona, Sammy 'The Bull' Gravano had

proved that there was after all life to be had after betraying John Gotti snr. Old Mafia watchers had seen Gravano give an impressive courtroom display. The former boxer had been with Gotti from around 1977 and, he later admitted, was the driver at the killing of Paul Castellano outside Sparks Steak house at 210 E 46 after which Gotti had taken over the Donship.

Gravano was a fairly rare flower. Formerly a member of the Colombo Family, after a dispute he had been allowed to transfer to the Gambinos. His rise in his adopted Family, under Gotti, had been almost relentless. He had taken over Castellano's interests in the construction industry and simply had his associates killed – Liborio Milito and Louis DiBono were two examples – if he thought they were being greedy. In 1989 it was estimated that the annual income of this man, born into a poor family from Sicily, was in the region of $¾ million.[11]

The blow fell on 12 December 1990 when Gotti was indicted on five murder conspiracies including the killing of Castellano and Thomas Bilotti. Also in the indictment were Frank Locascio and Gravano, as was Thomas Gambino, one of Carlo's sons. The indictments alleged that Castellano had been killed because he specifically disapproved of drug dealing and had imposed the death penalty for any member found so doing. He had come to learn that this was just what Gotti and his crew were doing and, at best, it was going to be broken up.

[11] For an account of Gravano's life with the Gambinos, see Peter Maas, *Underboss*. For an account of the trial of Gotti, see James Morton, *Gangland International*.

There was bad news for Gotti almost immediately. His lawyer, the flamboyant Bruce Cutler, was disqualified by the judge over a conflict of interest from acting at the trial and replaced by the Miami-based veteran Albert Krieger. Worse, there was a witness who could place Gotti outside the steak-house shortly before Castellano was shot. That was bad enough, but there was still more to come. Gravano defected. If convicted after a plea of not guilty and a trial, not only did he face 50 years but also the confiscation of his property. He was, however, the man who could unravel and expand on the hours of tapes taken from the bugs the police had placed in the Gotti hangout, the Ravinelli Club on Mulberry Street in Little Italy. It was cut a deal time or, as the French would say, *sauve qui peut*. The prosecution was also expected to call on the defecting Philadelphian mobster, Crazy Phil Leonetti, to tell the jury that Gotti had told him about the Castellano hit.

In the end Leonetti was not called but Gravano managed quite well enough. As might be expected, it was suggested that he was giving evidence for his own ends, which of course he undoubtedly was. The agreement he had reached was a maximum term of 20 years and a $250,000 fine. To a certain extent his fate was in his own hands. If he did well, Judge Glasser could give him less than twenty; if he was found to have lied, he could be prosecuted for any of the crimes he had admitted. What he did was catalogue a seemingly endless number of killings – 19 in all – of men for such diverse reasons as cheating, failing to show respect, lying, giving evidence to a Grand Jury and so forth.

The trial judge must have been enchanted because he sentenced Gravano to a little over 5 years. Gravano had sung sufficiently well to be released in early 1995. He was also well into the federal witness programme. In the spring of 1997, with the help of Peter Maas who had earlier assisted Joe Valachi, Gravano published his memoirs. The book was not entirely well received, particularly by the relatives of his victims who, perhaps understandably, thought some of the revenues should go to them. New York's Attorney General indicated he would be suing to ensure that Gravano did not keep the profits.

Moreover, the face-lifted Gravano has lived to tell his tale on television, appearing on such TV programmes as *PrimeTime Live*. Offers by an Illinois police union of a payment of $500 for spotting 'The Bull' in exile, something which could be interpreted as a bounty, went uncollected. In April 1997 a former Police Association President, John Flood, suggested that he expected Gravano to commit more crimes. He was not disappointed.

Eight years after his evidence had brought down Gotti, Gravano was again arrested – this time together with his wife Debra, his son Gerard and his daughter Karen along with 32 others including alleged white supremacist Michael Papa, said to be the founder of the Devil Dogs. Gravano had left the protected witness programme in 1995 and had been living in Tempe, Arizona, unmolested under the name of Jimmy Moran where he ran the Marathon Swimming Pool Company. He had, said the prosecution in February 2000, been overseeing an operation which sold 20–25,000 Ecstasy tablets a week. The police said he had also been acting as tutor to the Devil Dogs and other vendors and collectors, who had adopted a much more positive stance towards their debtors since Gravano became involved.

In December the same year Gravano, his son and Papa were linked to Ilan Zarger, an Israeli national with alleged ties with the Israeli Mob. Israeli crime syndicates were said to be the prime source of Ecstasy in the United States. In turn Zarger was alleged to have been linked to the Brooklyn Terror Squad, a group of men and women who robbed young people as they danced at raves. The allegation was that Zarger sold 40,000 Ecstasy tablets to the Gravanos. He had, it was claimed, bought them from Jacob Orgad, a high-ranking Israeli Mob member. It is Orgad who is credited with being the largest Ecstasy importer convicted in the United States.

The new indictment against Gravano and Co. suggested that he had bought 40,000 tablets from a New York drug gang. He had also tried to obtain control of the Ecstasy market in the Southwest. One problem spot was an Arizona night-club known as Pompeii in which Gravano jnr and Papa were alleged to have beaten up one of Zarger's dealers. Zarger promptly dispatched an enforcer named only as Macho to protect the dealer, and was then videotaped saying that if the worst came to the worst he had someone standing by to whack Gravano.

The worst did not come to the worst. The dealer was called to Uncle Sal's, a Gravano family restaurant in Scottsdale, Arizona, where he was told that Gravano owned Arizona and that he would be unable to sell pills in the state except through him. An accommodation was reached and it was agreed that Gravano would buy Ecstasy tablets at a discount of 25c per pill. In the spring of 2000 Zarger pleaded guilty to distributing Ecstasy over a 3-year period.

At the beginning of May 2001 Michael Papa called it a day. In return for a sentence of not less than 6 or greater

than 11, to run concurrently with any federal sentence
imposed in New York, he agreed to plead guilty and so avoid
the majority of 37 felony counts against him. In an exhibit
signed by him, he accused Gravano *père et fils* of running
the Ecstasy racket. He had been a partner with Gravano in
the pool construction business as well as the chief distrib-
utor in the Tempe-based Ecstasy operation.

It was only a matter of time before Gravano jnr turned
on his father. He wanted a separate trial in the New York
case, fearing 'All the evils that will be visited upon [his] fair-
trial rights will result solely from his father's presence in the
case.' Immediately after, the government released a 34-page
document claiming that Gravano had plotted to murder his
son Gerard's girlfriend because she had boasted of her relationship. He had also put a gun to Gerard's head for showing
disrespect. Michael Papa was said to have been under threat
after his agreement to plead guilty. There was also an allegation that he had tried to found the Arizona Mafia as a
chapter of *La Cosa Nostra*. Yet another allegation in the document was that he planned to murder Ronald Kuby, the New
York lawyer who was bringing civil actions on behalf of the
families of some of the 19 men whom Gravano acknowledged murdering. The idea had been to lure Mr Kuby with
the prospect of a new case and then kill him. This was something which Gravano's New York lawyer, Lynne Stewart, was
quick to deny. The request for a separate trial was refused.

A fortnight later it was all over. Both Sammy and Gerard
Gravano bowed to the inevitable and agreed to plead guilty
in New York, and by doing so limited their liability to 15
years apiece. That still left the Arizona charges. As for the

women, Debra Gravano received 5 years probation and Karen two years less.

Police corruption – what constitutes it, how to recognise it, how it flourishes and how to control or, better still, erad-icate it – has encouraged hundreds of academics to devote literally millions of hours to providing answers. There have been various suggestions: that corruption begins with accepting favours from local shopkeepers and is massaged by what is called the canteen culture of anti-Semitic, racist and sexist jokes over tea and coffee at the end of a hard shift. More control from senior officers and encouragement to younger officers to blow the whistle without fear of ostracism and often physical danger are just some of the antidotes. And probably there are dozens of others. There is no doubt whatsoever that, when they put their minds to it, because of their position of power and expertise and the reluctance of senior officers to expose the problem to the public, and with the support of the judiciary, police officers as groups can provide examples of outstanding criminal organisations.

There cannot be a single major police force in the world which has not at some time or another experienced corrup-tion on a massive scale, whether it is officers collaborating with thieves, falsifying evidence to obtain convictions or acting as an extra-judicial vigilante squad. New York suffered at the end of the nineteenth century and again in the 1970s with the Knapp Commission which exposed widespread corruption; London underwent a similar self-examination with inquiries into the Flying, Porn and Vice Squads following one another from 1969. From the end of the Second

World War until the 1990s the New South Wales police was regarded as endemically corrupt, with one commissioner regarded as 'the finest money could buy'.

In the last few years of the twentieth century there were equally stunning examples, in one of which the Los Angeles police featured. In April 2001, in perhaps the biggest corruption inquiry since the 1930s, US District Judge Gary A. Feess ruled that the police's city department could be sued as a racketeering enterprise. This followed allegations that Rampart station's anti-gang unit had allegedly robbed, beaten, framed and shot suspects.

More than 100 convictions have been set aside following the allegations made in 1999, and millions of dollars have already been paid out. The ruling came in a suit brought by D'Novel Hunter, who claims he spent 4 years in prison after being framed by former officer Rafael Perez on a charge of possessing cocaine with intent to sell.

The Perez fall-out began on 26 November 1996 when 19-year-old Javier Francisco Ovando, a member of the notoriously violent 18th Street Gang from South Central, was wheeled on a trolley into a courtroom in the Los Angeles County Hall of Justice charged with assaulting Perez and his colleague, Nino Durden, from the very tough Rampart division of Community Resources Against Street Hoodlums (CRASH), on 12 October that year.[12] According to the police

---

[12] Rampart, regarded as having little in the way of redeeming social features, is bordered by Sunset Boulevard to the north, Normandie Avenue on the west and two freeways. In an area of 7.9 square miles it had the highest population density, 36,000 per square mile, of any urban area west of the Mississippi. This did not include illegal immigrants.

evidence Ovando – holding a Tec-22 semi-automatic – had burst into the darkened room on the fourth floor of an abandoned block of flats from where the officers were keeping observation. Perez accepted that he (three shots) and Durden (one) had fired first, hitting Ovando with four shots. When back-up officers arrived Ovando was lying on the floor with his Tec-22 beside him.

Ovando (who had his gang number 18 tattooed on the back of his neck) had a different story and one which was difficult to believe. Basically it was that he, his pregnant girl-friend Monique Valenzuela and a friend Alex Macias (known as Nene) had been camping out rough in the building from which the officers were keeping observation. They had been told to move on but, once Perez and Durden had finished their shift, they returned. The next day Ovando and Macias were arrested again and handcuffed; Macias was told he could go and that Ovando would soon be released. Macias, who had rejoined Monique Valenzuela, then heard shots and fled.

Perez's story now changed slightly: he had heard voices outside the observation post and had turned in time to see his colleague Durden shoot Ovando. In turn he had fired three times. The now paralysed Ovando's story impressed Tamar Toister, the public defender, and, rather than accept the offered plea bargain of 13 years, she took the case to the jury. The trial lasted a week and on 20 February 1997 Judge Czuleger sentenced Ovando to 23 years' imprisonment, saying that he had shown no remorse. Czuleger had told the defence that if Ovando gave evidence he would allow cross-examination about graffiti reading 'LAPD 187' in the abandoned building. In LA street slang of the time 'LAPD 187' meant 'Kill Cops'. Ovando was wheeled off to prison.

Meanwhile the Puerto Rican-born Perez continued his upward career. He had come to Philadelphia as a child, and after graduating joined the Marines in 1985. Four years later he joined the Los Angeles Police Department. In 1995 he joined Rampart Crash where, partly because of his fluency in Spanish, he was regarded as a highly effective officer.

Then things began to conspire against him. The first was that on 6 November 1997 $722,000 was stolen from the Bank of America in South Central, of which Rampart is part. The money had been ordered by the service manager, Errolyn Romero, who when questioned admitted that the robbery had been organised by her boyfriend, police officer David Mack. The officer was a friend of Perez from the time when they had worked narcotics together before Perez went to Rampart. He and Mack had gone to Los Angeles two days after the robbery. Questioned, Perez said he knew nothing about the robbery but he spoke of his gratitude to Mack, who apparently had saved his life when he shot a drug dealer who had threatened him. Not everyone agreed with the story; two eye-witnesses said that Mack had shot the unarmed man. An LAPD inquiry found the shooting justifiable.

Romero received a sentence of 30 months, while on 17 March 1999 Mack drew 14 years for the federal offence of bank robbery. The stolen money was never recovered, but there were unproved suggestions that Perez might have been the second man who drove the getaway car.

On 26 February 1998 a gang member was brought into the Rampart substation and beaten until he vomited blood.

Instead of accepting the situation, he went to hospital and reported the incident. The officer said to be involved, Brian Hewitt, was dismissed.

The next difficulty which Perez faced, and one which proved fatal to his career, was when it was discovered that he had checked out 6 lbs of cocaine to take to court as evidence but had not returned it. In fact he had checked it out for a case which had already been heard. Further inquiries showed that he had done this in other cases, and he was arrested on 25 August 1998 in a well-orchestrated swoop. Tried in the December, he was perhaps fortunate to have a hung jury on charges of possession of cocaine for sale, theft and forgery. The jury was 8–4 in favour of a conviction. Now he faced a re-trial along with threats that his wife, a civilian officer in the police department, might be charged. His neighbours had thought he was a building contractor and his home had been extensively rebuilt. There were also deposits in his bank records which he could not explain.

Now his lawyer negotiated a plea bargain. He would receive 5 years and immunity from further prosecution; his wife would not be charged. This meant 16 months in jail, rather than state prison where he would have been seriously at risk. As always there was a *quid pro quo*, and in this case it was that Perez would expose the criminal behaviour of some members of the Rampart Crash. In the final shakeout Perez was sentenced to 2 years' imprisonment with a further 3 years' supervision after his release. He agreed to pay full restitution to his victims. He was released in July 2001 and it was agreed that, for his safety, he could serve his parole outside California.

Perez admitted that he had begun drug dealing in 1997 when he and Durden took 1 lb of cocaine, along with his pager, from a suspected dealer. When the pager had bleeped, Perez took an order for ¼ lb. However, instead of making an arrest they had simply sold the drug. As with all good snitches Perez maintained that the initial suggestion was not his but that it came from Durden, though he accepted that he went along with it. The deals from the 1 lb of cocaine netted the pair $10,000, and after that Perez looked to the police evidence lockers for further supplies. Now he admitted stealing the 8 lbs of cocaine from an evidence room, swapping it with flour and replacing it.

Then there was the brutality and the framing of suspects. It was, he said, commonplace in Rampart for gang members to be set up and had the full approval of the sergeant in charge, Edward Ortiz – who was, claimed Perez, the head. He and the others were simply the arteries. It was perfectly acceptable behaviour.

> These guys don't play by the rules: we don't have to play by the rules. They're out there committing murders and then they intimidate the witnesses, so the witnesses don't show up in court. So they're getting away with murder every day. When I planted a case on someone, did I feel bad? Not once. I felt good. I felt, you know, I'm taking this guy off the streets.[13]

---

[13] Quoted in Lou Cannon, 'One Bad Cop' in *New York Times Magazine*, 1 October 2000.

And framings led to shootings, escalating from three in 1995 to a dozen the following year. Celebrations took place at the Short Stop, a bar near Dodger Stadium. Throwdowns were carried to be left by the body of the victim.

One of the victims who survived was Ovando. According to Perez, he and Durden framed Ovando; Durden fired first and Perez then followed up. They had planted the Tec-22, so being able to claim self-defence. The semi-automatic had been taken from a gang member some days earlier and they had filed off the serial number. Ovando was released after 3 years in prison and has claimed $12.1 million in damages from the city. Judge Czuleger said, 'It was the worst day of my judicial career.'

It was a similar situation in Miami when in September 2001 13 current and former officers were charged with conspiring to cover up evidence in police shootings which had resulted in the deaths of 3 black men, including a 72-year-old man who died in a hail of bullets inside his home. The allegations were that after officers had shot at unarmed people guns were planted at the scene. The officers were then said to have given false evidence justifying the shootings.[14]

On a happier note the beginning of 2002 saw Suge Knight, the entrepreneur of West Coast gangsta rap, live to fight another day. Things had been seriously wrong in the industry and Knight and his label, Death Row Records, had been under a 6-year siege by the FBI with allegations of racketeering, drug trafficking and murder flying about the studios. Death Row's top star, Tupac Shakur, had been shot to

---

[14] *Globe and Mail*, 8 September 2001.

death in 1996 and his killing had been followed by that of his main East Coast rival Notorious B.I.G. Knight himself had served a 5-year sentence for assault, his ninth conviction in all. Now the criminal investigation was completed and under a plea agreement Death Row Records agreed to pay a $100,000 fine and an unspecified amount in back taxes.

Knight was pleased. 'I appreciate the fact that, after looking into these lies and finding nothing, they had the integrity to say, "OK, this guy broke no law" and called it off.'

Less happily, Stanley 'Tookie' Williams was still on Death Row. He had been sent there 20 years earlier after the killing of a teenage grocery clerk, shot in the back of the head in a robbery, and an Asian-American couple and their middle-aged daughter who were shot to death during a motel robbery. However, he had been nominated by the Swiss government as a candidate for the Nobel Peace Prize for 2001, for his work in weaning young men from street crime. Since 1993, after spending some 6 years in solitary confinement he had devoted his time to campaigning against gang life. His lawyers, who had previously run the seemingly conflicting rolled-up plea of alibi and mental impairment, argue that this shows a complete change of life-style. His critics say that he is being manipulative and that he has not uttered one word of remorse for the killings which he still denies. His supporters say that, rather as one must never admit liability after a road accident, if he did accept his guilt he would be signing his own death warrant. There are also unproved allegations that despite his championship of a new way of life for young people in deprived areas, he is still effectively controlling the local branch of the Crips inside and outside prison.[15] There is little doubt, however, that if Williams did wish to control the local Crips, his confinement would prove only marginally hampering.

[15] Richard Grant, 'The Nobel Prisoner' in the *Sunday Telegraph Magazine*, 22 April 2001.

23

Canada

By the twenty-first century Canada was gaining an unwelcome but possibly deserved reputation – as St Paul, Minnesota, and Hot Springs, Arksansas, had done in the 1920s and 1930s – for being a home-from-home for fugitive criminals. A declassified Canadian Security Intelligence Service document suggested that Canada was housing over 50 terrorist groups, ranging from the Tamil Tigers of Sri Lanka to supporters of Osama Bin Laden. At the beginning of the millennium a further report suggested that Canada was becoming a refuge for Asian Mob figures and a North American gateway for the Chinese mafia. Reasons given for this new home-from-home included a lackadaisical approach to illegal immigrants, underfunded law-enforcement agencies and generous social welfare programmes on arrival. In many cases, however, this latter would not be needed.

One of the older refugees was thought to be James J. 'Whitey' Bulger, brother of the Boston politician and long-time friend of Stephen 'The Rifleman' Flemmi. Flemmi was known to have contacts with Montreal's old West End Gang and had himself hidden out in Canada in the 1980s when wanted for the car-bombing of a Boston lawyer. There were suggestions that Bulger had money stashed away in both Toronto and Montreal.

A definite arrival, however, was Lai Changxing who, in 1999, had fled with the proceeds of his crime business from Fujian province in China and promptly bought himself a C$1.3 million home in British Columbia. He was alleged by China to be their most wanted fugitive who had, it was said, smuggled in the region of $6 million worth of vehicles, crude oil, weapons and computers into the province, corrupting thousands of officials with bribes of cash and women to ease his way.

His false passport was not noticed when he arrived in Vancouver in the August of 1999. Nor was any notice taken when he was banned from casinos in British Columbia for loan-sharking. Nor again when he was seen with Asian crime figures at the casinos near Niagara Falls where he was losing $600,000 nightly. In fact he remained unmolested until, on 23 November 2000, China demanded his return and with some speed he claimed asylum, saying he was a refugee from political persecution. Changxing will do well if he avoids extradition, though others back in China have not been so fortunate. The head of China's military intelligence, Major General Ji Shengde, received 15 years for his involvement with Lai. Others even less fortunate were executed. They are part of the 1,200-plus annual executions in China where public sentencing can take place in a sports stadium in front of a crowd of 30,000 and an execution is carried out almost immediately afterwards. There are nearly 70 crimes which attract the death penalty and they include murder, kidnapping, tax evasion, drug dealing, the theft of antiques and publishing pornography. If found guilty Changxing could expect an almost immediate bullet in the head, although some provinces are experimenting with lethal injections. Sometimes prisoners are offered a second chance; if they behave for 2 years in prison and show signs of remorse, then their sentences may be commuted to life imprisonment.

Meanwhile Changxing's home, dubbed the Red Mansion, has been opened to tourists in his home city of Xiamen where they ogle at the blood-red banqueting halls, sauna and massage parlour, karaoke rooms and private cinema, all of which had been staffed by 40 hostesses. Such has been the demand to see Lai's collection of tiger skins, gold bars and sports cars that the authorities limited the visitors to 1,000 a day.

Toronto

In recent years there have been suggestions that the Mafia, with decades of unchallenged power behind it, has lost its former absolute control. Amongst the leading criminal organisations there are now the Russian *mafiya*, Jamaican posses, bikers who have clubhouses in the east end of the city, Colombians selling large amounts of cocaine and the Vietnamese. Says a local cab driver:

You get them in taxis and they'll discuss things quite openly. 'I'll be rich after three years here,' they say, but at the time they are often small-level dealers to the Spanish community.

A lawyer friend of mine had a client who opened a bar on King Street and he hadn't been there too long when two Italian guys come in and start claiming him for $2,000 a week on behalf of their boss. There was a Russian guy sitting in the corner drinking vodka and the client says, 'He's looking after things, speak with him.' They go over and the Russian says, 'I know the Godfather. I'll call him now on the cellphone.' They said, 'Don't bother' and left.

What is certain is that an era of Ontarian crime ended on 31 May 1997 with the death by shooting of the grand old man of Hamilton, Johnny 'Pops' Papalia, extortioner, loan-sharker, gambler; a man who 'never let a deal slip by without making it a swindle'. It was quickly followed by the killing of his lieutenant, Carmen Barillaro, at his home in Niagara Falls where he was a crime boss in his own right. Barillaro had been a made man in the Magaddino Crime Family in Buffalo and had steadily worked his way up the Papalia hierarchy.

In his seventies, the immaculately dressed Johnny 'Pops' gave an interview to the crime writer Peter Moon in which he expressed his greatest disappointment in life as never having graduated from high school. He thought that had he been better educated he might not have turned to crime. 'It's been an interesting one,' he said of his life. 'But maybe I'd have liked it to be different.'

At his death Papalia had been seen talking to a white man aged about 35 years and walking with him through the car-park of the Papalia family-owned business, Galaxy Vending, on Railway Street. The man suddenly turned and shot him before fleeing in a green pick-up truck.

Two days after his boss's death, Barillaro spoke with Pasquale Musitano outside the Gathering Spot, a restaurant on Robert Street in Hamilton. He accused Musitano of being responsible for Papalia's death and when this was denied said that if he ever found out that Pasquale or his brother Angelo had been involved there would be swift retribution. Those words signed his death warrant. The old saw, 'twice blessed be he who gets his blow in first', proved correct. On 23 July, 35-year-old Kenneth Murdock and Angelo Musitano drove to Niagara Falls to look for Barillaro's two-tone Corvette. They found it in his driveway at 8 p.m. and, under the pretext that Murdock wanted to buy the car, rang the bell. When Barillaro opened the door Murdock pulled out a .9 mm handgun, said, 'This is a message from Pat,' and shot him.

Occasionally justice can be both swift and certain, and on 24 November 1998 Murdock – who, as it turned out, had taken out both Papalia and Barillaro – was charged, arraigned, pleaded guilty and sentenced to life imprisonment all in one day. Apparently he had not negotiated the price before his hit on Papalia, but later he received $2,000 and a quantity of cocaine.

Murdock, who was already in custody on charges of assault and extortion, saw the light when tapes indicating that he himself was marked for death were played to him, and he decided that prison was safer than the streets. Following his conviction for the murders along with the machine-gun killing in 1985 of Salvatore Alaimo, also in Hamilton, on which he will be eligible for parole in 13 years, he agreed to give evidence for the Crown. Pasquale (Pat) Musitano and his brother, Angelo, whose father Dominic and the family had been feuding with Papalia and others of the Toronto old school for years, were charged with the first-degree murder of Papalia. On 4 February 2000 both Musitanos pleaded guilty to conspiracy and received a 10-year sentence with the opportunity to apply for parole after they had served a third of their time. There was some criticism that the Crown had not pressed the murder charge, but it was pointed out that the only evidence was that of Murdock whose credibility would have been crucial. A plea in the hand is better than an acquittal in the court. Murdock was reported not to be pleased with the way things had turned out.[1]

Now the old hierarchy in Toronto changed, and with the change came the death of a long-time favourite, former boxer Eddie 'Hurricane' Melo, shot and killed in a Mississauga parking lot along with his friend Joao (Joe) Pavao on 6 April 2001.

Melo, who was 6 when his family arrived in Canada from the Azores in December 1966, had long been associated with the Montreal Mafia when it was led by Frank

---

[1] For an account of the career of Papalia and the feuds with the Musitanos, see Peter Edwards and Antonio Nicaso, *Deadly Silence*; Adrian Humphreys, *The Enforcer*; James Morton, *Gangland International*. See also Toronto *News*, 5 February 2000.

Cotroni.[2] Whenever Cotroni and his lieutenant, Tony Volpato, flanked by bodyguards came to Toronto, it was Melo who acted as chauffeur and guide. In their absence it was he who looked after Cotroni's gaming machine, drugs, loans and extortion as well as union interests.

Melo, who was described by former Canadian heavyweight champion George Chuvalo as 'a world-class puncher', began his boxing career as an amateur, running up nearly 100 fights with only a handful of losses before he turned professional. He had been coached by Sully Sullivan, a car salesman who signed his name with $ signs and who ran Sully's Gym or, to give it the grander title, the Toronto Athletic Club, on Ossington Avenue. Later Melo worked out in Queen City Gym and the Lansdown Gym, a home-from-home for gamblers and rounders where signs advised patrons that the police might have infiltrated the place and be listening. He wished to turn pro but, because the Ontario Athletic Commission required professional boxers to be aged 19 before they could do so, he appeared in unlicensed fights in Verdun, one of the working-class suburbs of Montreal. Before then, however, he had already made his first appearance in

---

[2] The leader of the Montreal Mafia, Paul Violi, was murdered in 1978. His logical successor, Frank Cotroni, was almost immediately imprisoned and Sicilian elements had taken over in the city importing heroin and cocaine through the Caruana-Cuntrera Family. On Cotroni's release he had regrouped, heading what remained of the Montreal branch of New York *mafioso* Joe Bonanno's empire. Frank Cotroni was sentenced in 1997 to 7 years' imprisonment for conspiracy to import 180 kg of cocaine into Canada. In July 2001 Cotroni was refused parole. He had, it was alleged, been visiting Mafia hangouts during his day-release from prison. For accounts of the rise and fall of the Cotroni brothers and the internecine struggles of the Montreal Mafia as well as their links with the Bonanno Family and his own power struggles, see Peter Edwards and Antonio Nicaso, *Deadly Silence*; James Morton, *Gangland International*.

court when he received probation for three counts of assault. The prosecutor alleged that the incident was an unprovoked attack 'by a professional fighter using a deadly weapon'. There was no suggestion that Melo's attack represented his usual behaviour, he said. But in time it would become so. In February 1978 he was charged with stabbing two men in a fight outside a Toronto bar which had ended with one man being kicked in the head and staying in hospital for twelve days.

His first pro fight was in March 1979, and Melo then won eight unlicensed bouts on the reel before he fought the Canadian middleweight champion, Fernand Marcotte jnr, whom he beat on a split decision. He was only 17 at the time. Marcotte ended the contest with five broken ribs. Melo lost a re-match with Marcotte in 12 rounds, having fought before a crowd of nearly 16,000 with a broken hand. Later his trainer rhetorically asked what else they could have done, adding, 'The promoter would have killed us if we had backed out.' Like so many young boxers, however, he had fought too many times too quickly and at too young an age. The last thing a boxer loses is his ability to punch and Melo, throughout his life, continued to dish out punishment both privately and on behalf of Cotroni.

The first thing to go is the ability to take a punch and it soon became apparent that, to use a boxing term, Melo could no longer take a shot to the head. Even so, by 1980 he had become the No. 2 contender for the legitimate Canadian middleweight title. He was a local celebrity and on 2 May 1981 he married Sine, the former Miss Montreal Alouette. Later a police source would comment, 'She met him on the way up. He was becoming rich and famous, and she was young and stupid.' Shortly before the birth of his daughter Jessica, he announced his retirement, saying that he would instead become a union representative and sell gaming machines. Many who thought that, translated, this meant he would become Cotroni's Toronto muscle, were reinforced in this belief when in August 1981 he was alleged to have held a gun to a barman's head saying, 'You don't want anything to happen to your wife or baby, do you?' A .38 handgun was found at his home; he said he kept it for Sine's protection. Later that year he was charged with firing a gun.

Two years later Melo was back in the ring fighting as a light-heavyweight, but his comeback win was spoiled with allegations that a glove had been cut. That year, as lap-dancing grew in popularity, he began to take over control of the strippers' agencies along with the Cotroni hitman, Real Simard. In November 1983 he and another associate, Elijah Anton Askov, were charged with threatening a stripper agent, Peter Belmont, with a knife and sawn-off shotgun. It took nearly three years for the case to come to court, at which time it was thrown out by Judge Michael Bolan as an abuse of process. The decision led to the dismissal of thousands of charges in Southern Ontario and Askov gave his name to the process of fighting a charge on the grounds of unreasonable delay, 'Askoving'.

After that Melo made regular court appearances. The same month, he was convicted of carrying a concealed weapon, and four months later he was acquitted after shots were fired at a man from whom he had wrested a gun. In April 1984 he was convicted of possessing an unregistered restricted weapon and the theft of union pamphlets. In September 1985 a second comeback in the ring failed.

Still more than useful outside the ring, in 1988 he was charged with aggravated assault on a man he had punched at a stag night. Despite the allegation that the man needed permanent screws and a plate in his face and had suffered what were described as 'extremely complex fractures in multiple areas of the facial skeleton', he served only 90 days in prison at weekends. He was also fined $500 for an attack on a man in a restaurant, when he had broken the victim's cheekbone, but a psychiatrist called on Melo's behalf told the court, '[He is] really a quiet person, a rather easygoing person who'd rather be left alone than get himself into difficulty.' At home, he was working out regularly on Sine, who filed for divorce and left for British Columbia.

The next year in November 1989 he and an Underworld associate, Frank Roda, were told by the Combined Forces Special Enforcement Unit that they had learned that there was a contract out for each of them. A former biker, John Avery, who had met Melo in the Don jail and liked him, said that back in 1985 he had been rather vaguely offered $10,000 by Danny Cappuccitti to kill Melo, but the contract had lapsed. It was renewed when Melo first gave what was described as a 'tune-up' to one of Cappuccitti's crew and then gave Larry Cappuccitti, Danny's younger brother, a public slapping in a College Street pool hall.

Two months earlier Melo, along with Roda, had been involved in the beating of a Toronto car dealer also named Frank. The salesman Frank had been owed money by Roda following a drug deal and, in an effort to get his money, he had refused to hand over a car to a woman friend of both Melo and Roda. Sweet-talking having failed to persuade the dealer to release the car, a beating in a Toronto tile factory was the 'tune-up' referred to.

The figure offered to Avery (which was to include Roda) was now $30,000. Melo's and Roda's bodies were to be wrapped in garbage bags around the neck with the heads covered and tied tightly so that no blood leaked out. By now, however, Avery was a police informer and was wearing a wire. The police took Melo and Roda into protective custody outside Toronto and two wrapped dummies were left in a van parked in the Yorkdale Holiday Inn car-park. When Avery met Danny Cappuccitti the following morning to ask for the balance of his money, he was asked for a full description of the killings, telling his paymaster how he had kidnapped the pair at gunpoint and then shot them on the floor of a stolen van. Danny Cappuccitti and his brother Vincent pleaded guilty to conspiracy to murder and received 8½ years and 3 years respectively.

Roda was unhappy over the sentences which he believed were far too lenient. On 8 July 1991 he and David Gabor Fisher blew themselves up while planting a pipe-bomb in a lane near to a Cappuccitti business. Roda lost a hand and Fisher suffered severe wounds to his leg. Both were later imprisoned for this failed enterprise.

At the time of his death Melo was awaiting deportation, something he had fought against for much of the 1990s. During that time he had in theory been working as what was described as an 'investor relations professional' for International Mineral Resources Ltd. In practice it was suggested that he was still working as an old-time protection racketeer on the gaming-machine circuit, handing out beatings to bar owners if there was any resistance to his installing machines and taking 70 per cent of the revenue. In 1995, a week after announcing yet another return to the ring, he was charged along with eight others in a police sting over a fraudulent loan scam. An illegal Tazer stun-gun along with .38 and .45 ammunition was said to have been found at his Lakeshire Avenue W condominium.

Whatever his faults, many still regarded him not as a double-crossing, wife-beating enforcer but as a man of some generosity and very considerable charm. On Maundy Thursday and Good Friday 2001, over 1,000 people attended the Cardinal Funeral Home where his body lay before his funeral.[3]

John Avery was still alive and living under a new identity. When asked about Melo and his death he commented:

> You'll probably have people lined up around the corner to spit on his grave, but I never had a bad moment with the guy . . . He treated me with the utmost respect. All I was was a street guy, but he'd cross the road to shake my hand.[4]

Melo's has not been the only death in the power struggle. In August 1998 Frank Cotroni's son, Paul, was shot outside his

---

[3] Police documents in Sicily show that Melo, despite his Portuguese heritage, was a member of the Siderno group. For a full account of the Cappuccittis, who were the sons of a wealthy Alliston, Ont., businessman, see Peter Edwards and Antonio Nicaso, *Deadly Silence*. See also transcripts of wire-taps of *Project Cappuccitti et al.*, 31 October–November 1989.

[4] Alan Cairns, 'Boxing in the Shadow' in *Toronto Sun*, 15 April 2001.

home in Montreal; and in June 2000 Gaetano Panepito was shot in his maroon Cadillac near his Etobicoke home on Smithwood Drive. Panepito, said the police, was a Mob enforcer who, appropriately enough, ran a business making discount funeral caskets said to be owned by the Montreal Godfather and alleged leader of the city's Mafia, Vito Rizzuto. He had opened the dealership in 1997 with the Frank Roda who earlier had blown himself up.

There were any number of suggestions regarding the death of Panepito, who over the years had made a series of enemies during his career as enforcer, slot-machine owner, drug trafficker and robber. One was the disappearance of two Calabrians who had been causing trouble in Panepito's illegal slot-machine racket and who were thought to be tied into Russian organised crime. James Dubro, an expert on Mafia affairs in Canada, thought otherwise, suggesting that it was a classic case of settling accounts over money due in the cocaine trade. Panepito's death was followed almost immediately by that of his clerk, Patti Real, who was executed in her own backyard.

As for the Musitanos, while Pat was serving a 10-year sentence he became involved in a libel action, which arose from the 1998 killing of Hamilton lawyer Lynn Gilbank and her husband Fred who were shot dead at their home in Ancaster on 16 November that year. Peter Montour, claiming that the police had falsely told Musitano that he (Montour) had informed on him, promptly filed a $4 million lawsuit.

Montour's action alleged that two detectives went to visit Musitano at the Collins Bay prison in Kingston, but when he refused to see them they left a note identifying him and another man as informants. The note ran: 'William [the surname is deleted] is bragging to everyone that he did the killing for you for $20,000 plus bombing La Cantina and La Costa.' Montour claimed that now he was in danger of retribution from Musitano. He had been in the wars with the courts himself. In 1997 he pleaded guilty and was fined $640,000 in a massive cigarette-smuggling operation. In 1998 the former restaurant owner was one of three charged in an extortion racket, but the charges were dismissed in the autumn of 2000; the Crown lodged notice of appeal against the dismissal.

If the note was genuine it referred to two bombings in November 1998 and February 1999. In the first the La Cantina restaurant suffered minor damage after only the detonator went off; but on 3 February 1999 a man and his sister were injured and a van badly damaged when a bomb exploded in an alleyway behind La Costa.

What was also happening in Ontario was a mirror of London's 'black-on-black' crime. Since 1996 there were thought to have been over 100 such killings, many drug- or revenge-related. Typical appear to have been the deaths of Paul Watson and Michael Lewis, killed at the end of July 2001 in what was suggested was revenge for the murder of Omar Christian the same day, or possibly for a fight on a boat the previous weekend. Of Toronto's one-a-week murders in the first half of 2001, thirty occurred in 51 Division and five of those were in the Regent's Park area. They included Yemi 'Yummy' Oduwole shot in the back on 5 March, Cleamart Calvin 'Mousy' Douglas shot behind a townhouse on Regent Street on 10 May, and Justin Sheppard, the half-brother of Jamaal Magloire, the Charlotte Hornets' basketball player, who was shot near Sherbourne TTC station near Bloor Street E on 24 June. The police in Rexdale were also investigating the murders of six people in 2001 which were linked, they believed, to a gang turf war.[5]

'200 plus black-on-black murders in 10 years and the politicians and the press avoid this, hanging fire like the plague. It will only get worse,' says Toronto writer Peter McSherry.[6]

One of the victims in 2002 of black-on-black crime was O'Neil Ricardo Greenland, known on the Toronto streets as Heavy D, who was killed in a shoot-out on 9 November outside the Danforth Road strip mall in Scarborough. Greenland had come to Toronto from Jamaica, supposedly entering Canada on a four-day visa in August 2001 as an entertainer at the Base, a night-club in Etobicoke. On the expiration of his short-stay visa he simply disappeared. Now it is thought that he had been brought from Jamaica as an enforcer for the Markham Crew which had been locked in a two-year struggle with the Versace Boys, who take their name from their predilection for the designer's clothing.

That quarrel began during a Caribbean community boat tour on Lake Ontario on 22 July 2001 during which shots were exchanged. One person was known to have been injured but no witnesses, nor indeed a victim, came forward. Two days later Omar Christian, thought to be a Versace, was shot dead in the parking lot of the Base. Retaliation was swift and

---

[5] See *Saturday Sun*, 28 July 2001.
[6] Letter to the author (undated).

the Versaces killed two young men in Lawrence Heights, an area known as the Jungle. Over the next 17 months there were over a dozen killings believed to be linked to the boat incident. Then in October 2002 things stepped up a gear and nine young black men were killed in shooting incidents. Greenland was believed to have killed two brothers, Kevin and Jermaine Ebanks, at the Club 94. Both were affiliated to the Versaces. The police believe that at about 1 p.m. on the Saturday of his death Greenland saw a car full of Versaces and opened fire. He missed and was shot dead.

Montreal

On 29 August 2000 a former Hell's Angels HQ went up in flames. The stone mansion on a small island in Laval had at one time belonged to the Lavigueur family, blue-collar Montrealers who won a $7.6 jackpot in a lottery in the 1980s. When disputes over money arose, the property was put on the market and purchased by the Hell's Angels who promptly turned the stone chateau into a fortress by installing iron fencing and surveillance equipment. Its last Angel occupant was Scott Steinart who disappeared in 1997, the year that the police confiscated the house under Quebec's proceeds-of-crime laws. It was two years before Steinart surfaced in the Saint-Nicholas River, identified only by tattoos on his arm. His wrists had been bound and he had been beaten to death before a plastic garbage bag was put over his head.

Efforts to sell the property had not been a huge success. The original asking price of $850,000 was down to just over £350,000 when a Taiwanese businessman, James Ho, bought it. He was reported to have intended to turn the building into a film studio, but met with opposition from the neighbourhood. Now it was in ruins. Saying he did not know whether Ho had insurance, Constable Guy Lajeunesse of the Laval police commented, 'A criminal hand did this. But for whose interests, which group, or for what reason, we don't know.' Some thought it was a message from the Angels, saying that although their property might have been confiscated no one was going to get any benefit from it.[7]

On 13 September 2000, veteran crime writer Michel Auger had the unenviable distinction of being one of the relatively few journalists in the Western world to be the victim of an attack by those who disagreed with his commentary on their activities. Two days before being attacked he had published a two-page article 'Pagaille chez les Caïds'[8] in *Le Journal de Montréal*, in which he surveyed the state of play in the Hell's Angels–Rock Machine war. Over the previous five years the war, centred primarily on control of drugs, had brought the deaths of 153 people, a further 172 attempts, 130 arson attacks and 85 bombings. Unfortunately 5 per cent of the victims were innocent bystanders.

In his weekly column Auger made a habit of totalling the gangster deaths and then providing a quarterly update. In the column before his shooting he commented that the senior echelons of both the Hell's Angels – which, with 100 chapters worldwide, was regarded as Canada's biggest motorcycle gang – and the Mafia were in disarray. In the April Normand

[7] *Globe and Mail*, 30 August 2000; *Toronto Star*, 17 September 2000.
[8] Translated as 'Chaos Among the Bosses' in *Le Journal de Montréal*, 11 September 2000.

'Biff' Hamel, a Nomad biker, had been killed and the police were looking towards the Rock Machine – numerically the Angels' biggest rivals, who were thought to be teaming up with the Bandidos – to find the killer. However, the police thought that the Angels themselves might be hiding the killers of the long-disappeared Louis 'Melou' Roy, who was the go-between with the Montreal Mafia. Roy, who was thought to be worth something in the region of $2 million, had vanished on 22 June.

Other notable losses during the spring and summer had been the former union boss André 'Dede' Desjardins killed on 27 April, a day after meeting Hell's Angels leader Maurice 'Mom' Boucher. Hell's Angels affiliate Stephane Hilareguy disappeared on 16 June, the day when his wife, Natasha Desbiens, was shot dead and their house torched. Other activities included Hell's Angels' sympathisers rioting in a holding jail in Montreal, trying to storm a wing housing Rock Machine members; the pepper spraying of a pub in Quebec City; and the beating of three after-hours drinkers by Hell's Angels in a protection racket display. There had been at least one success for the authorities – the breaking up by the police of a Hell's Angels' drug ring which sent cocaine and hashish by express post to Inuit villages in northern Quebec.

There was also the death of drug-importer Raymond Crag, shot while playing in a golf tournament on 29 August in Sainte-Adèle, Mafia country. The police said the killers must have had permission before carrying out a contract such as this.

After Auger had left the east-end shopping mall at Place Versailles (where he often met informants) and parked in the

lot of his paper, *Le Journal de Montréal*, he went to the boot
of his car to collect his laptop. It was then that a gunman
opened fire, hitting him in the back with five out of six
bullets. Before he collapsed Auger managed to dial 911 on
his mobile telephone; he underwent two operations and
survived. The whole episode had been botched. Not only
did the gunman fail to kill Auger but it seems that the radi-
ator hose in the getaway car, an old model Plymouth Acclaim,
broke and the vehicle had to be abandoned. In it was a
firearm and ammunition.

The would-be killer apparently did not survive. On 18
September the police found a burning car in woods near
Saint-Hippolyte. Inside was the body of 26-year-old Yanick
Girard, a member of the Rockers Motorcycle Club, a Hell's
Angel affiliate, who was due to appear in court the following
week on charges of drug trafficking and possession of
firearms. Another biker, Sylvain Payant – this time from the
Jokers, another affiliate of the Angels – was shot dead in
Saint-Jean-sur-Richlieu on 14 September.[9] On 28 September
2001 Michel Vezina, of St-Hyacinthe, Quebec, who had

[9] The risks in being an unsuccessful hitman or hitting the wrong person are high.
In 1987 lawyer George M. Aronwald was shot dead when he was hit by five
bullets near his Queens, New York, home. It was thought at the time that perhaps
he had been killed because of his son's career as a prosecution lawyer. It was
also suggested that he might have been shot by mistake. It seems the latter is
the more likely because in 1997 an informer told the FBI that he had heard
it had been a Mob hit by two brothers, Enrico and Vincent Carini. In turn they
had been killed for murdering the wrong man. *New York Times*, 29 July 2001.
   Another similar case occurred in Chicago in May 1999 when Leroy Williams
and Lavonne Carter were found dead in the Leydown Motel, Melrose Park. Carter
shot Williams and then turned the gun on himself. Earlier in the day they had
shot two men in Roosevelt Road, but they had survived. Carter had made 17
calls from the motel room before he shot Williams. He feared there would be
reprisals and blame for their botched job. *Chicago Tribune*, 5 May 1999.

supplied the gun used to shoot Auger, received a sentence of nearly 5 years following a plea bargain.

The shooting of Auger brought an immediate knee-jerk reaction, with suggestions for new anti-gang membership laws and a stinging riposte from Lorne Gunter:

> Apparently (and I confess I did not know this) it is perfectly legal in Quebec to shoot a journalist five times in the back. Well, OK, perhaps it's not 'perfectly legal'. But at best such behaviour seems to exist in some sort of grey legal area there.
>
> Also there seems to be some confusion about the legality of selling drugs, using bullets and lead pipes to enforce inter-gang pacts, smuggling, conspiracy, tax evasion, setting off car bombs, assassinating prison guards and so on.
>
> For if such activities were already legal, why would there be such a mad cry for all sorts of new laws to give police an arsenal of new powers (with which to trample on a host of old liberties) in the name of fighting the Mob and biker gangs?[10]

Meanwhile the alleged head of Montreal's Hell's Angels, Maurice 'Mom' Boucher, was having an unhappy time in the isolation wing of Tanguay prison where he was placed in October 2000. Acquitted in 1998 of charges that he had ordered the murder of two prison guards, that night he had attended a boxing tournament where the crowd applauded his appearance at ring-side. But in October 2000

[10] Lorne Gunter, 'New laws won't stop criminals' in *Calgary Herald*, 21 September 2000.

the Quebec Court of Appeal had ordered a re-trial, and he was arrested on 10 October as he and two of his lawyers left a Montreal restaurant. Apparently he had been on his way to surrender to the police, but 'I didn't want to give him that pleasure so we arrested him', said Commander André Bouchard of the Montreal Police Major Crimes Unit.[11]

Throughout the summer Boucher had been conducting something of a PR campaign – possibly, said some, to create an image which would be more acceptable when he faced a jury the second time around. He had been pictured with Ginette Reno, one of the most popular of quebecois singers, and there had also been an old photo of him with Robert Bourassa, a former Premier. More interesting was the September news that in a Montreal courthouse consultation room he had met with Frédéric 'Fred' Faucher, a leading member of the Rock Machine, a venue described by Premier Lucien Bouchard as 'totally unacceptable'. The men then dined together along with some 20 guests in the Bleu Marin, one of Montreal's more fashionable restaurants. It was an event for which the men had put on their club jackets, recorded for posterity by *Allo Police*, a crime magazine.

One of the problems so far as public relations and the Angels–Rock Machine are concerned has been the number of innocent bystanders who, over the years, have been blown up or shot by the players. Perhaps the most celebrated was 11-year-old Daniel Desrochers who on 8 August 1994 was killed when a bomb planted in drug dealer Marc Dube's Jeep went off. In the explosion a steel fragment went through the

---

[11] Quoted in *National Post*, 11 October 2000.

boy's brain and he died four days later. More recently some of the surviving victims, notably waitress Hélène Brunet, have started to fight back.

Ms Brunet had the misfortune to be used as a hostage in the Eggstra! restaurant in north-end Montreal at breakfast time on 7 June 2000. At one table was a man rather strangely eating a fruit salad and at another sat Normand Descoteaux who was joined by Robert Savard, loan shark and alleged confidant of 'Mom' Boucher. Almost immediately the salad-eater began making calls on his mobile telephone and just as swiftly a man appeared in the doorway of the restaurant, pulled on gloves and a face-mask and shot Savard in the back of the head. That, according to Ms Brunet, was when Descoteaux grabbed her as a shield. She was shot four times and suffered a broken tibia.

After being released from hospital, where she had spent a month under police guard, she finally found a lawyer who would act for her in bringing a civil claim against Descoteaux and the Angels. Descoteaux, himself hit five times and charged with extortion, uttering death threats, loan-sharking and possessing a 9 mm Glock pistol, denied he sympathised with the Angels. So far as he was concerned, the use of Ms Brunet as a human shield was a police invention.

There were also suggestions that the truce talks were designed to head off anti-gang legislation and were similar to those held in Denmark in 1997 where Hell's Angels and their arch-rivals, the Bandidos, were temporarily publicly reconciled in the face of legislation to outlaw both gangs. There the leaders of both gangs had bought television time to announce the end of their war which had included rocket attacks on clubhouses. The Danish legislation was never passed. In Canada it may have been the threat of legislation or it may have been pressure from the other powerful organised crime elements in Montreal, but a truce was signed between the Hell's Angels and the Rock Machine with terms not wholly favourable to the latter.

The truce would not last long because in December the Rock Machine suffered a reverse take-over when members, far from abiding by the terms of the truce not to treat with the Bandidos, agreed to become probationary members. The defection may have had something to do with the arrest of Frédéric Faucher, charged on 6 December with planting bombs between July 1996 and 8 March 1997 – the day when a Jeep packed with explosives was rammed through a fence at the Hell's Angels' bunker in Saint-Nicholas. The Jeep then exploded, damaging houses in the neighbourhood but causing little harm to the intended target.

Now, along with their patched-over new friends from Satan's Choice, ParaDice Riders, Lobos and Last Chance, the Angels began to move into Bandidos territory.

The first test of the controversial C95 1997 anti-gang law, which raised the maximum sentence for members of a gang found guilty of a crime, began when 13 bikers alleged to be either Hell's Angels or from their puppet group, the Blatnois, went on trial in Quebec City following their take-over of crime in Shawinigan. The group faced a total of 162 charges including kidnapping, extortion and illegal possession of firearms.

In March 2001 lawyers argued that Boucher's isolation in a cell – where he had no access to other inmates, but which was provided with two televisions, a washer and drier, a Nintendo games console and a Walkman, but only two videos a week – was making him confused and inattentive and consequently jeopardising his ability to defend himself properly on charges that he had ordered 13 killings including those of two prison guards.

His lawyer, Jacques Normandeau, referred to penal reforms in Denmark where solitary detention has been abandoned following studies which showed that there was a harmful effect. The judges were not impressed. Said Mr Justice André Biron:

> I see that inmates in Denmark are in an eight-metre cell. Here, Mr Boucher has a cell and a living hall. He has a TV in the living quarter and one in his cell. In Denmark there's a maximum of one-hour visit. Here, he gets personal visits with one, two, three, four, five people including his mistress, his children and his spouse. We know he gets to speak two to three hours on the phone every day. This seems far from the situation in Denmark.

His lawyers had suggested that Boucher be moved to Bordeaux prison, but this was certainly not acceptable. He had, said the government's lawyer, previously destabilised the prison population there and he now posed a security threat. When he had been in Sorel the warden's home had been burned, and that warden was now in charge of Bordeaux.

Later that month life became even worse for Boucher and the Nomads when, in a dragnet operation against the Quebec chapter, 2,000 officers raided clubhouses and homes in three provinces. In Montreal 87 people, mostly bikers, were arrested including Walter Stadnick and Richard 'Bert' Mayrand, two former Canadian national presidents, René 'Baloune' Ouellette-Charlebois, at whose wedding Ginette Reno sang, and most of the other Nomads. There were, however, some strange fish in the net as well and these included Gerald Matticks, reputedly a member of the West End Gang.[12] The charges against the bikers included murder, controlling prostitution, and conspiracy to commit murder. Boucher was charged with an additional 13 killings and three counts of attempted murder. His son, François, was charged with first-degree murder in eight of the same cases.

In the summer of 2002 Matticks pleaded guilty to drug-related charges. Nor were things that much happier for some other members of the West End gang. His son Donald was one of 15 men accused of importing $2.1 billion in drugs through the Port of Montreal. He had been working at the port as a checker, someone who verifies where containers are placed in the docks, and therefore plays an essential part in ensuring that drugs have a safe passage through the docks.

In March 2001 an alleged Mafia hitman, Gaetano Amodeo – who owned a Montreal jewellery store, Il Barone Dell'Oro on Alexis Carrel Street – gave up his struggle against deportation and was returned to Italy to face trial for two murders. He offered to pay for his ticket and told reporters, 'I think I have bothered Canada enough. I am leaving of my own free will.' The charges related to a killing

---

[12] Charged in 1994 with smuggling over 26 tonnes of hashish, Matticks had been acquitted when the judge stopped the case after allegations that the police had planted the evidence. The West End Gang, a group of criminals mainly of Irish stock, were traditional rivals of (and co-operators with) the Mafia.

on 12 January 1991 and the attempted murder of a man who survived the attack. He also faced a murder charge in Germany.

On 18 July, less than a month after he arrived back in Sicily, Amodeo was found guilty of murder and attempted murder by a court in Agrigento.

With the Rock Machine and its satellites virtually destroyed, all that stood between the Angels and absolute power in Montreal was Vito Rizzuto's old-style Mafia.[13] Now the police claimed that they had evidence that the Mafia had been supplying the bikers with cocaine and had agreed a re-sale price structure with them, but relations might have become frayed. On 14 July 2001 the police charged Christian Deschenes and Denis-Rolland Girouard with conspiracy to murder Rizutto and Francesco Arcadi as well as kidnapping Frank Martorano.[14]

The police, who arrested them when the pair were allegedly making a reconnaissance of a Mafia café in the St-Leonard district, then discovered a cache of marijuana plants at Girouard's home and an arsenal of weapons including a Kalashnikov-style automatic and two 9 mm pistols at the home of Deschenes. Originally the police had been investigating a series of robberies. Deschenes, who was serving a 23-year sentence imposed in 1993 for his role in the

---

[13] Vito Rizzuto, guided by his father Nick, was alleged to have taken over the reins of the Montreal Mafia from Frank Cotroni, and was allied to the powerful Siderno group in Toronto. For a short account of how the Montreal Mafia evolved, see James Morton, *Gangland International*, Chapter 24. For an in-depth assessment, see James Dubro, *Mob Rule*.

[14] Martorano, a car-dealer from Lorraine, was alleged to have close ties to Rizzuto. In 1994 he had pleaded guilty to his part in a car-theft ring which sold luxury cars stolen in Montreal to purchasers throughout Canada and America.

importation of drugs, had been on day parole earning $17 an hour as a construction worker. The 1993 case had been one of the largest seizures of cocaine and was believed, but never proved, to have been tied to the Rizzuto organisation. Deschenes was part of a team preparing a clandestine laboratory in Laval.

There was, naturally, some speculation as to why there should be an attack on Rizzuto, one line of thought being that it harked back to the killing in 2000 of Salvatore Gervasi, the son of bar-owner Paulo who had run the Castel Tina strip bar. Salvatore's body was found wrapped in a carpet in the boot of his Porsche in front of the family home; he had been shot in the head. Four months later his father survived a shooting as he came out of a bank on Jean Talon Street. At one time Paulo Gervasi and Rizzuto were thought to have been friendly, but Salvatore Gervasi had been a Rock Machine supporter.

In theory Rizzuto, in a case now being labelled as Canada's version of Al Capone, had perhaps longer-term – if less potentially fatal – problems. Revenue Canada was accusing him of failing to declare income totalling more than $1.5 million. The allegations were that he had taken and used this money and had organised a consortium of middlemen to invest in a small Alberta mining company, Penway Explorers Ltd, the stock of which then jumped tenfold. Investors had been buying $50,000 worth of shares with cash, said by one mortgage broker investor to have come from Mennonite clients. The stockbroker acting in the Penway Explorers dealings, Arthur Sherman, disappeared in 1988 and was declared officially dead so that his wife could claim his insurance. His secretary told a court in 1993 that Mr Rizzuto had visited Sherman accompanied by two 'very large and frightening thugs'.

The prosecution in the tax case had intended to subpoena Raynald Desjardins and introduce the criminal record of 'Mom' Boucher, a condition of whose bail had once been that he did not contact Rizzuto. But in fact it was Rizzuto's lucky year. In the end it all fizzled out when, the week before the trial was due to begin, an out-of-court settlement was reached. The details were not disclosed. 'He is an individual who has a right to confidentiality,' said a Revenue Canada spokesman.

Not so lucky were Francesco Vetri and David Belleville, killed at a meeting in the offices at Le Groupe Gem at 5600 Notre Dame St. W on 26 July 2001. Various members of rival clans from the Italian Mafia lost their tempers over a cache of 15 kg of marijuana which had somehow found its way into the basement. According to the police almost all of the 8–10 men were armed and shots were fired from at least five guns including an AK-47. Belleville was thought to have been part of a team of extortionists and Vetri, who was on probation when he was killed, was the brother-in-law of Agostino Cuntrera – sentenced in 1978 to 5 years for his part in a conspiracy to kill Paulo Violi – who had his eyes on control of the Cotroni Family.[15] A third man was injured. Within a fortnight Giancarlo D'Alessandro, who was related

---

[15] See Peter Edwards and Antonio Nicaso, *Deadly Silence*. In sentencing Cuntrera to 5 years' imprisonment the kindly judge paid tribute to his diligence in setting up a sandwich shop, Mike's Submarines, and treated the murder as a momentary slip in an otherwise impeccable life.

to the owners of Le Groupe Gem, surrendered with his lawyer. He, along with Peter Randolph Stuart, was charged with the murders.

There had been other spin-offs from the Auger contract. How, for example, had the bikers obtained the details of his car? The answer, said the authorities, was simple. Ginette Martineau had passed on information she received while issuing licence plates to her common-law husband, Raymond Turgeon. In turn he passed on the information at $200 (or rather less than £100) a throw.

The prosecution alleged that Michel Auger was not the only victim of the breach of trust. On 27 January 2000 Marius Poulin, a small-time drug dealer, had been shot in the hallway of his flat in Montreal only 109 days after it was alleged that Ms Martineau had pulled his file at the Quebec Automobile Insurance Board. In all she was alleged to have handed on information about 17 people and, according to the prosecution, she had been conducting her illegal searches since November 1999.

Meanwhile the bikers generally were expanding their territories with associate clubs set up in places as small as Antigonish, Nova Scotia. They were also expanding their business interests, hiring accountants and Internet experts. Unsurprisingly, in addition they were developing business relationships in South America as well as Europe. By the end of 2001 the total of biker-related murders in Quebec in the previous seven years had reached over 150.

On a more domestic level Dorval airport had the worst record for car thefts in 2001 with 222 stolen vehicles. Given that the total of users was only 10 million compared with seven times that number at Los Angeles (which only had 65) and JFK at New York (which had 35) there is an argument that the airport has been a training ground for young thieves. They also take advantage of the port of Montreal to ship out the stolen cars.

On 5 May 2002 Boucher was convicted of ordering the murder of two prison guards, which brought an automatic life sentence without the possibility of parole for 25 years. Appeals and new trials are still pending with counts alleging over 20 more murders and attempted murders. It is thought that Boucher will still remain an influential player for some years before his authority is inevitably weakened by his imprisonment. It is thought that there would then be further strife on a leadership battle.

In its annual report published in September 2002 the Criminal Intelligence Service Canada (CISC) said it believed that the Canadian mafia in the form of 'a Montreal-based Sicilian crime family' was coming out of hibernation and might well try to tighten its hold on traditional moneymakers such as prostitution, drug smuggling, stock manipulation and money laundering.

Vancouver

The end of the career of Bhupinder 'Bindy' Johal, Vancouver's most notorious if not most successful gangster, came shortly before Christmas 1998 when on Sunday 20 December he was shot dead in the Palladium night-club in the city. A gunman walked on to the crowded dance floor at about 1.30 a.m. and shot him behind the left ear. Despite security cameras on the exits, 300 people in the club and an abandoned semi-automatic on a barstool, no one was charged with the murder, one of 18 in Vancouver that year.

In March 1995 Johal and five others had been acquitted of the shooting of Jimsher and Ranjit Dosanjh, once Johal's cocaine-dealer bosses. The first of the brothers was shot on 24 February 1994, and the second on 19 April of that year.

Johal had a relatively brief but exciting career. The son of a mill worker, he arrived in Vancouver with his family as a boy. In 1988 he was expelled from Sir Charles Tupper High School for kicking the vice-principal in the groin; apart from his expulsion he served a 60-day sentence. After that he went to work for the Dosanjh brothers before leaving them to work with an old schoolfriend, Faizal Dean. About this time a mainly East Indian group of youths formed the Los Diablos street gang, an offshoot of the East Indian Lotus Gang, whose activities were initially home- and car-thefts before they moved into low-level cocaine dealing. 'We were the brown people and we didn't get much respect, so we decided to stick together for protection,' justified one former Los Diablos member.[16]

Known as Little Benji, Rajinder Benji was acquitted of the murder of Parminder Chana, stabbed to death with 54 wounds in 1991. The reason for the Chana killing was that he had been unwisely dating Benji's sister. The Crown did at least obtain a conviction against Faizal Dean. Perhaps the Crown case might have been stronger had not one of the

[16] Quoted in Neal Hall and Lindsay Kines, 'Bindy Johal, a notorious, violent and reckless thug' in the *Vancouver Sun*, 24 December 1998.

witnesses, Sanjay Narain, been thrown off the top of the Cleveland Dam into the Capilano River. There was speculation over the motive, although it was not seriously doubted that one of the 'chuckers' had been Johal. The only question was why, and the answer was probably that Narain had become a liability; he had been talking about the Chana murder and had developed too much of a liking for cocaine.

Rivalry between Johal – whose Diablos were now taking around $200,000 a week from the cocaine business – and the Dosanjh brothers escalated, and in February 1994 Jimmy Dosanjh was lured into an alley in East Vancouver. Cars were parked at each end and he was shot by at least three gunmen.

As is usual, there were various reasons for the killing on offer. One version is that a hit on him had been ordered from inside prison, but another and cogent suggestion was that Johal was launching a turf war. Clearly the surviving brother, Ron, thought that Johal was behind the killing because he appeared on television threatening to kill Johal. Instead his neighbour, Glen Olson, was shot twenty-nine times in mistake for Johal while walking his dog. The gunman, Terry Debour, who opened fire with an AK-47 and who had been an associate of the Dosanjh brothers, later died of a heroin overdose. Then in a pre-emptive strike Johal paid $50,000 for the murder of Ron Dosanjh who was killed when the truck he was driving was riddled with bullets from a semi-automatic in April 1994.

Prosecutions followed the next year, with Johal's brother-in-law Peter Gill and five others charged with and acquitted of the Dosanjh murders. Indeed, the only serious casualty of the prosecution was a divorced juror who received a short prison sentence after admitting having an affair with Gill while the trial was on; she had met him in a night-club. Johal left Vancouver on 17 December 1995, hours after a drive-by shooting at his sister's home. An hour later there was an attack on the home of Sun News Lal who had also been acquitted.

In 1996 Johal and Co. were charged with assaulting a man in a pool hall, but the charges were dropped. Prosecution witnesses, it was alleged, had been marched into a lawyer's office to withdraw their statements, and proceedings alleging obstruction of justice followed. These were no more successful. In the middle of the trial the prosecution stopped the case, saying that the identity of witnesses could not be protected if it proceeded. There was, said special prosecutor Bill Smart, 'an overriding public interest in protecting the lives of the confidential informants'.

There still remained charges relating to the kidnapping of Raymond Chan, the young brother of a member of the Lotus Gang who had been held for 56 hours and only released, admittedly unharmed, after the intervention of another lawyer.

By the end of 1988 contracts said to be worth $250,000 had been placed on Johal's head. Indeed, it had not been safe to be too close to him for some time. Mani Rezal, who was said to have been in the Chan kidnapping, was shot and paralysed. Another associate, Roman Danny Mann who had just started a luxury car hire business, was found dead in Richmond. Peter Gill went into hiding.

However, Johal's death may have been the result of the hijacking of a consignment of eight new Harley-Davidson motorcycles from Mann, who had just taken delivery of them. One theory is that Johal stole the machines from his partner Mann, and in turn when he was killed the bikes were stolen from him.[17]

Over the years there have been thoughts that organised crime in British Columbia was subtly changing, with an increase in drive-by shootings and home invasions. Asian gangs, preying on other Asians by demanding money to allow them to stay in business unmolested or else charging very high interest rates, were said to be making very substantial profits. From 1994 onwards there had also been something of a Pax Mafiosa, with more co-operation amongst families including Asian triads, said RCMP Staff-Sergeant Andy Nimmo.[18] If this was so, it bypassed both the Dosanjh brothers and Johal.

---

[17] For a detailed account of the comings and goings of Mann's business and the motorbikes, see the *Vancouver Sun*, 5 August 1999.
[18] Quoted in Greg Joyce, 'Gangs have long and continuing history in Vancouver' in *Canadian Business and Current Affairs*, 31 December 1998.

24

Mexico and South America

By the end of the twentieth century it was thought that of the 15–20 international drug cartels almost half were Mexican, the largest of which were in Tijuana and Cuidad Juarez, with drug lords controlling cells operating in the United States.

Another of the key players in the operation once run by Amado Carillo Fuentes – the so-called 'Lord of the Skies' who died after a botched operation for liposuction and plastic surgery in 1997 – went down in 2001 when Juan Jose Quintero, the 58-year-old uncle of Rafael Caro Quintero who is serving a 40-year sentence for the 1985 killing of United States DEA agent Enrique Camarena Salazar, was convicted on drug-trafficking charges. He received 17 years' imprisonment despite being acquitted of participating in organised crime charges. That still left Rafael's brother Miguel Caro Quintero, who was said to be shipping tons of Colombian cocaine from Sonora into California, Arizona, New Mexico and Texas.[1]

Shortly after, the ten-year reign of drug baron Alcides Ramon Mangana, a former federal police officer who operated out of Villahermosa, came to an end in June 2001. Based in Cancun and operating under the protection of Mario Villanueva, the governor of Quintana Roo for six years from 1993, Mangana – head of what was known as the Juarez mafia or the Juarez cartel – had shifted tons of cocaine from Colombia through the Yucatan Peninsula to the United States. His tenure lasted a little short of three weeks after the arrest of Villanueva, and both were indicted in New York with conspiracy to smuggle drugs worth $2 billion wholesale. It was claimed that for every shipment of cocaine through Quintana Roo, the Governor received $½ million.

Reports suggested that Mangana, who took over after Amado Carillo Fuentes' death, had originally struck the deal with agents at an airfield in Belize. Mangana, who even as a police officer had helped Fuentes, also changed his appearance as he flitted unhindered about Cancun for 4 years; he had lost weight, shaved his beard and he too had plastic

---

[1] One of the many drug routes from Mexico was through a series of tunnels from Nogales in Sonora and its twin town just the other side of the border in Arizona. The tunnels, one 25 feet long, ran under a dry stream-bed and connected to the sewage canals beneath an abandoned house. One raid produced more than 900 lbs of cocaine. Another series of canals and tunnels ran into a Methodist church in the Arizonan equivalent of Nogales.

surgery.[2] Imprisoned outside Mexico City, now he faced charges of racketeering, drug trafficking, possession of weapons and money laundering as well as the New York conspiracy indictment.

Another long-wanted man was finally traced in July 2001, but this time he was already in jail. Humberto Rodriguez Banuelos, known as 'La Rana' or 'The Frog', had been wanted since the shootout on 24 May 1994 at Guadalajara airport in which the Roman Catholic Cardinal Juan Jesus Posadas Ocampo was killed. He had died either in cross-fire or when his car was mistaken for that of the Arellano Felix brothers' rival, Joaquin 'Chapo' Guzan. Banuelos was also suspected of an attempt on the life of Amado Carillo Fuentes ten years earlier. Found in Tijuana, where he was facing other murder charges, Banuelos had been there three months before it was discovered that his false name and date and place of birth did not match official records. He had also had a facelift, hair transplant and successful liposuction. He was transferred to a federal prison in Guadalajara to face trial on charges of murder, organised crime and kidnapping.

Banuelos was the first of the top members of the Tijuana-based Arellano Felix gang to be arrested. The capture of 'The Frog' was swiftly followed by that of the man alleged to be their leading Colombian cocaine supplier – Gino Brunetti who, described as a key lieutenant, was found in Cancun. While there had been considerable success in weakening the

---

[2] It was not only the heads of the cartels who underwent plastic surgery. In 2001 it was reported that cocaine was being smuggled by way of breast and buttock implants. In one case a woman courier was arrested after police officers noticed that her buttocks were unusually large. *The Times*, 14 July 2001.

Gulf cocaine cartel, the previous recent failure to arrest any members of the very powerful Arellano Felix family had been criticised. It was all a bit unfortunate since General Jesus Gutierrez Rebollo, in theory Mexico's head of the National Institute to Combat Drugs, had been arrested in 1997. He had certainly cracked down hard on the Arellano Felix gang, but only in return for payments by a rival gang.

Not that the brothers Ramon, aged 36, and Benjamin Arellano Felix, 13 years older, could really complain about bribery. It was estimated that they spent about $75 million annually in bribes paid to the police, military and government officials. Since 1997 six Mexican generals have been jailed for their links to the brothers' operations.

At the border, posters advertising a reward of $2 million for the capture of the brothers went unheeded, while they moved their border trafficking from California to Arizona.[3] Their mules now include pensioners, often with motor-homes, who take the risk on the basis that they feel they are unlikely to be stopped. More likely the mule will be a Mexican who will earn between £300 and £400 for a run, the equivalent of several weeks wages. In the town itself there are thought to have been 1,000 murders which can be attributed to Arellano Felix operations there.[4]

Then in November 2001 two former policemen, Jesus Castro Pantoja and Adan Segundo Perez, were arrested. It

---

[3] Ramon Eduardo Arellano Felix, described as policeman, rancher and physician, was placed on the FBI 'Ten Most Wanted Fugitives' list in September 1997, where he remains.
[4] See Philip Delves Broughton, 'America fails to stem tide of drugs from Mexican Mafia' in *The Times*, 25 April 2001.

was hoped that they would have information on Joaquin Guzman, who had escaped from prison earlier in the year.

Meanwhile hopes that the Mexican Mafia, La EME, had been shut down were proving unfounded. The authorities claimed that it had been smashed when, in September 1996, heavy prison sentences were handed down to its leaders, but Hydra-like it had quickly grown another head. In November 1997 David Barron, from a *barrio* in San Diego, was killed when he attacked Jesus Blancornelas, editor of the crusading magazine *Zeta*, in Tijuana. Blancornelas's driver and body-guard were also killed. Barron had been a contract assassin on behalf of La EME, travelling back and forth across the border carrying out killings. He had also worked for the Arellano Felix brothers. The week before attacking Blancornelas, he had shot and killed two Mexican soldiers working with anti-drug police.

There were also fears that the violence displayed by the Mexican cartels might move north of the Rio Grande. In September 1998, 19 people were massacred near Ensenada. In an early-morning raid, men dressed in black pulled three families including their children out of bed, herded them on to a patio and shot them with AK-47s. The killings were the result of a feud between dealers. Three men linked to the Arellano Felix brothers were arrested.

At the turn of the century, drug-related killings were said to be running at several thousand a year and there were thoughts that this might spread north of the border where La EME controlled much of Los Angeles drug dealing. An estimated 40 per cent of the killings in Los Angeles County went unsolved because witnesses were intimidated.

In April 2001, federal prosecutors indicted members of the Nuestra Familia, the Mexican prison gang, some of whose senior members – including Gerald Rubalcaba, Tex Marin Hernandez and James Morado – had been serving long sentences in Pelican Bay state prison in California. Not that this had deterred them from continuing to direct operations over the past 12 years. They had been sending coded messages, known as kites or wilas, either in letters to their lawyers or having them carried out by their visiting wives and girlfriends.

The Nuestra Familia were not alone in organising matters from prison. In San Diego in 2000, Frank Madriaga, a leader of La EME, was convicted of narcotics trafficking and extortion conspiracy. He had co-ordinated the mailing of drug profits to the imprisoned La EME leaders at Pelican Bay.

But while life continued, albeit with restrictions, on the inside, it was not necessarily all sweetness and light for a released gang leader, as Mike Ison found to his cost. Ison, another leading member of the Mexican mafia, had survived 30 years in prison but seemingly lost his way when he was returned to the streets from Pelican Bay in 1994. His first felony conviction had been at the age of 21, and he then received an additional sentence for the manslaughter of another prisoner. He was thought to have killed (or at least tried to kill) several others. One of his victims was said to have been stabbed 51 times. In another murder, this time in the prison chapel at Folsom, he had cut open an inmate's stomach and thrown the intestines on to a pew.

Outside prison he struggled to adjust. He was, of course,

unemployable and had the old convict's fear of people. If someone brushed against him he tended to reach for a knife. If someone sat next to him on a bench, he was inclined to think it might be a police officer. Now he spent his life playing open-air chess. He died at the age of 54 after a fight in a bar, having been chased into a San Francisco alley and beaten with pool cues.

Kidnapping has long been an ingredient of Mexican criminal life. In 1999 Daniel Arizmendi received 50 years; he had been in the habit of sending his victims' ears to their relatives and friends to encourage the payments. He was followed the next year by Marcus Tinoco, who made something of a speciality of kidnapping Jewish widows and secretaries in Mexico City. Of the 11 kidnaps he carried out in the 15 months prior to his arrest, ten of the victims were Jewish. Most were held for a matter of hours, but one was a captive for 18 days. Tinoco had some legal training which he put to good use, pretending he had court papers to serve. Not an ear man, he preferred to snip off the ends of fingers to encourage the relatives.

The Ochoa brothers, who had served short terms in Colombian prisons in the 1990s, were in difficulties again when the youngest of them, Fabio – who ran the cocaine distribution end in Miami – was arrested and charged with helping to smuggle more than 30 tons of the drug monthly. He had been running that end of the trade since 1978 when he was described as being:

. . . just out of his teens, the boy smuggler dressed punk, wore his hair long and drove a Datsun 280Z car. But he was extremely mature, with fine manners and elegant Spanish.[5]

There had been a crackdown on Colombian drug dealers; Pablo Escobar was shot to death in 1993, four years after the death of Jose Gonzalez Rodriguez Gacha.[6] With short prison sentences on offer to wipe out a multitude of past crimes, the Ochoa brothers surrendered: Fabio in 1990, and his brothers Jorge Luis and Juan David the following year. They were all back on the streets by 1996. However, extradition to the United States which had been suspended in 1991 was reinstated in 1997. Any earlier immunity did not apply to crimes committed since the reinstatement, and Fabio Ochoa was arrested in 1999 along with 30 other Colombians suspected of participating in the syndicate.

In August 2001, the Colombian Supreme Court ruled that Ochoa could be extradited and President Andres Pastrana confirmed the decision. This was seen as the most significant extradition from Colombia since that of Carlos Lehder Rivas in 1987. Rivas had received a life sentence in the American courts, but this had been commuted to 55 years. The decision was seen as a severe blow to the Ochoa family who had been running an advertising campaign and a web site aimed at freeing their brother. Leaflets were dropped into

---

[5] Quoted in Guy Gugliotta and Jeff Leen, *Kings of Cocaine*. In his younger days Fabio Ochoa had fought bulls as a *rejoneador* in Portugal. In 1988 he was named but not charged in the indictment faced in the United States by General Manuel Noriega.

[6] For an account of the career of Escobar, see Guy Gugliotta and Jeff Leen, *Kings of Cocaine*. For an account of his subsequent deification, see Jan McGirk, 'My brother, brilliant villain of Medellin' in the *Independent*, 2 January 2002, and Roberto Escobar, *Mi Hermano Pablo*.

packed football stadiums, and on billboards a likeness of Fabio Ochoa appeared with the message: 'Yesterday I made a mistake; today I am innocent.'[7]

The brothers claimed that the charges were trumped up because Fabio had refused to become a government informer. Ochoa first appeared in Miami on 10 September amid scenes of high security, with masked agents closing down the main roads between the airport and the city's justice building.

There was other good news for the authorities when, in December 2001, it was announced that Miguel Caro Quintero had been arrested and was now facing extradition to the United States on charges of drug dealing and money laundering. In 1992 he was said to have used a combination of threats and bribery to have charges dropped against him, since when he had been acting with almost total impunity. He had even called a Hermosillo radio station to complain about allegations made about him by the Drug Enforcement Agency. On 20 December his immunity apparently expired when he was arrested in Los Mochis, Sinaloa State, and taken to the maximum-security prison in Mexico City. That still left Ramon Arellano Felix on the FBI's 'Ten Most Wanted' list.

However, there were signs of a rift in Mexican–United States co-operation when a Mexican court blocked the extradition of Agustin Vazquez Mendoza because the States would not give assurances that the man would not face life imprisonment. Vazquez had been one of America's most wanted men south of the border following allegations that he had

---

[7] *New York Times*, 8 September 2001.

masterminded the 1994 killing of Richard Faso, a DEA undercover agent shot in Arizona. At one time there was a $2.2 million reward for his capture. In the past United States prosecutors have accepted a condition that they would not seek the death penalty in return for extradition, but they are balking at ruling out life imprisonment.

There was also the question of whether one or more members of the Grupo Beta, the border-crime squad formed in Tijuana in the 1990s to protect migrants from drug smugglers and robbers, might have gone sour. In the week before Christmas 2001 Francisco Javier Arias, who worked out of the Tecate office, was found in Tijuana shot in the head; his eyes had been taped. There were reports in a Tijuana newspaper that Arias had been working for the Arellano Felix cartel.

At last in February 2001 came some good news for the authorities; Ramon Arellano Felix, 'El Mon', was reported to have been killed in a gun-battle with the police in Mazatlan on the Pacific coast. A car had failed to stop at a roadside check, there had been a chase, a shoot-out and two men were left for dead. The body of one was almost immediately claimed by relatives and, a month later, it became clear that it had been that of the younger of the brothers. Regarded as the enforcer of the clan his career included – it was believed – the killings of 300 people including judges, prosecutors and in all probability the Roman Catholic cardinal. His team of hitmen included what were called 'Narco juniors', sons of wealthy Mexican families who in return for supplies of cocaine inflicted cruelty at the highest level. One state prosecutor was shot over 100 times at his Tijuana home and a vehicle was then repeatedly driven over his body. A 3-year-old child was killed and his body stuffed with drugs before being driven across the border.

Then at the beginning of March the police followed a young girl to a house in Puebla, 65 miles from Mexico City, and arrested Benjamin Arellano Felix, 'El Min', the head of the clan. At his home was a shrine to his brother, and it appeared that he had been about to flee. It was, said DEA Administrator Asa Hutchinson, 'a great day for law enforcement'. The arrest of the brothers did not, however, entirely wipe out their administration, but immediately there were signs that others were prowling at the edges. On 19 March three bodies were found in Tijuana, and there were signs that the men had been tortured before their deaths. The same afternoon there was a shoot-out in the Los Olivos neighbourhood of the city in a zone from which the Narco juniors were often recruited. It was thought that the deaths might be part of a battle between the remainder of the clan and that of Ismael Zambada – regarded as being aligned to the Juarez cartel which, in recent years, has been hoping to make inroads into the lucrative Baja traffic.[8]

[8] Julian Borger and Ho Tuckman, 'Blood Brothers' in the *Guardian*, 11 March 2002; *The News* (Mexico City), 21 March 2002.

INDIA, AFRICA
AND AUSTRALASIA

25

India

Like so many basically agricultural communities, India has really only encountered urban organised crime in the period since the beginning of the Second World War. Which is not to say that sometimes there have not been bands of criminals, as in the case of the Thuggees, operating under a religious façade. The Thuggees, robbers devoted to the goddess Kali, were destroyed by Sir William Sleeman who, in a purge between 1831 and 1837, had over 3,200 imprisoned and 418 of them hanged. At a more secular level, in the nineteenth century the Zamindars used trained guards called Paiks to swoop and seize land and women. Indeed, the danger caused by itinerant gangs was recognised by the Criminal Tribes Act 1871 which was passed to deal with the extended families who would travel hundreds of miles to commit crime. The purpose of the Act was to restrict the movements of these tribes to a specific area. It was enforced in 1924 when the total number of gang members was thought possibly to be as many as 250,000.

Dacoity, basically the same as the Western world's armed robbery, has been an offence forming an inseparable part of Indian rural life from time immemorial. It comes from the Hindi *daka parna*, meaning to plunder, and there could be house dacoits and road dacoits as well as river dacoits. In 1929 it was described as 'almost invariably committed by large gangs, varying in number between fifteen and thirty or more, armed with guns and other firearms and weapons, the majority of which are not merely obsolete but prehistoric'. In law only five persons were needed to establish the crime, and by 1970 dacoity meant robbery committed by five or more persons animated by a common intent. Communities could be ravaged by dacoits, who were particularly prevalent in Jabua, Madhya Pradesh and Uttar Pradesh provinces – during 1960–64 in the latter, there were over 1,742 reported cases.

> They have spread a nerve-shattering fear in the villages. The chopped noses, half burnt faces, the brutally ravished female-folk, cold-blooded countless murders, orphaned families, the fallow lands and the ruined and deserted villages all tell the tale of their atrocities.[1]

Seemingly the only way to avoid these predations was by paying *tika* to the dacoits.

In recent times the most celebrated dacoit has been the

[1] Srikanta Ghosh, *The Indian Mafia*.

bandit queen Phoolan Devi, the subject of a number of books and a well-considered film. In turn she was a penniless villager, a child bride, a rape victim and a highwaywoman, before metamorphosing into a class warrior and folk heroine. For a time she was also a Member of Parliament for the Samajwadi Party.

She was born in 1964, one of six children of a lower-caste family and, at the age of 11, was the victim of an arranged marriage to an older man who beat and starved her. She escaped and then became involved in a family land dispute. Denounced by her cousin she served a short period in prison, being repeatedly raped and humiliated by the guards and then, according to her story, was kidnapped and again repeatedly raped by the dacoit leader Babu Gujar who operated in the Chambal ravines. It was then that his deputy, Vikram Mallah, killed him and became her lover.

The great days of their banditry were in the early 1980s – hijacking, kidnapping, looting villages and blowing up trains – but in turn Mallah was killed by two gang members. Devi seems to have had the same misfortune with men as did Sergeanne Golon's fictional Angelique because it was then that she was subjected to mass rape over a three-week period by upper-caste men from the village of Behmai in Uttar Pradesh where she was taken. She was also made to walk naked to the river to fetch water in front of a crowd of jeering villagers. But she escaped and became the leader of another gang of dacoits. In 1981 she and her gang were alleged to have lined up and killed the 22 upper-caste men in the village where she had been raped. Some accounts have the mass rape taking place before the death of Mallah, while others have the shooting as a reprisal for the village's refusal or inability to hand over the men who shot him. Later, however, she maintained she had killed no one.

Devi surrendered in 1983 on condition that she serve only 8 years for a total of approximately 70 cases of extortion, murder and kidnap. In a highly staged event, she and her supporters laid down their weapons in front of a portrait of Mahatma Gandhi and the goddess Durga. Thousands had walked miles to see the ceremony, but not everyone was impressed by the rather less than 5-ft-high queen.

> I was told she was a beautiful woman but when I saw her photographs I was appalled though perhaps I shouldn't have been. She was a gangster's moll servicing the whole gang. It was a tough life and it must have drained her.[2]

In fact she served 11 years and was released in 1994. Much of her time she had been in the same cell as male members of her gang who, to her fury, were released before her. In the year of her release she married a Delhi businessman. The film of her life appeared the following year and she later sued over the scenes of gang-rape and her portrayal as a victim. She recouped £40,000 but, it was said, her claim had been motivated by money rather than feminist principles. Interviews, as befitted a high-quality gangster, were given with her wearing a tiger-skin sari and vivid red nail polish. In 1996 she stood for Parliament for the Samajwadi Party

---

[2] Writer Khushwant Singh quoted in *New York Times*, 26 July 2001.

and became a symbol for the Dalits. But she failed to carry through her ticket for reform for the oppressed and for women's rights, and was defeated the following year.

However, like so many other gang leaders, Devi put pen to paper once too often and her status as a celebrity spurred relatives of the victims of the 1981 massacre to have the charges against her revived. At the end of January she disappeared after the court had refused her 'anticipatory bail' and the murder trial loomed. But it never materialised and she was re-elected to Parliament in 1999, pleading that her failures be pardoned and she be given a further chance on behalf of the voters.[3]

Devi was shot and killed under a neem tree outside her home on 25 July 2001. Having left Parliament during the lunch break, she was ambushed as she reached her front gate. Two days later, Sher Singh Rana was arrested in Dehradun. Already named as a prime suspect, ingenuously he called a press conference while on the run, claiming that he had had the killing in his mind for some time and by it he had avenged the widows of Behmai. According to his confession he had driven the Bandit Queen to Parliament that morning and later met with a relative who acted with him. They had lain in wait for her and shot her with a Webley & Scott handgun, and also shot her personal assistant. He had then gone to the Delhi bus station and made his way to Haridwar and then Rishikesh before arriving in Dehradun.

[3] See Mala Sen, *India's Bandit Queen*; Luke Harding, 'The Queen is Dead' in the *Guardian*, 26 July 2001. There is a not wholly flattering account of her by Amit Roy in the *Daily Telegraph*, 26 July 2001. Not all accounts of the Bandit Queen's life maintain the same historical sequence, and there is little doubt that she contributed substantially and enthusiastically to her own legend.

From a wealthy family, Rana also had a history of false claims, saying on one occasion that he had been kidnapped during student elections. Nor had he any immediately apparent links with Behmai. Immediately rival theories sprang up, with suggestions of politics and land disputes being the real reasons behind her death. The killing was set fair to become India's Kennedy assassination.

Bandit queens have been something of an Indian speciality. Archana Sharma, the convent-educated and one-time pop-singer daughter of a retired major in the Indian Home Guard, has led the authorities a merry dance. Initially recruited by Irfan Gogha, killed in Dubai in December 1999, she has been suspected of organising a crime enterprise which has made £6.5 million annually from kidnapping and extortion, playing a leading role herself. The technique has been simple and effective. She often seduces her victims, drugs them and has them abducted. In 1997 Lala Vyas, a hotelier, was ransomed for £700,000. Careless talk costs gangs, however, and while blindfolded he heard her speak of plots to kidnap another seven men in Delhi. A raid on her flat produced a cache of weapons as well as evidence to show she had been behind the kidnapping of a director of the Hyatt in Delhi. This time the ransom was £900,000. Sharma was arrested and absconded her bail. Next she retrieved another £700,000, this time from an oil magnate, and then her gang murdered a petrol tycoon whose family refused to pay the ransom.

At the end of 1998 her gang, paid with money from Dubai, killed a former government minister, Mirza Dilshad Beg, reputedly because he had links with another criminal organisation. Then in the December it was thought that she had been cornered. It was discovered that she had been tutored by one of India's leading gangsters, Baboo Srivastava, who had been advising her on a mobile telephone kept in a hollowed-out bed-leg while in prison. At the time, Srivastava was being held on 45 charges of murder, extortion and rioting. The authorities monitored 2,000 calls and traced the woman to a bungalow in Jodhpur Park, a smart Calcutta suburb, where she was planning to abduct another hotel owner. The idea was that she would drug him and, passing him off as a sick relative, take him to Katmandu. On 14 December, Srivastava gave the go-ahead. Four of her gang were killed in a gun battle, but she escaped to Nepal.[4]

In the 1970s and 1980s Charles Gurmuth Sobhraj, born in Saigon in 1944 to a Vietnamese woman and an Indian father, was something of a one-man crime wave himself, working outside the traditional parameters of organised crime in India. Brought up by a Frenchman in Saigon, when the city fell he was left behind with his natural father, as his mother went with the man to France. She then sent for him and Sobhraj grew up in Paris. He returned to Bombay in 1970 and began smuggling and black-marketeering. After a failed robbery in 1972 he went for a time to Kabul where he was sent to prison for not paying his hotel bill. It was now that he began to lay the foundations of a serious criminal career, drugging his guards and escaping. He hijacked a car, drugged the owner and put him in the boot where the man suffocated.

Now Sobhraj began to work the major cities of Europe

[4] *Sunday Times*, 31 January 1999.

and the Middle East. He would meet his victims in hotel bars, then drug and rob them. He was caught in Greece and escaped from prison on the island of Aegina, before returning to India.

It was in Kashmir that he improved on the drink-and-drug technique. Hippies were in plentiful supply in Thailand and they would be lured to the Kamit House in Bangkok where they would be drugged, robbed, stabbed or shot and their bodies burned. By the time he was traced to his flat in Bangkok in 1976, with eight murder warrants outstanding, he was gone – tipped off by a corrupt Thai official. In the flat, however, were the possessions of a number of his victims, now estimated at around 20 in all.

Now for the time being Asia's Most Wanted Man, he was back in India staying in the Bikram Hotel in Agra, where the 'kindly' Sobhraj would prescribe a remedy against dysentery for the many suffering tourists. He would then help them to their rooms and ransack them. Unfortunately on occasions he miscalculated the dose, and some fell down in the hotel lobby. Others accused him of trying to murder them.

In July 1978, standing trial for the murders of an American, Luke Solomon, and a drug courier, André Breugnot, he was convicted of culpable homicide and received 7 years' hard labour. Four years later in 1982 he was put on trial and received life imprisonment for the murder of a man found drugged and strangled in Calcutta. Again Sobhraj drugged his guards and escaped, but he was recaptured several weeks later and sent to the harsh Tihar prison.

In their book *The New Encyclopaedia of Serial Killers*, Brian

Lane and Wilfred Gregg wrote: 'And if he should ever be released from there, Thailand and Nepal have a number of outstanding murder charges for which they would like to try him.' It was an over-optimistic view. When he was released neither country showed much interest in spending money on him, and he was last heard of in Paris trying to rewrite his life story. Apparently he had not enjoyed the enthralling version of his life, *Serpentine*.[5]

From the turn of the century, *goondas* (gangsters) were in alliance with revolutionaries and smugglers, and the passing of the Bengal Goondas Act 1923 meant that they could be expelled from the province. Later in the 1960s they acted as strike-breakers after they had infiltrated the unions.

In the Second World War black-marketeering, black money and bribery became the keywords, with the population providing for various armies in India. Red light districts began to proliferate, and the kidnapping and abduction of women for the purposes of prostitution became prevalent. Urban gangs led by *dads* started to establish small power bases. A *dad*, or leader, would typically be 40–50 years old, semi-literate and married or 'living with a fallen woman'. He would collect funds for the gang and direct its operations.[6]

Gangsters who had not been active at the beginning of Independence were now used more and more as musclemen for politicians, and then as providers of funds for them and even as candidates. Kapil Deo Singh, a former cabinet minister, declared, 'I am honest enough to declare that I keep

[5] Brian Lane and Wilfred Gregg, *The New Encyclopaedia of Serial Killers*, pp. 339–41; Thomas Thompson, *Serpentine*.
[6] Srikanta Ghosh, *The Indian Mafia*, p. 9.

Goondas. For, without them, it is virtually impossible to win elections.' In 1997, 28 of the 85 MPs from Uttar Pradesh were alleged to have criminal records or to have serious charges pending against them.

In his account of organised crime in India, former senior police officer Srikanta Ghosh considered that police forces and courts had been neutralised with corrupt law-enforcement machinery and a clogged judicial system. As in Russia, businessmen turned to criminal organisations to resolve their disputes rather than spend their time and money in a wearisome trail through the courts.

In 1998 there were 81 shootouts in Bombay, leaving 88 people dead. Victims included a hit across the street from a police station; an estate agent shot, along with two bystanders, while reading his paper on a train platform; and the owners of a café who were shot at the till. Often the reason was a refusal to pay protection money. Suspected by the police of being behind some of the killings, something he denied, was Arun Gawali. He accepted that in the past he had indeed been a gangster, but now maintained he was a political leader emulating Gandhi and Nehru. Over a period of time he had been in prison for 6 years on remand but was never convicted. He had recently been released under a law which allowed the detention of suspects for a year.

When the police did crack down on organised crime, there were complaints about brutality. In 1995 nine people were killed when resisting arrest for what were said to be serious crimes. In 1996 the total was 56, and in the first nine months of 1997, 70 men were shot in these circumstances. It was the age-old dilemma. Libertarians said that rising crime was no reason for the police to act as exterminators. A police spokesman commented, 'Would you be happy if a policeman dies instead of a gangster? When the gangsters die it is their bad luck . . . We have the right to defend ourselves.' He pointed out that 226 gang members had survived arrest. There were also allegations that Shiv Sena had been using gang leaders to threaten their political enemies.

One industry which has suffered more than others at the hands of organised crime is the film industry in Bombay, India's Bollywood. One of the hit films of the 1999–2000 season was *Kaho na, pyar hai* (*Tell Me It's Love*), which starred the matinée idol Hrithik Roshan and was directed by his father, Rakesh Roshan. Soon after it opened the Underworld demanded protection money and, when Rakesh Roshan refused, five men burst in to his office and shot him. He survived, unlike producer Mukesh Duggal shot dead in June 1997, and two months later Gulshan Kumar, the king of Hindi film-music cassettes, killed outside a temple in the slum district of Versova where he grew up. A youth shot him in the head and two men followed up with a further 16 shots as he crawled towards a lavatory. Thought to be worth around £90 million, he had ignored a series of threats. In the meantime, director Rajiv Raj had survived an attack and left India. In the December Manmohan Shetty, another producer, survived.[7]

A music director, Nadeem Saifee, was charged in his

---

[7] It was not only Bombay film-makers who were at risk. In early 1997 Chidambara Setty was murdered in Bangalore after failing to pay the 1 per cent interest *per diem*. An actress, Urmila Bhatt, had her throat cut by men who broke into her flat. *Guardian*, 5 September 1997; *Los Angeles Times*, 21 November 1997; *Business Week*, 14 February 2000.

absence with Gulshan Kumar's murder, and extradition
proceedings from the United Kingdom were begun. Saifee,
who had been in England at the time of the killing, was at
one time close to Kumar, but they had fallen out when he
signed up with another company. Now the Indian police
alleged he had paid £44,000 for the death of Kumar. The
owner of a rival cassette company, Ramesh Taurani, was
bailed. The police alleged that Nadeem had used the gang
of the major criminal, Dawood Ibrahim, who operated from
Dubai and Karachi, to have Kumar killed. Ibrahim, regarded
as a Don of Dons, had left India a decade previously. Smaller
gangs were run by the Naik brothers, and by Chota Rajan
who had set up his own gang operating in north-east Bombay
and had links to Asian countries.

On 21 December 2000 Saifee walked free in London,
the High Court having ruled that the only evidence against
him was worthless and inadmissible. They believed that
documents against him had been fabricated. While they
rejected a claim that, as a Muslim, he would not have
received a fair trial, because of the breaches of conduct by
the police they did not believe he would get a fair trial on
the existing evidence. In January 2001 Abdul Daud Rauf
Merchant, a contract killer for Chota Shakeel, was arrested
as he went to buy a cash card for his mobile telephone,
and put on trial for the killing of Kumar. The police said
that, acting on a tip-off, they had checked ATM cards in
22 bank branches in Calcutta and had found an account
in Rauf's name with a deposit of Rs10,000 from Chota
Shakeel.

Rauf was said to have confessed to receiving £1,500 as a

down payment for the murder. He named a second hitman and a spotter who was also arrested. After the murder he was said to have gone to Dubai and to have stayed in a safe house provided for him by Qayuum, an intermediary for Ibrahim. He had travelled on an Indian passport in the name of Bimbal Das. Rauf told the police he had worked for Anees Ibrahim, Dawood's brother, in Dubai, and in 1999 had gone to Bangladesh and then into West Bengal before returning to Karachi. He had been told to stay in the Tiljala area and await instructions to return to Bombay for what was to be a major hit. Six months later India applied to Pakistan for Dawood Ibrahim's extradition for his involvement in the 1993 Bombay riots.

Before Rauf left Dubai, Anees Ibrahim had been arrested, charged with the murder of Irfan Gogha, the Asian kingpin of the drug mafia and believed to be behind a number of kidnappings. His body was found in early November after his wife reported him missing.

One theory was that the murder had been masterminded by Anees Ibrahim along with Chota Shakeel, Abu Salem and Sharad Shetty. The previous month they had all fallen out with Dawood Ibrahim to whom Gogha, along with another drug-lord Ejaz Pathan, had remained loyal. Dawood had apparently left his safe house in Karachi and travelled to Dubai in an effort to smooth things over, but he was unsuccessful.

Another theory was that 31-year-old Gogha, a mute who came from Saraimir village in Uttar Pradesh, had fallen out with a Gujarat businessman over a plot to smuggle gold into India from Dubai. After the gold was delivered, the price collapsed and the businessman refused to pay. Gogha then demanded double and the money was delivered via Hong Kong. Three men had been arrested in Bangalore in connection with the demand. The suggestion was that the businessman had had Gogha killed.

Gogha had an interesting if fairly brief career. Like many others, he began as a smuggler and contract hitman before graduating to kidnapping for ransom, including one unsuccessful attempt in 1995 to seize an industrialist, Ashok Mittal, at Nariman Point. He was thought to have masterminded the abduction two years later of R.D. Vyas, a bar and restaurant owner, using Arcana Sharna. Gogha had been a close friend of Baboo Srivastava and an associate of Mirza Ilshad Beg, the subordinate of Dawood Ibrahim who was shot in Nepal during 1998.

One reason for the grip of organised crime has been that despite some 700 films being made annually, the Indian government had refused to recognise the industry as a legitimate one, and consequently refused to bankroll producers. Money was therefore supplied by private financiers or the Underworld, which charged 50 per cent interest and demanded repayment even if the film failed at the box office. At the end of 1999 came the welcome news that Bombay's industry was now granted official status. However, this simply meant that the gangsters moved to straightforward extortion, as Roshan discovered.

What is clear is that politics and the Indian Underworld go hand in hand. Over the years allegations have included one that the one-time Minister from Bhagalpur harboured the dacoit, Sudama Mandal. When Kamed Singh, the darling of Bhumihar ministers irrespective of party affiliations, was killed in 1980 by police officers, they were transferred and politicians went to the gangster's house in person to offer their condolences.

The style and operation of the Underground, as it likes to be known, is modelled on the United States with, one suspects, more than a nod at the *Godfather* films. Indeed Haji Mastan, a one-time smuggler who has been named as one of the three leaders of the Underground, has acknowledged that he represented a combination of both Don Corleone and his son Michael. Like so many early gang leaders in England and America – the Sabinis in Clerkenwell and the early Italian gangsters in New York are both examples – Haji Mastan was sought out by the community for help.[8]

Smuggling has always been regarded as the bedrock of the criminal. Mastan made his start in life smuggling gold from the Persian Gulf and this has continued to be a stock in trade, with other commodities being added. Polyester fabrics and electronic goods were followed, slowly but inevitably, by drugs. In the 1980s Bombay and New Delhi were major staging posts for heroin as it travelled from Pakistan to the West. The other traditional Western forms of organised crime – extortion, protection and gambling – were all bedfellows along with the additional activity of eviction. There was also the use of gangs to force the electorate to vote the correct way. In Bombay, where housing was extremely scarce and money could be made out of renting property, organised crime was used to terrorise tenants into

[8] See *New York Times*, 14 October 1984.

leaving rent-controlled flats which could then be re-let
without control.[9]

Back in 1988, a time of gang wars in Bombay, Suraj Deo
Singh from Bihar was arrested with five others in a clean-up
of extortion rackets. But the officer authorising the arrest was
transferred and Singh was released.

On 12 March 1993, bombs killed more than 250 people
in Bombay. The outrage was described by the police as a
sloppy terrorist act which was set up, at least partly, by a
local Muslim family involved in organised crime. The police
claimed that two leading members of the accused family,
Yaqub and Ismail Memon, had been detained by the United
Arab Emirates government in Dubai where at least six of the
family went before and after the bombings. The two Memons
are described by the Indian police as gold, foreign currency
and narcotics smugglers.

In September 1996 the links between crime, religion and
politics were never clearer. Amar Naik, one of the Naik
brothers, now wanted in connection with 28 crimes including
murder, was shot by the police as he was driving a stolen
car. The news was greeted with a call by *Saama*
(*Confrontation*), the official daily newspaper of the Shiv Sena
Party which co-ruled in Maharashtra state – of which Bombay
is the capital and richest city – for the police to stop targeting
Hindu mafia Dons but to go after the Muslim ganglords

[9] The use of organised crime to force out tenants has continued. In July 1996
the body of Ramesh Kini was found in a cinema in Pune, Bombay. He was the
one tenant to resist efforts to make them leave an apartment building owned by
Laxmichand Shah, a friend of the family of Balasaheb Thackeray, the unofficial
leader of the Shiv Sena Party of which Kini was a member. See *Asiaweek*, 13
September 1996.

instead. The apparent reasoning was that since the city belonged to the Hindu majority, the Hindu gangs should be allowed to take over the Bombay Underworld.

When builder Natwarlal Desai was killed on 18 August 1996, there were suggestions that a new power was emerging. Over the years Dawood Ibrahim, then in Dubai, Chota Rajan, Arun Gawli and the Naik brothers had carved up the city between them, but now a new ganglord appeared. In what might be seen as a politically expedient move, Gawli was arrested, but now the unlikely named Ali Baba Budesh claimed responsibility from his Bahrain hideout. Desai had failed to pay the required protection money. Businessmen were quick to understand the message; they paid, and once again things quietened down.

Then in April 1997 Keith Rodrigues, a member of the staff at the Copper Chimney restaurant in Saki Naka, was killed. Two men arrived before the restaurant opened and, after Rodrigues had ordered them to leave, they returned 15 minutes later and shot him. It might have been an ordinary dispute, but then it turned out that the restaurant's owner had received a demand for Rs5 million from Budesh earlier in the year and had not responded sufficiently quickly.

But who was this Budesh? Apparently the son of an Indian mother and Arab father, he had been a pickpocket in the Bombay slums where he came into contact with Dawood Ibrahim's gang which he apparently helped. In turn, when Budesh went to Dubai, Ibrahim tutored him. The pair then quarrelled and two senior members – Subhash Singh Thakur and Dilawar Khan – defected, so beginning a steady erosion of the Ibrahim empire. The pace of the decline gathered when

Anees Ibrahim was arrested at Bahrain airport in 1996 following a tip-off attributed to Budesh. His release cost his brother Rs5 million.

He has followed the well-tested tactics of the extortionist, demanding fees or apartments from builders and deposits in numbered Swiss bank accounts from diamond merchants. He is also said to have bought high-ranking police officers. His main target has been Bollywood, and in 1998 he demanded Rs10 million from each of three producers who promptly went to the police for protection.

Then at the end of July 2000 came a new and outrageous demand, this time from the smuggler-cum-bandit Koose Maniswamy Veerappan who had been wanted for over 20 years. His men invaded the home of the legendary film star 72-year-old Raj Kumar and kidnapped him, leaving behind a video cassette tape.

Veerappan, who was believed to inhabit the 6,000 square kilometres of forest bordering Karnatake and Tamil Nadu, had been keeping a low profile for the past two years, but he and his gang were thought to have been involved in over 120 killings. He had begun his criminal career as an ivory poacher, switching to the illegal felling of the protected sandalwood tree. In 1987 he had been involved in the death of a forest ranger, and three years later tracking teams sent to dislodge him met with stiff resistance and the deaths of a number of police and rangers. In 1991 about 100 of his gang were rounded up, but Veerappan escaped and captured and decapitated the leader of the tracking force. Over the years more police and rangers were killed, as were local peasants suspected of being informers. Some were beheaded, some strangled and some boiled to death. Five were killed after they had helped in the arrest of his wife Muthalakshmi. Now he also became a sort of Robin Hood, helping villagers to build temples.

Veerappan's previous exploit before the abduction of Raj Kumar, which had been the kidnapping of six people including two photographers, was not a conspicuous success. The hostages were released unharmed after the editor of a local newspaper acted as an intermediary. The reports by the hostages did nothing to improve Veerappan's image. He told them he was tired of a life of banditry and wanted to surrender if there were guarantees of a short sentence and the rehabilitation of his relatives. 'He just stood there and wept,' said one hostage. 'It was a very strange sight.' Negotiations for his surrender came to nothing, however.

For once, Veerappan may have misjudged the mood of the public. News of the kidnapping of Raj Kumar prompted rioting in Bangalore and a curfew was imposed in one district. Meanwhile the tape was played and on it the moustachioed bandit could be seen giving the government eight days to send an emissary. The police responded, saying he would be captured dead or alive within 24 hours. Given their inability to track him down over the years, it was something of a misguided boast.

Two months later Chota Rajan was in the wars, narrowly escaping when an attempt was made on his life at a roof-terrace party in Bangkok. Six men wearing suits sprayed bullets killing Rohit d'Souza, Rajan's first lieutenant, and wounding d'Souza's wife. Rajan, shot in the arm and stomach, leaped off the roof, hobbling away before being taken to hospital. It was thought he then made his way in a hired aeroplane to Malaysia. It was also believed that Chota Shakeel had ordered the attack after obtaining permission from the senior Don, Dawood Ibrahim. Rajan, who began his life as a ticket tout, had assassinated Abdul Qujun on Ibrahim's behalf. The cricket-loving Qujun was well on the way to making a half-century when three youths walked in from the boundary and shot him dead. From then Rajan had been an Ibrahim protégé. This worked well with Ibrahim, rehoused in Dubai with Rajan running the shop in Bombay until the demolition of the Babri Masjid mosque in 1991. Although there were precedents galore for inter-religious gangland co-operation Ibrahim, a Muslim, and Rajan, a Hindu, fell out – the latter, now seemingly a Hindi patriot, becoming close to the powerful political Thackeray family.

Arrested in Bangkok on charges of passport fraud, Rajan was expected to be extradited. He had been taken into court strapped to a stretcher with a glucose drip. However, the Indian authorities seemed in no hurry to retrieve him. The heel-dragging was said to be because of Rajan's links with Bal Thackeray. In fact heels were dragged so long that Rajan escaped. He had been fined by the Thai courts for providing false information to obtain a business visa, but the long-awaited arrival of the extradition papers was thwarted when on 24 November Rajan, barely able to move because of his leg injuries, knotted his bedsheets and – skilfully eluding his guards – lowered himself four floors to the ground. That was the official story, but there were allegations by his Thai lawyer that a fee of around $580,000 was paid to facilitate him. Whichever was the correct version, it was followed by a wave of killing as his men and those of Dawood Ibrahim shot it out on the streets of Bombay. By the beginning of 2002 both were still at large, and although a treaty had been signed with the United Arab Emirates none of the other players seemed to have been extradited either.

Nor was Bollywood any less in the grip of organised crime. Eyebrows were raised when a small-time director, Nazim Rizvi, obtained three top stars for his newest film. Shortly before Christmas 2000 it became clear that he had been in league with Shakeel who had threatened actors if they did not co-operate with his protégé. Rizvi was arrested and charged with conspiracy to kill.

However, organised crime in India is not wholly about extortion and the protection of businessmen. The trade in child slavery and in prostitution (both generally and of children) continues in India where there are estimated to be at least 10 million prostitutes. Bangladeshi children have been smuggled to become jockeys in highly dangerous (for them) camel races. There is cross-border trafficking in women and children. They come from Bangladesh and Nepal – the latter's women being particularly favoured for their fair skin – and from South East Asia, and are exported to the Middle East. It may take 15 years for the women to be able to purchase their freedom. In raids on brothels in Bombay in 1996, 40 per cent of the 484 rescued girls were from Nepal. The red light district in Bombay was thought to generate a minimum of $400,000 million annually, prostitutes servicing an average of six men a day at $2 each. There is also a tradition of religious prostitution and, apart from being sold by their husbands or families, women are dedicated into prostitution for the goddess Yallamma.

A variant on straightforward prostitution is the 2,000 or more *hijras*, or eunuchs, sold to a sex ring and then castrated, often in a religious ceremony. The priest will create an artificial vagina with a folded strip of flesh. Eunuchs are also required to perform anal sex, and it is a common belief amongst Indian men that HIV cannot be contracted from them.[10]

[10] See, for example, Robert I. Friedman, 'India's Shame: Sexual Slavery and Political Corruption are leading to an AIDS Catastrophe' in *The Nation*, 8 April 1996; Soma Wadhwa, 'For sale childhood' in *Outlook*, 1998.

26

South Africa

All good things have small beginnings and diamond smuggling and its sister crime, illicit diamond buying (IDB), started when a nineteenth-century African miner hid a stone in his mouth instead of putting it on the conveyor belt and sold it outside for his own gain. By the middle of the 1950s the IDB business was worth in the region of £10 million a year. Over the years, the so-called 'white' market in diamonds has been controlled through the Diamond Corporation in London. The 'black' market, led by the belief that diamonds were a safe investment against inflation, and with relatively lenient sentences being handed down, has provided limitless opportunities for theft and smuggling.

Black-market diamond buyers have operated in Amsterdam and Beirut since the turn of the twentieth century. Originally all stones offered illicitly came from thefts by workers at the mine face but in time the European overseers have proved even more of a liability. Perhaps the first major case of theft and smuggling was in 1890 when a young and unsuccessful prospector saw the opportunity to steal two mailbags from the Dutoitspan post office. He made his way to Cape Town but unfortunately met one of his creditors to whom he offered to pay his debts in one fell swoop. The creditor reported the matter to the police and the diamonds were found in the barrels of three shotguns.[1]

Over the years diamonds have been hidden everywhere. The workers swallowed them, they hid them in self-inflicted cuts which were then bound up; in the middle of books; in the heels of shoes; in the tops of walking-sticks. The drug smugglers of today are only following a tradition at least a century old.

In 1953 De Beers decided that smuggling on an international scale had become out of hand and invited Sir Percy Sillitoe, the scourge of the Sheffield and Glasgow gangs and now retired from directing MI5, to set up the International Diamond Security organisation. It ran for a three-year period and by the middle of 1955 a clear picture had emerged. There were small leaks from the Kimberley mines and from the Consolidated Diamond mine at Oranjemund. There was also some leakage from what was then the Belgian Congo and Tanganyika, but mostly this was face-front security. Just as the Mafia skimmed money in transit between the tables and the weighing scales in Las Vegas, so did most of the losses occur between the mine-face and the manager's office.

---

[1] Sir Percy Sillitoe, *Cloak Without Dagger*, pp. 216–17.

The real river of theft was from Sierra Leone, brought about not wholly by organised smuggling but also by a collapse of the state. Now the Diamond Corporation set up machinery under which it could purchase stolen stones and take them out of circulation. With this and the government taking a stricter view on the issues of digging licences, the flow was to a certain extent stemmed.

The concept of the master criminal is naturally one which the authorities prefer to accept as a fiction. There have been a number in the IDB who have approached that status. In the 1950s one man operated out of Antwerp with three separate routes through what was the Iron Curtain and in 1957 it was said that during a fortnight in February he had smuggled £½ million-worth of stones to Russia. The diamonds had been collected all over the world and were smuggled through Germany. On their arrival a quarter were sent to China.

February 1992 saw the death of one of the most feared men in Kroonstad when George 'Wheety' Ramasimong, leader of the R3 Million Gang, and a number of his lieutenants were executed. The gang – reportedly adopted by security forces and used by the police as a killing machine to wipe out opponents of the state in the area – had been responsible for a series of murders, rapes and robberies. Roland Roy Petrus, alleged to be a commander of the Self-Defence Unit and who had opposed the R3 Million, received 14 years for Ramasimong's murder, and others had lesser terms imposed. In August 1996 they applied for an amnesty.

With the breakdown of apartheid and the move to rejoin the world came more violent street crime, which also brought with it non-disclosure by the authorities. At the end of January 1997 40 foreign tourists staying in the Backpackers Ritz hostel in the upmarket Dunkeld West suburb were robbed of cash and jewellery, passports and airline tickets by a gang of six men. Initially the information was withheld either because of its sensitivity or because so many foreigners were the victims, which many might think amounts to the same thing.

For a time in the 1990s drugs syndicates were, however, literally under fire from vigilantes such as PAGAD (People Against Gangsterism and Drugs), a predominantly Muslim group which burned one high-profile drug baron to death.[2] On 4 August 1996 Rashaad Staggie, leader of the Hard Livings Gang,[3] was shot and then set alight. The police turned fire extinguishers on Staggie, but even after his death the crowd, shouting '*Allah akbar*' ('God is great'), repeatedly fired bullets into his body and stamped on it. Unfortunately another road to hell was paved with good intentions and PAGAD degenerated into gangsterism itself. By 2001 a number of its members were on trial for terrorism.

His brother's death, however, did not deter his twin, Rashied Staggie (nicknamed 'Mad Dog'), who had served a 14-year sentence, and who maintained that apartheid had

[2] In the smart suburb of Yeoville, residents hired the Hell's Angels as protection. In White City in Soweto the streets were patrolled by Youth Action Against Crime. Another, non-violent, group is Domestic Workers' Watch whose members report suspicious incidents to the police. Even so only a quarter of reported crimes are solved and, where arrests are made, the conviction rate hovers at about 10 per cent.

[3] Also known as the Hard Livings Kids. Rashaad Staggie had sensibly cultivated a Robin Hood image, throwing banknotes as he drove down a street and, shortly before his death, handing out the equivalent of £700 at a local wedding.

given him little choice in life but to be a criminal. Holding a rally in the slum neighbourhood of Menenberg, he asked the audience, 'What would you do if you wanted to take care of your children?' The reply was unanimous: 'Smuggle.' He also held a parade by the N2 motorway in which he was driven in a red Opel Kadett – at walking pace and surrounded by some 200 of his supporters including members of the Americans, the Firm, the Dixie Boys and the Sexy Boys gangs who have dominated the Cape's coloured townships for over 10 years – to the police station to hand in a petition protesting against PAGAD.[4]

In South Africa the drug problem is seen as bad and likely to get worse. In April 1994 the city's airport serviced 20 airlines; by 1995 there were 120 including airlines from Thailand, India and Brazil. South Africa has 'long, porous borders and weak border controls, including undermanned ports and numerous secondary airports [which] give drug traffickers and other smugglers nearly unlimited access'. In the early 1990s heroin was almost unobtainable. By 1995 free samples were on offer when a purchaser bought cocaine or crack.[5]

---

[4] Other groups amongst the 100 or so operative street gangs included the Ugly Cats, the Nice Kids, the Naughty Boys, and the Genuine TV Kids. In 1995 nine people a week were murdered in South Africa's Western Cape. The Mongrels, whose motto was, 'We're dogs. We sleep in cars, anywhere. We don't care', were regarded as particularly vicious. See Ed O'Loughlin, 'Hard Living Kids' in *Irish Times*, 30 September 1995.

[5] Thomas Callaghan, 'United Against the Creeps' in *Living Africa*, November 1996. Sometimes, of course, the police had spectacular success; sometimes not. In August 1996 a Zairian, Martin Makengo Kinsombi, arrived on a flight at Johannesburg from Rio de Janeiro. His luggage was searched without success but an X-ray of his stomach showed he was carrying 92 thumb-sized packets of cocaine. While in custody he excreted all but one packet, and while in hospital joined the notable and ever-increasing band of escapers.

Traditionally, in the past Africa did not play a significant part in the international drug trade. It produced neither opium nor coca, and although it produced marijuana so did almost everyone else.

The trade began in the early 1980s when a group of Nigerian naval officers who were being trained in India put their spare time to good use and organised a smuggling ring bringing South-West Asian heroin to Europe and on to the United States. This was boosted in the middle 1980s with the collapse of the Nigerian economy, which in turn allowed smugglers to be recruited more easily and more cheaply.

Now it is claimed the Nigerians run some of the premier drug trafficking and organised crime networks in the world. They still rely heavily on individual couriers, or 'swallowers', who transport drugs by wrapping them in condoms or the fingertips of surgical gloves and then swallowing them. On arrival they are given a laxative. Although the quantity transported by this method is limited, the seizure of a mule means that the loss of a major shipment is avoided.

By 1995 a significant number of Nigerians had moved into the run-down Johannesburg inner city high-rise suburb of Hillbrow, around 60,000 entering since 1993. Many had arrived as tourists and then obtained South African identification books and applied for passports. By September 1995 there were thought to be 3.5 million illegal immigrants.

At the beginning of 1996 the Nigerian drug dealers in Johannesburg flexed their muscles and went on strike after two of their number had been shot by the police on Boxing Day 1995. Not surprisingly, the result was dismay among members of the white community who were their clients.

During the years of white-minority rule, cocaine use was confined to the affluent whites. For the majority the most favoured drug was 'white pipe', a mixture of locally produced marijuana and Mandrax. Now cocaine and crack use has effectively replaced 'white pipe' as the drug of choice. Mandrax cost £8 a tablet and a heavy smoker can get through six or more daily.

Back in 1996 it was estimated that there were 450 organised crime syndicates working in South Africa, and the police had 103 undercover operations running. Of these 37 were focusing on national and international narcotics syndicates, 7 on taxi violence, 24 on vehicle hijacking and related crimes and 6 on internal police corruption.[6]

By the end of that year it was estimated that organised crime was costing South Africa more than £5 billion annually. There were 18,000 unsolved murders outstanding – a murder was being committed every 29 minutes.

Gold smuggling is back in fashion – if indeed it was ever out. Wealthy South Africans, fearful of the instability of the economy, tried to get money overseas. As for the mines, there were said to be seven syndicates operating theft rings. In 1995 3,594 carats of stolen uncut stones were seized in Johannesburg alone. Usually the gold or diamonds are flown by small planes over South Africa's borders or sailed straight to Europe. In April 1996 David Friedman, the last member of the smuggling organisation known as Chemfix, was sentenced. Chemfix had been licensed to export restricted

---

[6] National Police Commissioner George Fivas, reported by *Agence France Presse*, 12 September 1996.

quantities of silver and gold, but the group camouflaged the gold as silver and used false documentation to export more gold than they declared. From June 1992 to May 1993 the amount declared was $2.7 million, while the amount actually exported was $25.5 million. The gold was bought with money obtained by crime and then sold to legitimate buyers in Europe.

Smuggling of both goods and people continued to be rife as lax controls allowed the international land borders to be open to whoever wanted to come or go. As a result, something in the region of £1.3 billion in uncollected duties accumulated annually. Guns came from Mozambique and Angola. Despite a more or less complete lack of basic facilities such as electricity supplies, storage, transport and living quarters at many of the border controls, 40,000 illegal immigrants were arrested, while over 1,000 stolen vehicles, 30,000 kg of cannabis and 1.5 million Mandrax pills were seized. The army made an estimated further 80,000 arrests of illegal immigrants.[7]

By May 2001 it was estimated that nearly 200 people had been shot in the gang war which rumbled across Cape Town's Cape Flats where there were thought to be more than 150 gangs with a membership, albeit fluctuating, of over 120,000. The traditional organised crime rackets of drug-dealing, loan-sharking, prostitution and protection flourish.

Setting the pace in an attempt to seize overall control are the street gang the Americans, three of whose members are in thorough disgrace. Having been convicted of the gang rape

---

[7] Etytienne Hennop, Institute for Security Studies, Pretoria.

and murder of a 14-year-old schoolgirl, they now face the jail gangs known as the various Numbers because of their specialities outside (the 26s, robbery; the 27s, contract killers) or their predilections inside (28s, buggery of other inmates). It is thought they will be lucky to survive many months before they are taken out with that traditional jail weapon, the sharpened spoon.

Overall, conditions in South African jails are criminal breeding grounds. There are mass dormitories for 40–60 prisoners who are locked down from 4.30 in the afternoon until 7 the next morning and, as a result, gang rape and prisoner-on-prisoner violence is a nightly occurrence. Some 1,500 prisoners are thought to be killed annually; nor is there any likelihood of immediate improvement.

'It is a question of survival. If they don't have gang affiliations when they come in then they do when they go out and the gangs are country wide,' says Brian Fellowes. 'There are three or four relatively new prisons in the public sector and two private prisons but the system will take 50 years to get rid of communal cells.'[8]

Nigerian enterprises are regarded as polycrime organisations with a high degree of adaptability. They include laundering money in Hong Kong, the purchase of cocaine in South America, prostitution and gambling in Spain and Italy and the infiltration of British businesses by the fraudulent letters-of-credit scam.

Some people never seem to learn. A former deputy Mayor

---

[8] Conversation with author, 11 December 2001. See Michael Dynes, 'Cape Town police lose war in gang ghetto' in *The Times*, 26 May 2001.

of Northampton found himself in a serious situation after he received one of the 78,000 letters sent to Britain in the last three years, inviting him to supply his bank details so that fraudsters who maintained they were working for the Nigerian Civil Service could transfer a large sum of money. The man would in return receive a commission.

He flew to South Africa to meet his future business partners in Johannesburg on 8 July 2001, when he was promptly kidnapped from the airport and taken to a house on East Rand where £20,000 was demanded for his release. A joint operation between the Northampton police, the National Crime Squad and the South African police ended when three men were arrested in Hillbrow, as they went to the bank to collect the ransom.[9]

A variation is that sometimes the investor does get to see a suitcase full of what appears to be his money. However, he is not allowed to take it with him and will be told that he may have it the next day after it has been dyed black to hide it from the inquiring eyes of the Customs officials. Sometimes he will have to make an additional payment to buy the stain remover. It is even possible he may be able to take away the suitcase full of dyed, cut newspaper.

However, it is the day-to-day lack of law and order which is the most worrying. Approximately 200 police officers were murdered in 2000, and the same dreadful figure is anticipated for 2001. Very often they are killed for their service weapons. In the suburbs of Johannesburg houses are fortresses with windows and doors barred, walls topped with

---

[9] *The Times*, 14 July 2001.

South Africa 507

razor-wire and driveways gated. Private security is the name of the game, with one major firm, Associated Intelligence Network, rivalling the government's law-enforcement and intelligence agencies in size. On the roads high-speed motorcycles without plates are ridden with impunity; the police cars are not fast enough to catch the riders.[10]

Two state departments, both concerned with crime prevention, jointly lost R1 million in the year to March 2001. Some of the losses were put down to all-embracing 'police activities'. The Department of Justice and Constitutional Development lost more than R½ million due to theft, fraud, break-ins and robbery. Overall there were nearly 600 separate incidents in which state money or assets were lost. Scheduled security improvements included solid wooden doors with locks. Meanwhile AIDS deaths spiralled, rising by 584 per cent in the 5 years to 2001. It was estimated that 45,000 would die in the next 10 years. Post-mortems showed that most of the 1,087 jail deaths reported in 2000 as being from natural causes were due to AIDS-related illnesses. In July 2001 the 236 jails designed to hold 101,000 were housing a total of nearly 160,500, almost a third of whom were waiting trial.[11]

There were also signs that members of the now disbanded African National Congress army, *Umkhonto we Sizwe*, or MK, had turned to crime. There was nothing new in this. When, after the Crimean War, soldiers were discharged in a long period of peace, there was an outbreak of violent street crime

---

[10] See Henry Kowalski, 'Gangster's Paradise' in *Globe and Mail*, 6 August 2001.
[11] Department of Safety and Security Report to 31 March 2001; *South Africa Times UK*, 3 October 2001.

in London which led to the so-called Garrotters Act. Now in South Africa robberies were being executed with military precision, and there were suggestions that former MK members were behind them – a suggestion which found tacit acceptance by the ANC. In 1997 something over £16 million was stolen from banks and around £7 million from SBV, a security firm specialising in transporting cash. At least 11 guards were killed in cash-in-transit robberies. There were about 400 robberies and over 50 attacks on automatic teller machines.

In October 1997 one of the biggest of the raids, which netted R12.9 million, took place at SBV headquarters in Pretoria, and shortly afterwards Hendrick Maloma was arrested. A former MK man, he was then a serving police officer. Another MK man, Colin Chauke, was also arrested but he escaped only to turn up – to the embarrassment of some – at the 40th birthday party for the Deputy Minister, Peter Mokaba. He left before the police arrived. Mr Mokaba protested that he had never met Chauke and would not have recognised him amongst the hundreds of guests. Another former MK man, Donovan Nel, was alleged to have threatened to blow up the headquarters of the National Intelligence Agency unless he received R10 million.[12]

The situation in Johannesburg, where in the first 34 days of 2001 there were 161 reported car-jackings, has led to the formation of paramilitary groups such as the Jewish-funded Community Service Organisation. Designed to protect the Jewish community, there were fears that it was exceeding its

[12] *Irish Times*, 17 February 1998.

role, also suggestions that the CSO had an anti-Arab bias.

After an attempted robbery at a filling station in the upscale suburb of Norwood, members of the CSO visited the offices of the *Jewish Report* minutes before the journal went to press to demand that the names of the garage owner and his friend be omitted. In fact the robbery was foiled when the owner, Johnny Glajchen, and the friend, David Miller, opened fire with semi-automatic weapons and killed one robber, critically wounding another. Unfortunately, it seems that a cashier was killed by what is euphemistically called 'friendly fire'. Commenting on the attempted robbery, Community Service Organisation National Chairman Mark Notolvitz said, 'Although I regret the loss of life, perhaps publicising this type of armed defence of property and life might teach criminals a lesson.'

Another member of the CSO, Wayne Dryer, was not so fortunate. He was found shot, with one bullet in the head, in his office at Nando's Chicken in February 2000. Very little had been stolen from the safe and the cash register was untouched. Indeed the incident carried the hallmarks of a mafia hit and there were suggestions that Dryer had been killed by members of a Lebanese gang operating out of a bar, Sam's Palace, where it was said that crack was the main commodity being sold. Dryer had been a customer at the bar where there was said also to be a lively small-arms trade.[13]

Nevertheless, Johannesburg must take some comfort from the reports released in the last 18 months which suggest that the level of danger on the streets of Nairobi (known locally

[13] *Jerusalem Post*, 9 March 2001.

as Nairobbery) was comparable with – and security was now slightly worse than – in Bogota and Beirut. Machetes, axes and clubs were the weapons of choice in a city where one in three could expect to be robbed with violence. Car-jacking is a common sport, with drivers forced into the back seat and, if they are fortunate, later dumped at the side of the road. Home invasions are common and residents may simply sit and see their televisions and other possessions disappear in the arms of gangs. One man named only as Kuldip, who refused to hand over his cellular telephone, had his hand sliced off at the wrist. He collapsed to the ground as his attackers ran off with both hand and phone.

Street gangs have developed a nastier version of the ketchup-on-the-shirt diversion. Armed with cans of faeces, they demand money from passers-by, threatening them with the contents unless they pay up. Matters have not been helped by a recent survey which showed that 98 per cent of over 8,600 residents interviewed thought the police were corrupt.[14]

[14] The United Nations Safer Cities Programme; *New York Times*, 29 November 2001.

27

Australia and New Zealand

Australia

Over in Australia a number of old villains have surfaced and submerged again and, over the years, they have done their best to thwart the efforts of the former Chief Constable of Norfolk, then New South Wales Police Commissioner. On his appointment Peter Ryan vowed to eradicate the corruption which had been endemic in the force for the past 50-odd years.

At the end of 1995 an amnesty was offered to corrupt officers if they agreed to tell all and provided evidence against their colleagues. This, said Mr Justice Wood, was, a once-and-for-all amnesty. Those who did not take advantage of it would not get a second chance; they had until 9 February 1996 to come out of the locker room. Resignation would be required, but they would be allowed to keep their superannuation, pension and ill-gotten gains. Ryan, who had been head-hunted from England where he also lectured at the Police Training College at Bramshill, announced in 2001 that his reformatory mission was now complete. In his earlier years in the force he faced a good deal of sniping on a professional and personal level, but he had weathered the storm. When interviewed shortly after his appointment, he was keen to dismiss suggestions that he did not have the depth of experience to deal with city detectives bent on hiding their misdeeds. 'People have overlooked the fact that there is a determination to clean up the act. It rests not only with me but with a widespread group of people.' There was now in place a Police Integrity Commission to root out corruption. In his first months he dismissed 20 officers, and 150 were suspended. 'When it was seen I was dismissing officers, there was a rush to hand in resignations.'[1] The force was now clean.

Unfortunately *Operation Florida*, a three-year sting mounted by the force's internal anti-corruption unit, told something of a different story in 2001. In a covert operation, in which microphones and cameras had been planted in lavatories in the North Shore suburb of Manley, the police were filmed as they met and dealt with drug dealers. One detective, Senior Constable David Patison, was filmed pushing banknotes down his trousers. He had found the money while searching the home of a cannabis dealer. Another clip of film showed three officers taking A$40,000 and laughing, 'Happy Days!'

[1] James Morton, 'Ryan's War' in *Police Review*, 29 November 1996.

Vince Caccamo, a senior heroin dealer of the North Shore area, paid over a total of $92,000 in bribes including a weekly $1,000 to Patison and Senior Constable Matthew Jasper in 2000. He was recorded complaining to an associate, Anthony Markarian, that he was being badly squeezed: 'Every cent I make goes to them.' Markarian thought it was like having a shop and paying rent. In another traditional police scam, another officer had arranged for a convicted burglar to rob the home of a man known not to be security conscious in return for a percentage of the proceeds.

Ryan, who had just negotiated a new $400,000 a year contract, was said to be very angry, as well he might be. Putting on a brave face, he told his force to, 'Wear your uniform with pride.' On the roads, it was back to the days when motorists in Chicago and New York carried $5 and $10 clipped to their licences. Now drivers stopped for speeding were said to be asking the police, 'How much?' Ryan said that the operation showed his reforms were working.

It is rare for barristers to have a knock-out triumph over a witness. At best it is usually a gruelling points decision but counsel for the inquiry, Peter Hastings, scored one when Sergeant David Hill said he planned to resign after giving evidence. 'Why wait?' asked Hastings and Hill complied.[2]

The police regrouped when on 23 October 2001 they launched a massive series of raids on the homes of suspected drug dealers, garnering a wide variety of drugs and other

[2] *Independent on Sunday*, 21 October 2001.

interesting property. It was denied that this was part of a publicity exercise.

On the national level, in December 2000 the chairman of the Federal Parliament National Crime Authority, Gary Crooke QC, admitted that he believed most of Australia's law-enforcement agencies had been infiltrated by organised crime. In his report to the Federal Parliament, he went on to say that the old Hollywood perception of the Mafia was long out of date. Images of gangs based on ethnic allegiances or territories no longer held true.

On 3 April 2002 Ryan resigned amid suggestions of governmental interference.

There were also plans for the nation's most celebrated criminals to provide mouth-swab samples for DNA testing; it was thought that between 20 and 30 per cent of the samples would match with outstanding crimes. Those to be tested included Earl Heatley, convicted in 1966 of murder and again in 1994 when a botched robbery at a factory on 1 October ended in two deaths, including that of his brother Paul; contract killers Gary Glasby and Lindsay Rose; and standover man and murderer 'Neddy' Smith.[3]

Of this sparkling quartet by far the most celebrated, with two books to his name, is Arthur 'Neddy' Smith. In the 1980s he had been one of the most celebrated of New South Wales' colourful characters and was sentenced to life imprisonment

---

[3] The Heatley brothers were somewhat unlucky men. Paul, who in the 1980s had worked with a team from Grenville as an armoured car robber, had shot himself in the leg in a failed hold-up in 1986. He had holed up and by the time the police retrieved him a week later his leg had gone gangrenous. He received a total of 16 years and had been released only five weeks before his death.

for the 1990 road-rage killing of truck driver Glen Flavell. With his partner Detective Sergeant Roger Rogerson, he was also regarded as being one of the three main gangs of heroin dealers in the city.

The early 1990s saw a new role for Smith, the drug dealer, rapist, robber and killer – that of assistant to justice. He had become an informer and was now the star witness at the hearings conducted by the Independent Commission Against Corruption. Much of his evidence was directed at his former solicitor, Graham Valentine 'Val' Bellamy, with whom he had had such a working relationship in the past that a Mercedes-Benz and a Rolls-Royce which belonged to him had conveniently been registered in the solicitor's name. One incident they shared, according to Smith, was the snatching of a bag containing $60,000, not once but twice in almost as many minutes. Around 3 p.m. on 17 September 1984 a black vinyl bag which contained the money withdrawn from a safety-deposit box of the Commonwealth Bank in Castlereagh Street was snatched as Mr Bellamy walked through Martin Place. A passer-by – some say it was Mr Bellamy's own father – chased after the thief and retrieved the bag with the help of an off-duty policeman. Sadly, the theft was repeated successfully almost immediately. This time the solicitor was punched in the stomach. Smith's version of events was that the robbery was a put-up job to cover Bellamy's withdrawals from the box on his own account. A fee of $10,000 had been paid to a police officer to help fake a report on the robbery.

As for 'Neddy' Smith, perhaps he had only himself to blame for his continuing troubles. On 22 January 1995 the *Sun-Herald* published a banner headline: 'I killed Six: Neddy

Smith.' Apparently Smith had foolishly been talking to a cell-mate who in turn, thinking it might do him some good, had reported the conversations to the authorities. One story he told about the police killing the solicitor's clerk, Brian Alexander, had been a blind. Along with five others, this murder was all his own work. It was he who had tied the law clerk to a gas fire on a boat and dumped him overboard.

In September 1998, Smith – who had been a thorn in the flesh of so many people over a long period of time – had been convicted of shooting the brothel manager, Harvey Jones, whose remains were found buried at Foreshore Beach in March 1995. He had been shot twice in the head. By this time Smith had recanted his confession and said that his cell-mate, known as Green, might have been paid to tell his story through a solicitor enemy of Smith identified as a Mr White. Smith's loyal wife said that all she knew to the detriment of her husband was that he might have been an illegal book-maker:

> People say I must have been so naïve, but Ned could have been leaving home at eight in the morning, coming home at five and said he was a doctor. I never asked, and he would tell me what I wanted to know.[4]

The Crown decided not to proceed with the prosecution for the murder of Brian Alexander.

In May 1999 Smith appeared in the Glebe Coroner's Court when an inquest was held into the disappearance of male model and cocaine dealer Mark Johnston. What was defi-

[4] *Daily News* (New Plymouth), 14 September 1998.

nitely known was that the last sighting of Johnston had been when Johnston called on Val Bellamy to collect $60,000 which the solicitor had been holding for him. Johnston's hired car, a Holden Commodore, was found eight days later at Maroubra after a tip-off by an anonymous woman. There were over 500 grams of cocaine in the car and some loose change. When Bellamy was seen by the police he told them he was constrained by client confidentiality from discussing the matter. However, he told them that Johnston had been to his home and had stayed about 15 minutes before leaving with his money.

What was less clear was what had happened to Johnston whose father, Arthur, had spoken to Bellamy a week after his son's disappearance. Mark had told his father that he tried to arrange three meetings with Bellamy to collect his money.

It all came back to those cell confessions. It was alleged that Smith had told his cellmate that he had killed Johnston at the solicitor's request. In the confession he said that he had handcuffed and then garrotted the drug dealer rather than spoil the carpet by stabbing him in the solicitor's new $3.5 million home at Dover Heights.

Detective Sergeant Neville Smith told the court that he believed Bellamy knew full well what had happened to Johnston, and found it difficult to accept that the money had been returned to him. When it came to it Deputy State Coroner John Abernethy ruled that Johnston was dead and that he had been killed at Dover Heights. He ordered the papers to be sent to Nicholas Cowdery, the Director of Public Prosecutions.

On 5 May 1999 Bellamy, now working as a telephone

clerk, was charged with fraud involving nearly $¾ million, including one charge of obtaining $350,000 from Broadway Credit Union.[5] In October 2000 he was sentenced to 4 years, with at least two to be served. He had pleaded guilty and in mitigation blamed his downfall on Smith. Justice Blanch took the view that he would be at risk from Smith in the prison system, and recommended that on his arrival he be transferred into some sort of protective custody.

Smith had been a long-time associate if not partner of the corrupt former detective Roger Rogerson, and as part of his general *mea culpa* back in 1996 had named Rogerson as being the killer of prostitute Lyn Cristene Woodward in a Sydney park in November 1981. Smith claimed that he had buried the body on his old friend's behalf. Rogerson, who had served a prison sentence for dishonesty, was called to the inquest on Woodward held in January 2000. Smith was a liar, he said:

> He hated me. It probably goes back to the fact that he was an informant of mine. He was the best informant that I ever had . . . and my situation had changed dramatically. He had been charged with serious crimes and I believe he decided to make allegations about police officers.

The coroner found there was no corroboration at all of Smith's evidence and that he 'appeared to have much to gain by making an induced statement and by implicating police, particularly a well-known person like Mr Rogerson'.

Smith's example, put at its most kindly to Rogerson,

[5] *Sydney Morning Herald*, 4/5 May 1999.

showed the dangers of getting into bed with one's informant, something Rogerson did almost literally. In Smith's book *Neddy* there is a picture of the pair of them with two girls at a hotel. A second picture shows Rogerson taking his clothes off. On 14 June 2000 Smith lost his appeal against his conviction for murder and the life sentence which followed it.

Another of the old-time criminals and one whom Smith had credited with introducing him to the heroin trade, Kenny Derley, was back in trouble. He had started his life of crime at the age of 13 and, with the exception of a spell as a lower-grade rugby league player for Balmain where he worked in the docks, he had done little else after joining the elite Double Bay Mob.

In November 2000 he pleaded guilty to commercial drug supply after having been found with a kilo of amphetamines in the boot of his car at Easter that year. He had been the subject of a bug planted in his car which picked up a conversation showing he was planning an overnight drive to Melbourne. Now, faced with a substantial term in prison, the man who was one of Sydney's earliest drug suppliers was said to have a heart condition which would mean he would almost certainly die in jail.

One old-timer, although at 47 he is still a relatively young man, has fared rather better. Mark Brandon Read, known as 'Chopper' because he sliced off parts of his ears – who has served long periods of imprisonment for robbery and, much as he protested his conviction, murder – was eventually paroled in 1997.[6] He had married in a jail ceremony on 22

[6] See Mark Brandon Read, *Chopper*.

April 1995. Rather sensibly he decided to stay in for the last six months because he did not want to be subject to any restrictions on his release. While in prison he became something of a celebrity, writing a number of highly colourful and successful books about his life which were turned into a film. He cleverly and generously sidestepped criticism about criminals making money from their misdeeds by donating the profits from the film to a police charity supporting children with cancer.

By the end of the twentieth century Australia had the second highest car-theft rate in the world, second only to England. Statistics showed that the average thief stole 47 cars before being sent to jail where, with remission, he would serve an average of 19 days. There was a fairly good record of catching opportunist or inexperienced thieves, but the chance of catching professional car thieves was remote. In 1998 Australia also had a higher ratio of burglary than the United States.

There has been a falling out amongst the drug dealers in King's Cross, Sydney, and one who fell was the Lebanese Danny Georges Karam, who gave evidence to the NSW Police Royal Commission telling of his role as an enforcer and how he protected other criminals. Possibly foolishly, he did this quite openly and without taking a codename. On 13 December 1998 he was shot and killed outside a block of flats in Riley Street. His killing was described by Superintendent Bob Inkster as 'an assassination, an execution'.

Around 9.30 p.m. Karam had left his Randwick home in his Toyota RAV4 to go to a meeting in Surry Hills, and it was thought that four men were waiting for him. They shot him through the open driver's window as he parked his car, hitting him with at least five bullets in the chest and lower body. The men ran down Fitzroy Street towards Central Station and as they did so another man ran to Karam's car and stole his wallet and mobile telephone. However, the man did not take a 12-gauge pump-action shotgun which was found on the back seat.

As the weeks went by a picture – if not a very clear one – emerged, and the police believed that Karam had been killed by members of the 10-strong gang of which he had been the leader. The gang, said to have been behind the killing of three innocent people in a drive-by shooting as well as one at the Lekemba police station, were also believed to have carried out up to 20 shootings across Sydney in the previous year. Karam had been the victim of a power struggle in his gang which specialised in drug dealing and extortion. His killing almost immediately followed a drive-by shooting at the EP1 night-club in King's Cross, when over 50 shots had been fired at the club.

Karam, once a commando in the Lebanese Christian Army, who had worked as a rigger after he migrated to Australia in 1983, had been the victim of a previous attack in 1993 at a time when he was said to be out of control and trying to feed a $1,000-a-day heroin habit. He was also alleged to have been having an affair with a woman whose husband decided he needed to be taught a lesson, if not a fatal one. Gunmen were hired to shoot him in the legs, but unfortunately they went to the wrong address. Instead of Karam being shot in the legs at number 50, 60-year-old Leslie Betcher at number 15 was shot in the stomach and died that night. It was not until 18 December 1998, the week after Karam's death, that Jon Leslie Baartman, who had been the lookout, was finally sentenced to 15 years' imprisonment. It was his third trial. Found guilty in 1994, he then obtained a re-trial at which the March 1998 jury could not reach a verdict. The actual gunman, Paul Thomas Crofts, had pleaded guilty. The hit had been worth $1,000.

Karam had been a regular court attender over the previous five years, including an appearance when he was fined after explaining that a pair of handcuffs were for sexual rather than criminal purposes. His transformation came in 1995 after a sentence for assault. During the time he spent in prison, at the very least he began to control his drug habit. Out he came to talk to the Police Royal Commission about his days with the King's Cross drug dealer, Billy Bayeh, in a form of the Murphy Game. Bayeh would find a client who wanted to buy drugs; Karam would rob him. He was, he said, being paid $5,000 a week to make sure than only Bayeh's men sold drugs on the street.[7] Bayeh went to prison in 1996, sentenced to 15 years after pleading guilty to conspiracy to supply a commercial quantity of heroin and cocaine. In November 2000 he lost his appeal against his sentence, which will expire in July 2011.

It was after Bayeh was sentenced that the wars began, and in July 2000 his brother Louis and two other men were shot outside the El-Bardowny Lebanese restaurant at Narwee. Louis was shot in the groin and thigh. Was this an attempted

---

[7] For an account of the drug dealing in the King's Cross area in Bayeh's time, see James Morton, *Gangland International*.

execution? At first the police thought so, but then it seemed to be something more in the way of a personal quarrel. Moustafa Laa Laa had been shot in the shoulder and Bayeh was arrested. According to his police file he had 46 aliases. There was still talk of a $200,000 contract.

At the end of January 2001 he pleaded guilty to demanding money with menaces from two brothel owners between 1989 and 1992. He admitted having taken up to $1,000 a week and a further $1,200 which, he said, was to go to corrupt police officers. In July, much to the displeasure of the judge, he managed to delay his sentencing by sacking his lawyers. It helped him by less than two weeks, and this 'man of public notoriety' received 3 years' imprisonment.

Karam had joined with Russell Townsend, who had been an associate of the legendary Lennie McPherson and the Double Bay Mob. Russell, twice Mr Australia and a world record powerlifter, was a notorious enforcer until in 1996 he was charged with manslaughter after a fight in King's Cross. Acquitted, he turned his back on crime, becoming a professional boxer in 2001. Weighing 115 kg, 15 kg less than his enforcing weight, he was regarded as a potential prospect. By the end of the year he had won his first four contests in a total of less than six minutes.

Memories of the golden days of Sydney crime surfaced again in May 1999 with the arrest of Joy Thomas, one-time friend of both Darcy Dugan and Lennie McPherson and the girlfriend of standover man Chikka Reeves, killed in 1979. DNA tests allegedly showed that she had licked the envelopes of extortion letters which temporarily caused the removal of

Arnott's biscuits from the shelves, leading to a $10 million loss.

Hers had been a colourful life. She was born into a boxing family and had been a showgirl. In 1968 she was sentenced along with her then husband, her son Ronald and another man after a bungled robbery at a Newtown postal depot in which a security guard died. She was released on parole in the late 1970s and when Ronnie escaped from Milson Island prison she was charged with harbouring him. Her cause was taken up by a group of radical feminists complaining that a mother should not be imprisoned for helping her son, and she was freed on appeal.

Then in 1991 Ronnie was again convicted, this time of the murder of the Gold Coast bookmaker Peter Wade and his girl-friend Maureen Ambrose – allegedly shot by him and another man in Wade's flat in Surfer's Paradise. In 1997 poisoned packets of biscuits and some letters turned up at the offices of a Queensland newspaper, as well as those of the Queensland Attorney General and the Criminal Justice Commission. There were the envelopes that Joy Thomas was accused of licking. The letters claimed that Ronald Thomas was innocent and demanded that the case be reviewed. The sender wanted the police officers involved to take lie-detector tests.

It all turned out well for her when on 26 April 2002 Joy Thomas, now aged 72, walked free. The Crown Prosecutor offered no evidence after a forensic biologist, who had allegedly matched a DNA sample, now accepted there might be a second profile after examining test results from the defence.[8]

[8] *The Gold Coast Bulletin*, 27 April 2002.

One thing of which French criminals do not have a monopoly is escape from prison by helicopter. In March 1999 off went John Reginald Killick from Silverwater prison where he was accused of attempted murder and armed robbery. His girlfriend had hired the helicopter for what the pilot thought was to be a joyride over the Olympic site; instead he found himself ordered at gunpoint to fly to the prison. When it was landing in the prison yard Killick jumped aboard. The pilot was later left bound with radio wires. The pair were thought to have left the state by boat. Killick obviously had a series of loyal girlfriends. In 1984 in Brisbane he had escaped when being taken to hospital for the treatment of an eye condition; on that occasion his then girlfriend, wearing a wig, held up guards at gunpoint.

By the end of 2001 the face of organised crime in Australia had changed. There was pressure on the government to organise a national cybercrime centre on the lines of those in America and Great Britain. In the previous 12 months over 400 e-crimes had been referred to the Australian Federal Police, of which 46 per cent were related to child pornography or paedophilia. The remainder of crimes ran the gamut, with hacking and unauthorised intrusions totalling some 17 per cent; another 7 per cent were viruses and denial of service attacks.

One new team of players appreciatively eyeing the charms of Australia was the Red *mafiya* who were reported to be buying homes and businesses, particularly cafés and restaurants, to launder money. Sydney, Melbourne and the Gold Coast of Queensland were seen as ideal spots. For the present the Gold Coast has been the most favoured, but there were thoughts that Sydney would become a prime target area. Age has withered the old so-called East Coast milieu and the Double Bay Mob has faded away. Youth gangs in Sydney are used as foot soldiers. The ethnic minority organised criminals are much more involved in the overall scheme of things; there is usually an Asian tier at some level in the organisations. Despite all denials, the police are still seen as facilitators in the drug market. Now there is much more interchange between operations. There are still renegade motorcycle gangs. In fact, it was much the same as elsewhere, if not better.

In 2002 the criminal career of a former England international, 'Champagne' Jimmy Neale, came to an end when he was convicted of an attempt to smuggle 270,000 Ecstasy tablets worth around £5 million into Australia in wine bottles. His career as a lawyer came to an abrupt halt in 1986 when his practice in Colchester collapsed with £1.3 million debts and he received three years at the Old Bailey. Then in 1995 he received another sentence, this time for a credit-card fraud. Neale moved to Hong Kong and it was there the plan to smuggle the drug in 940 bottles of claret was brewed. He and his fiancée had their Sydney hotel room bugged by the police and Neale, posing as a Hong Kong wine merchant, was arrested after 11 days' surveillance. He claimed that he had been forced to import the drug by Asian crime figures to whom he owed money but whom he, sensibly, did not name. His barman partner, Bruce Ridgway, received 12 years.

Griffith, New South Wales, scene of the death of anti-drug campaigner Donald Mackay a quarter of a century ago and a long time stronghold of the Calabrian mafia, was also the scene of the death of Antonio Romeo in the summer of 2002. He was shot in the back whilst pruning a peach tree. Although there were over 30 people nearby no one saw the killing. Romeo had been released from prison 6 weeks earlier after serving a 6-year sentence for conspiracy to import £3 million worth of marijuana from Papua New Guinea. One of his partners, Rosario Trimboli, from a local Griffith family, was still serving his sentence.[9]

Triad crime again surfaced in Sydney with a struggle between the Blue Circle and the Sing Wa for control of the restaurant extortion racket. The Blue Circle, with about 100 members, was thought to be trying to expand its interests at the expense of the Sing Wa. In the process the Superbowl Seafood Steamboat restaurant and the Y2K café were wrecked.

New Zealand: The Mongrel Mob Meets Black Power

Perhaps one of the more underrated gangs and certainly one of the lesser known has been the New Zealand-based Mongrel Mob, but in recent years it has been expanding both its activities and its image. It has also been involved in a biker war with its rivals, Black Power.

The ethnic gangs in New Zealand are principally Maori gangs – Black Power, the Mongrel Mob and the Nomads – and to some extent they align for profile purposes to the Maori

[9] For an account of the Mackay murder and the involvement of Robert Trimboli see James Morton, *Gangland International*.

activist movement. There is a fourth based in the Auckland region, a Polynesian gang called the King Cobras. Black Power and the Mongrel Mob have tentacles reaching throughout New Zealand and although the Nomads have a national operation their home bases are in Wairarapa, Horowhenua, Wanganui and Tokoroa. From 1993 to 1997 the police attributed 23 murders to gang activities. The Maori gangs control the cultivation of cannabis and a substantial part of the distribution, producing a multi-million-dollar industry.

One gang, the Mangu Kaha, a breakaway group of Black Power, has been regarded as developing a plan on strictly business lines. The police believe that a 40-year commitment is being called for from its members, and their town will be controlled by the traditional standover tactics of armed robbery, burglary, car theft and the distribution of drugs. There have also been signs that the Mongrel Mob has links with the 14K triad group. In 1996 an *Operation Strike Force* police investigation into a threat to kill a police officer showed ties between the organisations, with the Mongrel Mob being used to do the dirtier work of the 14K.[10] There are also suggestions that prison gang alliances have been formed whereby the Mongrel Mob protect triads who are serving sentences. The Mob's members have also been used as debt collectors and extortionists, and there are increasing drug networking links.

Of the Mongrel Mob, it was said by a former Auckland resident:

---

[10] Other triad organisations in New Zealand include the Sun Yee On and the Wo Shin Wo who have interests in real estate and prostitution. See for example Eamonn Fitzpatrick in *Courier International*, 15 May 1996.

It's not that they don't know the difference between right and wrong; it's simply they don't care a shit. On the other hand, if you meet them on a good day and you're out in the country and your tyre has burst, they'll change the wheel for you without even being asked.

This attitude has reflected the mistaken perception of the Mob as being rather wayward and wild boys who were essentially decent at heart. What was not realised for some time was that, far from simply being a little wayward, the Mongrel Mob were seriously into organised crime and had reached into politics and the police. There was some acknowledgement in 1999 that, as Detective Inspector Cam Ronald of the Drug Intelligence Bureau rather coyly put it:

> There were instances where some government departments, including police, may have had instances of, not infiltration, but . . . misdemeanours committed within departments which may have caused information to be leaked.

Two years earlier saw the first of the Mob's supergrasses. Anthony Hewison's lawyer Paul Drake said of the Mob, 'They know so much about the police and they have people in places that they should not have . . . They are incredibly well informed.'[11] What had happened was that Drake's client had turned informer and fled to Australia from where he was mounting an action for some $220,000 for breach of contract. He claimed that the police had failed to provide him with

---

[11] *The Dominion*, 16 December 2000.

sufficient money to start a new life; nor had they done everything they could and should to get him resettled in Australia.
This was the sort of action which has not gone down too
well with the British courts and it did not augur well in New
Zealand. The defection came at about the same time as Harry
Tam, a former front man for the Mongrel Mob, was hired as
a policy analyst for the Ministry of Youth Affairs. It occurred
the year after the rejection of his appeal against conviction
for assaulting his wife in front of their children.[12]

Hewison, who had been the acting vice-president of the
Upper Hutt chapter, had arranged for the surrender of
$40,000 of weapons and given details of the Mob's links with
the Chinese as well as its contacts with the Justice Department
and the police training college, along with its access to the
police computer. He also provided details of the Mob's
involvement in the drug trade.

In May 2001 a raid on Lower Hutt and Wainuiomata,
where 15 people were arrested, showed that the Mongrel
Mob had been trading in drugs in Wainuiomata, normally a
Black Power stronghold, reported the police. An $80,000
fishing boat with a 200 hp outboard motor was seized. This
was followed the next month by the trial of Napier president, Alexander Morrison Tamati, and 7 others on a variety
of charges including making, possessing and supplying

[12] In 2001 Mr Tam progressed further when he became a senior policy adviser
with the Corrections Department. There was predictable political outrage. The
Opposition Corrections spokesman said, 'This is part of the touchy-feely, intel-
lectual claptrap that is invading Corrections at the moment.' However Mr Tam
garnered support from an unlikely quarter when Women's Refuge chief executive, Merepeka Raukawa-Taot, said, 'Everyone has a right to change their behaviour. He obviously brings a different perspective because of his experiences in
the past.'

methamphetamine. Also in the dock were Tamati's lieu-tenants, Paul Laxon and Jeremiah Sua – the latter said to be high-ranking in the Palmerston North branch. Laxon, said by the court to be the ringleader, was sentenced to 8 years and Tamati to 6. Jeremiah Sua, who had racked up 61 previous convictions, received 4 years. In another later trial, racehorse trainer Dean Leslie Howard received 6 months. Asked by Laxon to obtain ephedrine, a constituent of methamphetamine, from his vet, he said he had supplied the drug because he believed that Laxon wanted it as a 'go-fast' for his horses.

Shortly after the raid came the news that Hewison had made some progress in his action, though on the way he had dropped his money claim. Both sides hailed victory, and for Hewison it was at least a partial one since the court ruled that the police could have done more to help him in his application to stay in Australia.[13]

Black Power lost one of its members at the end of July when 42-year-old Phillip Anaru Tangira Fox, known as 'Pip', was found dead at a house in New Plymouth. He had led an adventurous life. In 1989 he and another man were acquitted on a charge of murdering a Mongrel Mob member, Weina Wayne Kahotea, in a drive-by shooting. Three others were found guilty of his manslaughter. Six years later Fox was jailed for 6 years after robbing a woman in her New Plymouth home. His death was not regarded as suspicious, but it marked the outbreak of fresh violence between the Mob and Black Power.

[13] *The Dominion*, 8 June 2001.

Before that, however, Nevara Raymond Raheke – who had taken a $90,000 share of the $325,000 paid by the government to four Mob members who claimed they had been tortured by prison guards at Hawke Bay prison and left naked in solitary confinement on various days between 1991 and 1993 – received 3½ years for the gunpoint kidnapping of a Wellington couple. He had hijacked their car and forced the woman to drive to a cemetery. He then ordered the man out and the woman made a break for freedom. The man, running in the opposite direction, reached State Highway 1 and attracted passing motorists. Meanwhile Raheke took the car and was chased for 30 kilometres after ramming two police cars. He claimed he had been robbed by two people and had taken an air pistol to defend himself; when chased, he got into the couple's car.

Feuding between Black Power and the Mongrel Mob dated back 30 years. It began in July 1971 when Black Power members shouting 'Kill, kill, kill' broke into a public house full of Mob members just outside Auckland. Both sides were armed with axes, chains, cut-throat razors and aluminium baseball bats. Later in the year there was another pitched battle at Waikanae's Woodstock rock festival; this time guns were out and the festival closed early. Over the years there were sporadic incidents, such as the bombing by the Mongrels of a van in Northland in which there were thought to be Black Power members. But there were not, and a local resident was killed.

Now renewed violence which had been on the boil for over a year finally spilled on to Tuwharetoa Street in Taupo on 2 September 2001, when 60 Black Power members battled with the Mob's Hawke Bay chapter. They fought with whatever weapons came to hand including baseball bats, bottles, batons and even a cash register. Bars were locked up and customers kept inside as the gangs fought for an hour. The 8-strong police force had been relegated to the touchlines while reinforcements were brought from Rotorua and Tokoroa.

The war continued in early October with shots fired at a Mongrel Mob home in Palmerston North and, seemingly in retaliation, at a Black Power house in Pembroke Street. Now the Mayor Mark Bell-Booth took a hand, apparently successful in securing what was described as a groundbreaking peace at which apologies were given and *hogi* exchanged. The police had impounded the gangleaders' cars and so the Mayor lent them his wife's vehicle on the express understanding that it would only be used to buy food. In the 24 hours that the gangleaders had the car, it was stopped twice. Once the police confiscated a knife, and shortly after the other stop they arrested a man for possessing a loaded pistol which had not been found in the car. After collecting her car, the Mayor's wife said, rather breathlessly, that it 'was just like going around to my friend's place'. The peace lasted a little over a week.

The first breach was a fight in Napier's Clive Square after which two members from Black Power and two from the Mongrels were taken to hospital where a further fight broke out, this time with medical trolleys and rubbish bins as weapons. It was all fairly low key. Four days later there were fears of a national gang war with violence in Auckland, Christchurch, Rotorua and Turangi as well as in Manwatu

City. There had also been shootings in Castlecliff. Road-blocks were set up and cars were banned from that area.

However, both gangs appeared to be united when they condemned the raid and triple murder at the Mount Wellington-Panmure RSA on 8 December when the club president, a member and a cleaner were killed in what seemed to be a botched robbery. The club's part-time accountant received severe head injuries. Sonny Patua, a Mongrel Mob member, summed things up. 'Of all places they had to hit the RSA. Brother, you don't fucking hit a club for the old folks and war vets . . . It really annoyed us that they picked on the ones that could not really defend themselves.'[14]

Meanwhile, the police had struck a blow in what was seen as an all-out war on the country's methamphetamine problem with 78 search warrants executed by armed police over both islands. It followed the largest undercover operation for 10 years. Sixty people were arrested in Northland and a further 44 in Canterbury. Of the two operations in Wellington, *Operation Recon* targeted Class A and B drug dealers, with *Operation Visor* targeting career criminals including members of Black Power and the Mongrel Mob.

[14] *Truth* (Auckland), 14 December 2001.

28

Triads and Yakuza

Triads

Any city which has gambling and prostitution on a large scale is sure to attract organised crime at a proportionate level. So there has long been a triad presence in the former Portuguese colony, Macao, a 40-minute hovercraft ride from Hong Kong.

There, even the richest and most powerful have not always been exempt from the predations of others. One of these was Stanley Ho, or (to give him his Chinese name) Ho Hung-Sun, who, as the owner of nine casinos – reputed to bring in HK\$2 billion, of which 30 per cent went in taxes to the government – six hotels, television broadcasting and transport companies, was regarded as the richest man in Macao.[1]

---

[1] For a view of Ho, his career and influence in the territory, see Roger Faligot, *La Mafia Chinoise en Europe*.

Ho, a member of the wealthy Shanghai-Eurasian Hotung family, came to Macao in 1941 and married Clementina Leito, daughter of one of Macao's wealthiest families which owned the Hotel Bela Vista. Through his wife's connections he met the Fu family which then controlled gambling in the territory, but by the early 1960s he had taken over control from them. A talented ballroom dancer and a legitimate businessman, he was also regarded as a man who could fight his corner and was quite prepared to challenge his enemies on their own turf. His street name was Sun Goh (New Brother). While there is no suggestion that he was a triad member himself, his friend, the late Yip Hon, who became a director of Ho's Sociendado de Turismo e Diversoes de Macao, was said by the American government to have been a member of Hong Kong's Hung Mun.[2]

In 1978 Ho was held at gunpoint by a security guard demanding HK$125,000. In recent years there have been plots to kidnap him, and a robbery at his Hyatt Hotel in May 1984 netted $40 million. In 1989 the body of his personal secretary was found in Hong Kong's Causeway Bay district; a year later, his personal bodyguard was killed and his house burned down. Nobody has been charged with the murders. In 1994 the car belonging to his daughter Pansy, who then ran an exclusive jewellery store, Florina Hatton, was broken into. It was widely known that she used it as an unsafe safe. Within hours of the local television station giving details of the robbery, the jewels had been returned to Ho. Two days later the burned bodies of the thieves were found in a canal.

[2] 'Macao's Big Bet' in *Asia Inc.*, August 1997.

Of course, there has been no suggestion that anyone in the Ho family or their friends and helpers were in any way instrumental in those events.

In the late 1990s the 80-year-old Ho, who had made much of his early money in kerosene trading and then expanded into shipping metals and chemicals, was reported to be leaving Macao and following his wife and another daughter, Daisy, to Canada to open casinos there. He had attempted to break into Australian gambling and had been a member of the Hudson Conway consortium, but was forced to relinquish his stake when he was declared an unsuitable person to hold a casino licence during the bids for the Darling Harbour Casino in Sydney.

He had also failed to make any progress in an application to the Queensland government to participate in the Reef Casino in 1998. In 1992 he was found by a United States senate committee to have 'some connection with organised crime'. It was a finding he has bitterly contested.

Others less exalted have suffered from local violence. Indeed in 1996 and following the opening of the new airport, Macao endured 14 bombings, and later an assassination attempt was made on Lt-Col. Manuel Antonio Apolinario, a member of Macao's Gambling Inspection and Co-ordination Directorate, who was ambushed and shot in the head at point-blank range as he left his office. However, he survived. A casino worker at the splendidly rambling Ho-owned Lisboa, on the waterfront, had a hand chopped off and was scalped as he left work.

Casinos then recruited Gurkha soldiers as security staff for the junket tours, with players from both Taiwan and

Thailand pouring into the gaming rooms. The local triads have been keen to deny involvement in the shooting of the colonel and a possible leader of the gangsters was named as Wan Kuok-koi, Broken Tooth Koi, the Dragon Head of the 14K. Shortly before the assassination attempt he had been arrested for violating a casino entry ban.

Further violence occurred on a wet Sunday when on 4 May 1997 three 14K triads were shot to death as they sat in their Toyota in front of the Lisboa Casino on the fashionable Avenida da Praia Grande. The casino itself, built in appalling rococo style with tawdry decor, is generally packed wall to wall with gamblers and on the lower levels with prostitutes, pimps, moneylenders and triads all in a seething mass. In the VIP rooms the high rollers from Taiwan, Thailand and Japan play at tables with minimum bets of $10,000. It is here that the triads have wished to really establish themselves. They will provide security against armed intrusions by other triad groups, in return for which they will receive a percentage of the take. If anyone should think this is unnecessary they only need to be pointed to the case of the Hong Kong gambling king, Lam Pui-chang, shot three times in the stomach by the Hyatt Regency Hotel near the racecourse on Macao's Taipa Island in 1996 as part of a war for control of the high-level gambling.

The deaths of the 14K men brought the total to 14 for the year up to early May. The previous entire year had totalled a mere 21. Importantly, one was the 37-year-old Sek Weng-cheong, regarded as the right-hand man of Broken Tooth Koi (Wan). The killings were thought to be a warning to Wan that the 14K now faced a challenge from the Soi Fong, or Water Room Triad, also known as Won On Lok. The third of the prominent gangs was the Wo Shin Yee (Peace Victory Brotherhood). In return for the killings Wan promised a bloody war which would last until the take-over by the Chinese in December 1999. In the July of 1997 a fire-bomb was thrown at the governor's residence, cars were set on fire outside the Macao Jockey Club's headquarters and three workers at the Ho-owned New Century Hotel were shot in the legs.

The war was waged, said Wan, against Wai Ng who had run a protection racket in Hong Kong in the 1980s. Wan maintained that Ng objected to his rise to power and had promised Shui Fong a bigger cut from VIP gambling if they could dispose of Wan.

Wan was enjoying some personal good fortune. Warrants against him and four colleagues were dropped on 28 July 1997. The judge retired the next day for what were described as personal reasons. Macao's new anti-gangster law took effect on 4 August, and but for the action of the judge the warrants would have been valid.

The killings continued the next year. By April, 7 had died including 3 government officials. At the end of the month a bomb was planted in the car of a senior police officer, Antonio Baptista, who was saved because his dog sniffed it out as he was returning to the vehicle. The war ended with the Shui Fong leaving for Canada. Still banded against Wan, however, were four triad gangs with, it was said, the Macao chapter of the Big Circle Gang, formed by one-time Red Guards and People's Liberation Army officers.

It was probably the attack on Baptista which did for Wan. In early May 1998 he was arrested in the Lisboa as he was watching the Eastern gangster film *Casino* which he had financed and which was said to have been based on his exploits. In what was seen as a major strike against organised crime, he faced a variety of charges including involvement in some of the murders, drug trafficking and membership of a triad society. Five others were charged with him. His arrest was followed by a wave of arson attacks and a further 11 people were arrested. Wan was sent to the island jail of Coloane, where he had been before.

However, if the authorities thought they had things clamped down they were to be severely disabused when that month, in the fifth shooting in as many days, $775,000 was stolen from a clandestine bank dealing in illicit currency operations between China, Hong Kong, Taiwan and Macao. Wan's younger brother, Wan Kuok-hung, was subsequently arrested and both went on trial in the October along with six others. Wan said he was not a gangster but a businessman who had nothing to do with the 14K. His income derived from being a gaming-chip trader, a high-stakes gambler and a real estate investor.

Broken Tooth Koi was born in Macao in 1955 and, a member of the youth section of the 14K, had worked his way up as a street fighter. Over the years he suffered a number of injuries, including an arm chopped so that he is unable to straighten two fingers. His broken teeth have now been capped. In 1987 he was in the Philippines organising casinos, and later became director of the Wan Hao VIP Club at the Lisboa, arranging evenings for high rollers.[3]

---

[3] High rollers meant exactly that. In October 1997 it was said that one drug baron had lost $17 million in one of Macao's casinos.

In 1998 there were nearly 40 gang-related murders in the territory, including those of two Soi Fung members who were blown away by a remote-controlled nail-bomb as they left a restaurant in the early hours of a Sunday morning in August. Just as in American gangland 'two guys came in from Detroit', the killers often came over from mainland China and were back across the border within hours.

It was the second trial for Wan in 1999. In the first he was charged with intimidating casino workers. If so he had done his work well, for witness after witness said they knew nothing and he was acquitted. The second trial was largely based on police officers giving hearsay evidence of what they had been told by informers. Wan's lawyer, Dr Pedro Redhina, who had earlier spoken confidently of an acquittal, stormed out of court 'in protest against the violation of the human right to a dignified defence', complaining of the conduct of the trial. Unfortunately Wan also appears to have violated the unwritten law that gangsters should avoid the media, in that in the mid-1990s at the height of his power he had allowed himself to be interviewed.

On 23 November the 44-year-old Wan, wearing a grey pinstriped suit, smiled and chatted with his friends before the judgement of Judge Fernando Estrela was announced. He must have expected the guilty verdict because the newspapers had been predicting this during the month-long trial, together with a heavy sentence. Now he and 8 other defendants shouted abuse, alleging police corruption, as all but one were found guilty.

Judge Estrela jailed Wan for 15 years and ordered the confiscation of his assets. Convicted with him was a former police officer, Arturo Calderon, who received 10 years for running a criminal association and importing illegal firearms. Perhaps they were fortunate. On the day Wan was sentenced, the gangster leader Ye Cheng-jian and four others were reported to have been executed in Zhuhai at a People's Court. Their original convictions of robbery, murder and arms smuggling in Macao and Guandong province had been upheld and, as was customary, they were taken to the execution ground immediately after their sentences had been confirmed.

Ye Cheng-jian had followed in the footsteps of the 43-year-old Cheung Tze-keung, known as 'The Big Spender', who had kidnapped the millionaire Walter Kwok and Victor Li, the son of property tycoon Li Ka-shing in Gonganbu, ransoming them for a total of £120 million. According to reports, Cheung, the son of a farmer, had had Kwok run off the road. He had been under observation for months. In the case of Victor Li, he had actually moved into the boy's father's home until payment had been made.

It was after this that demands were made on President Jiang Xzemin to take steps against Cheung and his colleagues. He was arrested in Canton and his mother, wife and girl-friend, along with a dozen women accused of laundering, were held in Hong Kong. Assets said to be worth £12 million were frozen. There were suggestions that he should be returned to Hong Kong and tried in open court rather than under the semi-secret proceedings in China in which usually only the verdict is filmed for television. One Hong Kong radio presenter who suggested Cheung's return was attacked and nearly killed as he arrived at the studio. The wounds he received were said to be typical of Sun Yee On knife-cuts.

Unusually, some details of Cheung's trial leaked out. Asked why he had kidnapped Victor Li and not his father, he replied, 'because the father could write a bigger cheque for his son than the other way around'. This was not the display of penitence which might lead to a commutation of sentence. Cheung was condemned to death by a tribunal in Zhuhai and was executed on 5 December 1998.

It was thought that with the hand-over to the Chinese a very different form of policing would soon become evident in Macao where, despite the arrests of Wan and his friends, 37 people had been killed by the middle of November 1999. Certainly while the triads may still have a presence, they more or less stopped their internal war. Roger Faligot suggests that the turning point came in April 2000 with the death of another gangster, Chen Xingsheng. Now triad groups deemed to be the most patriotic – or, in plain language, who had the most to invest – drew up a non-aggression pact with the communist party.[4]

In fact they were merely sleeping. Shortly before Wan's appeal against his conviction was heard in February 2001, it was back to business with the kidnapping of the Portuguese lawyer Jorge Neto Valente, said to be one of the richest men in Macao. He had been returning to his home late on 28 February when the kidnappers on motorcycles stopped his car, shot him and dragged him to a waiting vehicle. He was released after the Macao police were advised by their mainland colleagues. The special Macao squad, known as the

[4] Roger Faligot, *La Mafia Chinoise en Europe*, p. 292.

Flying Tigers, arrested a man and in turn went to a building on Rock Street where they used explosives to get into a flat. In total 7 men were arrested and another suspect died after jumping from a seventh-floor window. Valente was found blindfolded, gagged and bound to a bed. He was taken to hospital where he underwent a six-hour operation to repair his leg which had been broken by the gunshot wound. There were suggestions, which were denied, that the kidnapping had been a 14K operation to put pressure on the courts over Wan's appeal.

Indeed Stanley Ho, who with an honorary degree liked to be known as Dr Ho, has also found it a very different world. In December 2001 it was announced that he was likely to lose his 40-year monopoly on the round-the-clock casino business there. Ho's licences expired at the end of 2001 and Macao is auctioning three casino licences in a move to attract operators from across the world as part of an attempt to convert the seedy prostitute-ridden image into a family-oriented Eastern Las Vegas. His competitors include the MGM Mirage and Aspinalls. Now Ho would have to bid along with foreigners. The King of Gambling believed, however, that one licence had been reserved for him.

By the end of 2001 there were reports that the Red *mafiya* might be trying to secure a foothold in the SAR. Prostitutes, paid about $3,000 a trip, were being sent from cities such as Vladivostock on 14-day tour visas to work in the entertainment districts of Wan Chin and Mongkok. The *mafiya*, said to be led in Macao by a former KGB major, had already established a network there and were now thought to have linked with the Wo Shin Wo and the 14K to export women to Hong Kong. The International Coalition Against Trafficking In Women said it had started receiving reports of Russian women moving into Hong Kong and when that happened the *mafiya* could not be far behind. Another sign was the $40,000 robbery of a Russian from Uzbekistan by a local gang in Mongkok.

Yakuza

The sign of a good criminal organisation is its willingness and ability to adapt swiftly so as to take advantage of any opportunity, however temporary. This the Japanese yakuza did with the craze in 1997 for the tamagotchi, the visual pet. With the toy retailing at around £10.50, people clamouring and stocks exhausted, the price moved to nearer £200 and the yakuza moved in. Workers at the manufacturers were threatened as the yakuza demanded that they be allowed to purchase supplies direct rather than going through the retail system. Employees were advised not to carry bags with the company's logo.

Overall, however, recession in Japan has caused problems for the yakuza gangs who were once again locked in internal fighting. Although membership of the Yamaguchi-gumi has increased slightly as it has absorbed smaller gangs, overall numbers have fallen and generally these have been hard times for the 83,000-plus yakuza. Smuggling illegal immigrants and the infiltration of companies has continued, although the number of *sokaiya* racketeers has fallen by half. However, income from another of the core businesses, bars and night-clubs, has been dramatically cut as companies slashed the expense accounts of businessmen who make up most of the clientele.[5]

In the autumn of 1997 there were signs that a power struggle might be imminent in the Yamaguchi-gumi. Four members walked into the coffee shop of a Kobe hotel and opened fire, killing *oyabun* (or Godfather) Masaru Takumi, the second-highest member of Yamaguchi-gumi, as well as a local dentist who was at a nearby table. Takumi had been instrumental in closing down some of the smaller Yamaguchi-gumi affiliates. In the past, when a boss retired or died a new one would be appointed. Now the remaining members had been dispersed amongst the organisation.

The killings immediately produced a series of reprisals from other gang members and also the police. There were a dozen gang shootings and Kobe and Tokyo residents demonstrated outside gang headquarters. About 700 people raided 91 gangster-owned buildings, and 8 people were arrested in Tokyo. Taro Nakano, the gangster thought to be responsible for the killings, was expelled.

Being a hostess in or even a visitor to a night-club could be a dangerous business. In Shinjuku, Tokyo's equivalent of Soho, 44 people had been killed earlier in the year in a fire which was believed to be part of a yakuza territory battle.

Over the last half-century the yakuza have always been

[5] One of the functions of a *sokaiya* is to disrupt company meetings, and another is to blackmail the company by threats to divulge sensitive information. Even the most powerful companies fall victim and in September 1997 it was alleged that Daiwa, Japan's second-largest broker, had (along with Nomura and Yamaichi amongst others) paid *sokaiya*. A month later a director of Mitsubishi Motors was arrested and accused of paying approximately $75,000 for shareholder meetings to go unmolested.

happy to trade in Western women. The trend started in the mid-1950s with Charlie Fischetti, a cousin of Al Capone, when he realised there was serious money to be made selling a blonde-haired, blue-eyed girl to the Japanese.[6] As with Colombian women the standard devices are used. The girl is to work in the 'entertainment' industry but, once in Japan, her passport is taken, her movements are limited and she has to pay exorbitant charges for laundry, bed and board and protection. Prostitution is the usual answer to her problems.

The use of blonde English and Australian girls as bar girls was highlighted when Lucy Blackwell, a 21-year-old former British Airways stewardess who had been working at the Casablanca club in Roppongi, Toyko, disappeared in July 2000. The club on the sixth floor of a building – which also accommodated a topless and bottomless gentlemen's club along with a transvestite bar – charged customers £150 to sit and have their drinks poured. The dividing line from prostitution in bars such as the Casablanca is thin. The hostesses are encouraged to have afternoon dates with the customers and then bring them back to the club for an evening's drinking. The girls can earn between £30 and £60 an hour as hostesses, and as afternoon dates can collect around £250. The manager of the Casablanca was quick to deny any yakuza connection, but there is undoubtedly a presence in many other similar bars.

Indeed the Casablanca had acquired what its manager would no doubt call an unjustified reputation in the middle

---

[6] Fischetti's other claim to fame is that he was the first to purchase machine guns for the Mob.

1990s when an American girl suddenly left the country, having been scared away by a customer who followed her, waiting for her in a large car with tinted windows as she left work.

When it came to it, however, there was not a straightforward yakuza connection to Lucy Blackwell's disappearance. She was simply one of many girls to have fallen foul of a Japanese businessman.

In August 2001 two hitmen from the Inagawa-kai, the 5,000-strong third largest of the gangs, opened fire killing Kazuhiro Maruyama and Takashi Endo while they were laying white chrysanthemums, traditional funeral flowers, on an altar in Tokyo. This was seriously bad behaviour. The dead men had headed the second largest gang, the Sumiyoshi-kai, whose membership was double that of their rivals. The killings were a sequel to the killing of another Sumiyoshi-kai leader who had been shot two days before in the doorway of his flat.

There was also the killing of Shigeyuki Harada of the Kokusuikai which was splitting up, divided by a fight for the diminishing profits. The recent wars had broken out over the highly prized Ginza district. The Kanamachi family moved on the territory of the Namai family, all part of the relatively small but well-organised Kokusuikai. Out went the Namai's Yujiro Shibasaki in a putsch. However, he was not one to stand back and a series of reprisals took place including drive-by shootings and attacks at funerals. In the summer of 2001 Shibasaki was expelled from the clan, something he did not take lying down, replying through the *Asahi Shimbun* newspaper that there would be no end to the dispute unless the expulsion was retracted and his Namai territory recognised.[7]

Taiwan

In late 1996 the Taiwanese government set themselves a deadline of February 1997 to disband the triad gangs which, apart from their other activities, were thought to have siphoned off $26 billion from public works contracts since the beginning of the decade. One of the challenges to carrying out this public-spirited work was the links which the ruling party, the Kuomintang, had with the triads. The spiritual leader of the Lo Fu-chu, the Heavenly Way Gang, had been appointed as chairman of the Judicial Affairs Committee which supervised the police and judicial budgets. The deadline came at a time when gunmen had walked into the house of Liu Pang-you, head of the Taoyuan county government, bound and blindfolded him and shot him, along with eight others, in the back of the head.

Naturally there were eulogies, but perhaps Mr Liu was not all he appeared to be. The previous August he had been indicted over a land appropriation and had previously been charged with forging his Master's degree. There were also two other land scandals outstanding.

His killing was followed by the murder of a high-profile feminist and the kidnapping and killing of the 17-year-old Pai Hsiaso-yen, daughter of the well-known entertainer Pai Ping-ping. A great show of strength was mounted and viewers

[7] *New York Times*, 10 October 2001.

were treated to the television *vérité* of the police surrounding and shooting one of the suspects.

Perhaps even worse, amongst the Taiwanese there was a wave of what was described as gangster chic. The leaders of the triads may have been indistinguishable from businessmen, but the street-level gangsters had a distinct uniform which was much admired and imitated – betel-nuts to chew; cigarettes to smoke; gold jewellery around the neck, to be shown off by an open-neck shirt worn loose; trousers either black or green; white socks and soft-soled trainers.

At least the government rushed through an anti-racketeering law. Now anyone convicted under the act would be banned for life from standing for elected office, and each political party which put up candidates would be required to guarantee their good behaviour. If in the next five years they were convicted under the act, the party would be fined.[8]

The clearance had some success. With *Operation Self-Renewal*, a 60-day amnesty, on offer, one in seven Taiwanese gangsters were thought to have turned themselves in. These included the 30-strong Heavenly Division, considered the most deadly unit of the strongest triad group, the Bamboo Union.[9]

One of the most wanted men in Taiwan, An-Lo Chang, said to be a leader of the Bamboo Union, continued to defy the

[8] Hardly organised crime, but prostitution does not always lead to an early grave. In Taipei an 82-year-old prostitute nicknamed 'Grandma' was arrested after taking a 52-year-old man to her flat. She had survived on the street by undercutting her younger rivals, charging only 300 Taiwan dollars (around £6) when her younger rivals were charging £60 to £120. According to an officer she appeared to be in good shape, merely looking like a 70-year-old. *Evening Standard*, 17 August 2001.

[9] Nisid Hajari, 'The Mob Takes a Fall' in *Time*, 17 March 1997.

police by choosing to remain in China. Chang had served a 7-year sentence imposed in 1986 before returning to Taiwan where he became involved in the building industry. He left Taiwan again and went to China in June 1996, ostensibly to set up a wig-making factory. On his return he was implicated in construction fraud and the murder of a Taiwanese legislator, and he fled back to China where he has remained. He claimed that the reason he left Taiwan was a governmental ban on him contacting his friends with organised crime connections. These included Chen Chi-Li who had been involved in the 1984 murder of journalist Henry Liu.[10] The same year that Chang moved to China, Chen fled to Cambodia from where reports linked him to smuggling guns, drugs and jewels.

There had also been ill-fortune for Chang in April 1998 when his son was stabbed to death in a night-club with a Four Seasons Gang member at a Taipei karaoke. Forty lawmakers and celebrities sent flowers to the funeral, which was attended by 2,000 gangsters, politicians, entertainers and businessmen.

For the present Chang, who denies any involvement in crime in the United States, may be regarded as an honoured guest who says he will return to Taiwan when the moment

---

[10] Henry Liu, a dissident journalist, was killed in a San Francisco suburb in the autumn of 1984. Chen Chi-Li and Wu Tun were both alleged to be members of the Bamboo Union. They had admitted killing Liu but now claimed that it had been done on the instructions of Taiwan's Chief of Military Intelligence, Vice Admiral Wong Hsi-Ling.

Liu had written a highly unflattering biography of President Chiang and according to Chen, the Vice Admiral had met him at a party and told him that Liu needed to be taught a lesson. Chen admitted he had been a member of the Bamboo Union but had resigned his leadership after being imprisoned for attempted murder in 1970.

is right. He may be living on borrowed time, however. In November 2000 Yang Kuang-nan, head of the Four Seasons, was arrested and expelled from China.

Whether the 1997 surrender under *Operation Self-Renewal* would have any long-term effect was moot. There had been a similar exercise back in 1984 when 3,000 gangsters were jailed. It was after this that the Heavenly Justice Alliance was born, which went on to become the third largest of the triad groups.

Thailand

Thailand has been gripped by a new form of methamphetamine, known as *yaa baa*, literally 'crazy medicine'. Produced in Laos and Burma where a farming family can earn £500 a year, one deal in a relatively small amount can produce half that sum. This addictive drug has swept through the nation and in turn has spawned the Death Angel squads of killer police officers whose aim it is to eliminate the dealers. In a possibly poorly thought through move, Lt. General Pichai Sunthorn Sunthornsajjabul announced that the police in his village, having failed to control drug dealing by acceptable means, had resorted to executing the dealers. Death Angel squads, named because of the belief that the Angel is an animist spirit which takes people straight to Hell, had already eliminated some 350 dealers and the General had plans to take the number to 1,000. Later, in the face of widespread criticism, he blamed a bad telephone line for his remarks. Meanwhile 19 traffickers had been sentenced to death en masse in July 2001.[11]

[11] *Daily Telegraph*, 28 July 2001.

At the beginning of 2003 the Interior Ministry announced that 993 people had been shot dead in the first 24 days of a campaign against drugs traffickers and producers. Many of the deaths were blamed on shoot-outs between rival organisations or the killing of potential informers. Human-rights groups, however, accused the police of operating a shoot-to-kill policy. The Thai Health Ministry estimated that 3 million people amounting to 5 per cent of the population regularly used methamphetamine.

Contract killings can be arranged in the country for as little as £1,000, rising to £15,000 for a famous person or a more difficult job. In March 1999 the Australian Michael Wansley, who specialised in insolvency and was working for accountants Deloitte Touche Tohmatsu, was shot outside a sugar mill whose owners had gone bankrupt. The first arrest in the case was that of a police officer accused of finding the gunman and providing a safe house after the shooting. In another case, after the murder of a millionaire property dealer, the police became involved in a shoot-out with the four killers – slaying one of them, an off-duty police officer.

One of the more rapidly increasing communities in Bangkok is the African one and African criminal gangs – often fronted by legitimate businesses – are increasingly using the city for heroin trading, human smuggling and the peddling of so-called blood diamonds. Unlike the strict hierarchies and codes of loyalty that bind, for example, the Italian Mafia or the Chinese triads, African crime syndicates are seen to operate in a much looser fashion and with minimal resort to gang violence. Additionally, the fluidity of their operations makes penetration difficult. There is thought to be a loose syndicate of around 20 Africans in control of the Thai heroin market. There is a feeling that, unless the crime is serious, Thai police will let things pass. Nor does there seem to be any real commitment to tackling the trade in either drugs or blood diamonds. Trade in these 'blood' or 'conflict' diamonds – dug out of mines in West Africa, often Sierra Leone, and used to finance rebel conflicts – is illegal.

Following a series of arrests of major drug traffickers in the mid-1990s, West Africans in Thailand were not regarded as major players. They also found that their main suppliers, the Chinese gangs, began transporting their heroin through Southern China rather than Thailand. Then, at the end of the millennium, Africans began to buy heroin direct from Afghanistan and Pakistan. An improved refining technique was the saviour. Heroin from Central Asia is brown coloured and much less pure than its Golden Triangle counterpart; it also fetches about a quarter of the price on the streets in the West. Now Central Asian producers have learned how to bleach their heroin white. West African crime syndicates can now move Central Asian heroin from Lahore to Bangkok, re-brand it as Golden Triangle heroin and re-export it to the West.

The drug also comes in from Laos and Cambodia. In the latter, smugglers from Cameroon have found that things have been tightened but Laos still provides a relatively safe route. Jakarta now has a thriving African culture too.

Overall, the African syndicates are now becoming more sophisticated. Caucasians and Asians are being used as mules.

Thai and Uzbek women are swallowing the heroin-filled condoms for as little as $250 a run. There are also serious opportunities in the blood-diamond trade.[12]

---

[12] See Shawn W. Crispin, 'Out of Africa' in *Far Eastern Economic Review*, 24 May 2001.

CLEANING UP

29

Laundering

With the massive amounts of dirty money now floating about, over the years traditional ways of money laundering have been improved greatly. In the 1950s money could be changed at racecourses and dog-tracks with no real difficulty. Some solicitors were reputed to give five shillings in the pound for money stolen from banks. Money marked by cashiers, and so traceable, could be donated to charity, shoved through letterboxes.

Now casinos have taken over as a simple way to clean the dirty money. Provided the washers stick to the boring job of playing red against black or odd against even, then, allowing for the house percentage of zero, money can be laundered relatively quickly; cash is converted into chips and paid out by cheque.

There must, however, be some minimal attempt to gamble

which is where the Irish drug dealer John Gilligan, 'The Warehouseman', fell foul of the Scheveningen Casino in The Hague. He and his associates, Brian Meehan and another man, arrived with 150,000 guilders and cashed them into chips. Unfortunately none of them made a bet and when Meehan, on behalf of the syndicate, turned up at the cashier's with all the chips and asked to have his winnings transferred to a bank account the answer was 'No'. The best the casino would do was to turn the chips back into cash. It also reported the affair to the Dutch Disclosure Office for Unusual Transactions. Gilligan also spent a great deal of money laundering it through betting shops. Accounts showed that hundreds of thousands of pounds had passed through the big bookmaking chains, laundered by Gilligan at a cost of around a highly acceptable 10 per cent.

The real danger for an organisation is that a washer will start gambling as if the money was his own, and the danger for the gambler is the retribution which will surely follow when the money is lost, as Brandon Hale discovered in London in January 1997. Given around £100,000 to launder, he lost the whole sum. He was found shot dead in Highgate Cemetery; he had been badly beaten before his death.

Not that racetrack laundering has been wholly neglected. In August 2000 four racetrack tellers who worked at Belmont and Aqueduct in New York and Saratoga were indicted. It was alleged that they had laundered more than $300,000 in six months.

Things have now become much more sophisticated. There is the bogus business, of which the empty restaurant is a good example. The books show that every night dozens of dinners have been sold. The money is then taken to the bank as part of the daily takings. The restaurateur becomes known as a businessman – perhaps a second restaurant is opened – and in turn larger deposits are not seen as suspicious.

Another popular way of washing large amounts of money has been the so-called rave. Says one East Ender:

> They're marginally legal and they're all cash. A good one can draw tens of thousands of people so there's no way anyone can check up exactly how many tickets were really sold. You simply 'sell' a hundred times more tickets at £20 a go than were actually sold. You've got the stubs to show to the bank. Then there's car parking at the venue. That's cash as well and you do the same. You pay out the legitimate expenses – band, disc jockeys, bar licence, security – then there's your own office and secretarial expenses. If you do it properly you can launder £100,000 at a time with no difficulty. And think what you can do with an outdoor rave in the summer.[1]

Another way in which money can be cleaned is through London hotels:

> You book into one of the big hotels for say three nights and give an address say in Cardiff. You ask the porter if there's a casino where you can play, and you while away the time and come back with a cheque. Then you ask for a ticket to be booked for say Zurich, and after that you ask them to get you Swiss francs. You then cancel the travel and ask if you can have a cheque for the Swiss

[1] P. M. in conversation with the author, November 2001.

francs you've bought. You paid a commission but you've got clean money. Do that in four hotels at the same time and think what you can clean.[2]

There are other scams. One is buying postage stamps. Many dealers will sell bags containing hundreds, so it is easy to have a lucky find of a stamp worth thousands. In reality such a stamp has been brought in from abroad.

Smurfing, named after the cartoon characters, is also popular if more time-consuming. With banks required to take notice of cash deposits of over £10,000 in the United Kingdom and $10,000 in America, depositors – very often students – are sent to buy bonds or make deposits of less than the reportable amount. If $7,500 is deposited in 14 banks a day, then over $500,000 can be laundered in a week. It has been estimated that between $500 billion and $1.5 trillion is laundered through banks alone every year.[3]

Another favourite is a service industry such as mini-cabs, again an almost wholly cash business. At least two of these cleansing operations have operated in the last decade in Glasgow. As with long-firm frauds, interlocking companies can be set up apparently trading with each other and making substantial profits, which in turn produce clean money on which an acceptable 30 per cent tax is paid.

Even so some of these are relatively small-time operations. At the other end of the scale are what are known as 'strings' and 'starbursts'. These are methods of hiding funds in a series of offshore accounts through nominees who will not neces-

[2] *Ibid.*
[3] *Time Out*, 28 November–5 December 2001.

sarily know the names of the beneficiary, or splitting the money into a number of accounts before joining them together again in a different tax jurisdiction. The funds then go through shell companies and more nominee accounts before they are reintegrated and resurface as cleaned money.

One new twist on how to launder money comes from the Russian *mafiya* through the Russian Orthodox Church. The French equivalent of MI5, the DST, discovered that Russian gangsters had attempted to send huge donations to the Church which in turn was to pass the money on to members on the Côte d'Azur.

Thinking of moving money from South Africa? Says one accountant:

> Basically there's three ways. The first is trade it out, the second fly it out and the third the Nun's knickers. The first you buy defunct sewing machines on letters of credit. You pay money into the South African bank and the letters of credit are handed over. The guy at the other end has to be in with it, of course. The money's clean and in London or Zurich or wherever you want, and the sewing machines get dumped in a harbour. The second way is to buy a plane and sell it at the other end. The third is through the Roman Catholic Church and the nuns and priests with Vatican passports. But that costs around 50 per cent. Really you only want to be paying 30 per cent to clean your money.[4]

Washington, DC, lawyer Don DeKiefer, whose firm acts for anti-laundering agencies, confirms the general principles:

---

[4] Conversation with author, November 2001.

A man in Russia wants to launder. He goes to a friend who goes to one of, say, 50 groups capable of setting up such a deal. He agrees to buy, say, $1 million worth of chocolate from the United States and goes through the regulations. With a bulk order discount he buys $1 million worth for $750,000. Letters of credit are established and once the chocolate is at sea, everything is paid. The chocolate goes to Antwerp, turns around and is then sold back in the United States at discount stores. The US company gets various credits in the form of tax reliefs.

One of the places for setting up these deals is the dining room of a hotel in Zurich where guys in combat fatigues look like caricatures from a Hollywood movie.[5]

In Canada it is far easier to launder money in smaller cities such as Regina and Hamilton than in Toronto and Montreal. For a long time Canada was more or less without money-laundering laws, but in October 1998 the police scored a notable goal when Alfonso Caruana, described as the Wayne Gretsky[6] of organised crime and whose family was said to be bankers to the Mafia, was arrested.

A wire-tap had been in place two years earlier on the telephones of the family, said to own large parts of Aruba, and once the coded messages had been broken, the police concluded that the Caruanas and their cousins the Cuntreras were running a drug pipeline between Colombia and Canada via Houston with the courier, John Hill from Sault-Ste-Marie, to collect a May shipment. The drug load was observed in

[5] Interview with author, November 2000.
[6] A celebrated ice-hockey player.

Houston and Hill was duly arrested with 200 kg of cocaine. The RCMP had anticipated that their taps would pick up some discussion on the arrest, but they were disappointed. It was business as usual.

On 15 July, after a further series of wire-taps and in the knowledge that the Caruana–Cuntreras were capable of upping sticks and leaving at a moment's notice, they raided Alfonso Caruana. In the sweep of 14 arrests, four were Caruanas.

Over the years the family had established a worldwide network operating in London, Geneva, Malta, Miami and Montreal. There had been some reverses, as when Gerlando Caruana was given 20 years in Montreal, and Alfonso fled from his home in Woking after a sniffer dog at Felixstowe docks had dug out 250 kg of cannabis in 1985.

Until the late 1980s there were no Canadian laws against money laundering and Alfonso had been using a smurfing operation, depositing money in the City & District Bank in suburban Montreal with people bringing in the money in shopping, paper and duffel bags. Their downfall came about through Sergeant Mark Bourque. After the 1985 raid which netted Gerlando Caruana, Bourque began to make inquiries into his bank accounts at the City & District Bank, where a cashier told him that the really interesting accounts were those held by brother Alfonso.

Bourque took 5 years to build a case at the end of which, shortly before he was transferred to protection duties, he was given the opportunity to present his findings to the Justice Department. He wanted the Caruanas then to be charged with smuggling, and the banks with aiding and abetting, but he was unable to persuade the authorities that it was worth-while. Instead he turned his information over to the Italian authorities which brought about the extradition and impris-onment of Pasquale Cuntrera who, in 1992, received 21 years in Italy after being deported from Venezuela. He was released by mistake in May 1988, but was recaptured five days later on the Costa del Sol.

The troubles of the Caruana family continued when in 2002 an associate, Nunzio Larosa of Montreal, allegedly responsible for arranging drug shipments and money laun-dering, was extradited to Texas to face drug-related charges. In 2000 his son Antonio had been imprisoned on charges of importing cocaine into Canada.

Still in Canada, on 30 August 1994 the 43-year-old Montreal lawyer Joseph Lagana was arrested and charged with 241 counts of having laundered proceeds from drug sales. He was caught with two of his employees in an RCMP sting when a foreign exchange was set up on the corner of Peel Street. Lagana had a very much hands-on approach, bringing sacks filled with small bills to the RCMP foreign exchange counter. However, the RCMP raids failed to include the man suggested as being the head of the Canadian and Montreal Mafia, Vito Rizzuto. Another former lawyer was, however, also in the frame. Jean-Paul Renaud, also known as Renault, a former fund-raiser for Les Ballets Jazz de Montréal who had been disbarred in the 1980s, faced 21 counts. In 1985 he had been sentenced to 14 years after Canada's first clandestine drug laboratory was found at a bungalow in Rosemere. Also rounded up was the long-serving Vincenzo 'Jimmy' Di Maulo, whose brother Joe had taken over as leader of Montreal's Sorrento Gang when Frank Cotroni was sentenced to 15 years in New York on drugs charges.[7]

The raids were the result of a long-running sting by the RCMP begun in 1990 when the exchange house was set up on the corner of Peel Street and de Maisonneuve Boulevard and which proved so popular that it was continued for four years and was even thought to have made a profit. The money laundered through the RCMP front was wired into more than 200 bank accounts in Europe, South America and the United States. Over the years many similar such operations have been established.

When the case came to court in June 1995 Lagana, who pleaded guilty, was described as the brains behind the $47 million money-laundering operation and the only man in direct contact with Vito Rizzuto, and received 13 years' imprisonment. The Crown announced that it would appeal and demand a longer sentence for Lagana and Luis Cantieri, said to be his immediate deputy in the scheme. The suggestion came to nothing. In August 1997 Lagana was released under new federal regulations which allowed a non-violent criminal serving a first offence to be released after serving one-third of his sentence.

There is no reason to abandon a winning formula, and in New York a brokerage house in the World Trade Center justified its reputation as being the place to handle illicit

[7] Frank Cotroni, the younger brother of Vic, was a key player in Montreal's Violi–Cotroni organisation which ran from the early 1940s. For an account of their influence and careers see Peter Edwards, *Blood Brothers* and James Morton, *Gangland International*, Chapter 24.

transactions efficiently. Money would be wired around the world to businesses and banks without the tiresome necessity of receipts and word was soon passed around reaching, amongst others, a mother and her two sons who, in due course, were arrested on 7 August 2001 and charged with laundering $8 million. The boys had picked up cash in as many as 40 different places which they then brought to the brokerage house in packets, shopping and duffel bags. The money was then wired to over 100 banks into jewellery businesses and insurance and investment houses. Unfortunately the brokerage house had been staffed entirely by undercover officers. 'We didn't advertise. They came to us,' said the sting's deviser Ronald Rose.[8] The trio faced a maximum of 25 years' imprisonment.

Being a money launderer – until you are caught at it, that is – is no bar to a judicial appointment. Once you are caught, however, your life tends to come apart, as Canadian judge Robert Flahiff discovered. Between 1989 and 1991 he spent a good deal of time commuting to Switzerland on behalf of his then client, Paul Larue, going to Europe on no fewer than 25 occasions and so cleaning $1.7 million in drug money which came back via Hong Kong, the Cayman Islands, Bermuda and Toronto. When, as the expression goes, it all came on top, a massive effort was made to save him from prison, with his lawyers citing the 'shame and dishonour' he had brought upon his family. At this point in the hearing, Judge Flahiff was reported as wiping his eyes. He may also have been reflecting on the cartoon in *La Presse* which

---

[8] *New York Times*, 17 August 2001.

pictured him at Bordeaux prison, where the prisoners are in thrall to the Hell's Angels, with a caption 'Hey, boys! A judge!' He received 3 years and resigned from the bench. A small consolation must have been that while he was on 'sick leave' for 2 years pending the hearing of his case he still drew his Cn$175,800 salary.

In England, Mike Calvert of the Office for Supervision of Solicitors, the Law Society's disciplinary arm, has evidence that organised crime families have targeted solicitors' firms and have infiltrated some on a long-term basis, ranging from putting bookkeepers in place to provide an early-warning system of an accounting investigation, to dishonest solicitors who are left as moles for future use. He is supported by reports that organised gangs are paying to put students through university and law school. NCIS has acquired intelligence in the West Midlands that this is happening with both law and accountancy students, some of whom are duped and some coerced. Most likely victims are Asian students who fall prey to Asian organised crime gangs who operate illegal immigration and smuggling rackets.

Calvert believes that, while the dangers are greatest for sole practitioners and one or two partner firms for whom a sudden cash injection may be the difference between survival and folding, the larger firms are not exempt:

If you have 300 fee earners, statistically at least one has to be significantly bent – probably five or six. There are those who are anxious to please the principal. They meet someone at the golf club who offers several millions pounds worth of work. 'Shall I cultivate him?' 'Of course.'

Then there is the senior partner who has lost his way and the Young Turks are baying at him. He'll be keen to introduce substantial business. They are both targets for the organised criminal.

He believes the majority are victims rather than professional criminals themselves and that there are about 100 firms targeted. They may be innocent dupes at first, but ultimately they will know what they are doing.

The temptations for a solicitor are endless:

He'll think 'Here's a new client with a large cash business. If I turn him away he'll only go next door.' Travel is a lure. The client says he's thinking of using a number of local firms. Will you be one of them? There's likely to be some travel abroad, possibly at short notice; meetings in Geneva.

Then there is the nature of the transaction. You will receive a sum of money from abroad. It is to be distributed in such and such a way. Now this is blindingly obvious. Why isn't he using a bank? Why am I being privileged enough to do what a High Street bank does ordinarily?

He recalls the case of a solicitor who took instructions from a man who set up a small jewellery business:

He said he had a small legacy to invest. These were the days when it was impossible to do much more than scratch a living as a small jeweller. He started turning over £2,000 a month using the solicitor as a bank, saying that he was arranging the moving of his account from one bank to another, and then it was suddenly £300,000 a month. The jeweller came from a London-based crime family.

As for payment?

There's no sentiment. You'll be paid very well. If you will supply other services the pay will be exemplary, but if you look nervous you won't be paid at all. You may be blackmailed. The best reward will be not to be beaten up outside a night-club.

Nevertheless, innocents apart, he thinks there are probably 20 firms actively and knowingly involved in money laundering, with 12 operating at any one time:

As with every business there are peaks and troughs. Some weeks there is a greater need than others. When the need is greatest dormant solicitors will be reactivated. They are professional criminals who happen to be solicitors and they will also be operating investment scams and mortgage frauds.

There is also the problem of the struck-off solicitor or dishonest clerk who prey on firms:

Every year ten or a dozen struck-off solicitors come to our notice involved in scams. In 2000 we intervened in 112 firms of solicitors. We reckon that 200 firms will have an actively dishonest solicitor. That's 200 out of 9,000. That's one in 45 that has a significantly dishonest lawyer in it.[9]

---

[9] Interview with author, 3 January 2001.

His fears were rather confirmed when the Serious Fraud Office disclosed that solicitors were involved in a quarter of the cases under investigation. Speaking at a conference in Cambridge, the head of the Office, Rosalind Wright, blamed the legal profession for helping drug barons to hide their cash.[10]

One solicitor who certainly did so was the middle-aged Louis Glatt who had a small practice in Mayfair and maintained a modest lifestyle in Southgate, North London. One of his major clients was Ellis Martin, described as a premier-league fraudster, who had made a fortune through a drink and cigarette smuggling empire which he continued to run while in prison. In 1996 he had received 6 years, and a further 9 years in 1999, coupled this time with a confiscation order of £10.7 million or 5 years in default.

Martin's assets had been made the subject of a restraining order, but between 1994 and 1997 Glatt helped to launder £28 million. Despite the order Martin was able to move money abroad and complete nearly 200 property deals including a distillery in Northern France.

Members of Martin's team were passed off as Glatt's clerks as they went into prison to take instructions from their leader. The men also supplied Martin with telephone cards so that he could maintain his contact with the outside world. In a five-month period in Wayland prison, Norfolk, Martin made over 1,000 calls with the cards Glatt supplied. 'On some days he was on the phone from 8 a.m. to 8 p.m. with scarcely a

[10] 19th International Cambridge Symposium on Economic Crime, 10 September 2001.

break,' said Mr Oliver Sells QC, prosecuting. It was estimated that in an 18-month period the loss to the Revenue from Martin's dealings was some £30 million.

It ended in tears and Glatt being convicted of conspiracy to evade duty in July 2001. He received a 6-year sentence, and a confiscation hearing was ordered to deal with his own assets. Glatt had told the court he thought that he had been moving the money on behalf of Martin's mother – a woman, it transpired, with an income of around £100 a week.

The end of one major money-laundering operation happened at the Old Bailey in June 2002 when a scheme allegedly run by the Cali cartel was broken. Using bureaux de change, one of which, located at the back of a sweet shop in Bayswater, washed £19 million in three years, the operation exchanged around £47 million. Louis Hurtado – born in Colombia but now a naturalised British citizen, who headed the scheme as a director of the World Express Bureau in Camberwell – received 8½ years. His brother-in-law Byron Carerra and others received lesser sentences. Customs officers thought there could be other, larger schemes working in Britain.[11]

At the beginning of the new millennium it was estimated that nearly 50 per cent of the Underworld cash was generated in the United States. This compared with 5.3 for Italy, 5.2 for Russia and 4.6 for China, with the United Kingdom down in ninth place at 2.4 per cent. The illegal gains were laundered mainly in the United States which catered for 18.9

[11] *The Times*, 18 June 2002.

per cent followed by the Cayman Islands with 4.9. Russia, China and Italy followed in that order. Britain did not feature in the world's top ten but – along with Liechtenstein, Luxembourg and the United States – was one of the most attractive places for holding offshore cash. The Seychelles were also thought to be lax over laundering regulations. At one time the islands had offered criminals an immunity from prosecution by any country for all offences unless they committed violence or drug trafficking in the Seychelles. This produced an international outcry and a warning to banks, whereupon the drug barons who had been packing their sun lotion put it back in the bathroom cabinet.

Countries used as cut-outs, so making tracing more difficult, were Mauritius, the Vatican City, Macao and Nauru, after which followed Luxembourg and South Africa. Then came the Isle of Man, Jersey, Guernsey and Sark. Indeed Britain came under some fire as being particularly vulnerable to money laundering and was said to be not actually doing enough.[12]

John Walker, a researcher into fraud, suggested that the world total of laundered money from crime was in the nature of £1,000 billion annually. Assessing the true figure is made all the more difficult by the fact that Russian criminals do not have bank accounts. They have banks – more than fifty of them.[13]

As legislation has become more and more restrictive over the last 15 years, so money laundering has become increas-

[12] *Guardian*, 10 October 2001.
[13] John Walker, *Inside Fraud Bulletin*.

ingly important. New laws have shifted responsibility to lawyers, accountants and bankers, making them responsible for reporting all suspicious transactions. NCIS had been disturbed by the lack of reporting by professionals in 2000. It believed solicitors and accountants had been used in more than 20 laundering operations and in over 200 cases the techniques used would have required the services of a solicitor or accountant at some stage in the proceedings.[14]

Of course, much may depend on the *savoir-faire* of the staff:

> I was in a branch of the Nat West a few years ago and the police were there so I started earwigging. They'd been called because a woman had tried to pay in £20 cash, and because she was on the social and couldn't explain how she'd got the money they called the police.[15]

[14] NCIS, *The Threat from Serious and Organised Crime*, 2001.
[15] B. P. Conversation with the author, 28 November 2001.

30

Yesterday, Today and Tomorrow

'Organised crime has disintegrated,' Professor Dick Hobbs is quoted as saying. 'Twenty years ago you could say here is a family, they own this particular territory. The days of them all having a manor that they stuck to are gone. If they run territory they are small scale.'[1]

With respect to the Professor, for whom I have the greatest admiration, organised crime has not disintegrated. Although the Krays are not a particularly good example and might be said to epitomise disorganised criminals, they would be astounded at the wealth some criminals and their families have accumulated through drugs and other enterprises. A

[1] Ruth Bloomfield, 'Bands of Brothers' in *Time Out*, 28 November–5 December 2001.

fine or confiscation order of £1 million is little more than a minor inconvenience to the top criminals of today.

Some organised crime remains the same as it has for centuries. On 5 December 2001 the New Zealand yachtsman Sir Peter Blake and his crew of the *Seamaster*, moored at the mouth of the Amazon while awaiting Customs clearance at the port of Macara, were attacked by an 8-man gang of pirates. They were at the start of a 5-year survey on global warming. Blake was killed, shot twice in the back; two of the crew were injured and a robber was shot in the hand. The attackers, who had been wearing balaclavas and motorcycle helmets, escaped with some watches, an outboard motor, two cameras and the equivalent of around £500 in cash. Seven of the pirates were arrested within a matter of 24 hours; apparently they had believed Blake's boat was that of a rich tourist.

Over the last decade, piracy large and small has increased exponentially. In 1996 there were 224 attacks recorded, as opposed to a more modest 90 in 1994. In the first six months of 1997 there were 79 reports. It is likely that by the end of 2003 there will have been around 500, most of them unreported by the world's press.

One difficulty in monitoring the frequency of attacks is that there are conflicting definitions of piracy. Under the United Nations Convention on the Law of the Sea, an act of piracy is an illegal act committed on the High Seas. However, since the majority of attacks take place within territorial waters they fall outside the definition. A second problem is that fear of massive losses for shipping companies reporting incidents means that the true picture is far from clear. Other difficulties stem from a lack of money to patrol the coastal waters of countries such as Brazil and Ecuador. However, those are not the most dangerous of places. A quarter of all reported incidents occur around Indonesia, Philippine waters and the Malacca Strait where there are many natural harbours for the pirates and where, in any event, the government has little control. Other problem areas are the seas around China and the coast of Somalia where crews of speedboats fire on passing ships. The International Maritime Bureau recommends that vessels there should pass at least 50 miles from the shore. Most pirate attacks take place between 1 a.m. and 6 a.m., with boarders climbing on the stern with grappling irons. There have been cases where boats travelling at 17 knots have been boarded.

Retribution, by the Chinese government at any rate, is harsh in piracy cases. In what was described as the biggest case of piracy since the founding of the People's Republic in 1949, on 16 November 1998 pirates posing as paramilitary police boarded the bulk carrier *Cheung Son*, clubbed 23 Chinese sailors to death, tied weights to their bodies and pitched them overboard. The vessel, which was carrying a cargo of furnace slag worth nearly £500,000 and was flying a Panamanian flag, was never found. Only six bodies were recovered when they were found by a fisherman off the coast of Shantou. In December 1999, 12 Chinese and one Indonesian were tried and sentenced to death in the Shanwei Intermediate Court. A number of them had told the court that the reason they participated was that the leaders had threatened to kill them had they not done so. That year some 67 people were reported to have been killed by pirates, the highest number for 10 years.

Dog-napping, in vogue at the beginning of the twentieth century, was still a popular (if minor) form of organised crime. Pedigree dogs were being stolen for ransom or on a temporary basis for breeding purposes. Some 150 thefts were reported in the first ten months of 2001 to Lurcher Rescue, an organisation for reuniting owners with stolen dogs. The dogs were often released exhausted after being used for stud, or ransomed. One breeder paid £2,000 to have a saluki returned, and a few weeks later three men were seen trying to lure away a second dog. There is little doubt that the thefts have not been isolated incidents but the work of a ring.

Much older was the use of *hawala*, employed over the centuries to transfer money by word of mouth but now thought to be a way of laundering. At the end of the twentieth century, Pakistani bankers believed that £2 billion annually was being transferred by *hawala*, double that coming in through conventional banking. *Hawala*, a banking system in which money is not always transferred, is based on trust and simplicity. The *hawaldar* tells an opposite number, usually in the Sub-Continent or the Middle East, that he has say £100 in his possession to be collected by his client's relation in Karachi. Once the second *hawaldar* has been notified, the relation goes to him and collects the money in local currency. The £100 may never actually be sent, but will be used by the second *hawaldar* to execute a similar transfer from Karachi. The cost is far less than through banks. One difficulty is proving the actual transaction in what is for much of the time a perfectly acceptable way of transferring money. So far there has been one successful prosecution in America when two Indian nationals were convicted of moving $5 million through corporate accounts using the system. The offence was not for using the *hawaldar* but for money laundering.[2]

Old-fashioned banditry still existed in 2001. Villagers of Nafitkhali in south Bangladesh reported being plagued by thieves who, en masse, appeared naked and stole from empty houses. The locals had been worried about the honour of their womenfolk, but the thieves proved impossible to catch because they had oiled their bodies.[3]

Few, if any, of the confidence tricks in current use are new. They are simply modern variations of the old tried and tested scams which have run for hundreds of years. Some of the more recent examples include an Oregon man who obtained something in the region of $100 million from Americans when he sold them calves as tax shelters. The herd was promised to provide huge profits when sold 10–15 years later. But when the authorities looked at it, each cow, far from being a cash one, had been the subject of multiple sales.

It was a not dissimilar situation with the British ostrich sales of the 1990s. This was to be the meat of the future and, apart from the protein, there would be spin-offs from highly prized ostrich feathers and skin which could be used for dusters and handbags respectively. Even the eggs were likely to be highly desired ornaments. The Ostrich Farming Corporation cleared £21 million from 3,000 investors. First, ostrich meat did not turn out to be the sought-after delicacy

[2] See Jonathan Calvert, 'Britain-Istan' in *Sunday Business*, 11 November 2001.
[3] *Sunday Times*, 30 December 2001.

suggested. The food critic David Fingleton describes it as, 'Nothing, a cross between veal and turkey.' Then there was a problem with the actual breeding. Ostriches in Northern Europe were not happy with the midwinter climate and started developing neurotic and anti-social tendencies such as pecking each other's skin and feathers, so ruining the potential market for dusters and shoes. Worse, there was no proper count of the number of ostriches in play. A director received 4 years.

A more recent swindle has been the Millennium Champagne scam. The thinking behind this scheme was that every house in Britain would be awash with champagne on the big night, blotting out fears of civil unrest caused by failed traffic lights and the like as systems failed at 00.01 hours. Twenty per cent profits were promised. Instead, apart from the fact that the traffic lights worked perfectly well, there was a surplus of genuine champagne and the hyped £30 a bottle turned out to be worth about a third of that sum.

The chain letter, known and loved for centuries, took on a new lease of life under the guise of a women's group, proving that the female is just as deadly as the male, if not more so, when it comes to swindles. Its advertising even suggested that it had the endorsement of the Citizens Advice Bureau, which it certainly did not. It worked so well that banks on the Isle of Wight imposed strict restrictions on the withdrawal of large sums of cash in March 2001.

On a smaller scale perhaps, but another long-running successful scam aimed at women is the home work scam. Women at home all day and desperate to earn additional money are invited to send off sums of up to £100 to do work at home such as addressing envelopes. Patricia Kelly, the barmaid who saw Ronnie Kray shoot George Cornell in the Blind Beggar, was perhaps one of the luckier ones. The scheme she paid into may have been sweated labour but it was genuine. She recalls:

> In the day I used to make Christmas tags and then after I finished in the pub I'd sit up addressing envelopes. I got something like £1 a thousand and I was working from a Welsh telephone directory. The Christmas tags which I had to thread were 4s. 6d. a thousand. It took ages. You had to cut the thread to the length. Then I'd walk to Hoxton with them on a pushchair. It wasn't a living but it was money.[4]

A recent offer invited customers to send for pornographic videos. Unfortunately, by the time their cheques were cashed the stock had run out and a cheque was enclosed refunding the money. Unfortunately again, the cheques were drawn on accounts with such pornographic names that people were too embarrassed to cash them. It might be wondered, *en passant*, what the banks were doing allowing accounts to be opened under these names in the first place.

However, as the years have passed so have some crimes. But, for every criminal activity which falls into disuse, another joins the pack. Some of those which have disappeared in the last hundred years, such as abortion and baby-farming, have done so because of changes in social attitudes and specifi-

---

[4] Mrs X, *Calling Time on the Krays*, p. 45.

cally the passing of the Abortion Act 1967. Thieves no longer target furriers and women no longer parade stolen jewellery as advertisements. In the past they were known as oysters. In part because of the activities of the likes of Bertie Smalls and his fellow bank robbers in the 1960s, the nineteenth-century Truck Acts, under which employees had to be paid in cash, have been repealed. Bank and building society robberies are now usually a way of funding a drug habit rather than major gang crimes, although there always will be exceptions.

Again, because we are moving towards a cashless society there is little point in safe-blowing. Quite apart from the difficulties in blowing the modern safe and the need to serve an apprenticeship – something the modern criminal is generally unwilling to do – in the past there was the likelihood of instant wealth. Now it is doubtful whether the safe will yield much more than a half-eaten and forgotten sandwich.

The trade in body parts has also grown steadily, and it was reported that a Chinese burns expert who was seeking asylum had taken the skin from over 100 dead prisoners. Apparently Wang Guoqi defected after being ordered to skin the still-breathing victim of a firing squad; the man's kidneys had already been taken. China has long been suspected of selling prisoners' organs to foreigners at up to £10,000 a time.[5] According to the Italian police the Mafia was now also heavily involved in what has become a multi-million-pound racket, with doctors and surgeons in their pay.

Russian families are currently selling children for their

---

[5] *The Mirror*, 29 June 2001.

body parts for very substantial sums indeed. One was trapped after demanding £64,000 from an undercover police officer for her five-year-old grandson who had been told he was going to Disneyland. In South Africa the practice of selling children for their organs is known as Muti.

In July 2001 Ferudtin and Alima Korayev and their son Dheykhum went on trial in Bukara charged with murder. In the dock with them was a doctor alleged to be an accomplice. In December 2000 the police had raided their flat, where they found bags containing human body parts from which the organs had been removed. They also discovered the equivalent of £60,000, along with 60 passports belonging to people who had vanished. Once the victims had been trapped by the promise of jobs in Canada and Australia, along with the necessary work permits for which they paid a small fee, they were given a diet of lemon juice to cleanse their systems prior to a lethal injection being administered. The organs were smuggled into Russia, believed ultimately to be destined for Turkey. The Korayevs admitted the killings, saying the victims owed them money, but denied trading in body parts.

In the autumn of 2001 it was reported that the United States was trying to curb baby-selling in Cambodia. Families were reported to be selling their children to gangs for around £50, the re-sale price to childless American families being in the region of £10,000. The American Embassy in Cambodia was refusing to issue visas for the children.

One crime on the increase at the beginning of the new century is that of people-smuggling. Regarded as safer for the organisers and meriting less in the way of sentences than drug-smuggling, it has long been profitable but by the late

1990s it had reached epidemic proportions worldwide. Interpol estimates that 4 million humans are smuggled across borders annually by transnational criminal syndicates.

In a heatwave on 18 June 2000, 58 illegal Chinese immigrants suffocated in a container lorry in Dover, following a long and expensive journey to their deaths. They or their families had paid £800 as deposits, against £18,000 to be paid on safe arrival in Britain. If – as was likely to be the case for many of them – they could not pay, the balance would have to be worked off in the form of sweated labour. On 7 June, 56 men and 4 women left their villages in the Fujian province in South China and were flown from Fuzhou to Beijing; from there they were flown to Belgrade, where they arrived on 10 June and were taken to safe houses. They were then put in a series of minibuses and driven across the border into Hungary, where they were transferred into a white van to go into Austria. Now their passports were taken from them. The next day in Austria they were given false Korean passports. On 16 June they were flown in small groups to Paris, from where the following day they went by train to safe houses in Rotterdam. Now their Korean passports were confiscated. On Saturday 18 June they were loaded into a container lorry in Rotterdam which, driven by Perry Wacker, left for Zeebrugge at 3 p.m., arriving three hours later. The ferry for England departed at 7.30 p.m. and arrived at 11.05 p.m. The bodies were discovered by Customs officers 20 minutes later. The travellers had been hidden behind boxes of tomatoes in the back of a sealed container. Two men survived and, on humanitarian grounds, were issued with visas to stay in Britain for four years. Before boarding the ferry Wacker had closed the only air vent on the trailer in an effort to avoid detection by immigration officials. Forensic evidence showed that when the air began to run out in the container the victims had started to bang the sides with their shoes, calling for help which did not come.

On 5 April 2001 Wacker, who stood to make £330 a head or a total of almost £20,000, was jailed for 14 years after his conviction on 58 counts of manslaughter and conspiracy to smuggle illegal immigrants. His contact in the UK, interpreter Ying Guo, was sentenced to 6 years for her part in the conspiracy. She would have been on call to arrange bail and process asylum claims. On 11 May in Rotterdam seven men were convicted of being grossly negligent and accessories to manslaughter, human smuggling and belonging to a criminal organisation. Gursel Ozcan, said to be the leader of a Turkish gang in Rotterdam, and his lieutenant, Haci Demir, each received 9 years. The run had been the third in a series. The defence claimed that the police knew about the fatal run but had allowed it to go ahead in order to obtain hard evidence against the gang. The Justice Ministry accepted that the police had been tracking Ozcan for some months, but denied knowing anything about the June operation.[6]

The run, one of any number, had initially been arranged by the Snakeheads, the gangs from the Fujian province who have switched from drug- to human-smuggling. The rewards are almost as high and the penalties substantially less. Perhaps the penalty in the case of Chen Xiaokong arrested in January

---

[6] This was not the only reported similar tragedy in 2001. On 20 October six Kurds from Iran suffocated near Foggia in a truck with Greek licence plates driven by a Bulgarian.

2001 might not be less, though. It was thought that Xiaokong, believed to be the brains behind the network, might be summarily executed to save the face of the Chinese authorities who have allowed the Snakeheads to become so powerful and also to protect those officials who have been dealing with them from damaging revelations at any trial.

In November 1997 a roll-call of recent activity in England included a lorry driver from Derbyshire who claimed he had been threatened at gunpoint in Germany to persuade him to try to bring 24 Asians through the Channel Tunnel. A rather more modest effort was that of Frenchman Mario Fernandez-Neira who in the August was jailed for 30 months for attempting to smuggle 9 Chinese also through the Tunnel. There was also a gang operating in the north of England providing false British passports to immigrants brought in through Holland and Belgium, and a forgery factory in Islington run by a Turkish group. For the better part of 10 years a Brazilian had been bringing girls into Britain to work in the sex industry. He had been using counterfeit Portuguese identity cards, while a Cuban national was masterminding the provision of forged immigration stamps. As part of an export drive a Briton had been producing thousands of forgeries of French and Belgian identity cards on a computer; these had mainly gone to Algerian nationals.

So far as Canada was concerned there had been a steady flow of illegal immigrants from Fujian province in operations controlled by the gangleaders, or Snakesheads. In the summer of 1999 an aircraft patrol spotted a rusting cargo ship off the west coast of Vancouver Island. On board were 190 would-be illegal immigrants. Poorly dressed, they had been at sea for 72 days; waste lined the deck, water had been rationed, there were no toilet facilities and little food. Three Chinese sailors – Yu Hua, Hong Ling Lin and Wei Quing Lin – were sentenced to 4 years' imprisonment each. The prosecution had asked for 8 years as a deterrent sentence. Meanwhile, a number of the 190 passengers who had been housed at the military base in Esquimault had vanished.[7]

Worldwide, the smugglers behaved with the same ruthlessness. In February 2001 a freighter carrying 900 Iraqi Kurds – others claimed they were Syrian Kurds – was said by French authorities to have been deliberately grounded on rocks off the Riviera near St Raphael. The crew then made off in an inflatable dinghy. The boat, registered in Cambodia, sank as it was being towed into Toulon harbour. A Turkish smuggling ring had crammed the refugees, over half of whom were children or elderly, into the hold. Charged up to £1,380 for the trip, they had been loaded from a Turkish beach a week earlier and fed on water and biscuits. Three babies were born during the journey.

That weekend the Italian authorities had picked up 130 would-be refugees, mainly Kurds but also Albanians, who had tried to make the journey in a variety of craft including motor launches and rubber dinghies. A number of others were thought to have died during high-speed chases. Because of the number of agencies involved – the police, *carabinieri*, navy coastguards and Guardia di Finanza – and the difficulty in co-ordinating their operations, Italy was a favourite target for smugglers.

[7] *Globe and Mail*, 17 March 2001.

On 8 December 2001 another run ended in tragedy when 8 refugees including 5 children were found to have died in a container dropped at Waterford, Ireland. Another 5 refugees were found to be semi-conscious; it appeared that they had been killed by falling furniture. The sealed container had left Milan by train on 30 November, and had gone to Cologne and then Zeebrugge where, police thought, the refugees had been loaded. The seal was removed and a second one fixed. The cargo ship then sailed on 4 December and arrived in Waterford two days later. It was collected on Saturday morning and driven to a business park in Wexford where the driver called the police.

Greece has also been regarded as a favourite landing place and was considered something of a soft touch until six Turkish seamen, who landed 224 Kurdish and Afghan migrants, received 10 years each in 2000. The coast near Tarifa, with its proximity to North Africa, was regarded as a suitable landing point in Spain. Chinese were sent through Belgrade airport, while Somali gangs processed illegals as they came through the Gare du Nord station in Paris.[8] It is estimated that in Paris alone there are 80,000 illegal immigrants working in sweatshops to pay off their triad-incurred travel debts. Five years is the average period before they are clear.

Immigrants have always provided an income for lawyers, some of whom have charged exorbitant fees and fabricated stories on their client's behalf. None more so, said the pros-

---

[8] *Daily Telegraph*, 19 February 2001. See also Frank Vivano, 'New Mafias go Global' in San Francisco *Chronicle*, 7 January 2001.

ecution, than Robert Porges, a Manhattan lawyer who ran the country's largest political asylum practice. In September 2000 he was charged in a 44-count indictment with helping to run a smuggling ring that had brought over 7,000 Chinese immigrants to the United States. He had, said the authorities, earned $13 million in fees.

The standard practice was for an immigrant to agree to pay between $40,000 and $50,000, part payment to be made before leaving. Those who evaded the INS and ended up in New York would be taken to Brooklyn. Illegal immigrants are entitled to apply for asylum and can be released on bail if they can show they have relatives with whom they can live pending the hearing of their cases. To facilitate their release on bail it is alleged that Porges and some members of his staff faked political asylum claims, one of which claimed that a Chinese woman had been obliged to undergo a forced abortion because of China's one-child policy. Those regarded as being the least intelligent were given the simplest of tales to learn to tell the INS. Staff would write out the final version in longhand and coaching lessons would be given. Fake documents were supplied from so-called relatives, often the smugglers themselves, and signatures were forged. Once the immigrant was released, Porges' firm would buy tickets for their transportation to a place designated by the Snakeheads where they would be held and forced to work until the debt was repaid.

In spring of 2002 Porges and his wife Sherry Lu Porges pleaded guilty together with a further 10 former Porges employees to racketeering and tax evasion. The Porges are scheduled to serve at least 6 years in prison and pay more than $8 million restitution. As a result of their activities, the United States government has been forced to review over 7,000 Chinese asylum cases.

Leaving the Channel Tunnel and taking the first exit on the A16 motorway in the direction of Boulogne, you come to a roundabout which leads to the coast. On a good day in March you may see hares living up to their name and leaping wildly through the fields. On any day in the year you will see clusters of unshaven men in *blousons* tramping up and down the road carrying plastic bags. They are some of the 5,000 refugees at the nearby Red Cross shelter at Sangatte, set back from the road, waiting to try and get into Britain – the home of social security milk and honey – by whatever means come to hand.

Many will try to sneak on to a Eurotunnel train. Potential immigrants who have paid up to £4,000 to gangs have been dropped in the Pas-de-Calais after being told they were now in Kent. In a television investigation when a reporter was sent to Turkey to pose as an asylum seeker, he found three gangs which agreed to smuggle him into Europe via Russia, Italy, Greece and Germany. One gang wanted £6,000 for the journey.[9] At the end of December 2001 the Kent police were called to the middle of the tunnel to turn back up to 150 immigrants who had broken through the extensive security surrounding the railhead.

On 29 March 2001, what were then record sentences were passed on Stephen, John and Darren Hobbs following their convictions for running a smuggling operation at Little Heath

[9] *Tonight with Trevor McDonald*, 23 August 2001.

Farm, Hemel Hempstead. Under cover of their removal business they had been bringing in illegal immigrants, having loaded them in wooden crates at a roadside lay-by in Germany. They were then unloaded at the farm and driven away in minibuses and a Range Rover. Unfortunately for the brothers, a neighbour had seen this operation disposing of 'Balkan-looking' people, and the police and Customs were alerted. In February 2000 a lorry driven by John Hobbs was stopped with 27 illegal immigrants on board. He denied knowledge of their presence and was released. Undeterred, the brothers organised another trip the same month and this time two vans driven by Darren Hobbs and Warren Charge were found with a total of 59 immigrants. Stephen Hobbs received 9 years, John was sentenced to 7½ years and Darren Hobbs and Warren Charge to 3 years each.

In September 2001, Kashmir Nanan, who ran a curry house, grocery store and four off-licences in Gateshead, was told he was facing a long term in prison after pleading guilty to trafficking, bringing people from India to Britain. He himself had arrived in Britain as an illegal immigrant, but had married an English woman and been granted indefinite leave to stay. His career as a human trafficker ended when he offered an undercover police officer £10,000 to drive a lorry bringing 21 immigrants into the country. He too had been operating with contacts in Germany. When arrested, he was found to be employing five illegal immigrants in his businesses.

In theory, French penalties on people-smugglers could range up to 5 years, but lesser sentences are generally imposed. Percentage-wise, however, there has been a great increase in the number of people now serving sentences in northern France. In the last three years 46 people have been imprisoned. In 1998 there were only four, but in 2000 the total had risen to 27. The offer to the smuggler was £2,000 a head and, correctly, they were told the penalties if caught were less than for drug-smuggling.

Some claimed they were themselves victims. A North London security guard served 10 months in Lille. He said he had been on a booze run buying cheap alcohol and cigarettes for Christmas in 2000. He and his friend, who received 6 months, willingly opened the back of their hired van as the ferry was about to leave Calais. There, to the men's amazement, was a total of 28 potential asylum seekers. The man did not know whether the people were Turks or Kurds or Albanians: 'We didn't speak to them and they didn't speak to us.' He thought the immigrants must have got into the van through an unlocked back shutter on one of the occasions when he and his friend had stopped to buy petrol, food and tickets.[10]

It was not always humans that were smuggled. Raymond Humphrey received 6½ years at Isleworth Crown Court on 18 January 2002 for smuggling, keeping and trading in endangered species and the theft of birds of prey. Sixty animals, dead and alive, were found from 14 endangered species. A second man received 22 months. None of the surviving animals was fit to be returned to the wild. Meanwhile, in America, indictments were brought in Missouri, Illinois and Michigan against a series of men and

[10] *Independent*, 12 November 2001.

women in the Midwest alleged to have illegally purchased, transported and sold tigers and leopards as well as black bears and mountain lions. The intention had been the introduction of meat and skins into the growing animal parts trade in America.

Another new sport has been carp theft and smuggling. These fish, which can live many years and can weigh over 50 lbs, are highly prized by coarse anglers. The fish are caught, weighed and thrown back. Gangs, one of which is said to be armed, are now stealing the fish which thrive in the warmer waters of southern France. They are stolen there, wrapped in wet sacking in which they can survive for 24 hours, and brought to England where, on the black market, about £5,000 will be paid for a 20 kg fish. In December 2001 Lewes magistrates imposed a record fine just short of £30,000 on a fish wholesaler for smuggling carp.

As one door closes another opens, and two of the more modern and rewarding businesses are raiding machines in amusement arcades – which is only a more lucrative version of the telephone box – and fly-posting. In April 1995 a man was shot in Manchester, a victim of what was estimated to be an industry worth £200,000 annually in the city. Christopher Horrox of Glossop died when he and another man were attacked by a gunman as they were pasting posters near the University of Manchester Institute of Science and Technology. His companion received four wounds at point-blank range but survived. The gunman had fired shots from a red Ford Transit van.

There were believed to be up to 120 teams fly-posting in London, with rock concerts and record releases being the most frequently advertised. Up to £1 a poster is paid and a skilled team can paste several hundred a night on whatever space is available, sometimes over legitimate advertising hoarding and, more often, over each others. Although there had previously been incidents of beatings, the Manchester shooting was believed to be the first occasion when a firearm was used to settle a territorial dispute.

As for the ravaging of amusement arcade machines, this is now a £50 million annual industry with, it is thought, about 20 gangs operating across Britain. Gangs of three or four tour constantly and will rob a machine of anything from £75 to £110. So far as the prospects of arrest are concerned, it offers little danger. The last big prosecution was in 1994 when a seven-strong gang from the West Midlands was convicted of stealing money from machines on cross-Channel ferries. Their downfall came when a bank cashier reported that they were changing thousands of pounds of coins into notes. It was estimated that they had cleared £300,000 in less than two years. More risk comes in the form of rival gangs anxious to maintain and protect their turf, and there are believed to have been three murders attributable to wars over amusement arcade machine raids since 1990.[11]

Another modern crime is called shoulder surfing. When the victim draws money from a cash machine outside a bank, the thief leans over his or her shoulder and snatches the card as it comes out of the machine. In the first half of 2001, 180

---

[11] Tony Thompson, 'Arcade gangs get away with yearly haul of £50 million' in the *Observer*, 19 August 2001.

such thefts were notified at Halifax and HSBC machines in Oxford Street alone. Down the road in Tottenham Court Road, 205 snatches were recorded in the first nine months of 2001, of which 54 took place in September. The trick is fairly standard. The thief tells the victim that a note has been dropped and as the person looks down the card is stolen. The PIN number has already been noted when the victim keyed it in, and the thief and accomplice hightail it to another machine which can yield up to £700.[12]

The first attack of Datastreaming, a new and fast-growing crime, took place in the spring of 2001. In essence, when a customer pays by credit card in a shop, the retailer holds the details of the card in the computer. Hackers enter the system and take the details, which are then used to create a counterfeit card which is sent abroad. It is only when a statement arrives and is checked that the fraud is discovered. Britain is an ideal target because, with something in the region of 127 million credit, debit and Cashpoint cards in existence, it has the largest card traffic in Europe. It was estimated that £400 million would be paid in 2001 over credit card fraud of one kind or another.

Threats to set fire to victims in armed robberies appear to be on the increase. There was horror when it was learned that the guards on the Security Express and Brinks-Mat robbery had been threatened in this way in the 1980s. Now it is almost standard procedure. At the same time, robberies of hi-tech equipment have also increased. In June 2001 two security guards were threatened when an armed gang stole more than £3 million-worth of mobile telephones from a warehouse at Heathrow. The guards were held for eight hours and forced to open the premises in the air freight area. The robbers all wore blue surgical gloves as well as an assortment of false beards, hats and masks. Ten thousand Nokia telephones were stolen. The raid followed similar robberies of hi-tech equipment in the South East. Earlier in the year in March a truck was ambushed on the M4 and the driver doused in petrol. In May another truck driver was bound and gagged and locked in the boot on the M40, while thieves took £120,000 of electrical equipment. The robberies continued, and in February 2002 hijackers sprayed a driver and passenger with CS gas before taking computer chips in Hampton, Middlesex. It was thought that as many as ten might have taken part in the raid.

At street level much of the robbery taking place is of mobile telephones, very often stolen by black youths from white boys too preoccupied with their calls to see what is happening until it is too late. Apparently, it is regarded as unsporting to steal from girls.

Smugglers have continued to devise novel ways of importing drugs. In recent years methods have included garden gnomes, 700 boxes of fake avocado pears and the arms of a mechanical digger. Another bizarre effort was the dissolving of drugs in alcohol and then absorbing the liquid in a suit. One woman had drugs taped to her head and then covered in an Afro wig.[13] Another used a hollowed-out

---

[13] The use of wigs as places of concealment is nothing new. At Bow Street Magistrates Court in the 1960s, one prostitute kept her used condoms under her wig.

wooden monkey which weighed 6.6 kg, and 666 grams of cannabis was found inside. It had been posted in Ghana by a witch doctor who then placed a curse on the doll after his arrest. The curse seems to have had some effect because a number of Customs officers have been injured either tripping over the figure, getting splinters from it or when it fell off a shelf, said Dover Customs spokesman Nigel Knott.

In January 2000 there were reports that crack-cocaine was being sold from hot-dog stands in the West End. The gangs work in threes: one armed with a knife, in theory for onion chopping, who cuts the drugs; a runner who collects the drugs and a spotter, or lookout man. A hot-dog stand, even without the sale of drugs, could be expected to gross £1,000 a night. A trolley costs £1,500. On New Year's Eve 1999, 22 unlicensed hot-dog stalls were seized.[14]

Drug dealers can operate out of the simplest of places. A chip shop on a North London estate near the Wembley Exhibition Centre was raided by 700 police on 20 September 2001, in response to complaints by local residents that a shopping precinct had effectively been taken over for the sale of drugs. There were hopes that a local 'Mr Big' would be scooped up but when he did not appear after an hour, officers swamped the estate. Fifty rocks of crack-cocaine were seized and 22 suspects were arrested in part of *Operation Claymore*, designed to run for 10 weeks and cut street crime.[15] Local communities are becoming more political in pressuring the police to take action against known crack houses. In a

[14] *Sunday Times*, 16 January 2000.
[15] *Evening Standard*, 21 September 2001.

raid in mid-December 2001 on the notorious Downs Estate in Hackney, 200 officers raided the three most active houses in an area known as the Pembury triangle. Following the raids, in which large quantities of crack were found, over 50 people faced drugs charges.[16]

Dealers were also alleged to be selling crack on board London buses. The customers hop on at prearranged stops, buy and hop off again. Transactions are arranged by mobile phone and suppliers restock the dealers. One popular route is the 73 which stops outside the London Library in the Euston Road en route to and from King's Cross, Stoke Newington and Islington, and one dealer became known as 'Brown and White' because he kept brown heroin in one side of his mouth and white crack cocaine in the other.[17]

There were also signs that the yakuza were beginning to make inroads into British organised crime, with a massive stolen-car ring in which expensive Japanese cars such as Toyota Landcruisers and Honda NSXs were being stolen to order, shipped out to Japan in containers and then forwarded to Dubai. It appears there is a whole industry of reconstructing the identities of Japanese cars which are then returned in their new guises to Britain. The scam first surfaced in Hampshire where, of imported Japanese-made cars stopped by the police, some 50 per cent were found to be stolen. It was thought that the scam might have made up to £1 billion.[18]

On 11 September 2001, with the deliberate attacks on

---

[16] *Evening Standard*, 18 December 2001.
[17] *Evening Standard*, 10 April 2001.
[18] 'The Biggest Car Fraud in the World' on BBC 1, 25 July 2001.

the World Trade Center in New York and the Pentagon in Washington, the world changed. Within a month Tony Blair had announced a raft of measures to be pressed through Parliament designed to combat terrorism, and at last it was recognised that organised crime was itself a form of terrorism. There had long been complaints about the British immigration system, which was not thought to weed out undesirables with any great precision. Despite opposition from some MPs, the Bill passed through the House of Commons on 26 November. It remains to be seen what success there will be in the coming years.

Following the atrocities, US Congress ordered the Secret Service to form task forces to combat cybercrime and cyberterrorism. One has been formed in Las Vegas. The resort hotels may not have been victimised by cybercriminals yet, but Lt. Steve Franks, head of Metro Police's financial-crimes unit, recalling the words of Willie Sutton, believed 'it was only a matter of time'.[19]

Decades ago when that notorious criminal was asked why he robbed banks, Sutton replied: 'That's where the money is.' 'It's a matter of time,' Franks said. 'If you want the money, the casinos are where to go.' There are also those who have tested the electronic locks, said David Shepherd, security director of the Venetian Hotel. 'There are always people trying to get into the system to see if they can do it.'

---

[19] Willie Sutton, known as 'The Actor' because of his ability to assume disguises, was thought to have made more than $2 million in 35 years as a bank robber. He wrote his biography, *That's Where the Money Is*, and he was then used to promote a new credit card. By the end of his career he had become a celebrity. He died on 2 November 1980 in Florida.

This was a battle which police and casino security directors were fighting well before the September attacks. But it is a battle that has taken on added importance. Investigators have found that terrorist 'sleeper cells were largely self-funding', Franks said, and they used credit card fraud and theft to finance operations.

Carter Kim, assistant special agent in charge of the local Secret Service office, said that his goal was to make contacts with the gaming industry before incidents happen. Electronic threats to a casino can come both from internal sources – for example, employees – and external hackers, Kim said.

According to Franks, so far cyberattacks in Las Vegas have been aimed outside the casino industry. In one case, when a hacker broke into a credit union's computer system, five separate banks were affected before the hacker was caught three hours later. In another case, a hacker broke into doctors' computer systems and stole patient lists. 'Once you take that, you have the credit card [numbers], and everything you need to do identity assumptions.'

Within casino systems, a wealth of records contain similar information for gamblers and employees. Business plans and high-roller lists can also be targets of industrial espionage. The risk for casinos, however, goes beyond stealing cash or information. There is also the risk of outright sabotage, especially since many of a resort's operations are controlled by computers. The degree to which criminals could do malicious things if they obtain access to networks is regarded as almost unlimited.

Las Vegas gaming lawyer Tony Cabot commented:

We're not just talking about cash, but some really malicious things that can affect people's health. Imagine
someone getting into a water-processing unit and changing
the amount of chlorine in the water.

'If you worry about bombs, you have to worry about the
security of your network systems. Saboteurs might have
blackmail on their minds as well,' Franks said. 'If I can make
an elevator shut down at a hotel on New Year's Eve, how
much would they [resort executives] pay to get it turned on
again?'[20]

But, said David Shepherd, Las Vegas casinos are prepared.
'When it comes to security on the Strip, all thoughts of
competition go out the door. This is not something where
you try to keep secrets from each other. How can you protect
your place if you don't protect the entire city?'[21]

Overall, however, it was thought that the old Mafia had
failed to adapt to modern technology, and were therefore
losing out to the more up-to-date Russian and Asian, let alone
Colombian, syndicates. According to Pino Arlacchi, director
for the UN Centre for International Crime Prevention, the
smaller, more flexible and less visible technology-based
networks are using corruption, infiltration and integration to
become richer and more powerful than their declining Italian-
American cousins.[22]

---

[20] The thought is not new. The electronic shutting down of a Las Vegas casino
for protection purposes was the denouement of the plot of John Camp's 1989
novel *Fool's Run*.

[21] David Strow, 'Casinos are at greater risk of cybercrime' in *Las Vegas Sun*, 20
November 2001.

[22] *Business FT Weekend* magazine, 27 January 2001.

The first Internet bank robbers in Britain were given relatively modest sentences on 7 December 2001 when Alan Ross received 30 months and estate agent Christian Palmer 2 years for their part in a scheme thought up, allegedly, by a former police officer, Roy Graham. Fictitious names and details were used to obtain credit cards from Internet banks, Cahoot and Egg. Empty properties on Palmer's books were used as addresses for applications by names such as Brown, Black and Green. The team made 111 applications with a 25 per cent success rate. Credit cards were issued with limits ranging from £500 to £15,000. Overall £130,000 had been obtained. Graham, who had resigned from the police on the grounds of ill-health, went to live in Majorca after he had been given bail. A warrant for extradition on another matter has been issued.[23]

By the end of 2001 the Russian *mafiya* was making inroads in hacking into e-commerce and banking web sites in America. Hackers had launched computer viruses but the real threat, said the FBI, was from organised crime. Nor were officials quite sure of the implications. According to the FBI, 40 companies in 20 states had been identified as targets for Eastern European organised crime groups, with over a million credit card numbers stolen. The Russian Ministry of Affairs estimated there were 5,600 criminal groups with more than 100,000 members involved in laundering, drugs and extortion. Hackers hired by the Russian *mafiya* were breaking into e-commerce computers and stealing credit card and bank account numbers. There was also a degree of extortion, with

[23] *Independent*, 8 December 2001.

threats to release data if the companies did not make pay-offs. In 2000 one Russian cyberthief, giving himself the name Maxus, stole credit card numbers from an Internet retailer. He then demanded a $100,000 ransom and, when this was declined, he placed 25,000 of the numbers on a web site.[24]

Weaponry has also changed. Whereas 50 years ago few professional criminals in England carried guns, now these are as necessary as mobile telephones. The anti-gun laws passed in a knee-jerk reaction to the Dunblane massacre certainly did nothing to stop a proliferation of guns on the London streets. Seizures ran at around 600 a year, with a 17-year-old being arrested after a laser-sighted AR-15 semi-automatic was found in the boot of his car. In 2001 one gunshot wound was treated every week in East London hospitals, and armed police responded to five incidents daily following calls involving the suspected use of guns. A fair number of these may have been false alarms, but it was still double the number three years ago.

Indeed German police have discovered mobile phone guns which can be fired four times by pressing the digits 5 to 8. Ten of the .22-calibre weapons were seized when a Croatian gun dealer was found trying to smuggle them into Switzerland.

Predictably the arrival of the Euro produced a series of opportunities for criminals, some of which have been taken. In the first days of its arrival, straightforward successful robberies took place in Germany, Spain and Italy. A bank in a German town near the French border was held up by men

---

[24] Laura Lorek, 'Russian Mafia Net Threat' on *Interactive Week*, 16 July 2001.

with a bazooka; while in Fuentesauco, Spain, a raid which lasted nearly half an hour netted E90,000. In Urzulei, Sardinia, a Fiat Uno was driven into the glass door of a bank and three men armed with pistols made off with E90,000. On 6 January the largest raid thus far took place when E500,000 was stolen from a branch of the Bank of China in Paris. The thieves seem to have climbed through an open window into an inner courtyard and, after disabling a security shutter, they then forced the locks on the bank vaults.

A less successful raid was in Borrisokane, County Tipperary, when in an old-fashioned counter-leap three men armed with a hammer and a knife stole around E3,500. Their success may be temporary, for they were not wearing masks and were recognised. Nor was a raid on 2 January 2002 – when two men in a stolen white van pulled out the window of the Berliner Volksbank in Friedersdorf, south of Berlin – any greater success. Unfortunately they set off the alarm and, in their haste, took with them the machine which prints bank statements and not the ATM they had wanted.

Life can imitate art. At the beginning of the Al Pacino film, *Sea of Love*, there is a police sting. Criminals have been sent invitations to come and see the New York Yankees baseball team. On arrival they are arrested. At the end of 2001 the Metropolitan Police concluded a very successful similar operation. Around 1,000 criminals were sent letters informing them that they had won big prizes, and some 350 went to collect their winnings and were arrested. They included a man wanted for the rape of an 11-year-old girl, but the majority were burglars and those accused of crimes of violence. The trick had earlier worked on a smaller scale, possibly because there is less crime in that part of the country, when the Avon and Somerset police netted 35 suspects.

On 18 February 2001, the Millennium Dome gang was convicted of conspiracy to rob and sentenced. Raymond Betson and William Cockram each received 18 years. Robert Adams and Aldo Ciarrocchi received 3 less and Kevin Meredith, convicted of conspiracy to steal, received 5 years. He was said to have been a hard-working fishing captain taking out charter parties of anglers, but had defaulted on a £14,000 loan from Cockram and this was to be his way of clearing the debt.

Adams, nicknamed 'Bob the Builder', had previously been sentenced to 6 years for the attempted murder of his wife and, back in 1984, had been sentenced in France for cocaine smuggling. Cockram had convictions dating back 30 years. Ciarrocchi had become involved when he started dating Cockram's daughter; he had only one conviction for shoplifting in 1992. The 40-year-old Betson was regarded as the ringleader. As a teenager he had learned how to drive a JCB and from the age of 25 he had been a career criminal, ending as a tobacco and alcohol smuggler. He was suspected of involvement in a £2 million raid on a Security Express van in Barking, and another on a post office in Hastings which had netted £5 million – both in 1996. The next year there was a robbery at Redhill on a Royal Mail van, and this was thought to have netted £5 million. In an abortive robbery of a Security Van in Nine Elms, the robbers escaped across the Thames in a stolen speedboat. The police believed that this method, if proved to be successful, would be used again. When it came to it, the police concluded that the diamonds housed in the Dome had been destined for the much-underestimated Russian *mafiya*.

As if, however, to prove that old-fashioned crime still has more than a small place in today's high-tech world, at the end of 2001 two robberies took place in London. The first was the theft of jewellery in the early hours of Christmas Day at Harvey Nichols, the department store in Knightsbridge. Three armed men broke in, tied up the staff and made off with jewellery said to be worth over £1 million. The second was an old-fashioned smash-and-grab raid at a Bond Street jewellers, again said to be netting something in the millions.

On Monday 11 February a grand old-fashioned robbery took place at London Heathrow – scene of so many major thefts, successful and unsuccessful. This time two men entered the secure cargo area and stole goods valued at £4.6 million. They approached the driver of a security van as he was transferring cash between planes, forced him to the ground and then loaded the money in their own van. They then drove to Spinney Drive in Feltham and transferred to another vehicle after setting fire to the one used in the robbery. It was thought that the thieves had inside knowledge of the security arrangements and that the money had left Britain within a matter of hours.

Perhaps there is life in the old crime yet.

Bibliography

Albanese, J., *Organised Crime in America* (1989) Cincinnati, Anderson Publishing Co.

Albini, J.L., *The American Mafia: Genesis of a Legend* (1971) New York, Appleton-Century-Crofts.

Alexander, S., *The Pizza Connection* (1988) New York, Weidenfeld & Nicolson.

Allighan, G., *The 65th Defendant* (1963) Cape Town, Howard Timmins.

Amorim, C., *Comando Vermelho: a historia secreta do crime organizado* (1993) Rio de Janeiro, Editora Record.

Anastasia, G., *Blood and Honour* (1991) New York, William Morrow.

————*Mobfather* (1993) New York, Zebra Books.

Arlacchi, P., *Mafia Business* (1988) Oxford, Oxford University Press.

Auger, M., *L'Attentat* (2001) Montreal, Editions Trait d'Union.

Balsamo, W. and Corpozi, G. jnr, *Crime Incorporated* (1988) London, W. H. Allen.

Barnes, T., Elias, R. and Walsh, P., *Cocky* (2000) London, Milo.

Behan, T., *The Camorra* (1996) London, Routledge.

Biaggi, E., *Il Boss e solo; Buscetta, la vera storia d'un vero padrino* (1986) Milan, Arnaldo Mondadori.

Bles, M. and Low, R., *The Kidnap Business* (1987) London, Pelham Books.

Block, A., *East Side – West Side* (1980) Cardiff, University College, Cardiff Press.

Blok, A., *The Mafia of a Sicilian Village 1860–1960* (1974) Oxford, Basil Blackwell.

Blumenthal, R., *Last Days of the Sicilians* (1988) London, Bloomsbury.

Bonanno, J., *A Man of Honour* (1983) New York, Simon and Schuster.

Booth, M., *The Triads* (1990) London, Grafton Books.

Borniche, R., *Flic Story* (1977) New York, Doubleday & Co.

Bottom, B., *The Godfather in Australia* (1979) Sydney, A.F. & A.W. Reed Pty Ltd.

Bradley, G., *The Wayward Lad* (2001) London, Green Water Publishing.

Brashler, W., *The Don: The Life and Death of Sam Giancana* (1977) New York, Harper & Row.

Bresler, F., *The Trail of the Triads* (1980) London, Weidenfeld & Nicolson.

————*Interpol* (1992) Harmondsworth, Penguin.

Brown, M. (ed.), *Australian Crime* (1993) Sydney, Lansdowne.

Campbell, D., *The Underworld* (1994) London, BBC Books.

Catania, E. and Sottile, S., *Toto Riina: Storia segrete, odii e amori del dittatore de Cosa Nostra* (1993) Milan, Liber.

Champlain, P. de, *La Crime organisé à Montréal, 1940–1980* (1986) Hull, Quebec, Editions Asticou.

Chandler, D.L., *Brothers in Blood: The Rise of the Criminal Brotherhoods* (1975) New York, Dutton.

Chicago Crime Commission, *Gangs* (1995) Chicago, Chicago Crime Commission.

————*The New Faces of Organized Crime* (1997) Chicago, Chicago Crime Commission.

Clarkson, W., *Killer on the Road* (2000) London, Blake Publishing.

Courtney, D., *Stop the Ride, I Want to Get Off* (1999) London, Virgin Publishing.

Coyne, H., *Scam* (1991) London, Duckworth.

Cretin, T., *Mafias du Monde* (1998) Paris, Presses Universitaires de France.

Cummings, J. and Volkman, E., *Mobster* (1991) London, Futura Publications.

Cyriax, O., *Crime* (1993) London, André Deutsch.

Davis, J.H., *Mafia Dynasty* (1993) New York, Harper Paperbacks.

Davies, N., *Dark Heart* (1997) London, Chatto & Windus.

Derogy, J., *Israel Connection: la première enquête sur la Mafia d'Israel* (1980) Paris, Plon.

————*Enquête sur les ripoux de la Côte* (1991) Paris, Fayard.

Dettre, A., Keith, G. and Walker, P., *Infamous Australians* (1985) Sydney, Bay Books.

Dubro, J., *Mob Rule: Inside the Canadian Mafia* (1985) Toronto, Macmillan of Canada.

Eddy, P. and Walden, S., *The Cocaine Wars* (1989) London, Arrow Books.

Edwards, P., *Blood Brothers* (1990) Toronto, McClelland-Bantam Inc.

Edwards, P. and Nicaso, A., *Deadly Silence* (1993) Toronto, Macmillan.

Eisenberg, U.D. and Landau, E., *Meyer Lansky: Mogul of the Mob* (1979) New York, Paddington Press.

Faligot, R., *La Mafia Chinoise en Europe* (2001) Paris, Calman-Levy.

Farrell, R.A. and Case, C., *The Black Book and the Mafia* (1995) Wisconsin, University of Wisconsin Press.

Fijnaut, C. and others, *Organized Crime in the Netherlands* (1998) The Hague, Kluwer Law.

Fleming, I., *The Diamond Smugglers* (1957) London, Jonathan Cape.

Follain, J., *A Dishonoured Society* (1995) London, Little, Brown.

Foreman, F., *Respect* (1996) London, Century.

Fox, S., *Blood and Power* (1990) Harmondsworth, Penguin.

Franceschini, R., *A Matter of Honour* (1993) New York, Simon & Schuster.

Frankos, D., *Contract Killer* (1993) London, Warner Books.

Fraser, F., *Mad Frank* (1994) London, Warner Books.

————*Mad Frank's Diary* (2000) London, Virgin Books.

————*Mad Frank and Friends* (1997) London, Warner Books.

Freemantle, B., *The Fix* (1985) London, Michael Joseph.

————*The Octopus* (1995) London, Orion Books.

Fry, C. with Kray, C., *Doing the Business* (1993) London, Smith Gryphon.

Galante, P. and Sapin, L., *The Marseilles Mafia* (1979) London, W.H. Allen.

Gambetta, D., *The Sicilian Mafia* (1993) Cambridge, Mass., Harvard Press.

Geher, R., *Wiener Blut, oder Die Ehre der Strizzis* (1993) Vienna, Osterreichischen Staatsdrucherei.

Gentile, N., *Background and History of the Castellamarese War and Early Decades of Organised Crime in America* (c. 1947). Unpublished.

Ghosh, S., *The Indian Mafia* (1991) New Dehli, Ashish Publishing House.

Glenny, M., *The Rebirth of History* (1993) London, Penguin Books.

Goldfarb, R., *Perfect Villains, Imperfect Heroes* (1995) New York, Random House.

Green T., *The Smugglers: An Investigation into the World of the Contemporary Smuggler* (1969) New York, Walker & Co.

Gugliotta, G. and Leen, J., *Kings of Cocaine* (1989) New York, Harper Paperbacks.

Gunst, L., *Born Fi' Dead* (1995) Edinburgh, Payback Press.

Hall, R., *Disorganised Crime* (1986) St Lucia, Queensland, University of Queensland Press.

Haller, M.H., *Life under Bruno* (1991) Conshocken, Pa., Pennsylvania Crime Commission.

Hammer, R.P., *Playboy's Illustrated History of Organized Crime* (1975) Chicago, Playboy Press.

Hoffa, J.R. and Fraley, O., *Hoffa: The Real Story* (1975) New York, Stein and Day.

Holden, A., *Big Deal* (1991) London, Corgi Books.

Home Affairs Committee, *Organised Crime* (1995) London, H.M.S.O.

——Police Corruption in England and Wales: An Assessment of Current Evidence (2002) London, H.M.S.O.

Humphreys, A., *The Enforcer* (1999) Toronto, HarperCollins.

Huston, P., *Tongs, Gangs and Triads* (1995) Boulder, Paladin Press.

Jackson, J. and Burke, W. jnr, *Dead Run* (1999) Edinburgh, Canongate Books.

Jones, M.D.B., *YBI: Young Boys Inc.* (1996) Detroit, H. Publications.

Katari., S.S., *Patterns of Dacoity in India* (1972) New Delhi, S. Chand & Co.

Kavieff, P., *The Purple Gang* (2000) New York, Barricade Books.

Kermoal, J. and Bartolomei, M., *La mafia se met à table: Histoires et recettes de l'honorable société* (1986), Paris, Actes Sud.

Kleinknecht, W., *The New Ethnic Mobs* (1996) New York, The Free Press.

Kuper, W. and Welp, J., *Beitrage zur Rechtswissenschaft* (1993) Heidelberg, C.F. Muller Juristischer Verlag.

Lane, B. and Gregg, W., *The New Encyclopaedia of Serial Killers* (1996) London, Headline.

Lavigne, Y., *Hell's Angels, Taking Care of Business* (1987) Toronto, Ballantine.

————*Good Guy, Bad Guy* (1991) Toronto, Ballantine.

————*Hell's Angels at War* (1999) Toronto, HarperCollins.

Lehmann, N., *The Promised Land* (1991) London, Macmillan.

Lehr, R. and O'Neill, G., *Black Mass* (2000) New York, BBS Public Affairs.

Lewis, N., *The Honoured Society* (1964) London, William Collins.

Longrigg, C., *Mafia Women* (1997) London, Chatto & Windus.

Maas, P., *Underboss* (1997) London, HarperCollins.

McAlaray, M., *Buddy Boys* (1989) New York, Charter Books.

Moffitt, A., *A Quarter to Midnight* (1985) North Ryde, NSW, Angus & Robertson.

Moldea, D.E., *The Hoffa War* (1987), New York, Paddington Press.

Mooney, J., *Gangster* (2001) Edinburgh, Cutting Edge.

Morgan, W.P., *Triad Societies in Hong Kong* (1960) Hong Kong Government Printer.

Morton, J., *Gangland* (1992), London, Little, Brown.

————*Bent Coppers* (1993) London, Little, Brown.

————*Gangland 2* (1994) London, Little, Brown.

————*Supergrasses and Informers* (1995) London, Little, Brown.

————*Calling Time on the Krays* (with Mrs X) (1997) London, Warner Books.

————*Gangland International* (1999) London, Warner Books.

————*East End Gangland* (2001) London, Warner Books.

————*Gangland: The Lawyers* (2001) London, Virgin Publishing.

Mueller, G.O.W. and Adler, F., *Outlaws of the Ocean* (1985) New York, Hearst Marine Books.

Nash, J.R., *Hustlers and Con Men* (1976) New York, M. Evans & Co.

————*World Encyclopedia of Organised Crime* (1993) London, Headline.

Newsday Staff, *The Heroin Trail* (1974) New York, New American Library.

Noble, T., *Untold Violence* (1989) Richmond, John Kerr Pty Ltd.

————*Walsh Street* (1991) Richmond, John Kerr Pty Ltd.

O'Reilly, E., *Veronica Guerin* (1998) London, Vintage.

Parker, J., *The Walking Dead* (1995) London, Simon & Schuster.

Pearson, J., *The Profession of Violence* (1985) London, Grafton.

————*The Cult of Violence* (2001) London, Orion.

Petacco, A., *Joe Petrosino* (1974) London, Hamish Hamilton.

Pistone, J., *Donnie Brasco* (1988) London, Sidgwick and Jackson.

Porter R. and Mikulas Teich, T., *Drugs and Narcotics in History* (1995) Cambridge, Cambridge University Press.

Punch, M., *Conduct Unbecoming* (1985) Tavistock Publications, London.

Read, L. and Morton, J., *Nipper: The Man who Nicked the Krays* (2001) London, Little, Brown.

Read, M.B., *Chopper* (1991) Melbourne.

Reid, E. and Demaris, O., *The Green Felt Jungle* (1963) New York, The Trident Press.

Renaud, F., *Le Nouveau Milieu* (1992) Paris, Ed. Fayard.

Robinson, J., *The Laundrymen* (1994) London, Simon & Schuster.

Roemer, W.F., *The Enforcer* (1994) New York, Ivy Books.

Rome, F., *The Tattooed Men* (1975) New York, Delacorte Press.

Roth, A., *Infamous Manhattan* (1996) New York, Citadel Press.

Ruggiero, V., *Organised and Corporate Crime in Europe* (1996) Aldershot, Dartmouth.

Schneider, A. and Zarate, O., *Mafia for Beginners* (1994) Trumpington, Cambridge, Icon Books.

Seiga, C., *Killer* (2002) London, Blake Publishing.

Sen, M., *India's Bandit Queen* (1995) New York, Harvill.

Short, M., *Crime In America* (1991) London, Mandarin.

————*Lundy* (1991) London, Grafton.

Sifakis, C., *An Encyclopedia of American Crime* (1982) New York, Facts on File Publications.

————*The Mafia File* (1988) New York, Facts on File Publications.

Sillitoe, P., *Cloak Without Dagger* (1955) London, Cassell & Co.

Silverman, J., *Crack of Doom* (1994) London, Headline.

Skelton, D. and Brownlie, L., *Frightener* (1992) Edinburgh, Mainstream Publishing.

Slatta, R.W. (ed.), *Bandidos* (1987) Westport, Conn., Greenwood Press.

Small, G., *Ruthless* (1995) London, Warner.

Smith, D.C., *The Mafia Mystique* (1975) New York, Basic Books.

Smith J.L., *Running Scared* (1995) New York, Barricade Books Inc.

Smith, N. with Noble, T., *Neddy* (1993) Balmain, Kerr Publishing Pty Ltd.

————*Catch and Kill Your Own* (1995) Sydney, Ironbark.

Sterling, C., *The Mafia* (1990) London, Hamish Hamilton.

————*Crime without Frontiers* (1994) London, Little, Brown.

————*Octopus* (1991) London, Touchstone Books.

Taoka, K., *Yamaguchi-gumi: Third Generation* (1973) Tokyo, Tokuma Shoten.

Taylor, L., *In the Underworld* (1983) London, Guild Publishing.

Thompson, Thomas, *Serpentine* (1979) New York, Doubleday.

Thompson, Tony, *Gangland Britain* (1995) London, Hodder & Stoughton.

Tyler, G. (ed.), *Organised Crime in America* (1962) Ann Arbor, University Press of Michigan.

Vaksberg, A., *The Soviet Mafia* (1991) New York, St Martin's Press.

Viccei, V., *Knightsbridge: The Robbery of the Century* (1992) London, Blake Publishing.

Vigil, J.D., *Barrio Gangs* (1988) Austin, University of Texas.

Whitton, E., *Can of Worms* (1986) Sydney, The Fairfax Library.

Williams, P., *The General* (1995) Dublin, O'Brien.

————*Gangland* (1998) Dublin, O'Brien.

Williams, E.S., *A Royal Commission of Inquiry into Drugs* (1980) Canberra, Government of the Commonwealth of Australia.

Wilson, D., *Big Shots* (1985) South Melbourne, Sun Books.

————*Big Shots II* (1987) South Melbourne, Sun Books.

Wisbey, M., *Gangster's Moll* (2002) London, Warner Books.

Articles etc.

Ruth Bloomfield, 'Bands of Brothers' in *Time Out*, 28 November–5 December 2001.

Raymond Bonner, 'Umbrage' in *New York Times*, 11 September 1999.

Alan Cairns, 'Boxing in the Shadow' in *Toronto Sun*, 18 April 2001.

Lou Cannon, 'One Bad Cop' in *New York Times Magazine*, 1 October 2000.

Edward Conlon, 'The Pols, the Police and the Gerry Curls' in *American Spectator*, November 1994.

Shawn W. Crispin, 'Out of Africa' in *Far Eastern Economic Review*, Volume 164, Issue 20, 24 May 2001.

Justin Davenport, 'Who pulls the trigger in London's gun war?' in *Evening Standard*, 13 June 2001.

——— 'London–Kingston: Twinned by Terror' in *Evening Standard*, 10 September 2001.

Robert I. Friedman, 'India's Shame: Sexual Slavery and Political Corruption are leading to an AIDS Catastrophe' in *The Nation*, 8 April 1996.

Mark Galeotti, 'Turkish organized crime: Where State, Crime and Rebellion Conspire' in *Transnational Organized Crime*, Spring 1998.

———'Albania Organised Crime: Europe's latest threat' in *Cross Border Control*, 1999.

Peter Gastrow, 'Organized Crime and the State's Response in South Africa' in *Transnational Organized Crime*, Spring 1998.

Sarah Gibbons, 'High Seas Piracy' in *International Police Review*, November/December 1997.

Richard Grant, 'The Nobel Prisoner' in *Sunday Telegraph Magazine*, 22 April 2001.

Joshua Hammer, 'Taming the Soccer gangs' in *Newsweek*, 14 April 1997.

Luke Harding, 'The Queen is Dead' in *Guardian*, 26 July 2001.

Angelo B. Henderson, 'Detroit Kidnapping Casts a Grim Light on a Shifting Crime' in *Wall Street Journal*, 18 April 2001.

Robert Kurson, 'The Chicago Commission' in *Esquire*, July 2001.

James Kynge, 'Something rotten in the rice bowl' in *Business FT Weekend*, 30 June/1 July 2001.

William Langley, 'The Parisian Job' in *Sunday Telegraph Magazine*, 10 June 2001.

Cal McCrystal, 'The Hit at the Royal Hotel' in *Independent on Sunday*, 8 August 1993.

Liam McDowall, 'Albania learns the art of wrecking' in *New Statesman and Society*, 13 December 1991.

Jan McGirk, 'My brother, brilliant villain of Medellin' in *Independent*, 2 January 2001.

Ron McKenna, 'Killer Instinct' in *The Scotsman*, 11 April 2001.

Marko Milivijevic, 'The Drug Threat from Eastern Europe' in *Jane's Intelligence Review*, November 1995.

Russell Miller, 'Unholy Macao' in *Night & Day*, 21 June 1998.

Dean Nelson, 'Adams Family Values' in *Gear*, September 2000.

L. Paoli, 'An Underestimated Criminal Phenomenon: The Calabrian 'Ndrangheta' in *European Journal of Crime, Criminal Law and Criminal Justice*, Volume 2, 1994.

Raphael F. Perl, 'The North Korean Drug Trade: Issues for Decision Makers' in *Transnational Organised Crime*, Spring 1998.

Tony Thompson, 'Arcade gangs get away with yearly haul of £50 million' in *Observer*, 19 August 2001.

Patricia Tourancheau, 'Neuf Balles au bout de la route du Belge' in *Libération*, 30 September/1 October 2000.

———'François le Belge, un mort bien nettoyé' in *Libération*, 14/15 October 2000.

David James Smith, 'The Mersey Killers' in *Sunday Times*, 14 July 1996.

Gus Xhudo, 'Men of Purpose: The Growth of Albanian Criminal Activity' in *Transnational Organised Crime*, Spring 1996.

Index

Gangland Today